*American and British Writers in Mexico*

# American and British Writers in Mexico, 1556-1973

DREWEY WAYNE GUNN

UNIVERSITY OF TEXAS PRESS, AUSTIN AND LONDON

THE PUBLICATION OF THIS BOOK WAS ASSISTED BY A GRANT FROM THE ANDREW W. MELLON FOUNDATION.

Grateful acknowledgment is made for permission to quote from the following poems:

Gregory Corso, "Mexican Impressions." From *Gasoline*, copyright © 1958 by Gregory Corso. Reprinted by permission of City Lights Books.

Hart Crane, "Havana Rose," "Purgatorio," and "The Broken Tower." From *The Complete Poems and Selected Letters and Prose of Hart Crane*. Copyright © 1933, 1958, 1961 by Liveright Publishers, New York. Reprinted by permission of the publisher.

Allen Ginsberg, "Siesta in Xbalba." From *Reality Sandwiches*, copyright © 1963 by Allen Ginsberg. Reprinted by permission of City Lights Books.

Langston Hughes, "Mexican Market Woman." Copyright © 1926 by Alfred A. Knopf, Inc. and renewed 1954 by Langston Hughes. Reprinted from *Selected Poems* by Langston Hughes, by permission of the publisher.

LeRoi Jones, "The New World." From *Black Magic Poetry 1961–1967*, copyright © 1969 by LeRoi Jones, reprinted by permission of the publishers, The Bobbs-Merrill Company, Inc.

Denise Levertov, "The Weave" and "Overland to the Island." Denise Levertov, *The Jacob's Ladder*. Copyright © 1958, 1961 by Denise Levertov Goodman. Reprinted by permission of New Directions Publishing Corporation. *The Jacob's Ladder* is published in England by Jonathan Cape, London.

Robert Lowell, "Mexico." From *Notebook*, 3rd ed., 1970. Reprinted by permission of Farrar, Straus & Giroux, Inc. and Faber & Faber Ltd.

Malcolm Lowry, "Sestina in a Cantina." From *Selected Poems of Malcolm Lowry*, copyright © 1962 by Margerie Lowry. Reprinted by permission of City Lights Books.

Archibald MacLeish, "Conquistador." From *Collected Poems 1917–1952*. Reprinted by permission of Houghton Mifflin Company.

William Carlos Williams, "The Desert Music." William Carlos Williams, *Pictures from Brueghel and Other Poems*. Copyright © 1954 by William Carlos Williams. Reprinted by permission of New Directions Publishing Corporation.

Library of Congress Cataloging in Publication Data

Gunn, Drewey Wayne, 1939–
   American and British writers in Mexico, 1556–1973.
   Bibliography: p.
   1. American literature—History and criticism.
2. English literature—History and criticism. 3. Mexico in literature. 4. United States—Relations (general) with Mexico. 5. Mexico—Relations (general) with the United States. I. Title.
PS169.M4G8          820′.9′32          74-8840
ISBN 0-292-70307-4

# CONTENTS

# ACKNOWLEDGMENTS

The formal research for this study was completed between 1967 and 1973 primarily in libraries at the University of North Carolina (where the Josephus Daniels collection provided an important nucleus of materials), Duke University, The University of Texas, and Texas A&I University, and in public libraries in Greensboro, Kingsville, Corpus Christi, San Antonio, Mexico City, and New York City. Too many people have contributed bits of knowledge for me even to remember them all, but the following deserve special mention: Joyce Bowden, Latin American history scholar; William Doxey, writer and professor of English at Western Georgia College; José Gutiérrez of Hebbronville, Texas; Jo Carolyn Harper (Hoggins), poet and former editor, now teaching English at Rockingham County Community College; Helen Haydon, professor of English at Texas A&I; Harry Hude, graduate assistant in English at Texas A&I, who proofread the manuscript; Jack Lampe, political science instructor at Southwest Texas Junior College; Fredericka Martin of Cuernavaca, revisor of *Frances Toor's Guide to Mexico*; Raúl Ortiz y Ortiz, professor of philosophy at the National University of Mexico and translator of Malcolm Lowry's *Under the Volcano*; Harry Russell, professor of English, now retired, at the University of North Carolina; Orlan Sawey, critic of Southwestern literature and professor of English at Texas A&I; Max Steele, writer who lived in Mexico and professor of English at the University of North Carolina; Lini de Vries of Cuernavaca, associated with the Centro por Intercultural Documentación; and Forrest Wassermann, English scholar. But especially I want to thank Daniel W. Patterson, professor of English at the University of North Carolina, and Norma Beth Drake, English instructor at Texas Southmost College, for their indispensable help and encouragement. Other people will be cited in appropriate chapter notes.

# INTRODUCTION

Mexico as either a multifaceted symbol or a concrete reality has stirred the imaginations of American and British writers since shortly after the Spanish Conquest. From 1569 until the present these writers have published nearly 600 travel books recording their visits there, the majority of them appearing in the last 150 years. Starting in 1805 over 450 novels, plays, and narrative poems—including historical romances about Mexico and the American Southwest of Mexican days—plus an unknown number of short stories, essays, and lyrical poems scattered in books and magazines have explored Mexican materials. And if the reader turns to American and British works on Mexico outside the realm of belles-lettres, he is buried under the mass of books that have appeared since 1741. Some of these writers never saw the country, but the majority, including some of the most outstanding in American and British literature, wrote from personal experience. Mexico often had a striking effect on them, marking the beginning, the end, or a turning point of their careers. But the importance of Mexico to English and American literature has gone relatively unobserved, being eclipsed by investigations of Continental influences.

A number of bibliographies have revealed the English-speaking world's interest in the country,[1] but real critical attention began only in 1955 when Stanley T. Williams published his two-volume study *The Spanish Background of American Literature*, a wide-ranging look at possible influences of Spanish and Spanish American culture on

---

[1] The most important bibliographies have been: Cony Sturgis, *The Spanish World in English Fiction*; A. Curtis Wilgus, *Latin America in Fiction*; Charles E. Babcock et al., *Children's Books in English on Latin America*; C. Harvey Gardiner, "Foreign Travelers' Accounts of Mexico, 1810–1910," *Americas* 8 (January 1952): 321–351; and Drewey Wayne Gunn, *Mexico in American and British Letters*.

that of the United States. In 1956 *Western Review* printed an essay by George Woodcock (a Canadian who later wrote a Mexican travel book), "Mexico and the English Novelist," which discussed four writers' reflections. And in 1963 Cecil Robinson published his sociological study of the Mexican and the Mexican American as characters in American literature, *With the Ears of Strangers*. At least two unpublished studies explored this interest: a thesis completed by Mary Caroline Estes at The University of Texas in 1961, "American Travellers in Mexico, 1810–1940," and a dissertation written by Donald Lewis Zellman at Ohio State University in 1969, "American Intellectual Attitudes toward Mexico, 1908–1940."[2]

Neither Williams nor Robinson distinguished carefully between the Mexican and the Mexican American cultures. Nor did either pay much attention to the differences found in the writings of those who actually knew Mexico, those who knew only the Mexican American culture in Texas and the American Southwest, and those who wrote solely from their reading and imagination. But obviously the border and the physical experience of crossing it—as Woodcock realized—are important. Graham Greene, in his Mexican journal, noted the exciting aspects:

The border means more than a customs house, a passport officer, a man with a gun. Over there everything is going to be different; life is never going to be quite the same again after your passport has been stamped and you find yourself speechless among the moneychangers. The man seeking scenery imagines strange woods and unheard-of mountains; the romantic believes that the women over the border will be more beautiful and complaisant than those at home; the unhappy man imagines at least a different hell; the suicidal traveller expects the death he never finds. The atmosphere of the border—it is like starting over again . . .[3]

But the border was as often frightening. The American and the British writer left behind their language, their legal systems, their customs and rituals—sometimes, it seemed to them, their very safety.

Many writers tried to enter deeply and fully into the Mexican culture; as many simply saw Mexico as a retreat, a momentary place of isolation where they could obliterate the past or solve whatever problems confronted them. But no writer could escape an intense

---

[2] I appreciate Zellman's letter to me concerning his work, March 25, 1969.
[3] Graham Greene, *Another Mexico*, p. 13.

awareness of Mexican culture. In both travel books and fiction the reader generally finds an outsider, the writer or his projection, standing in strong contrast with the Mexicans' world. For some writers Mexico became a prison. Surrounded by various patterns which they were able only partly to understand, these writers whirled around, at times appearing to move in a meaningful direction but actually going nowhere. Sometimes the apparent simplicity of the natives seemed to hold a possible answer to their problems, but at other times the natives came to represent demonic or at best purgatorial forces. Yet other writers moved toward some understanding of themselves, their potentials, and their limitations. Physical journeys developed into explicit spiritual or mental pilgrimages. Mexico, having presented certain values whereby to judge later events, became a point of departure.

Unlike expatriates to the Continent (and American expatriates to England) during the nineteenth and twentieth centuries, in Mexico the best writers generally sojourned alone or in the company of non-literary types. Still, each tended to read what his predecessors—and sometimes his contemporaries—had to say and was often influenced by their comments, so that we do have a series of relationships. But the foreign writer in Mexico was singularly affected by events within the country itself. Whereas the foreign writer in Paris, for example, found a rather hermetic culture in which the significant events were the display of a painting, the opening of a play, or a ballet, or the publication of a book, the writer in Mexico, cut off from his own kind, was more attuned to political, social, and economic movements. He often felt the need to ponder the significance of the everyday world around him. However, the Mexican artistic renaissance of the 1920's did have a profound effect on several writers.

The relationship of the American and British writers with Mexico divides naturally into the same general periods as the country's history. The three hundred years of Spanish rule (1521–1810) saw a few travel works of interest. But Mexico did not really become a part of the American-British imagination until the nineteenth century. The hundred years between the Mexican War of Independence, 1810–1821, and the Revolution of 1910 split into three periods: the Santa Anna era (1822–1855), from which came many travel works of enduring merit and a fumbling attempt to create fiction based on Mexican themes; the years of Juárez and Maximilian (1855–1876), which had practically no immediate impact on American-British literature;

and the Díaz era (1876–1911), during which the general quality of travel literature declined but in which fiction worthy of note finally found its way. Mexico as a modern nation began with the Revolution of 1910. The war years (1910–1920) attracted only journalists and political observers, but with the cultural flowering of the 1920's and 1930's Mexico as a theme for American and British literature flowered too. A list of the significant writers who then visited the land becomes impressively long, and they contributed outstanding works in almost every genre. D. H. Lawrence and Katherine Anne Porter were especially important. Since World War II, concern with Mexico among American-British writers has declined but has shown no signs of disappearing, and important works based on Mexican experience continue to appear.

*American and British Writers in Mexico*

# 1. British Travelers in New Spain

Few of the earliest American or British visitors to Mexico were primarily authors. Consequently what writing they left us consists mainly of relatively straightforward accounts of their travels. Because such narrations display many different approaches, travel literature can be defined only as writing done from first-hand observations about a relatively strange place. Most travel accounts intimately record the personal impressions of the author, but some examples are quite formal, emphasizing such concerns as politics, culture, science, or religion. The traveler is generally caught up in the moment, no matter what his approach, and seldom makes historical judgments. Such accounts have proliferated in the twentieth century; almost every Mexican visitor seems to think about publishing his impressions, and a large number succeed. But few of these modern journals can match the early chronicles either in the interest of literary history or by intrinsic value. C. Harvey Gardiner has theorized that the ease and speed of modern travel induce overly hasty conclusions and prevent the visitor from knowing the country as intimately as early writers could.[1] Modern writers also suffer in part because Mexico changes

[1] C. Harvey Gardiner, "Foreign Travelers' Accounts of Mexico, 1810–1910," *Americas* 8 (January 1952): 322.

slowly and the earlier writers have mapped out the territory so well.
Many of the early narratives continue to be almost as true as when
they were published.

The very first accounts, published between 1569 and 1648, appeal
to us now mostly because of their historical value.[2] Whereas later
works reveal a land in which Spanish and Indian cultures had fused
into something peculiarly Mexican, the earlier ones show European
institutions dominating the Indian ways of life. For the English the
Catholic dogma was unacceptable, the churches and clergy too showy,
and the tortures of the Inquisition, real and imagined, too menacing.
Otherwise they seem to have felt at ease. As a result their descriptions,
though lively and filled with a sense of discovery, are less vivid than
we might expect. Many later visitors, meeting a culture unexpectedly
alien, felt a certain persistent disquiet and wrote more discerningly.
But if the earliest accounts now seem pertinent only in their revelations about the Indians, the landscape, and the beginnings of some of
the basic Mexican institutions, that information, coupled with the
ability yet to entertain, should keep a number of them—particularly
a book by Thomas Gage—for a long while before the reading public.

Charles I and subsequent Spanish kings jealously sealed off their
empire while the rest of Europe, especially England, looked on with
envy at the rich flood of gold and silver coming across the Atlantic.
Still, a surprising number of British visitors came to Mexico during
the sixteenth century; for example, a Scot named Thomas Blake had
arrived in Mexico City by 1534, but he left us no account of his adventure. This was just thirteen years after Hernán Cortés had completed his awesome march into the heart of Mexico, to discover there
the complex and essentially alien civilization of the Aztecs and thence
to destroy it. Several Englishmen probably were admitted during the
brief marriage of Philip I to Mary, 1554–1558, but the largest number were unwilling visitors as a result of John Hawkins's ill-fated
voyage into the Gulf of Mexico in 1568. Eight accounts from these
British visitors—four by merchants, one by Hawkins (who, however,
never set foot on land), and three by survivors of his voyage—have
come down to us, mainly through the efforts of Richard Hakluyt. In
1589 Hakluyt printed seven of these works, only one of which had
been published before, in the first edition of *The Principall Naviga-*

---

[2] As such they have been paraphrased by William Mayer, *Early Travellers in
Mexico, 1534 to 1816.*

*tions, Voiages and Discoveries of the English Nation*; for later editions he dropped one account and added the eighth. Besides Hawkins we know nothing about the men other than what they have told us.

Of them Robert Tomson, a merchant from Andover, arrived earliest, landing at Veracruz in April 1556. He had resided with another English merchant, John Field, and his family for a year in Cádiz, where they all had become intrigued by "the fleetes of shippes come out of the Indies" and decided to see "that rich countrey from whence such great quantitie of rich commodities come." After weathering an almost fatal storm in the Gulf of Mexico, they were warmly welcomed ashore by one of Field's Spanish friends and outfitted for their trip to Mexico City, only to have Field and several more of the party sicken and die shortly after their arrival in the city. Tomson himself lay ill for six months. Upon recovery he was impressed by the city's size and stateliness; the great activity that he witnessed led him to predict that it would in time become "the most populous Citie in the world." Thus he decided to remain and with the aid of Thomas Blake found service under Gonzalo Cerezo, one of Cortés's attendants during the Conquest. The problem of religion shortly presented itself. At a dinner Tomson was asked if it was true that the English "had overthrown all their Churches and houses of Religion" (apparently only the vaguest rumors about any part of the Reformation had then crept into Mexico), and he defended his country by quoting scriptures. One of the guests, "a villanous Portugal," reported this conversation to Archbishop Montúfar; consequently, Tomson was imprisoned seven months. In July 1558 he and others were then brought to do penance before a great crowd of people gathered in front of the cathedral. But these common people, he wrote, would not believe the greatness of the crimes with which the men were charged. Nowhere in his narrative does he show any bitterness about his treatment in Mexico (or his subsequent imprisonment in Spain), though clearly he had little use for Catholicism. A year after his release in 1561 he married a Mexican heiress. This sudden wealth proved to him, as he carefully pointed out at the end of his short narrative, that God was still on his side. Because of his freshness and naïveté his account remains one of the most attractive of the early ones.[3]

The other merchant narratives are much more impersonal and

3 Richard Hakluyt, *Principal Navigations*, VI, 246–263.

much less valuable as literature. Roger Bodenham, who had lived several years in Seville, spent nine months in Mexico, 1564–1565. But he begged off setting down many of his findings, saying that the Spanish histories were "full of those observations." John Chilton and Henrie Hawks were more generous with details about the country, especially those that would interest other merchants, but even more vague than Bodenham about personal matters. Chilton spent seventeen years, 1568–1585, in New Spain, Peru, and the West Indies and saw almost every corner of Mexico during his travels. His account is scarcely more than a catalogue of the places he visited, with a short appendix about the economic situation in Mexico. Hawks wrote a yet more impersonal survey "of the commodities of Nova Hispania, and the manners of the inhabitants" that he had witnessed during a five-year stay, spent mostly in the central part of the country sometime before 1572. Both men barely mention religious matters, and nowhere did either seem to encounter any antagonism because he was an Englishman, although the Hawkins incident occurred while both were in Mexico.[4]

In September 1568 nine ships under the command of John Hawkins (1532–1595) dropped anchor near San Juan de Ulúa at Veracruz. The adventurer had found on two previous voyages that a sizable profit could be made by seizing Negroes along the African coast and selling them to the Spanish colonists. On his third voyage he decided to penetrate the Gulf of Mexico, which Englishmen had not yet explored. There he encountered two great storms, which so crippled his fleet that he was forced to put into harbor. The Spanish authorities were none too happy with the situation, looking upon the English rightfully as pirates. To complicate matters the Spanish fleet, with the new viceroy, Martín Enríquez de Almansa, aboard, came into port at the same time. Hawkins later wrote that he feared the Spaniards' "accustomed treason," and indeed a week later they opened fire against the English. Two ships escaped: the lighter, under the command of Francis Drake—who spent the rest of his career avenging the battle—sailed home easily; but Hawkins's ship, overcrowded and with scarce supplies, wandered lost in the Gulf. Many of the starving sailors desired to be put ashore; Hawkins finally set off over a hundred near Tampico. His narrative of these events, *A True Declaration of*

4 Ibid., VI, 263–296.

*the troublesome Voyage of Mr. John Hawkins to the Partes of Guynea and the West Indies in the years of Our Lord 1567 and 1568,* was first printed in 1569.[5] Naturally Hawkins saw nothing of Mexico except what he could observe from shipboard, but of the men he put ashore three left rather full narratives of their adventures.

One of these, by Miles Philips, shows real literary talent. By his vivid choice of words and selection of detail he can thoroughly entertain the reader with his life in Mexico, made especially hazardous through repeated attempts to escape the country and its hated Inquisition. Shortly after the men were set ashore, Philips recalled, they met a tribe of Indians, who stripped them of all their brightly colored clothes. The English castaways, some dressed in somber black and others "starke naked," attempted to make their way through the brush and "noysome" mosquitoes to the Río Pánuco. One group decided to strike out northward. With these men went David Ingram, whose confused account of an incredible two-thousand-mile journey into present-day Nova Scotia was included by Hakluyt in the first edition of his collection but omitted subsequently under suspicion that much of it was fabricated. Most of it is probably true, but his journal, though touching briefly on Mexico, really belongs more to a history of travel in the United States.[6]

Philips's group continued to the south, coming to the Pánuco, where they were taken prisoners by the Spanish. In Tampico they were reviled as both "English dogs" and "Lutheran heretikes" and forced to march to Mexico City. Still, Philips could gratefully praise the care that one old Spaniard took of them and the courtesy they received at a hospital in the capital. They were then imprisoned and later, after having attempted to escape, sold as servants or slaves. Many of the Englishmen, having none of the prejudices of the aristocratic Spanish against work, proved valuable overseers at the mines and other operations and gradually rose in wealth. But in 1574 the "bloodie and cruell Inquisition" was formally established in Mexico and the English Protestants were seized as its first victims. From then on Philips had no pleasant memories of the country.

Three of Hawkins's men were burned and some sixty given penance. Philips was bound over to an order of the Dominicans and ap-

5 Ibid., VII, 53–62.
6 *Voyages and Travels Mainly during the 16th and 17th Centuries,* I, 161–172.

pointed overseer of a body of Indians building a church. Learning the workers' tongue, he found them "a courteous and loving kind of people, ingenious, and of great understanding," who "hate and ab-horre the Spaniardes with all their hearts." Upon fulfilling his period of service Philips was freed, with the knowledge that he would be carefully watched thereafter. Nevertheless, he struggled to leave the country and was twice more taken prisoner. In 1579 he was in Acapul-co, hoping to find Drake (who had raided the port in March) so that he might be, as he wrote, "freed out of that danger and miserie where-in I lived, and should returne to mine owne countery of England againe." Finally in 1582 he took the arduous road to Guatemala and from there made it to Europe. Several of these later episodes, especial-ly one in which we find him sawing off his irons while an Indian fixes the broken wheel of the wagon in which he is being returned to Mexico City, have something of the flavor of a swashbuckling novel.[7]

In 1591 appeared a third narrative by a survivor, *The rare Trauailes of Iob Hortop, an Englishman, who was not heard of in three and twentie yeeres space*; it was reprinted in the next edition of Hakluyt's *Voyages*, 1600. Job Hortop, who was also put ashore at Tampico, adds little to the facts as Philips presented them. And staying only two years in Mexico before being shipped as a prisoner to Spain, he saw little of the country. Yet his narrative is interesting in the way it so often smacks of the medieval interest in marvels; Hortop mentions every strange animal and plant he saw or thought he saw in Africa and Mexico. After the modernity and ease of Tomson's and Philips's narratives, this one (like Ingram's and to some extent Hawks's) re-minds us what a strange world these men were encountering.[8]

To the English, whose ships always entered the Gulf of Mexico from the south after having traversed the entire Caribbean Sea, Mexico still seemed quite remote. After the defeat of the Spanish Armada in 1588 and the opening of British colonies along the north Atlantic sea-board, perhaps it also seemed less important. For over a hundred years only one other English book about Mexico appeared: *The English-American his Travail by Sea and Land: or A New Svrvey of the West-India's, containing a Journall of Three thousand and Three hundred Miles within the main Land of America*, 1648. But that book, by

---

[7] Hakluyt, *Principal Navigations*, VI, 296–336; comments about Indians, p. 323. Philips's story was reprinted separately in 1724.

[8] Ibid., VI, 336–354.

Thomas Gage (1603?–1656), was the first systematic survey of Mexico to be published in any language and still remains one of the six or seven most important accounts about that country written in English.[9] It is an odd work, since Gage felt that in addition to describing his travels he must also convince his Puritan readers of two things: first, that he had completely forsaken the Catholicism he had earlier embraced—so he heaped much abuse on the Church and its clergy; and second, that the British held a moral responsibility to rescue the Americas from the various evils the Spanish had visited upon them. Scholars have questioned Gage's sincerity.

Educated in Spanish schools and ordained a priest in the Dominican order, Gage along with his good friend Antonio Meléndez had volunteered in 1625 to join a mission to the Philippines. In spite of his clerical position, however, the Spanish government still looked upon him first as an Englishman, and he had to hide "in a barrel that was emptied of biscuit to that purpose." In the same fleet as the new viceroy, the Marqués de Cerralvo, and the inquisitor who had been sent to investigate a civic disturbance caused that year by quarrels between the former viceroy and his archbishop, they arrived at Veracruz in September. Gage and his fellow friars traveled thence to "that famous and gallant city" of Mexico to rest before they joined the fleet at Acapulco. He was greatly taken by the beauty of the place, concluding, "There is nothing in Mexico and about it wanting which may make a city happy." He remained there five months, inquiring carefully about the country and about the islands to which he was going. A friar who had just escaped the Philippines represented the clergy there as so dissolute that Gage, Meléndez, and two others finally determined to slip away to Guatemala instead. Thus in February 1626 the four secretly left the Dominican house on a devious route designed to throw any pursuers off their true direction. Then they rode south, stopping at Oaxaca, "a fair and beautiful city to behold," where Gage would have liked to stay. But the friars there were unlikely to welcome them, and they pressed on, crossing the pass at Macuilapa after a wait of three days for the fierce Pacific winds to subside and thus arriving in Chiapas. In Ciudad Real (now San Cristóbal de las Casas)

9 For information about Gage's life, see Thomas Gage, *Travels in the New World*, including introduction by J. Eric S. Thompson, pp. xiii–lii. A. P. Newton's edition of Gage's *The English-American* and George Conway's monograph *An Englishman in Mexico* were helpful.

the tired refugees were befriended by Father Pedro Alvarez, one of the few priests whom Gage mentions with admiration, and there he remained from April until the end of September teaching Latin. His account of the experience indicates that it was pleasant.

In the spring of 1627 Gage arrived in Guatemala, where he remained nearly ten years, part of the time working with the Pokoman Indians, a branch of the Mayas. His stories of witchcraft in the country and his search for the idol of an ancient god hidden away (an incident retold by Aldous Huxley)[10] must have mildly titillated the imaginations of his Puritan readers. It was during this period, he related, that he came to have grievous doubts concerning certain points of Catholic dogma, and he asserted he was shocked by the life led by the clergy in Mexico and Guatemala. Upon his arrival in Mexico he had observed the "vanity and worldliness" of a richly clad Franciscan and the priests' obvious delight in cards and dicing. Examples of such behavior multiplied during his long stay. He concluded: "Sin and wickedness abound in Mexico, yet there are no more devout people in the world toward the Church and clergy."[11] Such conditions caused him to reappraise his profession. At the same time Gage was longing to see Europe again. When a transfer did not seem forthcoming soon, he decided to flee once again, and departed, like Philips, on a dangerous journey into the jungles of Central America and thence along the Pacific coast to Portobello in Panama. From there he served as chaplain on a ship leaving for Spain and in 1640 arrived back in Britain, barely able to "speak some few broken words" in English. Three years later he renounced his faith and threw in his lot with the Puritans.

Gage appears to have kept some kind of journal during his twelve years in New Spain, for *A New Survey* contains remarkably few factual errors. He described fully the countryside through which he passed and the people he met. The way of life he observed in the isolated stretches of Chiapas and Central America has changed relatively little since the book was published, as many subsequent visitors have noted. The strange vegetation especially fascinated him, and he devoted one entire chapter to a discussion of chocolate and *atole* (a corn drink). In order to substantiate his observations about Mexico

[10] Aldous Huxley, *Beyond the Mexique Bay*, pp. 131–132.
[11] Gage, *Travels in the New World*, pp. 44, 70.

City and its history, Gage incorporated segments of his own translation of Francisco López de Gómara's *Historia de la conquista de México* (first translated into English in 1578), and he must have consulted many other sources for his rather full knowledge of Mexican history and geography, including information about areas he did not see. Much space in the book is taken up with objective redaction of these materials.

Throughout he carefully remembered, of course, his propagandistic purposes, and some of the government officials in England must have read the work attentively. In 1654 Gage was invited to submit a memorandum, "Some briefe and true observations concerning the West-Indies, humbly presented to his highness, Oliver, Lord Protector of the Commonwealth of England, Scotland, and Ireland." Since the Civil War was over, Cromwell late in 1654 determined to send an expedition to the Spanish Main. Before it left, Gage prepared another edition of *A New Survey*, probably in order to spur enthusiasm for the undertaking. Gage himself was aboard one of the ships as its chaplain. Cromwell decided, however, to attack the Caribbean islands rather than the mainland as Gage had suggested. In 1655 the first assault, on Hispaniola, was a dismal and costly failure. The fleet easily took Jamaica, however, and then sailed home. Gage remained behind, dying on the island the next year.

In the next sixty years four more editions of his book were published in Britain, and in 1758 a seventh edition appeared in New Jersey, both as a serial in the *New American Magazine* and as a book. The reading public then largely forgot about it, although Robert Southey used it as a basis for the Mexican part of his epic poem *Madoc*, 1805. In 1928 A. P. Newton finally reissued the book in an abridged form. This text was reprinted several times. The currently available edition, *Thomas Gage's Travels in the New World*, first appeared in 1958, edited by the Maya archaeologist J. Eric S. Thompson. He decided to omit all the excerpts from Gómara since they concerned Mexico of the century prior to Gage's visit; he modernized the language and some of the sentence structures; and like Newton decided to censor those portions of the text that might offend Catholic readers, including three entire chapters dealing with polemical statements against the Church. Thus part of the contemporary flavor is missing, though Gage's rich description of the land is perhaps better served.

Gage was the last Englishman, for 170 years, until the Mexican War of Independence, to penetrate the interior of New Spain and to publish his observations. But at least ten British naval officers—from William Dampier in 1697 to George Vancouver in 1798—and the American captain William Shaler, in 1808, gave their impressions of the Mexican and California coasts. A British diplomatic envoy, one Lieutenant James Cook, in *Remarks on a Passage from the River Balise in the Bay of Honduras to Merida,* 1769, described a mission through Yucatan.[12] And the American lieutenant Zebulon Pike (1779–1813), as a result of his straying into Spanish territory and being captured, saw the area from Santa Fe to Chihuahua, an adventure described in *An Account of Expeditions,* 1810.[13] Only Pike's narrative created much excitement; Americans were already desiring to expand westward.

As a result of such paucity of information, Mexico remained almost a blank for the average English reader and seems to have touched his imagination only as a vague symbol of wealth, error, and high adventure. The country figured at moments in reports of colonial rivalries, and a few of the New England divines—Cotton Mather, who talked with one traveler from Yucatan, and Samuel Sewall—wished that it could be saved from Catholicism.[14] A number of reviews of Spanish chronicles appeared in the *Gentleman's Magazine* in London. In 1741 John Campbell published *A Concise History of Spanish America . . . Collected Chiefly from Spanish Writers,* and in 1777 William Robertson issued his important two-volume *History of America.* But both Scottish historians touched mainly on the matter of the Conquest. The translator of Humboldt's monumental study of New Spain in 1811 observed how empty Robertson's comments on the land turned out to be when set against an eyewitness account. More dismaying was Robertson's complete unwillingness to believe the truthfulness of the Spanish *conquistadores.* Thinking that they had inflated their descriptions of the Aztecs in order to make their conquest seem

[12] Mayer, *Early Travellers in Mexico,* pp. 117–119; Edward G. Cox, *A Reference Guide to the Literature of Travel,* I, 42–49, II, 30–31; *Dictionary of National Biography,* XVII, 147–148, XVIII, 46–48; Cecil Robinson, *With the Ears of Strangers,* p. 33; *Dictionary of American Biography,* XVII, 19.

[13] W. Eugene Hollon, *The Lost Pathfinder,* pp. 136–157, 176–178.

[14] Stanley T. Williams, *The Spanish Background of American Literature,* I, 3–20.

more marvelous, Robertson insisted that the Indians had really been ignorant barbarians who lived in the rudest circumstances. Bernal Díaz del Castillo's simple and straightforward memoir, *Historia verdadera de la conquista de Nueva España*, finally translated in 1800, revealed something of the truth. But not until the advent of Humboldt's work, followed rapidly by the overthrow of Spanish rule and the opening of the territory to foreigners, would the myth of Mexico really become matter for American and British writers.

## 2. The Followers of Humboldt

Beginning with Alexander von Humboldt's encyclopedic wealth of information—political, scientific, historical, and cultural—published in French in 1811 as *Essai politique sur le royaume de la Nouvelle-Espagne* and translated into English the same year, the nineteenth century began to discover real, contemporary Mexico and to gain some sense of the greatness of its Indian heritage. The mystery of Mexico would vanish slowly (it has not yet completely disappeared), but the country would never again be an almost complete cipher. Humboldt, a German scientific explorer already well known for his studies, was accorded in 1799–1804 a royal welcome to all Spanish America.[1] His four-volume study of Mexico excited much attention (Humboldt's entire survey of the new world made him one of the most famous men in all Europe) and remains a standard source of information about late colonial Mexico. He described the mining operations at Taxco, volcanic activity in Michoacán, and archaeological ruins around Mexico City and at Cholula. In the next several decades after its publication, many visitors to Mexico read the book

---

[1] Alexander von Humboldt, *Political Essay on the Kingdom of New Spain*, and idem, *Vues des cordillères*; Helmet de Terra, *Humboldt*, pp. 149–171, 217; Germán Arciniegas, *Latin America*, pp. 278–280.

eagerly and often quoted it with approval in their own travelogues. Joel Roberts Poinsett wrote of it: "When I turn to the work of this extraordinary man, I am disposed to abandon my journal. He has seen more of the country, and described it better, than any other can hope to do, and he has left almost nothing for the future traveller, but the narrative of his own adventure, and a record of his own feelings and impressions."[2]

In 1810 Humboldt had also issued a book of plates, *Vues des cordillères*, which contained for the first time many reproductions of pre-Columbian art and architecture. The expensive book was never published in the United States or Britain, but it seems to have had a small circulation in both countries and likewise influenced the remarks of later visitors.

But without realizing it Humboldt chronicled the end of an era. In 1810 Father Miguel Hidalgo precipitated Mexico into rebellion. Having learned that the authorities were about to arrest him for his political activities, he summoned the Indians to Mass and aroused them to arm. The *grito de Dolores* is reenacted each September sixteenth by the president of Mexico to commemorate the event. The resulting wars dragged on until 1821, threatening to lay the country utterly waste. William Davis Robinson (1774–1822?) published in 1820 in Philadelphia his eyewitness account of part of the struggle, *Memoirs of the Mexican Revolution*; and Captain Basil Hall (1784–1844) included a brief history of the wars in his popular work *Extracts from a Journal Written on the Coasts of Chili, Peru, and Mexico*, published in Edinburgh in 1824.[3] The United States naturally sympathized with the revolutionaries and then watched in dismay as independent Mexico remained in a state of anarchy. Its ultimate liberator, Agustín de Iturbide, had proclaimed himself emperor as soon as he dared. In early autumn 1822 Joel Poinsett (1779–1851) took a semiofficial tour of Mexico to discover what attitude the American government should take toward Iturbide. Poinsett, a thorny republican, was naturally against Mexico's new monarch but foresaw correctly that he would fall. Poinsett published *Notes on Mexico* anonymously in 1824. It is unfortunate that the man is remembered by the public today chiefly

---

2 Joel R. Poinsett, *Notes on Mexico Made in the Autumn of 1822*, p. 43.

3 For information about Robinson and Hall, in addition to their books see *National Cyclopaedia of American Biography*, XVIII, 185–186; *Dictionary of National Biography*, VIII, 942–943.

for the Mexican flower that he introduced into the United States, for
the book is a rather delightful survey of Mexico and its people.[4]

For thirty-four years, until 1855, the government was changed by
one coup after another as Mexican history followed its most confusing
course. The only constant figure throughout the period was General
Antonio López de Santa Anna, who sided first with one faction and
then another, paying attention always to his personal benefit and little
to that of his country. Weak as a result, Mexico suffered invasions by
Spain in 1829 and 1861, by France in 1838 and 1862, and by the
United States in 1846, as well as rebellions in Texas and Yucatan. A
more subtle war for economic advantages was waged by foreign representatives within the capital as the various impoverished presidents
slowly mortgaged Mexico away. The United States and Great Britain
engaged immediately in a hard-fought struggle for commercial gains;
Henry George Ward, the British chargé d'affaires from 1824 to 1827,
proved to be more effective than Poinsett—who served as minister to
Mexico from 1824 until 1829, when that government requested that
he be recalled. Ward (1797–1860) also published a survey of the
country, *Mexico in 1827*, with illustrations by his wife. But he must
take second honors as an author.[5]

Ward noted in his introduction that most Englishmen were quite
ignorant about Mexico. A surprising amount of attention was nevertheless being paid to the country in those years. Between 1816 and
1836 American and British visitors published at least eighteen travel
accounts; the next ten years saw nineteen more. In general, Humboldt's followers tended to be less objective than he. Whereas religious
differences had plagued the early British visitors, cultural pride now
became something of a hindrance, especially for Americans.

Thus it was with Albert Pike (1809–1891), a New England school
teacher and poet who, hoping to make his fortune in the West, joined
a trading expedition en route to Santa Fe in 1831. He lived in the
area for nearly a year before returning to settle in Arkansas, where
he prepared for publication *Prose Sketches and Poems Written in the
Western Country*, issued in a limited edition in 1834. A second edition,

---

[4] See Poinsett, *Notes on Mexico*; J. Fred Rippy, *Joel R. Poinsett*, pp. 35–68, 90–
131, 226–230; Edward T. Tayloe, *Mexico, 1825–1828*. Grace E. Heilman and Bernard S. Levin prepared a bibliography.

[5] See Henry George Ward, *Mexico*; *Dictionary of National Biography*, XX, 773–
774.

including additional stories Pike had published in Boston and Little Rock newspapers, was prepared only in 1967, but the book is historically important as the first creation of English fiction and poetry based upon actual experiences within Mexican territory. The verse, most of it revealing Pike's homesickness rather than his actual surroundings, today seems dated, although his attempts to imitate Comanche and Navaho Indian songs have their moments. The prose sketches include personal observations about his journey west and life in New Mexico as well as three short stories.[6]

The short stories, though so uncertain in structure and characterization as to render their literary value slight, provide the chief interest. "A Mexican Tale" describes the sorrows of two lovers, separated from each other by a calculating priest who had been bought off by another suitor of the girl. It ends dramatically with a triple murder. "The Inroad of the Nabajo" relates an American's comic surrender of his sweetheart to a Mexican who loved her more. The third, "Refugio," concerns the heroic endurance of an American, unjustly accused of murder, at the hands of the local authorities. The previously uncollected stories deal with a miner who is taken by the Navahos, two more love stories with happy endings, and an Indian battle.

In all these Pike displayed a low regard for the Mexicans. He conceded that "they have some generosity and hospitality," but continued: "They will all lie and steal, to be sure, and have no idea of gratitude. There is neither honor among the men nor virtue among the women. In fact, honor in New Mexico would be apt to lie on the owner's hands. Character is a mere drug, a valueless article; and he who has little of it is as well off, and as rich, as he who had much. The men most in honor now in that country are such as have either stolen, perjured or dishonored themselves."[7] Pike implies repeatedly that the natives stood in awe of the more manly Americans. His modern editor commented, "Pike anticipated the Anglo-American attitudes of cultural superiority toward Mexicans which would find final expression in the twin concepts of Manifest Destiny and Mission,

[6] See Albert Pike, *Prose Sketches and Poems Written in the Western Country*, pp. 92–162, 183–202, 240–241, with introduction by David J. Weber, pp. ix–xxv. Other biographies are not particularly useful. Ray Baker Harris prepared a bibliography.

[7] Pike, *Prose Sketches and Poems*, p. 187.

and result in the loss of Mexico's far northern frontier to the United States."[8]

Several other authors felt the need to deal with Mexican themes even when they had not seen the country. In 1826 the first American novel set partly in Mexico (which Pike criticized for the inaccuracy of some of its details) had appeared: *Francis Berrian, or The Mexican Patriot*, by Timothy Flint. Washington Irving in *Adventures of Captain Bonneville*, 1837, and James Fenimore Cooper in *Jack Tier*, 1848, used Mexicans as incidental characters. Aware of themselves now as citizens of the United States rather than as colonists from Europe, Americans also saw Mexican history as part of their own—Cortés's march represented the opening of the new world that Columbus had discovered. In 1829 William Gilmore Simms had finished a long poem, *The Vision of Cortes*. Robert Montgomery Bird, who planned to visit Mexico but had to give up the idea, turned out two historical romances covering the discovery and siege of Tenochtitlán: *Calavar, or The Knight of the Conquest*, 1834, and *The Infidel, or The Fall of Mexico*, 1835.[9] Among British writers Robert Southey had published *Madoc*, and Captain Frederick Marryat used a Mexican setting for one of his books for children, *Narrative of the Travels and Adventures of Monsieur Violet in California, Sonora & Western Texas*, 1843.[10]

Irving also had begun work on a history of the Conquest, but when he learned that William Hickling Prescott was interested in the same subject he turned his materials over to him. Since the publication of *History of the Conquest of Mexico* in 1843, Prescott's narrative has become for Americans and British alike the authorized version of that adventure. The history can be compared only with great novels and epics in an attempt to appraise its artistry, though it represents astute scholarly research, incorporating much material previously buried in Spanish and Mexican archives. Prescott was objective in his presentation, giving both the faults and the virtues of Cortés. Yet the Spaniard obviously became a heroic figure for him; he could not bear to end

---

[8] Weber, in ibid., pp. xv–xvi.

[9] Cecil Robinson, *With the Ears of Strangers*, pp. 22–24; Stanley T. Williams, *The Spanish Background of American Literature*, I, 218–221, 246; James K. Folson, *Timothy Flint*, pp. 107–118; Curtis Dahl, *Robert Montgomery Bird*, pp. 72–84. Flint edited in 1833 *The Personal Narrative of James O. Pattie*, which describes Pattie's visit to Mexico.

[10] *Dictionary of National Biography*, XII, 1086–1088.

the story with the completion of the Conquest but continued it until the *conquistador*'s death. In Indianized Mexico, Cortés has lately been denounced as the destroyer of a noble civilization, but for the average English reader he stands as one of the great heroes of the age of exploration. Prescott is probably responsible for our continuing interest in the man.

Since Prescott spent the first section of his history re-creating as fully as he could the life of the Aztecs before the Conquest, he excited further interest in that civilization. Moctezuma became for Prescott a man almost as great in stature as Cortés. Nor did Prescott hold up either the Aztec or the Spanish civilization as particularly better or worse than the other—except in one way. The New Englander could not be sympathetic with Aztec sacrifices and represented the blood-stained priests as pure villains. Our awareness of the savage cruelty of the Aztecs, a characteristic that many later writers (most notably D. H. Lawrence) have insisted continues to permeate Mexican blood, possibly comes from Prescott.

Another important sourcebook about Mexico's Indian past, *Antiquities of Mexico*, was being published in London from 1830 to 1848, large volume by large volume. Although the set was too expensive to be well known, it still influenced a number of writers. In these volumes Edward King, Viscount Kingsborough, an eccentric Irishman who never saw Mexico, magnificently reproduced examples of pre-Columbian art and literature together with various accounts of the life of the Indians.[11]

But the works from this period that must interest us most are four firsthand accounts of travel in various sections of Mexico: a book by Richard Henry Dana, Jr., about a voyage along the California coast, two by John Lloyd Stephens about expeditions through the wilds of Chiapas and Yucatan, and one by Frances Calderón de la Barca (Scottish in spite of her married name) about life in the great interior of the country. These works not only rank among the best descriptions of Mexico in our language, they are also esteemed by lovers of American and British travel literature as classics.

When Dana (1815–1882) published *Two Years before the Mast* in 1840, it was an instant success and has remained continuously in print since. He left Harvard at age eighteen and signed up as a common

---

11 J. Eric S. Thompson, *The Rise and Fall of Maya Civilization*, pp. 33–34.

sailor in the merchant marine in an attempt to strengthen his weak eyes. The book primarily records his life aboard ship, but for seventeen months, 1835–1836, he was helping load hides along the coast of California, then still part of Mexico.[12] Although he did not travel far into the country, merely touching port at San Diego, San Pedro, Santa Barbara, Monterey, and San Francisco, his observations are a major source of information about the area during this time, for Dana saw more than most visitors. He borrowed a Spanish grammar and dictionary; aided by the other languages he knew, he could converse after a fashion with the native Mexicans. Consequently the ship's captain often sent him ashore on various errands. Dana discovered a region still sparsely settled—although the various Spanish and Mexican governments had long promoted colonization of the area in fear of Russian expansion southward—and a region where the resources were scarcely tapped by anyone but the energetic Americans and British emigrants already streaming into the land.

Reared as a New England gentleman, Dana tried to be calmly objective in all that he wrote about the Mexican culture. He understood well that American life could appear incredibly stupid to an outsider. Thus, although he obviously admired the enterprise of the American settlers, he balanced his picture of them with accounts of several rascals who had drifted to the West Coast. He tried to show the good and the bad in the Mexican character. He admired greatly the Mexicans' brilliant appearance and their elegant manners and diction, common even to the lowest classes. He resisted the impulse to ridicule an impoverished grandee, who insisted on acting as if he had all the money he needed, and set him tellingly against the "fat, coarse, vulgar, pretending fellow of a Yankee trader" who preyed off him. But in almost every way Dana revealed himself to be American to the core, insulated and somewhat dubious about the worth of a strikingly different way of life. He unconsciously shows this in his selection of details. For the New England teenager horseraces, cockfights, flirtations, and other apparent and real signs of moral laxness stood out. He found it amusing that a friar would not let him pay for a meal at the mission but would easily accept whatever offering he wished to make. Dana, like Pike, simply assumed that the women had "but little vir-

[12] See Richard Henry Dana, Jr., *Two Years before the Mast*, pp. 66–352, 462–490. An edition by John H. Kemble helped greatly. Robert L. Gale, *Richard Henry Dana, Jr.*, will place the trip in perspective.

tue" and refused other men only because "the jealousy of their husbands is extreme, and their revenge deadly and almost certain."[13] Having imagined that the dancing would be more exotic, he was disappointed in the formal patterns followed at a wedding fiesta. The show of gaiety displayed at a child's funeral quite bewildered him. Sometimes he became explicit in his judgment, and he summed up by saying that the Mexicans were "an idle, thriftless people" on whom "a curse had fallen, and stripped them of everything but their pride, their manners, and their voices."[14]

Dana more urbanely balanced his political observations, amusedly comparing the Americans' "*caucusing*, paragraphing, libelling, feasting, promising, and lying" with the Mexicans' "muskets and bayonets." He barely mentioned the rebellion in Texas and nowhere betrayed the growing sense of Manifest Destiny, which would shortly sweep the nation. However, after summing up the ill use that the Mexicans were making of the area, he exclaimed: "In the hands of an enterprising people, what a country this might be!"[15] And when he returned to California in 1859–1860 to review the changes the Americans had brought, although he remembered the lonely wilderness with nostalgia, he was delighted by the bustle he found. He appended a sketch of this visit, "Twenty Four Years After," to the 1869 edition of *Two Years before the Mast.* He now had more praise for the Mexicans whom he found still residing in the area. But he did note that one was a state senator because the Americans respected the brave manner in which the man had resisted them, "not a common thing among the Mexicans." By this time Dana had seen another part of Spanish America, having visited Cuba earlier the same year. *To Cuba and Back,* 1859, however, lacks the exuberance and artistry of the earlier book.

*Incidents of Travel in Central America, Chiapas, and Yucatan* and *Incidents of Travel in Yucatan,* two works by John Lloyd Stephens (1805–1852), are as exciting as Dana's work. That they have not achieved the popularity of the earlier book may perhaps be explained by their size and the expense of reproducing them. For without the carefully drawn engravings of Frederick Catherwood (1799–1854), the impact of many of the chapters, especially in the second set of

---

[13] Dana, *Two Years before the Mast,* p. 215.
[14] Ibid., pp. 94, 97.
[15] Ibid., pp. 212, 216.

volumes, would be lost. Stephens, an American, was a lawyer by profession but an explorer by temperament. He had already published two popular travel accounts about relatively unknown countries of eastern Europe and western Asia before he came to Mexico and Central America in company with Catherwood, an English artist and architect.[16] Stephens held a commission from President Van Buren to the government of the Confederation of Central American States, but his real interest was to view the few ruins of the ancient Maya civilization that had come to light. At that time no one even suspected that there had been such a civilization, rivaling in splendor the well-known Aztec and Inca empires. To be sure, various Spanish explorers had seen the remains of several of the Maya cities, a few of which were still inhabited; but most of their reports were yet unpublished. Stephens read everything that he could find. Beginning in 1773 several persons had explored Palenque. Among them were Antonio del Río, whose story was first published in London in 1822; Capitán Guillermo Dupaix, whose expedition was revealed in a volume published in Paris in 1834; and the French count Jean Frédéric Waldeck, who unfortunately altered his drawings of the ruins at Palenque (not published until 1866) and at Uxmal, published in 1838, in accord with his belief that the builders had been Roman or Phoenician. An Irish soldier of fortune, writing under the pseudonym "Juan Galindo," published "The Ruins of Copán" in an American journal in 1838; he also visited Palenque.[17] But Stephens was the first to realize the extent of the civilization of the Maya, stretching from present-day Honduras to Yucatan, and to point out that it had arisen from the ancestors of the same Indians who still inhabited the region. Moreover, the popularity of Stephens's two books brought this information to the widest possible audience and created an interest in learning more. For these reasons Stephens is often called the father of Maya archaeology.

After a brief stop in Belize, with which the Central America book begins, Stephens and Catherwood set out early in November 1839 from Livingston, Guatemala, on the dangerous search for the con-

---

[16] John L. Stephens, *Incidents of Travel in Central America, Chiapas, and Yucatan*; idem, *Incidents of Travel in Yucatan*. Also Victor Von Hagen, *Maya Explorer*; idem, *Frederick Catherwood, Arch^t*. Ann and Myron Sutton (*Among the Maya Ruins*) provide a light redaction of Stephens's books with superb illustrations.

[17] Thompson, *Rise and Fall of Maya Civilization*, pp. 32–35; Victor Von Hagen, *World of the Maya*, pp. 13–18, 214–215.

federation government. Roads were poor; the native Indians were suspicious of strangers. But the reason for the American government's sending Stephens on his journey in the first place provided the chief danger: the area was embroiled in civil war. The trip toward Guatemala City forecast the constant and confusing problems that would beset him and Catherwood: they were arrested, released, met by surly or indifferent officials, greeted with customary Spanish politeness, admired for their medicines, soaked through by the rain, almost killed through various natural calamities, annoyed by insects, and threatened by fever. But Stephens and Catherwood, in spite of politics and climate, were excellent explorers. When they were in town they attended bullfights, cockfights, the theater, and religious festivities, scurrying by sentinels who might any moment shoot them for no reason. In the country a mountain was to be climbed, a lake was to be seen, and all rumors of ruins, no matter how far off their path, had to be checked out.

Even on the way to Guatemala to present his credentials, Stephens showed his true interest in coming to the area; the route was carefully chosen to lead them by Copán. The site included a collection of ruined pyramids, fallen buildings, statues, and carved stones. These monuments, Stephens wrote, "put at rest at once and forever, in our minds, all uncertainty in regard to the character of American antiquities, and gave us the assurance that the objects we were in search of were interesting, not only as the remains of an unknown people, but as works of art, proving, like newly-discovered historical records, that the people who once occupied the Continent of America were not savages." With growing excitement they began clearing the brush away so that Catherwood, aided by a camera lucida, could begin drawing. The artist had difficulty at first as "the designs were so intricate and complicated, the subjects so entirely new and unintelligible," but he soon mastered the problems and reproduced such exact detail that archaeologists have since depended upon his drawings in order to reconstruct works subsequently destroyed. While Stephens proceeded on his mission, Catherwood remained behind, making scores of drawings at considerable risk to his own health. Hearing of other ruins at Quiriguá, he journeyed there, making the first report ever about this ancient city. He and Stephens together would encounter several more ruins in Guatemala, notably at Santa Cruz del Quiché. Their sense of awe seems to have grown with each new discovery. Of Copán, Stephens wrote: "Of the moral effect of the monuments themselves, standing as they do in the depths of a tropical forest, silent and solemn, strange in design, excellent in sculpture, rich in ornament, different from the works of any other people, their uses and purposes, their whole history so entirely unknown, with hieroglyphics explaining all, but perfectly unintelligible, I shall not pretend to convey any idea. Often the imagination was pained in gazing at them."[18]

In April the two men, accompanied by Henry Pawling (an American who had come to Guatemala with Handy's Traveling Circus and stayed on to run a cochineal plantation), rode north into Mexico. Their ultimate destination was Palenque and Uxmal. Riding through southern Chiapas, well off all the usual trails, provided all the excitement of the earlier journeys, with the added difficulty of even steeper mountains. When they arrived at Palenque they discovered that John Herbert Caddy and Patrick Walker, whom they had met in Belize, had stopped there a few months earlier.[19] Now Stephens, Catherwood, Pawling, and their native servant excitedly set up residence in the building called the Palace. "For the first time," Stephens wrote, "we were in a building erected by the aboriginal inhabitants, standing before the Europeans knew of the existence of this continent, and we prepared to take up our abode under its roof." Working under atrocious conditions, Catherwood began copying the carvings and structures. By the end of May, Stephens remembered, "he was wan and gaunt; lame, like me, from the bites of insects, his face was swollen, and his left arm hung with rheumatism as if paralyzed."[20] Nevertheless, they now had proof that this place was built by the same race as had worked at Copán: the hieroglyphics were identical.

From Palenque, Stephens and Catherwood descended to the coast, leaving Pawling behind to make plaster casts of the sculpture at the ruins (he finished some thirty, only to have the local authorities destroy them), and embarked for Sisal in Yucatan. Catherwood was still ill with malaria, but he insisted that they explore Uxmal. The pair plunged into another revolution. Yucatan and Tabasco had declared their independence of the rest of Mexico. But the men made it without incident to Mérida, where Stephens called upon Simón Peón, a de-

---

[18] Stephens, *Central America*, I, 102, 120, 158.

[19] Their reports, including Caddy's drawings of the ruins, were finally published in 1967 by David M. Penderast in *Palenque*.

[20] Stephens, *Central America*, II, 292, 334.

scendant of the powerful Montejo family and present owner of the ruins, whom Stephens had met in New York. Uxmal overwhelmed them, both because of its inherent grandeur and because the ground around the buildings had been cleared so that they could finally see one of these ancient sites in perspective. The Governor's House, Stephens felt, was "not unworthy to stand side by side with the remains of Egyptian, Grecian, and Roman art." But before Catherwood could scarcely begin, he collapsed. On June 24, 1840, they left the country. By now, though they had seen only four cities and other scattered ruins, Stephens was convinced that these buildings had been erected by the same people "who occupied the country at the time of the invasion by the Spaniards, or of some not very distant progenitors." Modern archaeologists accept his conclusion.[21]

Back in New York, Stephens began quickly rewriting from his journals while Catherwood supervised the making of the engravings from his drawings. By the middle of the next year *Incidents of Travel in Central America, Chiapas, and Yucatan*, with seventy-eight illustrations, was ready for the printers. The details about the exploration of the ruins were by no means the only high points in the two-volume work. Stephens's meetings with political personages, his descent into the crater of an extinct volcano, his and Catherwood's exploration of Lake Atitlán, their encounter with a forest fire, the description of the death of a child, and his farewell to his mule also stand out. The public was understandably excited about the book. Prescott, who was well into his history of the Conquest, was pleased to find confirmation of what he had deduced from manuscripts and sent off a copy to the Calderóns in Mexico.

*Incidents* finished, Stephens and Catherwood itched to return to Uxmal and to visit another site they had heard of, Chichén Itzá. In late October 1841 they landed at Sisal, accompanied by Dr. Samuel Cabot, an amateur ornithologist. Before they left in May of the next year they had discovered "the crumbling remains of forty-four ancient cities," all "lost, buried, and unknown, never before visited by a stranger, and some of them, perhaps, never looked upon by the eyes of a white man."[22] In general, this trip was almost peaceful, certainly in comparison with the former one. Yucatan was still in a state of

[21] Ibid., II, 430, 442–443.
[22] Stephens, *Yucatan*, II, 306–307.

rebellion, toying with the idea of uniting with Texas; but they traveled everywhere in perfect safety, welcomed warmly since copies of *Incidents* had preceded them. Their willingness to take daguerreotype portraits and Cabot's surgical skill in remedying cross-eyes (a particular affliction of the Maya) also helped them. They covered an enormous circuit of ground, but as a result of these conditions Stephens's second book, *Incidents of Travel in Yucatan,* is less adventurous and more descriptive of local color. He discussed among other matters the lottery, bullfights (he appreciated the element of danger involved and disliked the precautions that had recently been introduced), life on the hacienda, the killing of an iguana, the small weaknesses of the priests, a funeral wake, fiestas. His lively eye roved unabashedly in search of the beautiful women. He recorded a humorous incident in which a man at a dance had harangued him in the Maya tongue to the delight of the crowd, only to be put down by Stephens's answering oration in English and Greek; they agreed to stick to Spanish. By now Stephens was more adept in this language, although he never learned to spell it well (as Mrs. Calderón noted). He had read several Mexican histories in search of data about the conditions existing when the Spaniards arrived. The three explorers, however, seriously needed knowledge of Maya. In some sections no other language was spoken.

Before they could return to Uxmal, they heard of Mayapán and detoured there briefly. Then for six weeks they slaved at getting Uxmal on paper in reproductions and words. Stephens wrote, "The freshness and enthusiasm with which we had first come upon the ruins of an American city had perhaps gone, but our feelings were not blunted, and all the regret which we had felt in being obliged to leave was more than counterbalanced by the satisfaction of returning."[23] The daguerreotype proved unsatisfactory because of the strong relief of the carvings, casting heavy shadows, so that Catherwood was forced to return to the camera lucida. Once again the place turned out to be unhealthy; all three men left wracked with malarial fever. These were strong explorers, however; they quickly recovered under the care of a village father and moved on to other sites, discovering always "the same strange mingling of old things with new." Among other places they saw Kabah, with its solitary corbeled arch (rediscovered

[23] Ibid., I, 89.

only in 1941) and carved wooden lintel; Labna, with its arched gateway; Chichén Itzá, "presenting a spectacle which, even after all that we had seen, once more excited in us emotions of wonder";[24] and Tulum, in its picturesque setting overlooking the Caribbean. Along the way they also explored caves and *cenotes*, including the deep well at Bolonchén and the sacrificial well at Chichén, and they came upon traces of the ancient roads that had connected the Maya cities. In the villages Stephens searched the archives, discovering a number of treasures at Maní.

Catherwood had already opened in New York an exhibit displaying panoramas of Jerusalem and Thebes. Upon their return he added copies of the new Mexican drawings, a unique sculptured beam with hieroglyphics from Uxmal, the lintel from Kabah, and various other artifacts. The last day of July 1842 the building caught fire; all the contents were destroyed. Despite the irrecoverable loss, Catherwood threw himself into supervising the engravings for the new *Incidents*. When the two-volume work was published in late winter 1843 it contained 126 illustrations. In addition the book included the first accurate map of Yucatan and the first publication (in translation) of Juan Pío Pérez's important contribution to working out Maya chronology. The whole work received the same enthusiastic response as the earlier volumes.

Stephens planned one more book, a four-volume survey of American antiquities to contain articles by Humboldt (whom he was shortly to meet), Prescott, himself, and others, as well as drawings by Catherwood. The scheme unfortunately fell through. Thereupon, Catherwood decided to issue a collection of twenty-five lithographs of the Maya artifacts. *Views of Ancient Monvments in Central America, Chiapas, and Yvcatan* appeared in London in 1844, dedicated to Stephens. One of the plates depicts the only known likeness of Catherwood as well as figures of Stephens and Cabot. For the work Catherwood wrote a brief introduction, making the same points about the probable origin and general appearance of the ruins as Stephens had made. After this both men turned to other projects that took them back to the Caribbean area, Stephens to Panama and Catherwood to British Guiana and Panama and across central Mexico. But, unfortunately, no more books were forthcoming from either.

[24] Ibid., II, 182.

The narrative of Frances Calderón de la Barca (1804–1882) is not nearly so lively as those by Dana and Stephens, but *Life in Mexico during a Residence of Two Years in That Country* possesses a warm charm all its own.[25] Charles Flandrau called it "the most entertaining as well as the most essentially true book on Mexico that I have been able to find."[26] Because of her position Mrs. Calderón probably saw more of Mexican life than any traveler had since Humboldt. Born in Scotland, she had in 1831 emigrated with other members of her family to the United States. There some seven years later she had met and married the Spanish minister to the States. Within a year he was chosen as the first Spanish envoy to Mexico. The country received the couple with much show when they arrived in the winter of 1839–1840; they were the visible symbol that Spain had finally acknowledged Mexico's independence. Consequently, in addition to the Mexicans' natural good manners, the social and political powers had every desire to accommodate the wishes of the minister's wife. Her curiosity was practically boundless, and her feminine viewpoint and sometimes almost malicious tongue provide a contrast to Humboldt's scientific observations.

She visited all the chief tourist attractions of Mexico City: the great cathedral, with the Aztec calendar stone then affixed to it, and the national palace on the Zócalo; the shrines of the Virgin of Guadalupe and the Virgin of Los Remedios; Chapultepec and its environs; Tolsa's Minería, in which various historical and scientific collections were poorly kept; the Viga Canal, which ran into the city from Xochimilco. (A modern-day traveler would have trouble recognizing some of her city since the Zócalo was a park, the stately buildings around the Alameda were not yet erected, and the magnificent Paseo de la Reforma dates from Maximilian's period.) Included always with her observations about these places is a brief account of their history. As she wrote, "Here, everything reminds us of the past; of the conquering Spaniards, who seemed to build for eternity; impressing each work with their own solid, grave, and religious character; of the triumphs of catholicism; and of the Indians, when Cortés first startled them

[25] Frances Calderón de la Barca, *Life in Mexico during a Residence of Two Years in That Country*, from which all quotations come; idem, *Life in Mexico*, with biography, pp. xxi–xxix, and bibliography, pp. 629–630, edited by Howard T. and Marion Hall Fisher.

[26] Charles M. Flandrau, *Viva Mexico!*, pp. 147–152.

from their repose, and stood before them like the fulfillment of a half-forgotten prophesy. It is the present that seems like a dream, a pale reflection of the past."[27] In preparation for her visit she had read Humboldt (in Spanish), to whom she often refers, Poinsett, Ward (she particularly admired Mrs. Ward's sketches), and various Mexican histories. From her Mexican friends she picked up many other stories.

Like Stephens she was witnessing history. She attended the consecration of the first Mexican archbishop since the war against Spain (the mother country having recognized Mexico, Rome could no longer refuse recognition of Mexico's church). She met Guadalupe Victoria, Mexico's first president; Anastasio Bustamante, the current chief of state; and Santa Anna, fresh from his defeat in Texas and his triumph against the French at Veracruz and still the real power in Mexico. Though in July 1840 a part of the army tried to unseat Bustamante, Santa Anna chose to sit this attempt out. As in so many of Mexico's revolutions, Mrs. Calderón observed that "both parties seem to be *fighting the city* instead of each other; and this manner of firing from behind parapets, and from the tops of houses and steeples, is decidedly safer for the soldiers than for the inhabitants."[28] But when another pronouncement was made against the president in late summer 1841, Santa Anna joined with the army against Bustamante and soon moved into the national palace. The Texas question was also intermittently on everyone's mind during this period; Mrs. Calderón saw one detachment of the Texas Santa Fe expedition, which had been seized and marched to Mexico City.

*Life in Mexico*, however, appeals more for the chance remarks about lesser personages—such as María Ignacia Rodríguez, whom Humboldt had called "a sort of western Madame de Staël"—and their daily habits. She shows us much of the home life of the aristocratic Mexican. She commented about most of the religious festivals, especially those connected with Holy Week, the Day of the Dead, and Christmas. In many of these remarks she showed herself a Protestant who would shortly convert to Catholicism. Rather unusual for a visitor, she saw "every hospital, jail, college, and madhouse" in the city, leaving us records of their appearance. She attended the theater and

[27] Calderón, *Life in Mexico*, p. 357 (p. 432 in Fisher ed.).
[28] Ibid., p. 231 (p. 300 in Fisher ed.).

the opera and was as much depressed by the former as she was delighted by the latter. "But music in this country is a sixth sense," she observed. Her discussion of street cries is superb. About the bullfight, which she had to attend as wife of the Spanish minister, she confessed that, "though at first I covered my face and could not look, little by little I grew so much interested in the scene, that I could not take my eyes off it."[29] But cockfights and the gambling tables at San Agustín (now Tlalpan) continued to distress her since she observed that too often the losers further swelled the hordes of beggars and robbers, too prominent products of "the disorganized state of the country." Like many visitors to Mexico at this time, she finally learned to take both groups—like a third, bad servants—philosophically.

Nor did the robbers prevent her from making several expeditions out of the city in company with her husband. She visited silver mines, pulque haciendas, ranches at branding time, archaeological remains at Teotihuacán and Cholula. With others they traveled around the volcanoes from Cuernavaca to Puebla and then later out to Michoacán through Morelia as far as the Indian village of Uruapan. On this last trip especially Mrs. Calderón proved her sturdy spirit, writing, "I am happy to say that we are generally the discoverers of our own pathways . . . and this kind of journey has something in it so independent and amusing, that with all its fatigues and inconveniences, we find it delightful—far preferable even to travelling in the most commodious London-built carriage."[30] When they left Mexico in January 1842, they stopped in Tampico. On all these trips the scenery and climate continued to delight, especially vistas by moonlight and at dawn.

Her letters reveal a gradual change on her part from perplexity, approaching antipathy, to warm admiration for the country and its people—except its politicians. When she first landed she thought Veracruz was most "melancholy, *délabré*, and forlorn," but when she left she excused the sorry conditions of the city as a result of the recent war with France. She found Mexican cookery first detestable and then delicious; pulque at first the drink of Pluto but later a beverage she would find it "very difficult to live without!" Of the architecture, she wrote, "The houses, which at first appeared gloomy,

[29] Ibid., pp. 365, 79 (pp. 441, 129 in Fisher ed.).
[30] Ibid., p. 482 (p. 568 in Fisher ed.).

large, and comfortless, habit has reconciled us to, and experience has taught us that they are precisely suited to this climate of perpetual spring." At first she had had problems adjusting to the apparently unsophisticated society. The women were plain, overdressed, and exceedingly lazy, she thought, not to mention the fact that they smoked in public. But as she became friends with many of them, visiting often in their homes and holding soirées in hers for them to attend, she perceived their true worth and respected fully their quiet involvement with their homes, their religion, and their various charitable organizations. She thus concluded, "How necessary for a traveller to compare his judgments at different periods, and to correct them!"[31] Many Mexicans at the time of the book's publication did not read so far in their copies and were outraged at her earlier remarks. Now, however, her portrait hangs in the country's museum of history—the only foreigner besides Humboldt thus to be honored—and her book is treated with great respect.

*Life in Mexico*, though dated 1843, actually appeared in the last days of 1842. The author was identified merely as "Madame C—— de la B——"; but most readers could have guessed her full name readily, and indeed Prescott plainly revealed it in his glowing review of the book for the *North American Review*. Undoubtedly Prescott was largely responsible for its publication (he also prefaced it with a short note of appreciation). He had met her in Boston before her marriage and had contacted her husband in an effort to obtain materials from Spain for his *History of the Conquest*. While the Calderóns were in Mexico, they corresponded with Prescott at some length.[32] Prescott also arranged through Charles Dickens for the book's British publication and cited it several times in footnotes to his history. Mrs. Calderón's observations had been useful for his description of Cortés's ascent into the highlands, just as the book would shortly prove useful for General Winfield Scott's advance during the Mexican War. *Life in Mexico* was reprinted several times during the century and then allowed to go out of print.

In 1915, however, Everyman's Library included it among its titles. In the introduction to this edition, Henry Baerlein (later the author

---

31 Ibid., pp. 523, 528 (pp. 609, 614 in Fisher ed.).

32 Roger Wolcott (ed.), *Correspondence of William Hickling Prescott*, pp. 128–133, 167–170, 220–223, 247–254, 263–265, 284–288; C. Harvey Gardiner (ed.), *The Papers of William Hickling Prescott*, pp. 172–173.

of a Mexican novel) noted that unpublished material existed, but he declined to edit it. Finally in 1966 Howard T. Fisher and his wife published a compilation of Mrs. Calderón's original journals and the first edition. This new edition reveals that Mrs. Calderón had polished many of her pithy comments (rather modern in their cadence) to match the acceptable literary style of the day; it fills in the names so annoyingly left blank in the original; and it shows that the minister's wife was even sharper in her first remarks against the country and the Catholic church than she had allowed to appear. Part of her problem at first, as she recognized, had been coming so suddenly from the United States. In reworking her journal she had left the statement: "If anyone wishes to try the effect of strong contrast, let him come direct from the United States to this country."[33] The Fishers' edition presents ultimately a more sympathetic figure, direct and open, than her own edition does.

All these works should have built up much good will on the part of Americans toward Mexico, but instead a seemingly unavoidable conflict between the two countries was growing. As Alexis de Tocqueville noted on his visit to the United States in the early 1830's, Americans held it their right to extend their boundaries to the Pacific, and the undeveloped Mexican holdings represented an obstacle.[34] Texas provided the opportunity to change the situation. American emigrants there had in 1835–1836 rebelled against the corrupt Mexican government and formed their own republic. Then both sides proceeded to make a series of blunders, all of which created resentment against Mexico in the United States. Walt Whitman in writing "Song of Myself" in 1855 still remembered the massacres at the Alamo and at Goliad. One of the first acts of Waddy Thompson as American minister to Mexico, 1842–1844, had been to intercede on behalf of the prisoners from the Texas Santa Fe expedition. In 1841 this poorly equipped group had set out for New Mexico ostensibly on a trade mission but in reality to rouse the people there to join their rebellion. Instead they had been seized by the Mexican authorities and cruelly marched to Mexico City via Chihuahua; several prisoners were killed along the way. The founder of the *New Orleans Picayune*, George Wilkins Kendall (1809–1867), had joined the group in search of a

---

[33] Calderón, *Life in Mexico*, p. 355 (p. 431 in Fisher ed.).
[34] Alexis de Tocqueville, *Democracy in America*, I, 430–431.

story and gotten it.[35] He published his *Narrative of the Texas Santa Fe Expedition* in 1844 and helped to stir up more anti-Mexican feeling. Nevertheless, Kendall returned to the United States less bitter than might have been expected, considering the treatment the prisoners had received. He carefully mentioned the sympathy they had had from the lower classes and praised the women and such groups as the muleteers. He detested the enslavement of the Mexicans by the military and ecclesiastical powers and seemed amazed at the Mexican unwillingness to admire and adopt the vigorous American system, but the book does not severely counter the views of Mexico offered by Mrs. Calderón (whom he praised) or Stephens. But Americans read it in a different light then.

Racial feelings undoubtedly played their part in the emotional build-up toward war. When John Charles Frémont (1813–1890), a Southerner, published his *Report of the Exploring Expedition* in 1845, he expressed freely his rather low opinion of the darker Mexicans.[36] Waddy Thompson (1798–1860), another Southerner, likewise showed some distaste for the "primitive" people in his memoir, *Recollections of Mexico*, 1846.[37] Both men were obviously unconscious of their prejudices, however; Thompson, for instance, performed his duties as minister well and joined Poinsett (also a Southerner) in a campaign against the war with Mexico when it came. Moreover, this feeling of superiority was apparently easy to hold despite one's origins. The British Halliburton of the century, George Frederick Ruxton (1820–1848), felt the same way. Journeying through Mexico during the actual fighting, he later wrote in his *Adventures in Mexico and the Rocky Mountains*, 1847: "I cannot remember to have observed one single commendable trait in the character of the Mexican; always excepting from this sweeping clause the women . . ."[38]

When President Polk declared in 1846 that a state of war existed, the abolitionists were dismayed, seeing it as an attempt to gain addi-

---

[35] George W. Kendall, *Across the Great Southwestern Prairies*; Fayette Copeland, *Kendall of "The Picayune,"* pp. 51–238.

[36] John C. Frémont, *The Expeditions of John Charles Frémont*, I, 597–709; Allan Nevins, *Frémont, Pathfinder of the West*, pp. 127–185, 200–326; Charles Preuss, *Exploring with Frémont*.

[37] Waddy Thompson, *Recollections of Mexico*; Henry T. Thompson, *Waddy Thompson, Jr.*, pp. 17–31.

[38] George F. Ruxton, *Ruxton of the Rockies*, pp. 105–162; comment on Mexicans, p. 105.

tional slave territory. Henry David Thoreau went to jail rather than
contribute his taxes to such an effort and as a result wrote "Of Civil
Disobedience." And Ralph Waldo Emerson in his "Ode Inscribed to
W. H. Channing" spoke angrily of

> ... the famous States
> Harrying Mexico
> With rifle and with Knife!

But the American army from the Mississippi Valley marched enthusiastically into Mexico, which they imagined in all its pre-Conquest
splendor as described by Prescott. Among the foreigners were Lewis
Wallace (1827–1905), who had already begun a historical romance
entitled *The Fair God* (finally published in 1873) as a result of reading Prescott, and the Englishman Thomas Mayne Reid (1818–1883),
who would write a number of Mexican novels, mostly for boys, including *The Rifle Rangers*, 1850, *The Scalp Hunters*, 1851, and *The
White Chief*, 1855.[39] No important works, however, came directly out
of the war, although some fifty journals and collections of letters by
soldiers and sailors have been published to date and a number of
historical romances about the event have been created.

As a result of the treaty signed in 1848, Mexico ceded to the United
States more than half its territory—not only Texas but almost all that
area now comprising the American Southwest. Dana and Frémont
had created excitement about California. Frémont had covered the
area between San Francisco and Kansas City on his expedition with
Kit Carson in 1844; his *Report* dispelled the myth of an impassable
desert barring the way west just as it spoke glowingly of the beauties
of the Pacific Coast. Similarly a number of works had greatly stimulated American interest in New Mexico. The foremost of these remains *Commerce of the Prairies*, published in 1844 by Josiah Gregg
(1806–1850).[40] A perceptive and balanced survey of life on the Santa
Fe trail and of the inhabitants and nature of the land, Gregg's book
was based on observations and readings made during his four expeditions into the area between 1831 and 1841. Of course, many
citizens at the time felt that the United States should annex all of

---

[39] Lewis Wallace, *An Autobiography*, I, 88–91, 101–192, 196; Irving McKee,
*"Ben-Hur" Wallace*, pp. 9–12, 90–114, 122–127; Stanley J. Kunitz and Howard
Haycroft (eds.), *British Authors of the Nineteenth Century*, pp. 517–518.

[40] Josiah Gregg, *Commerce of the Prairies* and *Diary and Letters of Josiah Gregg*.

Mexico and establish republican order there for good. Obviously the country's politics would always be affected in some way by American policies, though no one could see then the wide interpretation of the Monroe Doctrine that the American government would later find possible.

During the year of the treaty, as if to signal the rightness of American actions, gold was discovered in California. The great rush westward began, and by the next year California was applying for statehood. Early in the summer of 1849 Horace Greeley commissioned Bayard Taylor (1825–1878) to tour the area. On his way home from California, Taylor, like many of the prospectors, took the Mexican route, landing in Mazatlán in December 1849. From there he headed for Veracruz on muleback and by coach. Some of the Mexicans, many of whom in truth had welcomed the American invasion as an end to the confusing turmoil in their country, or who had aristocratically disdained even to think about military matters, greeted him warmly and spoke of Scott and Zachary Taylor (now president) with admiration. Bayard Taylor was robbed by bandits just outside Guadalajara, but he had expected that. The acridity of Thompson and Ruxton is completely missing from his report, *Eldorado, or Adventures in the Path of Empire*, 1850; Taylor especially praised life in the capital in glowing terms.[41] We also have over fifteen other journals about the gold rush trails through Mexico, several of them quite lively.[42]

A period ended with the war and the gold rush. The United States was now moving inexorably toward its Civil War. And France, under Napoleon III, would shortly interfere with Mexican life decisively by placing Maximilian and Carlotta on imaginary thrones there (thus creating a story that would rival the Conquest in the imagination of historical novelists). By then Mexico had also gone through a great reform period and the important government of Benito Juárez. Lewis Wallace returned to help Juárez overthrow the French, but all he accomplished of significance was two magazine articles, the first published in *Harper's* in November 1867 and the second in *Scribner's* in March 1879. No major writers were influenced directly by this period. When American and British visitors arrived after the fiasco, life

---

[41] Bayard Taylor, *Eldorado*, pp. 245–331.

[42] Ferol Egan, *The El Dorado Trail*, made a study of these and unpublished items.

would be markedly different, and their work would be equally distinctive from that of their predecessors.

Why did not more American or British writers, in a period in which so many wrote travel books of great merit, visit Mexico? As many visitors pointed out, conditions in the land were quite primitive in comparison with eastern United States or Europe. Wallace observed:

It requires no little philosophy to transfer one's self from the United States to Mexico with a view to the enjoyment of travel. The differences are past realization by those who have not tried the experiment. Mules take the place of horses; carts and carriages serve instead of cars; and, as a consequence, locomotion works impatience, discontent, ennui, and the whole family of like ills. To the above may be added a total absence of hotels, inns, travelers' rests, or places of entertainment of any kind for man and beast, such as delight wayfarers in more favored lands. . . . Altogether it may be doubted if the things to be seen in our sister republic, even the most interesting, are worth the discomforts of going to see them.[43]

These "discomforts" also included robbers, murderers, disease, filth, and corruption.

Nor is it surprising that no real attempts, except Pike's, at creating fiction or poetry came out of the visits that were made, even when we remember that few of these writers were professionals. The literature of one country about another often seems to begin with such travel notes. It is as if more creative work cannot be set easily in a foreign locale until the area has somehow become domesticated through familiarity.

[43] Lewis Wallace, "The Mines of Santa Eulalia, Chihuahua," *Harper's* 35 (November 1867): 681.

## 3. Fact, Fantasy, Fiction

American and British travel writing about Mexico in the period between the French intervention of 1862–1867 and the Mexican Revolution of 1910 was considerably different from the works of the first part of the nineteenth century. Accounts continued to appear, some by such outstanding writers as William Cullen Bryant and Stephen Crane; but as entrance into the heart of Mexico became easier because of improved highways and newly opened railroads, the general quality of travel writing deteriorated, with one notable exception by Charles M. Flandrau. As the sense of discovery ebbed, skill in writing became as important as content, and few skilled writers attempted the subject. In fact, some important visitors were not moved to write anything. Henry Adams (1838–1918) dwelled at length in *The Education of Henry Adams*, 1907, upon his impressions of Europe, but he dismissed his two trips into Mexico, 1894–1895 and 1896, in exactly two sentences, merely saying of the second trip, in which he met the president and other officials, that he had returned "to study the charms of *pulque* and Churriguerresque architecture." All else we know of his observations was made in letters published after his death.[1] More sig-

[1] Henry Adams, *The Education of Henry Adams*, pp. 350, 355; idem, *Letters of Henry Adams*, pp. 58–64; idem, *Henry Adams and His Friends*, pp. 331–335, 363–367. Biographers add nothing else.

nificant than the travel books for subsequent literary history were the
efforts made by a number of visitors to create fiction out of their experience. Especially important are two romances by Rider Haggard and
some eight short stories (six by Stephen Crane) that begin in the
same tradition as Pike's autobiographical tales and finally move into
pure fiction.

Also as earlier, authors who had never seen the country continued
to use Mexican characters or to explore Mexican themes. Such uses
are found in Henry Wadsworth Longfellow's last poem, "Bells of San
Blas," 1882; Edward Everett Hale and his sister Susan's children's
book *A Family Flight through Mexico*, 1886; Gertrude Atherton's
stories of old California, *Before the Gringo Came*, 1894; O. Henry's
(William Sidney Porter's) short story "He Also Serves" and his book
for a musical, *Lo!*, both 1909; and Joseph Conrad's *Victory*, 1915.[2]
These six writers, however, seem to have had no influence upon those
writing from actual experience, then or later.

After Juárez returned his government to Mexico City, a minor cultural flowering occurred. The elite of Mexican sciences and letters
were gathered into the Sociedad Mexicana de Geografía y Estadística.
In 1872 this group invited William Cullen Bryant (1794–1878) to become an honorary member. Late that winter he sailed to Veracruz,
pausing on the way to revisit Cuba, and took a stagecoach to Mexico
City, where he was greeted with acclaim.[3] He thought the arts were in
ill health, but he found a kindred soul in José Rosas Moreno and
translated some nine of his *Fábulas* (printed in Bryant's *Poetical
Works*, 1883).[4] Stanley Williams noted that Bryant was thus "the
first major American poet to recognize the achievements of his Mexican brothers" and that finally "a poet of Mexico received in the United States the most substantial of recognitions, namely, adequate trans-

[2] Newton Arvin, *Longfellow*, p. 316; Gerald Langford, *Alias O. Henry*, pp. 101–
106, 193–194; Eugene Current-García, *O. Henry*, pp. 31–32, 90–94; Jerry Allen,
*The Sea Years of Joseph Conrad*, pp. 19–46. I can find no evidence in two biographies that Hale visited Mexico. O. Henry was in Honduras, 1896–1898; Conrad
sailed the Caribbean in the seventies.

[3] William Cullen Bryant, *Prose Writings of William Cullen Bryant*, II, 148–
185; Parke Godwin, *A Biography of William Cullen Bryant*, II, 318–322; Clara C.
Chapin, "Bryant and Some of His Latin American Friends," *Bulletin of the Pan
American Union* 78 (November 1944): 609–613.

[4] William Cullen Bryant, *The Poetical Works of William Cullen Bryant*, II,
353–359.

lation into the English language."[5] Bryant also corresponded with another poet, Guillermo Prieto. But at this late point in Bryant's life Mexican poetry could have no influence on his own.

Bryant did send back to the *New York Evening Post* a series of reports about his findings (reprinted in his *Prose Writings*, 1884). They are chiefly interesting because of the man who wrote them, but still they have been unjustly neglected by students of Mexican history. Bryant was quite struck by the dignity of Juárez, and he complimented the country in a number of ways. Yet in general his disapproval of the lottery, the immorality of the clergy, the great number of robbers and beggars, and the many other ills that Mexico suffered outweighed his descriptions of the happier aspects of the land. He was pleased to learn that the excesses of the Church were being curbed and that bullfights had been outlawed. An American democrat always, he wrote in one dispatch, "Who shall say that the country which has made these advances may not yet accustom itself to submit quietly to the arbitration of the ballot, as a lesson learned from a long series of bloody experiences?"[6]

Bryant's hope was premature. A few months later Juárez died, and his successor proved inefficient. In 1876 Porfirio Díaz launched another revolution, and for the next thirty-four years, either directly or indirectly, he ruled Mexico with a tight hand. Under him peace came, for Díaz proved to be a superb politician who could control all the other politicians, the army, and the Church. He brought order to the land through his *rurales*, described by Crane as "that crack cavalry corps of the Mexican army which polices the plain so zealously, being of themselves the law and the arm of it."[7] Thus Díaz turned Mexico into a semi-modern nation flourishing, as Adams noticed, under an "extraordinary prosperity." But Díaz balanced his national budget ruinously by granting concession after concession to foreign investors without doing anything to safeguard the rights of his people. His advisors scorned the Indians and allowed their lands to be taken away; they sold alleged criminals into slavery and an early death on tropical plantations; they allowed the cost of living to rise far beyond the

[5] Stanley T. Williams, *The Spanish Background of American Literature*, II, 139–144.

[6] Bryant, *Prose Writings*, p. 173.

[7] Stephen Crane, *The Complete Short Stories and Sketches of Stephen Crane*, p. 248.

means of the poor. Soon Americans and Englishmen owned mammoth ranches and plantations, mines and oil fields, and all sorts of industries.

Under the new calm, tourists became a common sight. By 1894 Adams was complaining that Mexico "was overrun by Americans and English. At the hotels, even in small places, English is more common than Spanish."[8] The first guidebooks had appeared in the 1880's, and in the last two decades of the century nearly sixty books of travel were published by American and British writers, the best of these in C. Harvey Gardiner's opinion being *Face to Face with the Mexicans*, 1887, by Fanny Gooch Iglehart (1842?–1913?). Few tourists were coming to explore the ancient Indian monuments, which were mostly in ruins, inaccessible, or undiscovered. (Tula, a major site not far from Mexico City, remained unknown until just before World War II.) What remnants were visible appeared too alien for most visitors; rather it was the Spanish heritage, the new works created by Maximilian and Díaz, the scenery, and the local color that attracted tourists.

The new phenomenon of the mass-circulated American magazine brought forth many travel accounts. Four writers, though minor, are worth mentioning in this connection. Mary Hallock Foote (1842–1938), one of the local colorists of the West, published a three-part article in *Century*, 1881–1882, describing a journey she had made with her husband, a mining engineer, to Morelia. Illustrated with her own sketches, it charmingly tells of their ride in a stagecoach there, her stay in a wealthy home in the city, and their return by horseback to Mexico City. Helen Hunt Jackson (1831–1885), who was to write *Ramona*, a historical romance of old California, visited El Paso del Norte (now Ciudad Juárez) late in the summer of 1882 and published a romantic vision of the town in *Atlantic* the next March, writing that to be there "on a Sunday is to escape from America and the nineteenth century as from place and time forgotten." Charles Dudley Warner (1829–1900) reported his rail trip across Mexico in 1887 in *Harper's* and then collected the five sketches with others in *On Horseback*, 1888. He was obviously delighted by the country, though he considered many of its people immoral, felt that Mexico demonstrated "the depressing outcome of miscegenation," and distrusted the dicta-

---

[8] Adams, *Henry Adams and His Friends*, p. 332.

torial powers of Díaz, warning investors away. His mood later changed, however, for when he returned in 1897 and 1898 he reported in dispatches to *Harper's* that he could think of no one "who shows more goodness, firmness, and wisdom in ruling a people" than Díaz. Frederic Remington (1861–1909) published four light essays in *Harper's* in 1893–1894 about his trip into northern Mexico and collected them in *Pony Tracks* the next year. They are still pleasant to read, but the painter's illustrations of Mexican ranch life, which accompany them, are naturally more interesting.[9]

At the same time a number of serious scholars were carrying on the work of Prescott and Stephens. Most of their writing had a subliterary quality, though Hubert Howe Bancroft (1832–1918) clearly hoped that several of his works—including *Native Races*, 1874–1875; *History of Mexico*, 1883–1888; and a Spanish life of Díaz, based on interviews with the dictator, 1887—would merit consideration with those of earlier historians of Mexico.[10] The collection of materials remains a standard service for the scholar, but few people are likely to read it for pleasure. Of the many archaeologists of the period, Adolph Francis Alphonse Bandelier (1840–1914) perhaps possessed the most literary talent. The Swiss-born American was in and out of Mexico throughout the 1880's, chiefly studying the ancient ruins and modern cultures in northern Mexico and around Oaxaca as well as researching the archives of Mexico City. *The Gilded Man*, 1893, entertainingly described the Spanish pursuit of gold. A series of travel letters, written in German for an Illinois newspaper in 1880–1881 and giving a more human picture than his formal *Report of an Archaeological Tour in Mexico in 1881*, was finally translated and published in 1949 as *A Scientist on the Trail*. A passing glance should also be paid Alfred Percival Maudslay (1850–1931), explorer of Maya ruins in Yucatan

[9] Mary Hallock Foote, "A Diligence Journey in Mexico," *Century* 23 (November 1881): 1–14; idem, "From Morelia to Mexico City on Horseback," *Century* 23 (March 1882): 643–655; idem, "A Provincial Capital of Mexico," *Century* 23 (January 1882): 321–333. Also Helen Hunt Jackson, "By Horse-Cars into Mexico," *Atlantic* 51 (March 1883): 350–362; Ruth Odel, *Helen Hunt Jackson*, p. 197; Charles D. Warner, *On Horseback*, pp. 155–304, and idem, "Editor's Study," *Harper's* 95 (June and July 1897): 146–150, 312–314, and *Harper's* 97 (June and July 1898): 150–154, 312–316; Annie A. Fields, *Charles Dudley Warner*, pp. 153–154; Frederic Remington, *Pony Tracks*, pp. 58–130, 149–161.

[10] John W. Caughey, *Hubert Howe Bancroft*, pp. 131–133, 168–181, 248–249, 299–300, 367–368; Hubert Howe Bancroft, *Literary Industries*, pp. 384–402.

and Guatemala. In 1899 he published with his wife *A Glimpse of Guatemala*; it obtained some degree of popularity. Even more important was his translation in 1908 of Bernal Díaz's *Historia verdadera* for the Hakluyt Society. Curiously, unlike the other writers of this period—save Flandrau—the works of these three men did influence later writers' views of Mexico.

The first English writer of note in these years to see the fictional possibilities of a Mexican experience was Robert Bontine Cunninghame Graham (1852–1936)—explorer, former soldier of fortune in South America, and friend of the Edwardian literati—although he did not get around to publishing his short story until 1900, in a collection *Thirteen Stories*.[11] The Cunninghame Grahams came in 1879 to Texas to start a ranch but, disliking Americans, decided to take a herd of cattle to Mexico City. Mexicans they also found disagreeable, and Apaches proved a real threat. Moreover, when they arrived, the price of cattle had fallen so low that they were forced to sell at a loss. But Cunninghame Graham was still glad to be out of the United States, and he and his wife opened a school in an attempt to recoup their losses. Finally they decided it was wiser to return to Texas, however, and in October 1880 they joined a mule train headed for the border. It was then that he found his story, "A Hegira." His wife, Gabriela, published her account of the experience in *The Christ of Toro*, 1908.

In his story, eight Apaches have been captured near Chihuahua and brought to the capital, where they are kept like wild animals on display in Chapultepec Park. Shortly after the narrator departs, they escape, "making northward, as a wild goose finds its path in spring, leaving no trace of its passage by the way." Through a series of accidents all but three—a man, a woman, and a youth, accompanied by a dog—are killed. The narrator's imagination becomes excited by the singleness of their flight, and at each step of his journey he pictures them, now ahead of the train, perilously going their way, until finally

---

[11] Robert B. Cunninghame Graham, *Thirteen Stories*, pp. 110–132; Gabriela Cunninghame Graham, *The Christ of Toro and Other Stories*, pp. 73–104; Aimé Felix Tschiffely, *Don Roberto*, pp. 142–174. Leslie Chaundy prepared a bibliography. See Robert B. Cunninghame Graham, *Progress and Other Sketches*, pp. 1–61 (for review of *Tomochic* by the Mexican novelist Heriberto Frías), and idem, *Brought Forward*, pp. 106–119 (for a story retold from Cortés's journey into Guatemala).

he hopes that they are safe with their own people. And then he meets a garrulous Texan, who among other unsavory comments mentions how his party has shot and killed three Indians just the day before, leaving the dog sitting disconsolately on the mass grave. It is an imperfectly told story, suffering the limitation of vision that all Cunninghame Graham's work does, but its straightforward design marks a great advance over Pike's similar tales and points the way toward Stephen Crane's even more effective use of autobiographical fiction.

It is difficult to know just how many short stories set in Mexico were being published either in the United States or in Great Britain during the last three decades of the nineteenth century, although the number of novels and historical romances is easier to estimate. Certainly fewer works of fiction than travel accounts came out; still there were a surprising number. Between 1866 and 1900 we find at least thirty novels set in either contemporary or pre-Conquest Mexico or in the Mexican days of the American Southwest, just twice the number that had appeared during the previous forty years; the first decade of the twentieth century saw at least twenty-two more. Several of these were based on personal experience. For instance, Frances Christine Fisher Tiernan (1846–1920), whose works achieved some popularity in the States, lived for ten years, 1888–1898, in Mexico, where her husband had mining interests. Among the novels that reflect her knowledge gained there are *The Land of the Sun*, 1894, and *The Picture of Las Cruces*, 1896, both published under her pseudonym, "Christian Reid."[12]

More important are two romances by Henry Rider Haggard (1856–1925). In January 1891 this already famous author came with his wife by train from Ciudad Juárez to Mexico City.[13] Two years earlier he had met in England the director of a Chiapas copper mine, J. Gladwyn Jebb, and through him became interested in Mexican mining operations. But what actually lured Haggard to the country appropriately enough was Moctezuma's lost treasure. Jebb thought he had discovered the site at which the hoard had been buried by

---

[12] *Dictionary of American Biography*, XVIII, 531–532.

[13] H. Rider Haggard, *The Days of My Life*, II, 39–71, and his introduction to Mrs. J. G. Jebb, *A Strange Career*, pp. xv–xxv; Lilias R. Haggard, *The Cloak That I Left*, pp. 151–156; Merton Cohen, *Rider Haggard*, pp. 130–134. J. E. Scott prepared a bibliography.

Cuauhtémoc, the last Aztec ruler. He enlisted Haggard's aid, an adventure Haggard described in his introduction to Mrs. Jebb's biography of her husband (*A Strange Career*, 1895) and in his own posthumously edited autobiography (*The Days of My Life*, 1926). The two men were never to approach the supposed burial place, however, for the day before they planned to leave for the site Haggard received word that his only son had died in England. The news threw him into a profound depression, and though he decided to remain in Mexico two months longer, he had lost all interest in Aztec gold. The rest of the trip became for him "a kind of nightmare," but he did receive from it the ideas for the two novels, *Montezuma's Daughter*, 1893, and *Heart of the World*, 1896.

The first work he dedicated to Jebb and in it used the legend of the treasure. Also, Haggard acknowledged in his autobiography that the grief his hero feels upon losing a child was "what myself I felt." The plot concerns the adventures of an Englishman who becomes involved in the Spanish Conquest on the side of the Indians. The narrator tells his own story, replete with hairbreadth escapes, marriage into Aztec royalty, and melodramatic meetings with La Malinche, Cortés's Indian mistress, with Cuauhtémoc, and with Bernal Díaz before all ends in tragedy. Though hardly great literature the book is exciting to read. (Graham Greene credited it with influencing his travels, saying: "And surely it must have been *Montezuma's Daughter* and the story of the disastrous night of Cortez' retreat which lured me . . . afterwards to Mexico."[14]) Haggard subordinated all historical details to his plot, but those details, gained from Prescott and Mexican historians, were handled convincingly. The landscapes were based on his own observations of the Valley of Mexico, the Pinal mountains of Querétaro, and the Tabasco area.

Haggard accompanied Jebb into southern Mexico after the news of his child's death in order to escape all thought; he described the trip as "the roughest piece of journeying that has come within my experience in any part of the world." The two men went down to Veracruz, where they took an untrustworthy boat to Frontera. Suffering from insects and other ills, they then proceeded up the Río Grijalva. For some reason they gave up their plans to explore nearby Palenque,

[14] Graham Greene, *A Sort of Life*, p. 53.

though the idea of the ruins obviously—from the number of references in the two novels to them—continued to fascinate Haggard. He caught some glimpse of the mistreatment the natives endured on the secluded plantations and sympathized with their plight. The dangers of such a lawless area intruded on the travelers' consciousness more dramatically while they were staying at one of the haciendas far up country; they narrowly escaped being murdered for the money that Jebb was taking to the mine workers. As if all this were not enough, their voyage back to Veracruz nearly ended in disaster as a result of the poor condition of the boat and a storm they encountered. But besides anxiety, Haggard took back much of the material for the opening of his second novel.

Unfortunately *Heart of the World* has almost none of the virtues of *Montezuma's Daughter*. It again concerns an Englishman, though the story is narrated by an Indian noble. But the novel never focuses clearly on either and at once loses power. Many of the early events—discovery of a dangerous mine, a storm, and an attempted murder—seem merely padding rather than an essential part of the plot. By taking the story outside history (it apparently takes place early in the nineteenth century, but the major part of the novel really occurs external to time or space) Haggard lost control of his imagination. On his Chiapas trip he had apparently heard the same legend that Stephens recorded, about an enchanted city in Guatemala where the Indians carry on a stately existence as before the Conquest. The two heroes of *Heart of the World* meet the ruler of this imaginary city and his daughter and return with them. There follow the usual battles and a romance between the Englishman and an Indian maiden, in the midst of the most improbable costumes and temples and a mysterious cavern—the kind of stuff Lewis Wallace had used. One new element does appear: an examination of the racial prejudice that Haggard had observed. In the novel those of Spanish blood freely disdain even the Indian noble (he is the last descendant of Cuauhtémoc). Unfortunately, Haggard's prejudice was no more liberal; he easily held that Englishmen were superior to Spaniards and Indians alike and had his narrator say that "among companions of a coloured race a white man of gentle birth is always acknowledged to be by right of blood" the leader.

The first American writer of real talent to be attracted by the fic-

tional possibilities of Mexican life was Stephen Crane (1871–1900).[15]
He arrived in late March 1895 on a Western tour sponsored by a
newspaper syndicate. Coming down by railroad from Nuevo Laredo,
he stopped several weeks in Mexico City. While staying at the Hotel
Iturbide, he met an American engineer, Charles Gardner, and set out
with him to explore the sights of the capital. Then Crane went on
alone into the wilds south of the Valley, returning to Puebla in early
May. There he became so homesick that he decided to return to New
York. Out of these experiences came five articles, published irregularly
and out of chronological order in the *Philadelphia Press* and other
newspapers, and rough drafts for three others, first printed in 1967
(all reprinted in *Stephen Crane in the West and Mexico*). More important were six short stories, the three major ones collected in *The
Open Boat*, 1898, and the others in *Last Words*, 1902. Little is known
about Crane's adventures outside the information contained in these
works; almost no Crane letters from the period exist, and no one
seems to have commented on his presence in Mexico.

The articles are all rather ill-written and appear to have been
dashed off in some haste. As we might expect, Crane was most impressed by the color and movement of the people. He wrote: "In
Mexico the atmosphere seldom softens anything. It devotes its energy
to making high lights, bringing everything forward, making colors
fairly volcanic."[16] He apparently admired the pulque shops, brightly
decorated then with murals inside and out. Of tourist attractions he
wrote little. One of the articles he left unpublished described a visit
to Xochimilco, but the activity of the boatmen, vendors, musicians,
and little parties of natives interested him more than the actual gardens. Obviously he was disturbed by the appalling poverty of the
people, their fondness for strong drink, their cruelty to animals, and
their petty thievery and confidence games. These matters occupy a
prominent place in his notes. Yet he wrote, "I refuse to commit judgment upon these lower classes of Mexico." He realized that foreigners
have a hard time understanding another country, especially Mexico:
"Above all things, the stranger finds the occupations of foreign peoples
to be trivial and inconsequent. The average mind utterly fails to

[15] Stephen Crane, *Letters*, pp. 55, 63, 86, 103, and idem, *Stephen Crane in the
West and Mexico*, pp. 41–91; Thomas Beer, *Stephen Crane*, pp. 112–119; R. W.
Stallman, *Stephen Crane*, pp. 140–150.

[16] Crane, *West and Mexico*, p. 47.

comprehend the new point of view and that such and such a man should be satisfied to carry bundles or mayhap sit and ponder in the sun all his life in this faraway country seems an abnormally stupid thing. The visitor feels scorn."[17]

Still Crane found himself embroiled in the contradictions into which all foreigners in Mexico seem to fall, and throughout the articles he adapted a satirical view of the Mexicans to the point of accepting stereotypes. Perhaps he was deliberately catering to public taste (his more perceptive comments are in the unfinished articles), but the following anecdote from his first newspaper article is typical:

The Indians, however, must have credit for considerable ingenuity because of the way they have invented of assisting a fallen donkey to its feet. The Aztecs are known to have had many great mechanical contrivances, and this no doubt is part of their science which has filtered down through the centuries.

When a burdened donkey falls down a half dozen Indians gather around it and brace themselves. Then they take clubs and hammer the everlasting daylight out of the donkey. They also swear in Mexican. Mexican is a very capable language for the purposes of profanity. A good swearer here can bring rain in thirty minutes.

It is a great thing to hear the thump, thump of the clubs and the howling of the natives, and to see the little legs of the donkey quiver and to see him roll his eyes. Finally, after they have hammered him out as flat as a drum head it flashes upon them suddenly that the burro cannot get up until they remove the load. Well, then, at last they remove his load and the donkey, not much larger than a kitten at best, and now disheveled, weak and tottering, struggles gratefully to his feet.[18]

The short stories are much better. Two of them, comedies of the Anglo-American colony in Mexico City, concern the exploits of a "New York Kid" (obviously an extension of Crane), a "San Francisco Kid," and a man named Benson. "The Five White Mice," published in the *Westminster Gazette* in 1897, consists of two episodes in which the New York Kid is called upon to show his composure. He loses in a game of dice—the title of the story comes from a gambler's charm he uses—and has to take everyone to the Circo-Teatro Orrin. In losing, however, he has displayed great coolness by challenging

[17] Ibid., pp. 77, 74.
[18] Ibid., p. 53.

everyone to lay more money on the last turn in so convincing a manner that no one will take him up. After the circus he encounters the Frisco Kid and Benson, both drunk. On the way home Benson jostles a Mexican, and again the New York Kid is called upon to show his courage. The Mexican—"a yellow mask, smiling in eager cruelty, in satisfaction, and, above all, . . . lit with sinister decision"—and his two friends challenge the Americans. Before the New Yorker's revolver, however, the Mexicans reveal that they do not wish "for too bloody a combat" and, having shown such "equality of emotion," back away. Benson finally is on his way, completely oblivious that "nothing had happened." In the second story, "The Wise Men: A Detail of American Life in Mexico," published in *The Lanthorn Book* in 1898, the two Kids discover that an old bartender is a fine runner, but his appearance so belies the fact that they are sure they can rook everyone into betting against him in a race with another bartender. The race is on the Paseo de la Reforma, "a broad, fine avenue of macadam, with a much greater quality of dignity than anything of the kind we possess in our own land," before a record crowd from the Anglo-American colony. The old man, clad only in his underwear, easily takes the other man. The Kids are triumphant, but Benson, a perfect scapegoat, has lost a tidy sum as well as the handkerchief he had tied to the finish line.[19]

The best of Crane's Mexican tales remains "Horses—One Dash," published in the *Philadelphia Press* and other periodicals in 1896. Crane based it on his own experiences in southern Mexico. He and his guide, Miguel Iturbide, had run into one of the flamboyant bandits who still infested isolated stretches, one Ramón Colorado. In the story Richardson, a New Yorker, and his Mexican guide stop for the night in a small village in which a fiesta is in progress. Some of the revelers drink too much and decide to kill Richardson for his possessions. But Richardson confronts them calmly, holding his revolver under the blanket: "Ah, well, sirs, here was a mystery. At the approach of their menacing company, why did not this American cry out and turn pale, or run, or pray them mercy? The animal merely sat still, and stared, and waited for them to begin. Well, evidently he was a great fighter; or perhaps he was an idiot. Indeed, this was an embarrassing situation,

---

[19] Crane, *Short Stories*, pp. 408–429; description of Mexican, p. 415, of Paseo de la Reforma, p. 427.

for who was going forward to discover whether he was a great fighter or an idiot?" They retreat, and the next morning Richardson and his badly frightened guide sneak out at dawn and flee in a wild chase across the plain. Now that they have revealed their weakness, they are pursued by the bandits. Luckily Richardson and his guide encounter a band of *rurales*, who quickly dispatch the outlaws. Crane's colorful description of the countryside, houses, and people and his interest in the psychology of Richardson at a moment of great stress are reminiscent of similar methods he had used in *The Red Badge of Courage*.[20]

Crane also wrote three fables, sold by his agent to *Pocket Magazine* as "Mexican Tales." These were "The Voice of the Mountain," 1896, "How the Donkey Lifted the Hills," 1897, and "The Victory of the Moon," also 1897. The first two tell how Popocatépetl and the donkey were tricked by man into submission. The last shows the insignificance of man.[21]

Crane's achievement, impressive as it was at this time, was surpassed by a man now virtually forgotten in the literary world but loved by all who know Mexico intimately, Charles Macomb Flandrau (1871–1938). His book *Viva Mexico!*, published in 1908 and frequently reprinted, is one of the most charming travel books ever written about the country.[22] It does not contain the reams of information to be found in Mrs. Calderón's letters, and it lacks the sense of adventure that fills the pages of Dana and Stephens, but for genial insight into Mexican life it provides an ideal starting point. Flandrau was both involved with the people—at their fiestas and in their sufferings—and objectively detached. He based *Viva Mexico!* on a series of visits between 1903 and 1908 to his brother's coffee plantation near Misantla, Veracruz, and farther up country to Puebla, Mexico City, and Cuernavaca. He seems to have grasped Mexican psychology as deeply as any foreigner can hope to. He noted the difficulty of essaying such a work after repeated contact with the country: "After traveling for three weeks in Mexico, almost anyone can write an entertaining and oracular volume, but after living there for several years, the oracle—unless subsidized by the Government—has a tendency to

[20] Ibid., pp. 239–249; description, p. 242.

[21] Ibid., pp. 312–314, 359–364.

[22] Charles M. Flandrau, *Viva Mexico!*, including a biography by C. Harvey Gardiner, pp. xi–xxv.

become dumb."[23] Luckily for his readers, he was no oracle, simply a very sensitive man. Mexico in many of its contradictory moods emerges solidly from his pages.

Some of the clichés are there—perhaps he invented a few—but usually he saw Mexican life in the round. What he said of the Church is typical of his viewpoint in general: "So one's attitude toward the Church in Mexico becomes at the last curiously ill-defined. The Church is corrupt, grasping, resentful; but it unquestionably gives millions of people something without which they would be far more unhappy than they are—something that no other church could give them." He never plumbed the depths that D. H. Lawrence would, though he never made as many absurd statements either. One can trust Flandrau; and having read him, one's view of Mexico is forever subtly altered. Little phrases from the book constantly float to mind as one explores; for instance, of churches: "The use of gold leaf in decoration is like money. A little is pleasant, merely too much is vulgar; but a positively staggering amount of it seems to justify itself." And of one native fruit he recorded perfectly that "without a plate and a knife and a spoon, a papaya, like a mango, can be successfully managed only while naked in a bath tub." In such unitalicized moments his insight displays itself completely.[24]

Certain larger scenes also stand out: an afternoon in the *sala* of a Mexican family, a quarrel with a bishop for christening Flandrau's godchild with a girl's name rather than the proper male one, groups of American tourists fluttering about and generally disgracing themselves then as now, a typical day on the plantation. Many readers have been especially delighted with the chapter on the Trawnbeighs. This very British family had come to Mexico on a business mission that fell through and left them impoverished. Finally they came into a small inheritance that enabled them to buy a coffee plantation near that of Flandrau's brother and there to re-create life on an English estate, including teas and formal dress for dinner. Without benefit of money and servants they had to do everything themselves: tea tables were whisked in and out of the "garden" (that is, among "three tattered banana trees") by one of the family; Mr. Trawnbeigh rang the dressing bells; Mrs. Trawnbeigh cooked the meals and then appeared

---

[23] Ibid., p. 21.
[24] Ibid., pp. 47, 277, 181.

elegantly at the table. One night while Flandrau was visiting them—
he was put in "the north wing," a storage room for equipment—a
storm came up. Rain poured, and the wind howled, blowing open a
window. He ran in to close it, "but before I reached it, I stopped short
and, as hastily and quietly as I could, tiptoed back to the 'wing.' For
the next room was the kitchen and at one end of it Trawnbeigh, in a
shabby but perfectly fitting dresscoat, his trousers rolled up halfway
to his knees, was patiently holding an umbrella over his wife's sacred
dinner gown, while she—bebangled, becameoed, beplumed, and
stripped to the buff—masterfully cooked our dinner on the brasero."[25]

Several of these chapters first appeared in *The Bellman*. Flandrau
collected two more essays about Mexico in his volume *Loquacities*,
1931; both possess the same low-keyed charm as *Viva Mexico!*, but
neither adds measurably to the impression gained from that book.[26]
Of great interest, however, is a short story, "Wanderlust," collected
in *Prejudices* in 1911. More perfectly told than even Crane's short
stories, it recounts the experiences of two Americans, Lansing and
Hayward, whom fate overtakes in Veracruz, destroying Hayward.
The Americans become fascinated by the thought of the tropics as a
result of various strolls along the New York wharfs. They ship out on
a steamer, eventually arriving in Veracruz, where they are paid off.
Unfortunately it is the same time that swarms of tramps who have
drifted south for warmth are looking for jobs to take them home; the
two men are mistaken for tramps and are turned away. Too poor to
return to the States, they are trapped physically and emotionally:
"They could not walk in any direction without soon coming to the
water or to a hot and dreary stretch of sand, and in their unconsciously blasé New York fashion they had become, by the second day,
hardened to ragged Indians, enormous straw hats and scarlet *sarapes*."
Finally destitute, they decide to stow away on a ship. Lansing apparently makes it, but Hayward is dragged out and returned ashore.
There he dies and is dumped "into a hole with an Indian who had
been stabbed in a drunken row the night before." Flandrau told the
story easily with none of the excesses that naturalism had brought
into fiction, though the story line lent itself readily to naturalistic

---

25 Ibid., pp. 230–246.
26 Charles M. Flandrau, *Loquacities*, pp. 159–170, 230–232; idem, *Prejudices*,
pp. 210–211.

touches. It is simply an anecdote, more satisfying by being under-stated.[27]

Except for Crane's and Flandrau's work, and perhaps Haggard's, these years saw, then, several important names in Mexico but little of real literary significance for the English-speaking world. Thus one of the peculiar things about the relationship between American and British writers and Mexico shows up for the first time clearly: under times of great political stress in Mexico, as the government threatens to fall apart and all sorts of hardships develop though not war itself, American and British authors produce their best writing about the country, whether fiction or nonfiction; but in periods of quiet they flounder. The same phenomenon occurs in the early years of the 1930's and again after World War II. At the end of the nineteenth century, when any American, instead of scurrying off to Europe, could have headed south and found a remarkable degree of ease, or when an Englishman could have discovered Aztec and Maya ruins more peaceful than the beauties of India and surely more interesting than enormous stretches of Africa, authors chose to stay away or wrote such stuff as we have seen.

[27] Flandrau, *Prejudices*, pp. 43–66.

# 4. American Radicals and the Revolution of 1910[1]

Various wars, including some in which the United States took no active part, such as the Spanish Civil War, have so excited the imagination of American writers that it seems surprising the battles of the Mexican Revolution, between 1910 and 1920, influenced American literature so little. The Revolution was the first great social upheaval of this century, and the United States had, so to speak, a front-row seat for the event. Many Mexican leaders were in exile in the States at one time or another, and twice the American government directly engaged in military actions against some faction in the Mexican Revolution, not to mention the number of times battles and raids of one sort or another spilled over onto American territory. For years American newspapers, led by William Randolph Hearst's chain, thundered that the United States government should direct the internal affairs of Mexico. Such an action would have harmonized with the prevalent interpretation of the Monroe Doctrine; between 1898 and 1916 the American government pressured six Latin American countries around the Caribbean to take directions it desired. Thus many American in-

[1] Part of this chapter appeared in somewhat different form in *Southwest Review* 55 (Autumn 1970): 393–410. I am grateful for the encouragement of Margaret Hartley, the editor.

terests were quite vocal in their disgust when Woodrow Wilson withdrew troops from Veracruz in 1914 and called back General Pershing's expedition in pursuit of Francisco Villa in 1916. A very few American writers championed the direction of the Revolution, but from the published evidence—or rather the lack of it—it would seem that the majority agreed with the rest of the nation that the movement was simply another Latin American riot calculated to annoy.

Katherine Anne Porter caught a glimpse of the Revolution's inception, but her literary relationship with Mexico really dates from the 1920's.[2] Otherwise only minor writers became caught up in the movement, particularly Jack London, Ambrose Bierce, John Reed, and Lincoln Steffens. But their involvement reveals the limitations and strengths that authors display when confronting a complex and alien social situation, and it shows again the confused attitudes that America has taken toward Mexico. The work of London, Bierce, Reed, and Steffens anticipates the work of several later and more impressive writers who used Mexico as a setting. Besides, there is something rather charming about them, especially Reed and Steffens—without whose help the course of Mexican history might have been different.

On September 16, 1910, when Díaz celebrated the centennial of his country's declaration of independence, all seemed calm and prosperous. To commemorate this event and the celebration of his birthday the day before, the eighty-year-old dictator had set aside the entire month for festivities in which thousands of guests from the world over were invited to join and to laud the progress they found. Eighteen days later the man whom Charles Flandrau had hailed in 1908 as "an acute, patriotic, and enlightened president" began his eighth term.[3] Indeed, Díaz was convinced that he was doing the best possible for Mexico's development. Neither his circle of advisors nor any outsiders seemed to have anticipated what lay ahead. But already the revolutionary forces were at work in Mexico. As John Kenneth Turner (1879–1948) pointed out in his clear and simple exposé, *Barbarous Mexico*, 1910, under the façade of prosperity the mass of the people

---

[2] Katherine Anne Porter, *The Collected Essays and Occasional Writings of Katherine Anne Porter*, p. 355.

[3] Charles M. Flandrau, *Viva Mexico!*, p. 19. Ethel B. Tweedie (d. 1940) in *Mexico as I Saw It*, 1901, and Edith Louise O'Shaughnessy (d. 1939) in *A Diplomat's Wife in Mexico*, 1916, also praised Díaz.

lived in utter poverty.[4] Even Flandrau had pointed out that the Mexicans "have been treated, one would be inclined to say, like so many head of irresponsible cattle, if cattle, as a rule, were not treated more solicitously."[5] More than 90 percent of the land was owned by a relatively small number of *hacendados* and foreign speculators. The foreigners had brought in much capital, but they tended to enrich the country itself very little. As a result of such a lopsided economy many of the people were living, as Turner recorded graphically, in a state of actual slavery. Solutions, however, were being found. Even as Díaz celebrated in the capital, the illiterate Emiliano Zapata—whom John Dos Passos and John Steinbeck would celebrate—was making plans to acquire for the people of Morelos *tierra y libertad*, land (that is, the haciendas) and liberty.

Meanwhile, the leader of the Revolution had appeared—Francisco I. Madero. Madero suggested that if Díaz chose to run again the people at least should choose the vice-president since clearly the old leader might not live out his ninth term. When Madero announced his candidacy for vice-president, his following was so enthusiastic that Díaz ordered him jailed. Released, he went to San Antonio, Texas, there published in early November a denunciation of the recent election, and called for a new one. At first nothing happened, although *maderistas* continued to mill, even in the capital. The battle finally began in earnest when Francisco Villa and another general opened fire against the *federales* early in 1911; Madero hurried back to Mexico and persuaded them to let him lead the rebellion. In May they took Ciudad Juárez, and Díaz soon resigned.

Other forces besides Madero's and Zapata's had been instrumental in undermining the government. These gained the attention of Jack London (1876–1916), a friend of Turner and the first prominent American writer to record what the Revolution was about. The Flores Magón brothers had established a series of juntas in the United States that had engineered several strikes and other reprisals (of which even Flandrau had been vaguely aware) against Díaz's various forms of oppression. In January 1911 the brothers seized Mexicali and other

[4] John Kenneth Turner, *Barbarous Mexico*, including introduction by Sinclair Snow, pp. xi–xxix. *Barbarous Mexico* was much praised by Mexican revolutionists, and David Alfaro Siqueiros included Turner's portrait in a mural of Mexican heroes.

[5] Flandrau, *Viva Mexico!*, p. 61.

towns in Baja California in order to create a socialist republic there.[6] The entire action so excited London, the professed socialist, that he composed an open letter to his "dear, brave comrades of the Mexican Revolution." It was published in February and widely reprinted in the socialist press. In part he wrote:

We socialists, anarchists, hobos, chicken thieves, outlaws and undesirable citizens of the United States . . . are with you heart and soul in your effort to overthrow slavery and aristocracy in Mexico. . . . All the names you are being called, we have been called. And when graft and greed get up and begin to call names, honest men, brave men, patriotic men and martyrs can expect nothing else than to be called chicken thieves and outlaws.

So be it. But I for one wish that there were more chicken thieves and out-laws of the sort that formed the gallant band that took Mexicali, of the sort that is heroically enduring the prison holes of Diaz, of the sort that is fighting and dying and sacrificing in Mexico today.

I subscribe myself a chicken thief and revolutionist.

In an interview he expressed the hope that the United States would not seek to invade Mexico, but he added, "It might end the Revolution, but it certainly cannot crush the revolutionary spirit in Mexico."[7]

This statement was followed in the August 19, 1911, issue of the popular *Saturday Evening Post* by a short story, "The Mexican" (re-printed in *The Night Born*, 1913). It tells the story of a youth, Felipe Rivera, who mysteriously pours money into a junta in Los Angeles to help the Revolution, especially the rebellion of Baja California. It is revealed that Rivera has earned at least part of the money as a fighter, and the last part of the story recounts his melodramatic en-counter with one of the name fighters of the day. The match lasts seventeen rounds; the referee, displaying the prejudice of some Americans against Mexicans, does all he can to throw the bout against Rivera. But the boy triumphs and gains the money needed for the rifles. In this part of the story, probably influenced by Turner's de-

---

[6] Joe Hill (Joseph Hillstron, 1882–1915), the Swedish-American Wobbly and song writer, fought in one of these battles. See Wallace Stegner, "Joe Hill: The Wobblies' Troubadour," *New Republic*, January 5, 1948, p. 22.

[7] Joan London, *Jack London and His Times*, pp. 338–339. Hensley C. Wood-bridge and others prepared a bibliography. I appreciate letters from Miss London, Jack London's daughter, dated September 7, 1967, and Woodbridge, dated Septem-ber 13, 1967.

scriptions, London projected through Rivera's mind memories of actual conditions in the industrial slums of Mexico and the aftermath of a strike against a number of textile mills in 1906:

The strike, or rather, the lock-out, because the workers of Rio Blanco had helped their striking brothers of Puebla. The hunger, the expeditions in the hills for berries, the roots and herbs that all ate and that twisted and pained the stomachs of all of them. And then, the nightmare; the waste of ground before the company's store; the thousands of starving workers; General Rosalio Martinez and the soldiers of Porfirio Diaz; and the death-spitting rifles that seemed never to cease spitting, while the workers' wrongs were washed and washed again in their own blood. And that night! He saw the flat cars, piled high with the bodies of the slain, consigned to Vera Cruz, food for the sharks of the bay. Again he crawled over the grisly heaps, seeking and finding, stripped and mangled, his father and mother. His mother he especially remembered—only her face projecting, her body burdened by the weight of dozens of bodies. Again the rifles of the soldiers of Porfirio Diaz cracked, and again he dropped to the ground and slunk away like some hunted coyote of the hills.

Such memories provide Rivera the motivation for his battles, and from them London artistically secured a powerful propaganda value not even approached by other writers who felt equal sympathy for the aims of the Revolution.[8] London's identification with the Mexican cause at this time was clear. But these two pieces were all he ever wrote in favor of the Revolution—and apparently the last pieces of propaganda he ever wrote for a socialist cause. When he finally came to Veracruz to cover the invasion of Mexico in 1914, he was quite changed.

Meanwhile, Madero had been duly elected to the presidency, and some measure of peace returned to Mexico. During this interval Zane Grey (1875–1939) slipped in for some fishing at Tampico and to explore one of the wild rivers that fell to the coastal plain near there. From these experiences came *Ken Ward in the Jungle*, 1912, and a section of the nonfiction *Tales of Southern Rivers*, 1924. Another novel, *Desert Gold*, 1913, reflected his observations about life in Sonora, through which he had entered the country.[9]

---

[8] Jack London, *The Night Born*, pp. 243–290; quotation, pp. 271–272. See Anita Brenner, *The Wind That Swept Mexico*, photograph 42.

[9] Frank Gruber, *Zane Grey*, pp. 100–103, 115; Zane Grey, *Tales of Southern Rivers*, pp. 135–249.

The Revolution, however, was just beginning, for Madero proved incapable of meeting the terrible demands of the office. All the ills that had been building up for forty years demanded instant solution; off in the provinces rebellions continued, most notably under Zapata. To complicate Madero's problems, the American ambassador, Henry Lane Wilson, proved trying in his insistent demands for protection of American lives and property. Finally, in February 1913, after ten days of terrible fighting in Mexico City itself, the villainous Victoriano Huerta emerged as the real leader. Madero was murdered four days later. Wilson, who seems to have had no small part in the coup, announced that Mexico had been saved. The country, in fact, was in worse shape than it had been in the days of Díaz, but the people now were aroused. Venustiano Carranza and Alvaro Obregón, two powerful leaders in northern states, moved to join Villa; together the three, under Carranza's leadership, formed the Constitutionalist army.

In the fall of 1913 Ambrose Bierce (1842–1914?) journeyed south to witness the activity of this army.[10] He left little by way of comment about the situation he found, merely a few letters to friends; but because of the publicity that accompanied his disappearance, he has become for Americans forever part of the myth of Mexico. He set the archetypal pattern for the several writers who would later go to the country in order to lose themselves in drink or drugs, in saturnalia, in obscurity, or in death. One can never be sure of the facts, but the journey of the seventy-one–year–old man, suffering from asthma and tired of living, into a desert country torn by violence seems to have been a form of suicide. Certainly several of his letters indicate his willingness to die there. Just before he left home, for example, he wrote his niece: "Goodbye—if you hear of my being stood up against a Mexican stone wall and shot to rags please know that I think that a pretty good way to depart this life. It beats old age, disease, or falling down the cellar stairs. To be a Gringo in Mexico—ah, that is euthanasia!"[11]

Bierce may have been interested in the ideas behind the Revolution. He has generally been characterized as an archfoe of revolutions; but

[10] Carey McWilliams, *Ambrose Bierce*, pp. 314–326; Paul Fatout, *Ambrose Bierce*, pp. 310–319. I appreciate the help of M. E. Grenander, professor of English at New York State University, in a letter dated August 1, 1967.

[11] Ambrose Bierce, *The Letters of Ambrose Bierce*, pp. 196–197.

if we can trust the statements of Adolphe Danziger, his sometimes friend, he had often condemned the tyranny of Díaz. In 1913 he apparently corresponded with Carranza; at least he told his friends that he liked the man. But he could not believe all the news he read and wanted to go to Juárez to see for himself. He told his daughter, "In America you can't go east or west any more, or north, the only avenue of escape is south."[12] Beyond these statements he was vague, but his daughter felt there was more to it than a mere desire to see Mexico.

After he left the States he remained in constant communication with his secretary, who destroyed all the letters but jotted down in a notebook the dates and significant facts in them; thus a skeletal journal of his movements has been preserved. Having attempted to cross at Nuevo Laredo, he finally reached Ciudad Juárez in late November, where he obtained credentials as an observer attached to Villa's army marching to Chihuahua. Bierce rode south, carrying approximately two thousand dollars in gold through a countryside teeming with bandits. The weather was bitter; there was much talk of the *jornada del muerto*. At the battle of Tierra Blanca (November 24–25) he was received with suspicion. To relieve himself, Bierce took a rifle, walked to the top of a ridge, took careful aim, and dropped a Mexican. But the spirit of the Civil War was gone. "Poor devil! I wonder who he was!" he wrote.[13] The Mexicans, whom he described as fighting like the devil though in a most unmilitary fashion, were duly impressed anyway and presented him a sombrero as a token of acceptance. By December 16 he was in Chihuahua, eight days after Villa's forces had occupied the city. On Christmas Eve he sent a short note to a friend, asking him to pray for him. His last letter, to his secretary, was postmarked December 26; she noted its essence: "Trainload of troops leaving Chihuahua every day. Expect next day to go to Ojinaga, partly by rail."[14] The rest is mystery; no further word was ever received from him.

After some time his daughter requested the American authorities to investigate; the U.S. commander on the Mexican border instigated a search but received no positive information. Much later Carranza conducted an investigation under the direction of Major Gaston de

[12] McWilliams, *Ambrose Bierce*, p. 316.
[13] Ibid., p. 324.
[14] Tom Mahoney, "The End of Ambrose Bierce," *Esquire* 5 (February 1936): 150.

Prida, Richard Harding Davis's interpreter at Veracruz. Prida found a soldier who was positive Bierce had accompanied Toribio Ortega's detachment to Ojinaga when the siege began (January 1–11, 1914) but was unable to discover what had happened to him. In the midst of a civil war it is not surprising that Bierce should simply disappear, but in lieu of facts rumors spread wildly. One critic summed up the situation succinctly: "Obscurity is obscurity, but disappearance is fame." For years a story about Bierce's death could easily be placed with some periodical, and many people, most notably the correspondent George Weeks and Danziger, tracked down all sorts of stories about his end. Danziger came up with the most spectacular, that Bierce had been murdered by Villa.[15] After that the rumors became more and more improbable and were finally taken over by science fiction and mystery fans.

The Bierce legend, however, did not assume shape for years, being lost at the time in the deluge of Mexican news that came from newspapers and magazines. With the excitement generated by Villa and Carranza, other radical writers became interested in the Revolution. John Reed (1887–1920) was the first to arrive, coming in mid-December of 1913 and staying for nearly four months.[16] He was then an editor of *Masses*, but this trip was sponsored by the *Metropolitan* magazine and the *New York World*. In the spring of 1914 Reed turned out sixteen signed articles and a short story. Many of the articles were incorporated into a book published late in the summer entitled *Insurgent Mexico*, one of the most objective works, if a limited one, ever written about the country. The journey also gave him the facts by which to appraise the invasions of Veracruz and northern Mexico in a number of later articles and the germ for one more short story.

Reed first saw Mexico by wading across the Rio Grande from Presidio to Ojinaga in order to interview the defeated *federales*, who had

[15] Mahoney, "End of Ambrose Bierce," pp. 62 ff.; Edward L. Tinker, "The Devil's Lexicographer," *New York Times Book Review*, July 23, 1967, p. 4; George F. Weeks, *California Copy*, pp. 327–328; Adolphe de Castro, *Portrait of Ambrose Bierce*, pp. 326–338.

[16] John Reed, *Insurgent Mexico*; Granville Hicks, *John Reed*, pp. 112–147, 207–208, 218–219; Gregory Mason, "Reed, Villa, and the Village," *Outlook*, May 6, 1925, pp. 11 ff.; "Reed and Companion Had to Escape from the Front," *New York World*, March 31, 1914, p. 2.

retreated before Villa. He then returned to El Paso and followed the same trail to Chihuahua that Bierce had taken a month before, arriving December 25. Villa received few reporters warmly, but Reed quickly obtained several interviews with him and was attracted to the man; Reed appreciated Villa's democratic spirit and his genuine love for the poor, including his feverish attempts to give them land, money, and an education. Reed was convinced that Villa could save Mexico from chaos or exploitation. Reed was never blind to the fallibility of the Mexican people; he realized how complicatedly dangerous they could be and barely escaped death several times when someone became suspicious of the gringo; he recorded honestly that some would rather fight than do anything else, as many Americans were asserting. But he also saw what John Kenneth Turner had pointed out: that Americans and other foreign exploiters, backed by Díaz, had brought about the conditions that made it more enjoyable to fight than to work. Reed understood fully that there could be another culture completely different from the American culture, yet no less valid. For example, he did not reject a peasant soldier's definition of liberty as the right to do what he wanted; instead, he pointed out that in America liberty was only the right to do what the courts wanted. He loved the primitive gaiety and the deep passion of the people. Knowing that "already around the narrow shores of the Mexican Middle Ages beat the great waves of modern life—machinery, scientific thought, and political theory"—Reed romantically hoped that Villa could bring these things to the people and still preserve their cultural integrity.[17]

Reed was taking notes all the while he traveled, and he had already picked up the ideas for his two Mexican stories, both of which were published in *Masses* and reprinted in his posthumous collection, *Daughter of the Revolution*, 1927. "Endymion," not published until 1916, roughly sketches a doctor who charges a quarter for every service from delivering a baby to setting a broken arm, and a drunk who came out of Mexico when the Revolution began. Doc seems to have known all the famous people of England around the middle of the century and to have traveled throughout the world, until some obscure relationship with a woman (who called him her Endymion and gave him his only tangible memento of her, a copy of Keats's poem) reduced him to his present state. Still the Americans and Mexi-

17 Reed, *Insurgent Mexico*, p. 326.

cans alike stand in awe of Doc. Reed is not a great writer, but the discrepancy between Doc's potential achievements and his present setting conveys quiet pathos.[18]

"Mac—American," published in April 1914, came from a discussion Reed had with three Americans in a bar in Chihuahua. In it he attempted to show the discrepancy between American ideals and actual practices, a point he and Steffens made several times. The men speak with scorn of the immorality of the Mexican women and praise the purity of the American, but one lets slip that he thought he had caught a venereal disease from some Kansas girl. Next Mac relates a fierce fight he had had with his pacifist brother in Vermont over a girl, won by kicking his brother in the groin, after which Mac had gone to the South, to see at one point a Negro torn to pieces by hounds. But Mac ends the story saying, "I wouldn't like to live down here in Mexico. . . . The people haven't any Heart. I like people to be friendly, like Americans." The forced propagandistic purposes weaken the story; still it stands out like a monument among the distorted accounts that Hearst and most other newsmen were handing their readers.[19]

Little was happening in Chihuahua in January 1914, and besides, Reed wanted to see more of the people. Thus he decided to accompany the prototype for Mac south. Reaching Jiménez by train, Reed hired a Mexican soldier on leave as a muleteer and pushed on into the state of Durango. He was the lone gringo among the Mexicans, forced to make his way by his own personality. He visited in the home of the soldier and attended a passion play at Santa María del Oro. The play was stopped several times by the audience's arguments over its themes, by an announcement of an army victory, and by a stray dog. Reed was fascinated. He then joined General Tomás Urbina at Las Nieves and saw his first battle shortly thereafter. It seemed like "a page out of Richard Harding Davis" at the time, but most of his friends were killed or wounded, and he had to walk miles across the desert to escape. He returned to El Paso in February. There he became totally disgusted with the Americans he met—reporters, detectives, spies, business agents—set so sharply in contrast with the simplicity of the Mexicans he had known, such as the gentle one who did not want to go to New York when he found that there were no sheep or cattle in

---

[18] John Reed, *Daughter of the Revolution and Other Stories*, pp. 53–63.
[19] Reed, *Daughter of the Revolution*, pp. 43–49.

the streets. Reed left for Nogales to interview Carranza, with whom he was unimpressed, and then joined Villa's army for the raid on Torreón in late March. Most of his articles for the *World* were reports of this campaign. The killing, however, became too much for him, and he returned to the States before the city was taken.

The few pieces that had appeared had already earned him a reputation; Walter Lippmann enthusiastically wrote Reed that reporting had begun with his work. Dos Passos, who praised *Insurgent Mexico* when it appeared, summed up in *Nineteen Nineteen* his appreciation of Reed:

> Pancho Villa taught him to write and the skeleton mountains and the tall organ cactus and the armored trains and the bands playing in little plazas full of dark girls in blue scarfs
> and the bloody dust and the ping of rifleshots
> in the enormous night of the desert, and the brown quietvoiced peons dying starving killing for liberty
> for land for water for schools
> Mexico taught him to write.[20]

*Insurgent Mexico*, growing out of the articles, has great faults. It is carelessly structured; portraits of Villa and Carranza are inartistically interspersed with Reed's own narrative; three short sketches, which seem more like appendices than a final coda, end it. Since the story is not told chronologically, the reader gains little sense of progression. But within each section Mexico in war is rendered graphically. Reed may have had little understanding of the economic or even the political issues at stake, but he understood the people and their inarticulate desires for land and liberty. Without ignoring their faults he managed to convey their nobility, a grace that few Americans would concede for many years. Moreover, Reed's irony became more controlled, as in his picture of American soldiers of fortune in Jiménez—"hard, cold misfits in a passionate country, despising the cause for which they were fighting, sneering at the gaiety of the irrepressible Mexicans"— soon set in contrast to two starving peasants who joined the camp— "courteous, loving, patient, poor, so long slaves, so full of dreams, so soon to be free."[21] Reed editorialized about such individual scenes, but he let the reader see for himself the differences between one group

20 John Dos Passos, *U.S.A.: Nineteen Nineteen*, pp. 14–15.
21 Reed, *Insurgent Mexico*, pp. 160, 170.

and the other. *Insurgent Mexico* has been overshadowed by his book on the Russian Revolution, but after London's story it is the next important piece of literature to come from the Mexican Revolution.

Shortly after Reed's return to the States the Veracruz incident occurred. Several American sailors had been detained for a few hours at Tampico. Reports to Woodrow Wilson concerning the seriousness of the affair were confusing; besides, the president wished to see the disposal of Huerta and did not realize that any interference would cause the Mexican people to rally around their president, whatever their private feelings about him were. Thus in April 1914 the American navy took Veracruz, and shortly afterward American army troops were shipped in to occupy the town. Reed quickly wrote two articles, one for the *New York Times* and the other for *Masses*, urging the United States not to interfere in Mexican politics. In "The Causes behind Mexico's Revolution," published in the *Times* April 27, he acknowledged that a great many Americans sincerely wanted to help the Mexicans but pointed out how little Americans understood the Mexican temperament. The Mexicans were waging a true fight for better conditions, he insisted, and American interference would only stifle justice. The article was reprinted as a pamphlet and in *Metropolitan*. For the June issue of *Masses* Reed contrasted the hovels that the American Smelting Company had raised for its employees to the homes that the Mexican National Mines had given their workers at Magistral. He recommended the newly published book *The Mexican People* by Lázaro Gutiérrez de Lara (who had accompanied Turner on his fact-finding expedition) and Edgcumb Pinchon as the most truthful picture of Mexico available. And since American interests were citing the murders of American citizens in Mexico as justification for intervention, Reed concluded by reminding his readers how many Mexicans had been wantonly killed in Texas and California.[22] Meantime, he persuaded Joseph Pulitzer of the *World* to support nonintervention, and in June he expounded his views to President Wilson.

The invasion itself was covered by some of the most notable correspondents of the American press. Besides London, who was working for *Collier's*, there were Robert Dunn (1877–1955), Frederick Palmer (1873–1958), who had published in 1910 *Central America and Its*

---

[22] John Reed, "The Causes behind Mexico's Revolution," *New York Times*, April 27, 1914, p. 4; idem, "What about Mexico?" *Masses* 5 (June 1914): 11, 14.

*Problems*, and Richard Harding Davis (1864–1916), who was making his first trip to Mexico though he had traveled in other parts of Spanish America and had written *Three Gringos in Venezuela and Central America* in 1896. It was not the old London who was with them, however, as he indicated by having along his wife, who included an account of the adventure in her *Book of Jack London*, as well as his valet! When the London party arrived over a week after the naval invasion, they learned that President Wilson had accepted an offer of mediation. Davis has written how charming Veracruz appeared when they first arrived and how hot, moist, and overcrowded with refugees it seemed when they learned there might be no war; the correspondents had not come to file stories of local color, and soon they were strained for copy. Palmer later reminisced: "Soon we were suffering utter boredom, with nothing to do except to walk around the plaza and pass the time of day with Jack London, who sat at his favorite table in the cafe hour after hour in the apparent conviction that inertia was an aid to stoicism."[23]

In the Russo-Japanese War the adventurous London had slipped away against orders to the battle front, but it was now Davis who added a touch of glamour and excitement to the aborted invasion.[24] Back in the States an editor came up with the brilliant idea of sending his reporter from Veracruz to the capital for an interview with Huerta. It would have been a sensational scoop, but the reporter prudently declined to risk his life. Many Americans were being killed in Mexico every day without provocation. As Davis remarked, the Mexican could not "grasp the nice distinction between occupying his territory and invading it."[25] Thereupon, the editor passed the idea on to Davis's syndicate, which cabled him. In less than two hours the reply came:

[23] Richard Harding Davis, "When a War Is Not a War," *Scribner's* 56 (July 1914): 47–48; Frederick Palmer, *With My Own Eyes*, p. 293.

[24] Davis, "When a War Is Not a War"; Charles B. Davis (ed.), *Adventures and Letters of Richard Harding Davis*, pp. 354–367; Fairfax Downey, *Richard Harding Davis, His Day*, pp. 236–245; Gerald Langford, *The Richard Harding Davis Years*; Robert Dunn, *World Alive*, p. 197; Medill McCormick, "Just Out of Jail," *Harper's Weekly*, May 30, 1914, pp. 6–7; John T. McCutcheon, "With Davis in Vera Cruz, Brussels, and Salonika," *Scribner's* 60 (July 1916): 91–97; Palmer, *With My Own Eyes*, pp. 293–295. Henry C. Quinby prepared a bibliography.

[25] Richard Harding Davis, "Tells Story of Arrest," *New York Tribune*, May 12, 1914, p. 1. Altogether Davis published twenty dispatches in this newspaper between April 30 and June 23, 1914.

"Leaving Mexico to-morrow afternoon at 3 o'clock." There are several versions of the ensuing story; Davis was willing to embroider upon the truth for the sake of a better yarn. It would seem that he and Medill McCormick left Veracruz on May 8 with letters to the Brazilian consul and to General Joaquín Maas. Palmer accompanied them, although he had only an American passport.

At Paso del Macho they were taken off the train and carried to jail. McCormick and Palmer agree that Davis conducted himself like a hero, and Davis himself wrote afterward:

Everything they did to us I had written and copyrighted. The serial, dramatic, and "movie" rights were all in my name. But . . . I found acting it much more difficult than writing it.

For instance, in the same situation my hero always says to the spigotty general: "Release me, or I'll bring a warship here and blow your dingy republic off the map."

I recalled the line perfectly, but, somehow, could not hear myself saying it. The moment seemed inopportune.[26]

But apparently he refrained only because Palmer and McCormick restrained him. The Gibson profile had aged, and he had gained weight, but Davis played his role to perfection. Finally the letters worked their release, and Davis and McCormick proceeded; Palmer returned to Veracruz and filed a page-one story that caused Washington to pull what diplomatic strings it could. In Mexico City Davis and McCormick were arrested again; the next day they were on their way to Puerto México (now Coatzacoalcos), where they took a steamer back to Veracruz—without the Huerta interview. It was the most sensational story of the entire expedition, and the closest any of the reporters came to danger. Davis's newspaper account was reprinted in the *Literary Digest* and he retold it for *Scribner's* magazine in its July issue.

London did slip away from Veracruz once; he went with Oliver Madox Hueffer in late May to Tampico.[27] London was struck by the industry of the oil fields, which reminded him of his Klondike days;

[26] Davis, "When a War Is Not a War," p. 50. The line was used in his Latin American novel *Soldiers of Fortune*, 1897.

[27] Joan London, *Jack London and His Times*, pp. 348–353; Charmian London, *The Book of Jack London*, II, 289–299; Oliver Madox Hueffer, "Jack London: A Personal Sketch," *New Statesman*, December 2, 1916, pp. 206–207.

he saw a part of the Constitutionalist army and watched two drunks shoot it out at a local bar, but otherwise the trip was uneventful. It did have two important effects, however. There he probably picked up the bacilli that laid him low with dysentery, hastening his departure from Mexico and perhaps his death as well. And the final article he wrote, concerning the Tampico trip, indicated to the socialists that he had sold out. Certainly the London who had subscribed himself a chicken thief with the revolutionists was gone completely. Now he himself looked upon them as chicken thieves, calling them "skylarking boys on the rampage, these rebels who had exchanged the tedium of the day's work for a year-long picnic."[28]

In all fairness the description was not totally inept, as Reed had shown; but London was most irritated, as so many tourists had been and would be, that in four hundred years the Mexican had achieved no civilization that reflected the more desirable British-American culture. This attitude permeates all seven articles he wrote for *Collier's*. He blamed the failure on the half-breed, who had kept Mexico, he thought, perpetually in a state of chaos and slavery. Yet the full-blooded Indian received only occasional sympathy from London, and then for the wrong reasons (from a socialist's point of view), as when he praised the honesty of those at Tampico who had kept the oil fields going for the departed Americans or when he expressed an admiration (which Davis also felt) for the Indian Huerta. Usually London spoke of Indians as "merely descendants of the millions of stupid ones who could not withstand the several hundred ragamuffins of Cortez and who passed stupidly from the harsh slavery of the Montezumas to the no less harsh slavery of the Spaniards and of the later Mexicans." Some strong man must lead Mexico to London's idea of civilization; but looking around, he saw none who could take the place left vacant by Díaz. Therefore, the United States should logically interfere in Mexico's internal affairs: "Mexico must be saved from herself."[29] In his last article he praised the accomplishments of the oilmen in Tampico; throughout all he wrote, he was clearly impressed by the clean appearance of the American military forces and by the efficiency with which they made Veracruz a town closer to the typical American one.

28 Jack London, "Our Adventures in Tampico," *Collier's*, June 27, 1914, p. 6.

29 Jack London, "With Funston's Men: Our Army and Navy in Peaceful Action," *Collier's*, May 23, 1914, p. 10; idem, "The Trouble-Makers of Mexico," *Collier's*, June 13, 1914, p. 25.

At one point London admitted that Americans tend to look at other people as if they should think exactly as Americans do; then he forgot his own warning and showed how little he understood the psychology of a conquered folk by assuring his readers that the citizens of Veracruz would appreciate the American invasion and long to be conquered again.

The socialists back in the States who read these articles kept some hope, because numerous rumors had spread that London was leading a band of insurgents in northern Mexico (someone apparently was using his name there).[30] But London emphatically stated to the press that under no circumstances would he do such a thing. Two years later he openly resigned from the movement. Dunn commented that London had always been "more egotist than either individualist or socialist."[31] And Hueffer held that, consciously or not, London worshipped the Anglo-Saxon. London's wife attempted to defend him by saying that he always saw the big picture; if he could admire the hopes of the socialists, he could also see the remarkable efficiency of the military and the oilmen. But she admitted that six weeks in Veracruz did not strengthen "his already weak regard for the Latin Americans."[32] Certainly London was more closely aligned with Theodore Roosevelt than with the radicals who came to Mexico or with the expatriates already headed for Europe. Ironically, in the 1920's he became one of the most popular American writers in all Latin America.[33]

London the creative writer gained nothing from the Mexican experience. He wrote one piece for *Collier's*, "Law-Givers," about the new law court presided over by the American military, in which he described in detail the characters of the many Mexicans brought before the court for various misdemeanors. He showed most interest in the liars, such as Francisco Hernández, who invents a story to explain why he has rolled a barrel of wine down the street from a shop; and a dark woman who swears that she was not drunk though a soldier affirms that she was; and Alonzo de Xara Quemada, who denies his wife and his five children—"all memory of them and responsibility

[30] See Jack London, *Letters from Jack London*, pp. 422–425, 450.
[31] Dunn, *World Alive*, p. 202.
[32] C. London, *Book of Jack London*, p. 296.
[33] Arnold Chapman, *The Spanish American Reception of United States Fiction, 1920–1940*, pp. 42–56.

for them"—when his suit for adultery against his wife results in his being made instead to take care of his family. Nowhere does London show any real understanding of the bewilderment that a new system of law had thrust upon the *veracruzanos* or a realization that another system of justice could exist. He simply noticed that the Americans were blond and that the judge was impartially exact. Nothing more than a series of vignettes, "Law-Givers" was still the only Mexican piece in which he revealed his skill as a writer of fiction.[34] Dunn says that he asked London about material, "and his hands went up. 'Too much. An idea every day.' But none were ever written . . . and he looked peaked, yellow." In Tampico he told Hueffer that he wanted to write a novel about the Revolution and started searching for material.[35] If the work had been written, it would undoubtedly have resembled his earlier work very little. The Mexican experience contributes nothing positive to the London legend.

President Wilson recalled the troops from Veracruz in the summer. Shortly afterward Lincoln Steffens (1866–1936), a less impassioned but more prestigious defender of the Mexican Revolution than Reed, joined Carranza in Veracruz, where the general had come after American troops pulled out.[36] That summer Steffens had become discouraged with the beginnings of World War I. The war was not the economic revolution that he felt had to come soon; meanwhile he was convinced by the confusion that he needed to prepare for it. Mexico was the logical place for Steffens to visit. Huerta had fled in July, and the battles, which did not interest Steffens, were temporarily at a lull. He could observe the political and economic developments as Carranza attempted to make a permanent gain from the Revolution. Steffens had already come to the conclusion (partly through a visit to Wall Street, which supported Villa because supposedly Villa could be bought) that Reed and the other revolutionists were wrong in putting their faith in the bandit general. Carranza might be bourgeois, but he seemed to be the only independent leader. He was not easy to interview, because of his "healthy hatred" for Americans, yet Steffens—

[34] Jack London, "Law-Givers," *Collier's*, June 20, 1914, pp. 15–16 ff.

[35] Dunn, *World Alive*, p. 202; Hueffer, "Jack London," p. 206.

[36] Lincoln Steffens, *The Autobiography of Lincoln Steffens*, pp. 712–740; idem, *The Letters of Lincoln Steffens*, pp. 351–352, 361–370, 551–566; idem, *The World of Lincoln Steffens*, with notes, pp. 1–4. *Letters* contains a bibliography, pp. 1053–1058.

by showing that he wanted to learn, not to teach as every other American seemed to want—finally won Carranza's confidence. In 1921, a year after Carranza had been assassinated and Obregón had come to power, Steffens made a third visit to Mexico and concluded that Carranza had failed because he did not have a true sense of economics. But in 1914 Steffens was impressed by Carranza's concern for history and his intentions to restore land and liberty to the people by righting their economic ills first and then worrying over the political problems.

In his *Autobiography*, 1931, Steffens set forth his conviction that economic forces ruled every revolution. Yet he was not a pure Marxist, since he became equally convinced that revolutions always wanted to return to their starting point unless the antirevolutionists forced them somehow into a spiral movement. His only active purpose in the Mexican Revolution, however, was to state to the American people, as clearly as he could, the Mexican position, so as to allow Mexico to solve its internal problems with as little outside interference as possible. His first essay, "The Sunny Side of Mexico," appeared in the *Metropolitan* in May 1915 (reprinted by his wife in *The World of Lincoln Steffens*), several months after his return to the States. Like Reed, Steffens offered a balanced view of the Mexican people, trying to let his readers see the American position from the Mexican viewpoint. He quoted a Cuban, chafing from sixteen years of American occupation of Cuba:

"Suppose," he said, "suppose you were having a family quarrel in your home, and a stranger came in and beat you, all of you; and restored order; and then, looking over your house, found it not to his taste. Dirt here and there, perhaps; left by the servants. And suppose the stranger cleaned it all up . . . and ran the whole family for a while to show you how he ran his home. Not nice, what? . . .

"And then suppose . . . that you heard that he didn't really run his own house that way; that there were family rows in his home, and dirt . . .

"But suppose . . . you didn't care how he ran his own house. Suppose you didn't like the way he ran his house and suppose you preferred to run your own house in your own way."

. . . I said that I supposed he meant that his people felt about the American intervention as we Americans would feel if the Germans came over to the United States, licked the Mexicans for us, organized our army, regulated our railroads and trusts, cleaned out Tammany Hall and cleaned up New York.[37]

A year later Steffens would also remind his readers that Americans began their nation with a war and that once there had not been such a discrepancy between what Americans said and what they actually did.[38]

In early November Steffens returned to Mexico for his second visit and was invited to join Carranza on a rail tour of northern Mexico. Again the Mexican leader took Steffens into his confidence; their discussions may have led to the decision to declare state ownership of all mineral rights in the Constitution of 1917, although Steffens denied it. Steffens was pleased that the Wobblies were gaining control of Mexican labor. In December he left the train at Saltillo to go to Mexico City with Dr. Atl, the painter (Gerardo Murillo), for whom he wrote an article published in *Acción Mundial* on February 5, 1916, warning the revolutionists of the dangers of corruption.[39] Steffens liked everyone, even the people whose policies he hated. He got along now equally well with the Americans he met in the capital, though he gently chided them for their greediness and their lack of understanding of a country in which they had lived so long. He rejoined the Carranza caravan in the Chapala region and then left for the States in March.

As he prepared to leave Veracruz, Steffens learned that President Wilson had authorized General John J. Pershing to enter Mexico in search of Villa, who had split with Carranza the year before. Although Villa was probably the purer revolutionist, Obregón had decided that Carranza was stronger than Villa. Piqued by Wilson's support of the Constitutionalists and having nowhere really to turn, Villa raided Columbus, New Mexico. Although the evidence is scanty, both Reed and Steffens said that American business may have lured Villa into the States in a deliberate attempt to force war. Now the Church too had joined Wall Street's cries for intervention. Wilson still did not want to go to war against Mexico, but he felt that some measure had to be taken to defend American honor.

[37] Steffens, *World*, pp. 4–20; quotation, p. 10.
[38] Lincoln Steffens, "A Talk across the Border," *Masses* 8 (July 1916): 14.
[39] Lincoln Steffens, "The World's Interest in the Mexican Revolution," *Acción Mundial*, February 5, 1916, p. 2 (?).

Most of the outstanding correspondents were now in Europe. Robert Dunn joined the Punitive Expedition, however, and so did a newcomer, Damon Runyon (1880–1946). Runyon wrote some twenty syndicated dispatches for Hearst's *New York American*, mostly colorful incidents from the soldiers' lives, as well as several jingles designed to arouse his employer's version of patriotism.[40] To be fair, the *American* was at the same time publishing Reed's objections to the invasion (March 13, April 16, 1916). In these Reed warned that the stereotyped view of the Mexicans as cowards was wrong, that Mexicans hated Americans because of the shabby way they treated Mexicans and Mexican Americans, and that the Mexicans would see the American expedition as an open invasion and would fight to defend their land at the cost of much American labor, time, and money and many Mexican lives. He repeated the same assertions in an article for *Masses* in June, and in the same issue published an exposé of American persecution of the Flores Magón brothers. These were Reed's last articles on "the Mexican tangle."[41]

Steffens echoed Reed in an article for *Everybody's* in May, but he quickly returned to his native humor. In July he published in *Masses* an allegorical conversation between Uncle Sam and Don José in which he made light of the situation. But already he had obtained an interview with Woodrow Wilson; in July and August Steffens wrote a thoughtful summary of his position for *Collier's*[42] and a chapter on Mexico intended for the Democratic platform. The plank was rejected, however, as too radical. He spent that fall lecturing across the States about the need for a better relationship with Mexico. By then the American troops had been withdrawn.

Actually Carranza, in spite of Steffens's admiration, ruled a rather corrupt administration. Still Carranza consolidated, almost by acci-

---

[40] Ed Weiner, *The Damon Runyon Story*, pp. 96, 111–113; Edwin P. Hoyt, *A Gentleman of Broadway*, pp. 125–129, 132. Also Damon Runyon, *Poems for Men*, pp. 196–199, 243–244; idem, dispatches in *New York American*, March 23–May 27, 1916.

[41] John Reed, "Bandit in Mountains Can Hold His Retreat," *New York American*, March 13, 1916, p. 3; idem, "U.S. in Danger of Mountain Ambush," *New York American*, April 16, 1916, pt. 2, pp. 1–2; idem, "The Mexican Tangle" and "Persecution of Mexican Refugees," *Masses* 8 (June 1916): 11, 22–23.

[42] *Collier's*, November 25, 1916; reprinted in Steffens, *World*, pp. 20–31.

dent, the spirit of the Revolution. In an attempt to win popular support he made a series of promises for reform, and on February 5, 1917, with the backing of Obregón, he promulgated a new constitution, which voiced the objectives of the long fight. For a long time its promises were only promises, but the foundation for a new Mexico had been laid. All that was needed was a leader who could begin to make the reforms actualities. Although such a leader was already present, Obregón would not come to power for three more years. Meanwhile Mexico was left free by the United States to work out its own destiny. Americans were preoccupied by the war in Europe; only the exposure of the Zimmermann telegram in 1917—the supposed offer from Germany to help Mexico invade the United States—reminded them vividly of their recent worries in Mexico.

During this same period, 1916–1917, Steffens published three Mexican short stories in *Everybody's*; two more, which were apparently written about the same time, appeared in *Collier's* in 1921–1922. None has been collected, and they are now of more value to the critic and historian than to the general reader, although the last two stories are pleasant reading. All five used stereotyped characters, essentially that of the amoral but lovable rogue, and the same general structure. In none do we see Mexico or Mexicans in the heroic light that plays across Steffens's other writing.

Two of the stories are about Tommy Tyler, a Texas correspondent based on the real figure of John W. Roberts, who also appears in Reed's *Insurgent Mexico*. Gregory Mason, another correspondent (and later writer of several Mexican books), described Roberts as "one of the most picturesque amalgams of the delightful and the unscrupulous ever produced by the Border."[43] Steffens's first story—" 'Thirty-Threed,' " 1916—revolves around the problems Tyler is having with Carranza because of Tyler's previous association with Villa. The title refers to an article of the old constitution that gave the government the right to deport all undesirables. "The Battle of Celayo," 1922, tells how Tyler, just to win the affection of a stenographer, dictated from El Paso his story of the entire battle (in which Obregón had defeated Villa in April 1915), including an account of the reporter's being wounded, without his having been close to the clash. Ironically it had

[43] Mason, "Reed, Villa, and the Village," p. 11.

turned out to be his best battle piece, and he is now indignant that some fellow correspondent is pointing out its fraudulence.[44]

The other three stories are about Major d'Alegro (given the more proper Spanish name "de Alegre" in the last one), a figure similar to an officer Steffens had described in his first essay. The major's name describes one of his main characteristics, but in addition to being happy he is also vain and greedy. Yet he is so honest about his intentions that one must like him. The situation is the same in all three stories: de Alegre wants money from the narrator, but the narrator will respond only with receipt of a story. In the first encounter, "Bunk," 1917, the major tells how he escaped a firing squad that morning. First, he had handed out all the bunk he could about patriotism, motherhood, and the joy of life, but when he offered to treat the captain to an evening on the town, he won. He needs the money to keep his promise. In "The Last Great Moment," 1917, the major relates how one of his captains had arranged to kill a group of federalist cadets in the public square, first giving each cadet a speech about patriotism and then having each lean forward so that when he dropped he would fall in a military line with the others. The cadets loved it, but the major felt he had to stop the exhibition. Higher officials did, in fact, order the major to execute the captain. Deciding to let the punishment fit the crime, the major made the mistake of carrying him out to the square to be shot in the same manner. Again there had to be speeches, and when they turned to questions of land and liberty, the major realized that he was no longer the center of attention and envied the nobility of the captain's death.[45]

The stories are obviously not propaganda; de Alegre is almost the personification of the American view of the typical Mexican. Yet in the second story, Steffens introduced the issues at stake in the Revolution and suggested other kinds of leaders. In "The White Streak," 1921, he found a way to integrate these ideals naturally into the plot and to invent a symbol of the Revolution showing both its success and its ultimate failure. De Alegre has also changed. He is still the honest

[44] Lincoln Steffens, " 'Thirty-Threed': A Tale of Our Border To-day," *Everybody's* 35 (July 1916): 41–51; idem, "The Battle of Celayo," *Collier's*, March 11, 1922, pp. 3–4 ff.

[45] Lincoln Steffens, "Bunk: A Story of Revolutionary Mexico," *Everybody's* 36 (February 1917): 200–211; idem, "The Last Great Moment," *Everybody's* 36 (March 1917): 350–361.

rogue who admits that he is yellow with just a troublesome white streak, and when at the end we find that he has taken part of the gold with which he was entrusted, the action seems consistent with those in the other stories. Nevertheless, he has heroically returned nearly thirty thousand dollars when he could easily have caught a ship with the entire amount at Veracruz and skipped the country forever. And when the train he had confiscated had gotten out of control, the runaway engine, he remembers,

. . . made me think of Mexico. She didn't know where she was going, but she was on her way, free. She wasn't fit to be free, not yet; but she didn't realize her dependence on foreign intelligence, and she didn't care for it. She loved liberty, and she was after it. And—but, just like Mexico, what she didn't know was that she couldn't have liberty and stay on the narrow, crooked road you damn foreigners had laid out for her, and so, like Mexico, she jumped the track. She sprang off into space and went crashing back into barbarism . . . a free and glorious wreck.[46]

The decade ended on a downward note with respect to American literary interest in Mexico: Bierce, London, and Davis were dead; Reed was dying in Russia; Steffens, though writing such stories as these, was involved in other matters. One other important American radical appeared in Mexico during the period—Michael Gold (1894–1967). But when he waded the Rio Grande in 1917, he was merely trying to escape the American draft. One biographical source states that "much of his writing stems from his Mexican experience, and his life there confirmed him in his political views," but only an unsuccessful play, *Fiesta*, seems to have reflected the Mexican period of Gold's life directly.[47] However, with the Revolution's battles finished, greater things could now occur in Mexico, and these events would attract much attention.

[46] Lincoln Steffens, "The White Streak," *Collier's*, January 15, 1921, pp. 5–7 ff.; quotation, p. 29.

[47] For information about Gold in Mexico, see Stanley J. Kunitz and Howard Haycroft (eds.), *Twentieth Century Authors*, p. 547, from which the quotation comes; Daniel Aaron, *Writers on the Left*, p. 86; and Carleton Beals, *Glass Houses*, pp. 35–37. A synopsis of the play is given by Burns Mantle (ed.), *The Best Plays of 1929–30 and the Year Book of the Drama in America*, p. 396.

# 5. The Expatriate Scene

The 1920's brought a new mood to Mexico: Anita Brenner remembered in *The Wind That Swept Mexico*, her history of the Revolution: "There was a lift, a stirring feel, . . . a sense of strength released: much work to do, everything at the beginning . . ."[1] What happened now brought renewed attention from the United States and Great Britain. As peace settled, as the railroads were repaired and roads opened up, tourists came fast, most clutching their copy of *Terry's Guide to Mexico*, quickly revised by its author, Thomas Phillip Terry (1864–1945), to meet the changed scene. Among them traveled a number of first-rate writers. If Paris continued to be the major literary magnet for the world, Mexico City now saw such expatriates as D. H. Lawrence, Katherine Anne Porter, John Dos Passos, and Somerset Maugham exploring its streets, branching out into the country, and jotting down their impressions for publication. With them came a sizeable number of other writers: some hacks; some important only in their day, such as Witter Bynner and Joseph Hergesheimer; and others of wider-ranging talent, such as Langston Hughes, Kenneth Rexroth, and B. Traven. Almost all were influenced considerably by

[1] Anita Brenner, *The Wind That Swept Mexico*, p. 62. See John W. F. Dulles, *Yesterday in Mexico*.

Mexican politics during an eight-year period in which Alvaro Obregón and Plutarco Elías Calles began to realize to a limited degree the goals of the Revolution; the writers were even more powerfully stimulated by Mexico's artistic renaissance, which began in 1922–1923.

Obregón was the ablest leader to come from the civil wars; his inauguration on December 1, 1920, began an era of reconstruction. Revolts still broke out sporadically, and Obregón himself was assassinated in 1928 by a religious fanatic, but the tremendous bloodshed of the previous decade was finished and even Obregón's assassination did not plunge the country into disorder. "Obregón meant to restore peace and prosperity, and he made the Revolution respectable," Lesley Byrd Simpson summed up in *Many Mexicos*, adding, "Everyone became a Revolutionary with a capital R."[2] Since Mexican rhetoric now echoed that of Russia, the United States, moving prosperously under Warren Harding's administration, became so frightened that it refused to recognize the new government. Ironically, Mexico, for all its socialist propaganda, was encouraging the growth of a native capitalism as much or more than it was encouraging collectivism. While in some areas the native culture, to the delight of people like Lawrence and Traven, was exalted, in most areas the natives attempted to be as modern as their northern neighbors. All this confusion is indicative of the troubled path that Mexico followed as Obregón and Calles attempted to solve the country's multiple problems.

Agrarian reforms were freed somewhat from the restrictions that Carranza had placed on them, but Obregón, too, feared radical measures. Moreover, under threat of physical violence from the *hacendados* and spiritual reprisal from the clergy, few of the poor requested land, and, as Dos Passos noted, little was given away. Other causes also conspired against the poor. For example, Rosalie Evans, a British subject, angrily withstood expropriation, defending her land with guns, until she was ambushed in 1924. Her letters, published two years later, stirred English readers and added international pressure against redistribution. Few outsiders shared Katherine Anne Porter's conviction that Mrs. Evans was "avaricious, with an extraordinary hardness of heart and ruthlessness of will; and she died in a grotesque cause."[3] Greatest gains for the landless were made in Yucatan under

[2] Lesley B. Simpson, *Many Mexicos*, p. 308.

[3] Katherine Anne Porter, *The Collected Essays and Occasional Writings of Katherine Anne Porter*, p. 420.

the leadership of its governor, Felipe Carrillo Puerto, but he was killed in 1924. Labor reforms under the strong leadership of Luis Morones, head of the official labor union, made a more promising start. Working conditions were markedly improved through the threat of strikes backed by the power of the constitution, as Traven shows in his novel *Die Baumwollpflücker*. But the leaders often failed, finding it personally more lucrative to blackmail the owners than to hold the strike, and the workers became cynical. Thus, although powerful steps were taken by peasant and laborer, the objectives of the Revolution remained more talk than actuality.

Foreign speculators, especially oilmen, created another major problem that was temporarily settled by compromise. The constitution had declared that Mexico owned all subsoil rights; the investors in the rich oil fields around Tampico vehemently protested and tried every way possible to direct the government as they chose. Primarily because of this controversy, Harding, influenced by his oil-hungry advisors, refused to recognize Obregón's administration. For a while it made no difference; Mexico's sense of pride was strengthened by its ability to launch a new government without the aid of the United States. But when the election of 1924 approached, Obregón, fearing a rebellion, decided he must gain American backing. Therefore, in July 1923 he agreed that the constitution was not retroactive; his government was recognized by Calvin Coolidge in August. The manipulations of the oil companies, including outright forging of documents, would continue to plague the Mexican government for fifteen years and would elicit varying responses from American and British authors. In the manner of London, Hergesheimer tacitly defended the oilmen (Evelyn Waugh would later implicitly defend them); but Miss Porter, Traven, and Carleton Beals protested their methods, and Traven and Beals wrote entire novels to expose their corruptness.

The final major contention came from within—the Church. The quarrel began in January 1923 when Obregón interpreted the dedication of a monument to Christ at Guanajuato as a challenge to his government. He deported the Pope's representative to the ceremony; the faithful placarded their homes with the slogan *¡Viva Cristo Rey!* Then in January 1926 the clergy republished a statement against the anticlerical clause in the constitution. Calles answered by deporting all foreign priests, ordering all native priests to register, and closing all Catholic schools and convents. In July, the priests went on a three-

year strike. Fighting broke out between self-seeking generals and the
*cristeros*, who were especially active in the area around Lakes Pátzcuaro and Chapala and who burned public schools, killed federal
employees, and finally dynamited the Mexico City–Guadalajara train.
D. H. Lawrence was gone from Mexico before the split became so
violent, but if we may trust the evidence of his Mexican novel,
Lawrence like Traven understood much of the tense situation and
would have supported Calles's reaction.

The great accomplishments of the period were made in the pro-
grams under the direction of José Vasconcelos, a remarkable philosopher who united classical learning with a love of his native culture.
As minister of education he created a rural school system that was
designed to serve all the needs—practical and aesthetic—of the village
in which a school was located. In 1926, after Vasconcelos had resigned, John Dewey (1859–1952) was invited to Mexico to advise the
government on its educational progress. He wrote four articles concerning his trip for *New Republic*; these he collected in *Impressions
of Soviet Russia and the Revolutionary World*, 1929. In general he
applauded the directions the Revolution had taken and in particular
the work of Vasconcelos, commenting that "there is no education
movement in the world which exhibits more of the spirit of intimate
union of school activities with those of the community than is found
in this Mexican development." He also found the attempt to incorporate the Indians into the national life reassuring and noted the freshness of concept that the minister had brought to all he touched.[4]

For the expatriate writers, Vasconcelos's encouragement of Mexico's
artists was his most important act. In 1922 he commissioned Diego
Rivera and others to decorate the education ministry. Rivera's furious
activities at the ministry and at the college in Chapingo and his
strange murals, all inspired by forgotten or ignored native forms, appeared so horrible to the Mexican establishment, trained to like the
academic style of the nineteenth century, that the frescoes quickly
became news and for a time a verbal civil war was waged about their
worth. In the middle of the battle the sensitive Mexican press realized
that these desecrations against the nation were being greeted with
overwhelming enthusiasm by critics elsewhere and were bringing

---

[4] John Dewey, *John Dewey's Impressions of Soviet Russia and the Revolutionary
World*, pp. 113–141; quotation, p. 124. Milton Halsey prepared a bibliography.

great fame to the country; the press reversed its position. The critics, after their initial awe of Rivera, saw the other artists: José Clemente Orozco, who developed slowly into Mexico's greatest artist, a giant even in world art; David Alfaro Siqueiros, whose paintings are exciting even though often unfinished, since their creator was always being thrust in jail for his political activities; and an uncountable number of lesser figures. The excitement produced by the muralists, above everything else that came from the Revolution, attracted visitors. Few American or British writers failed to comment on the muralists' work, and many of them—Miss Porter, Lawrence, Rexroth, Dos Passos, Hughes, and later Hart Crane—spent some time in the company of one or more of the artists.

Historian Henry B. Parkes concluded: "The most striking and unique achievements of post-revolutionary Mexico were, in fact, not practical but aesthetic."[5] Scores of books and articles have been written about the artistic renaissance, including much nonsense. Among the more informative have been those by Alma M. Reed (c. 1890–1966), who has also earned a romantic spot in Mexican history.[6] She first came at Obregón's invitation because of her work on behalf of Mexican Americans in California, and then returned slightly later to report on the Carnegie Institute's exploration of Chichén Itzá. There she met and fell in love with Felipe Carrillo Puerto, governor of Yucatan. In her honor he commissioned Luis Rosado Vega to compose "La Peregrina" (music by Ricardo Palmerín), now one of the country's popular songs. After Carrillo Puerto's assassination Mrs. Reed stayed on in Mexico and discovered the work of Orozco. She wrote two biographies of the artist (1932 and 1956) and also prepared *The Mexican Muralists*, 1960, a rapid survey of the lives and works of all the outstanding painters, as well as *The Ancient Past of Mexico*, 1966.

In addition to the excitement provided by Rivera and Orozco, many writers came in search of the primitive and looked upon the popular arts and crafts of the Indians with awe. Miss Porter wrote one of the earliest surveys of this aspect of Mexican life, but the first thorough history from pre-Columbian forms through the beginnings of the renaissance in the 1920's was *Idols behind Altars*, 1929, prepared by

[5] Henry B. Parkes, *A History of Mexico*, p. 381.

[6] H. Allen Smith, *The Pig in the Barber Shop*, pp. 92–104. See Alma Reed's obituary in *New York Times*, November 21, 1966.

Mexican-born Anita Brenner (1905–).[7] In a very personal way she attempted therein to relate the artistic development to the people's cultural and religious history. From the early fifties to the early seventies Miss Brenner continued to share her interest through her magazine for tourists, *Mexico This Month.*

All this attention naturally led to renewed interest in the ancient Indian civilizations. Under the leadership of Manuel Gamio, Mexico's first major anthropologist, exploration of Aztec and Maya ruins resumed, revealing more fully to the world the high artistic values of these cultures. Most of the books written by American and British explorers—foremost among them George C. Vaillant (1901–1945) and J. Eric S. Thompson (1898–)—interest only a select audience, but a few had wider appeal. Thomas Gann (1867–1938), for example, wrote six books in a popular vein, including *In an Unknown Land,* 1924, and *Ancient Cities and Modern Tribes,* 1926.[8] These relate to his discoveries in Yucatan and British Honduras, where he was stationed as a district medical officer. Though Oliver La Farge (1901–1963) utilized his archaeological experiences in Guatemala as a basis for several fictional works, from his experiences in southern Mexico in 1925 we have only his scholarly collaboration with the Danish archaeologist, Frans Blom, *Tribes and Temples,* 1927, and a few scattered comments in his autobiography, *Raw Material,* 1945.[9]

With such diverse intellectual and emotional currents sweeping Mexico, the country needed a Humboldt to put the scene in some sort of order. None was forthcoming, unfortunately. Ernest Gruening (1887–) among writers in English came closest to succeeding with his topical survey, *Mexico and Its Heritage,* 1928. Mention must also be made of the varied writings of Carleton Beals (1893–).[10] He had ar-

[7] I appreciate Anita Brenner's letter, September 2, 1969. In addition to her survey of the arts and her history of the Revolution, Dr. Brenner has published several children's books set in Mexico (with illustrations by Jean Charlot) and translations of novels by Mariano Azuela, Gregorio López y Fuentes, and Mauricio Magdaleno.

[8] Vaillant wrote *Aztecs of Mexico,* 1941, and Thompson, *The Rise and Fall of Maya Civilization,* 1954. For Gann's life see *Dictionary of National Biography, 1931–1940,* pp. 305–306; a review of one of Gann's books was by Katherine Anne Porter, "Maya Treasure," *New York Herald Tribune Books,* February 8, 1925, p. 9; other reviews of his books came from Gregory Mason and Robert Redfield.

[9] Oliver La Farge, *Raw Material,* pp. 77–91, 166–176, 207; Everett A. Gillis, *Oliver La Farge,* pp. 4–5.

[10] See Carleton Beals, *Glass Houses;* idem, *The Great Circle.*

rived in Mexico about 1918—moneyless, friendless, and knowing little Spanish—and within a year was on his way to becoming one of its leading popular authorities. He seems to have known almost everyone worth knowing, both natives and foreigners, politically or culturally. He helped Frances Toor edit *Mexican Folkways*. His own work includes a biography of Díaz, several travel journals, and various social-political interpretations, including *Mexican Maze*, 1931, which was illustrated by Rivera. Basically a conservative with radical fire running through him, Beals tried in all these works to evaluate the nation as objectively as possible. His writings often displeased authorities in both Mexico City and Washington, but his integrity and high prestige impressed them. Although the books do not add up to the thoroughness and exactness of Gruening's volume, they undoubtedly reached a wider audience.

For literary historians the most interesting of Beals's writings are four memoirs—*Brimstone and Chile*, 1927; *Glass Houses*, 1938; *The Great Circle*, 1940; and *House in Mexico*, 1958—which, along with the first volume of the *Daybooks*, 1961, of the photographer Edward Weston (1886–1958), give great insight into the day-by-day affairs of Mexico City. Beals also wrote two novels: *Black River*, 1934, an exposé of the oil industry based on documents he had accumulated, and *The Stones Awake*, 1936, the story of an Indian girl in the Revolution. Miss Porter, reviewing *The Stones Awake*, commented, "He might have been a fine novelist if he had had time to stop and learn." Like other reviewers, she felt that Beals stayed too close to facts and could not "follow his characters into the closed doors of their hearts and minds because he did not create them." Still she spoke warmly of his overall contributions to the literature about Mexico.[11]

The first important writer to arrive in Mexico during this period was Langston Hughes (1902–1967), who came in the spring of 1919.[12] His father, upset by discrimination against Negroes in the United States, had emigrated to Mexico during the last years of Díaz's dictatorship. Hughes's mother became so homesick, however, that she returned with the children to the States. When the Revolution began,

[11] Katherine Anne Porter, "History on the Wing," *New Republic*, November 18, 1936, p. 82.

[12] Langston Hughes, *The Big Sea*, pp. 15–16, 34–80; James A. Emanuel, *Langston Hughes*, pp. 11, 23–24. Donald C. Dickinson edited a bibliography.

his father, because of his color, experienced none of the dangers that white Americans did. But ironically he became what he hated. Like a typical American he set about acquiring property in Mexico City and a ranch near Toluca and became the general manager of an electric plant in Toluca. He disliked the Mexican peons as much as he had come to hate people of his own race; his friends were three aristocratic creoles in the capital, the Patiño sisters. But young Hughes, knowing none of these things, thought of his father as a symbol of freedom from racial lines and the tenement life. Thus, when his father asked him to return to Mexico after an absence of eleven years, he readily accepted.

Meeting his father, he found that he hated him and later recalled that summer in his autobiography *The Big Sea*, 1940, as "the most miserable I have ever known." At one point the youth seriously contemplated suicide; in August he fell ill with a fever and took delight that the American hospital in Mexico City to which he was carried cost his father twenty dollars a day. Nevertheless, since his father had hinted that he would help with his college education, Hughes came again the next summer. His father was kinder, perhaps calmed by a German housekeeper, whom he later married. But Hughes, who had quarreled with his mother in returning, remained miserable. He turned to poetry for solace and sent some of his work to *Crisis*. This magazine accepted many of his poems over the next few years. Several of them have a tropical setting, but only one is indisputably Mexican (Hughes later spent some time in Cuba and Haiti): "Mexican Market Woman," published in March 1922 and collected in *The Weary Blues*, 1926. Only seven lines long, it suggests the freedom for which both Hugheses sought. In a recording the poet recalled the circumstances: "In Mexico once I wrote a poem about . . . an Indian peasant woman from the hills. I lived in Toluca where there was a big market. And this old woman had come into town one day with a bag of vegetables on her back that she spread out on the earth in the market place to sell. So I wrote:

> This ancient hag
> Who sits upon the ground
> Selling her scanty wares
> Day in, day round,
> Has known high wind-swept mountains,

And the sun has made
Her skin so brown."[13]

In December 1921 *Crisis* had also published his prose version of the
legend of the Virgin of Guadalupe. Earlier, *Brownies' Book*, a magazine begun by the *Crisis* staff for children, had published three other
articles. "Mexican Games," his first piece in a national magazine,
appeared in January 1921. It simply gives three games that he had
seen the children in Toluca playing. Later in the year "In a Mexican
City" and "Up to the Crater of an Old Volcano" appeared. Since both
are in a language appropriate for children, they do not give us much
indication of Hughes's great skill with the rhythms of American
speech. In the one he takes a tourist's view of Toluca, speaking particularly of the fiestas, the homes, and the markets; in the other he
tells about a walking tour he made with students from the Instituto to
the nearby Nevado de Toluca.[14] *The Big Sea* provides a more interesting view of life in the provincial town.

Actually the year turned out better than the one before. Hughes
became independent of his father by teaching English at a local business college and at a private finishing school for girls. In his new
position he met the town's leading citizens. Almost every weekend he
went into Mexico City to attend plays and to watch the bullfights. He
became as enthusiastic an aficionado as Hemingway, although he
found that he could never capture the spectacle in words. Finally his
father, probably impressed by Hughes's several publications, agreed
to send him to Columbia University. Unfortunately a series of trage-
dies, including one melodramatic episode in which Hughes only acci-
dentally escaped being murdered, occurred to mar his leaving Mexico
in September 1921. And he had to turn his classes over to a young
woman from Arkansas, who expressed surprise at discovering "an
educated Negro."

Hughes did not return to Mexico for ten years; then, while he was
on a lecturing tour across the United States, he stepped over the border

[13] Langston Hughes, *The Dream Keeper and Other Poems*, Folkway Records,
1955; idem, *The Weary Blues*, p. 91.

[14] Langston Hughes, "The Virgin of Guadalupe," *Crisis* 23 (December 1921):
77; "Mexican Games," "In a Mexican City," and "Up to the Crater of an Old Volcano," *Brownies' Book* 2 (January, April, and December 1921): 18, 102–105, 334–
338. Virginia Spencer of Howard University Library located these last three for me.

to Juárez for a temporary respite from the problems of color. He could not really use Mexico as his father had; wherever he went he always had to return in his poems and his fiction to his own people. Yet he would live there one more time. In the late fall of 1934 he learned that the elder Hughes, whom he had not seen since he left for New York, had died. He went to Mexico City to settle the estate. All the property had been left to the Patiños, but since he was completely broke, he accepted, at their urging, the money on deposit. Although he traveled as far away as Guadalajara, he remained mostly in the capital through the late spring. When he wrote his second volume of autobiography, *I Wonder as I Wander*, 1956, he thought of the period as one of the most delightful in his life.[15]

It was a Bohemian time. Because his friends, especially the irrepressible estranged wife of Rivera, embarrassed the Patiño sisters, he moved into a tiny flat near the Lagunilla market with Henri Cartier-Bresson, the French photographer, and Andrés Henestrosa, a Mexican poet, novelist, and student of Indian languages. The bullfights again attracted him; he became friends with a Spanish matador. He knew all the leading artists of the mural renaissance: Rivera, Orozco, Siqueiros, Rufino Tamayo, Roberto Montenegro, who had a studio across the street from him, and Miguel Covarrubias, whom he had known in Harlem when the caricaturist had designed the jacket for *The Weary Blues*. He renewed his friendship with a Cuban diplomat to Mexico, José Fernández de Castro. The latter published a long article informing the Mexican public that Hughes was one of the most distinguished poets in the United States. There followed sessions with newspaper interviewers and photographers. Xavier Villaurrutia, José Mancisidor, and Rafael Heliodoro Valle wrote articles about him; *El Nacional* devoted a page to his poems. Requests for speeches finally began to bother him so much that in June 1935 he returned to California.

This trip had less direct influence on his work than the earlier visits. Yet it was important in a number of ways. He worked to perfect his Spanish and later translated several Mexican pieces, including a short story by Antonio Acevedo Escobedo, poems by Nellie Campobello (Francisca), and some of the Indian poetry in Covarrubias's *Mexico*

---

[15] Langston Hughes, *I Wonder as I Wander*, pp. 63, 285–300; Emanuel, *Langston Hughes*, pp. 36–37.

*South.*[16] (He also translated the poetry of Federico García Lorca and Gabriela Mistral.) And he read *Don Quixote,* a work that he felt much influenced his delineation of Simple, a character in a series of short stories. *I Wonder as I Wander* also offers many sidelights to Beals's and Weston's revelations about Mexican cultural life.

Two other poets of some note came to Mexico in the early twenties. The visit seems to have had little effect on the development of Kenneth Rexroth (1905–), and his two poems that reflect the experience— "Oaxaca 1925" and "Gradualism"—are insignificant. In *An Autobiographical Novel,* 1966, he like Hughes gives us a glimpse of Bohemian life in Mexico City. When Rexroth arrived in autumn 1925 he plunged into the artistic ferment. Rivera he found "simply dreadful," but the personality of Siqueiros and the "lonely greatness" of Orozco impressed him. Weston's beautiful photographer friend, Tina Modetti, stirred him in a different way. After a short while he went with one of her friends, an Austrian prostitute, to Oaxaca. But after two weeks there he fled to Chicago; in the forty years following, he wrote, "I have never had any desire to go back to Mexico."[17]

Witter Bynner (1881–1968), on the other hand, was happily composing in Chapala the poems that would make up *Indian Earth,* 1929. He had fallen in love with the area when he first explored it with the Lawrences in 1923 and maintained one home there the rest of his life. Some of the poetry is heavily overshadowed by Lawrence's personality, but generally the voice is Bynner's own: an elegant, rather weary tone speaking of the essential loneliness of man and attempting to find refuge in either the comforting music of the people or the sharp images of the Mexican landscape. Other Mexican poems—he wrote some sixty in all—found their way into later volumes or were left uncollected. Unfortunately the man's personality was not forceful enough to keep interesting the two or three poems that are good; they seem lifeless in spite of their technical perfection, almost Oriental in nature.[18]

[16] Antonio Acevedo Escobedo, "Fire in the Rain," *Rocky Mountain Review* 2 (Spring 1938): 8; Dudley Fitts (ed.), *Anthology of Contemporary Latin-American Poetry,* pp. 213–219; Miguel Covarrubias, *Mexico South,* pp. 18–20, 31–35, 312–318, 330–335.

[17] Kenneth Rexroth, *The Collected Shorter Poems,* pp. 7–8; idem, *An Autobiographical Novel,* pp. 344–345.

[18] Witter Bynner, *Caravan,* p. 46; idem, *Indian Earth,* pp. xv–xvi, 3–57; idem,

Fiction about Mexico fared much better, both in quantity and in quality. If the work of Josefina Niggli and Hergesheimer ranks with that of Beals and if some critics despair of Traven's inept style, the work of Lawrence, Miss Porter, Maugham, and Dos Passos retains vitality and marks in the case of three of them a turning point in their careers.

Josefina Niggli (1910–) was born in Monterrey and spent the years 1920–1925 in the nearby village of Sabinas Hidalgo, where her father managed a cement plant.[19] When she returned to the United States she carried with her intense memories of her childhood in the Mexican village—its people, its history, especially during the Revolution, and its folklore. From these grew the series of interrelated stories about a Mexican American who returns to his roots, *Mexican Village*, 1945, and a novel about the conflicts in a wealthy Monterrey family, *Step Down, Elder Brother*, 1947. They represent two of the few attempts in English fiction to move into the life of northern Mexico. She also wrote ten poems printed in *Mexican Silhouettes*, 1931, five one-act plays collected in *Mexican Folk Plays*, 1938, and a children's book, *A Miracle for Mexico*, 1964 (with illustrations by Alejandro Rangel Hidalgo).

The fall 1924 visit of William Somerset Maugham (1874–1965) as part of his tour of Latin America has been remarked chiefly for an altercation with Lawrence. When Beals asked Maugham if he were going to see Lawrence while they were both in the capital, Maugham in agitation stuttered: "Is he in Mexico? He's one man I never want to see again. I shall leave Mexico at once." Beals tried to soothe him by saying that Mexico was a big country, but Maugham retorted, "No country is big enough to hold that creature and me."[20] Maugham left for Cuernavaca the day that the Lawrences arrived, but they soon met at a dinner in Mexico City. From this distance it would be impossible to say which man was at fault, but certainly Lawrence through a series of misunderstandings snubbed Maugham. Lawrence wrote in a

*Against the Cold*, pp. 83–92; idem, *Take Away the Darkness*, p. 97. Eight poems were left uncollected. Robert O. Lindsay prepared a not altogether helpful bibliography. Mary Austin reviewed *Indian Earth*.

[19] See *Current Biography 1949*, pp. 455–456; *North Carolina Authors*, pp. 85–86. Miss Niggli's first name has been spelled "Josephine" and "Josephina." Reviews of her books were written by Carleton Beals and Bertram D. Wolfe.

[20] Carleton Beals, *House in Mexico*, pp. 196–197.

letter that Maugham was "disagreeable, with no fun left in him, and terrified for fear he won't be able to do his next great book, with a vivid Mexican background, before Christmas."[21] Early in November, Maugham left for Yucatan to visit the Maya ruins; soon afterward he continued on his journey to Central America.

Mexico did not greatly impress Maugham, but he had contracted with *Cosmopolitan* magazine to supply it with a number of two-page stories, and between 1925 and 1929, in the course of meeting this obligation, he used three anecdotes set in Latin America, two of which he had definitely picked up in Mexico (all collected in a volume called *Cosmopolitans*, 1936). Maugham always wanted simply to tell an interesting story well, generally with a slight touch of humor for even the most tragic situation. These stories illustrate his usual methods. In all three a person who seems to be modeled clearly on himself narrates the incident.

Had Beals not told us the origin of the first, "The Man with the Scar," we would not have known that the idea came from Mexico, because Maugham changed the setting to Guatemala City. The same night on which Beals had mentioned Lawrence, Maugham had become intrigued by a waiter in the Hotel Regis who had a frightful scar running down his face. Maugham began inventing stories to explain the injury and soon had the rest of his dinner guests thinking up possibilities. Beals asked the waiter the truth; it turned out that a case of carbonated water had blown up in his face. In Maugham's short story the narrator and a Guatemalan companion are at a hotel bar when the scarred man, a seller of lottery tickets, comes in. The narrator learns that the ticketseller had been a Nicaraguan general who had failed to pull off a coup and had been sentenced to die. At the firing line he had requested that he be allowed to bid his wife goodbye and had thereupon killed her. The commanding officer demanded an explanation; the condemned man replied that he loved her. For such a noble gesture the officer deported him. The Guatemalan becomes silent; the narrator finally asks how he received the scar. He answers that the man had been opening a bottle of ginger ale and it had blown up. With that unexpected twist the story ends. Maugham revealed a

[21] D. H. Lawrence, *The Letters of D. H. Lawrence*, p. 621; idem, *The Collected Letters of D. H. Lawrence*, II, 816. See Frieda Lawrence, *"Not I, but the Wind . . .",* pp. 147–148.

similar haughty attitude in "The Closed Shop," now extended to American women as well as Spanish American men. He probably picked up the idea for this story—about the troubles an unidentified country has when it creates an easy divorce law—later on his journey.

"The Bum," the last of the *Cosmopolitan* stories, takes place in Veracruz. The narrator is delayed on a trip to Yucatan by a strike on the Ward boat line. Without anything to do he puts up at the Hotel Diligencia and watches the dull routine of the city. One of the beggars catches his attention; the man is an undernourished gringo, about forty years old, with brilliant red hair and beard. When he comes to the narrator's table to beg, the narrator is convinced that he has seen him before. Finally he remembers that some twenty years earlier the redhead had been one of the many American and British artists at work in Rome. The artist had spoken often of Central America, but mostly he had prophesied with arrogance his immediate success. When the narrator sees the artist again, he asks the man if he remembers Rome. There is no answer. Perplexed, he hands him a bill; the man crumples it into a ball and throws it away. The episode is ended. The story is inconsequential, but it is intriguing when one remembers that at the time Maugham met Lawrence, Lawrence was nearly forty, was suffering from his fatal sickness, and certainly had red hair and beard. If the beggar is some sort of projection of Maugham's anger, his spleen at least did not get the better of the craftsman. The story is a well-told variation on the old theme of the unsuccessful artist.[22]

Maugham also used a Mexican character in one of his *Ashenden* series: "The Hairless Mexican," 1927. Ashenden, a British agent, must prevent an enemy agent from coming into Italy. To achieve this end, British intelligence has hired an accomplice to dispose of him, choosing a refugee from the general rout that had accompanied Huerta's fall. It is a typical Maugham yarn: a man is murdered, but at the end Ashenden discovers that they have killed the wrong person. Throughout the story the Mexican chats about his country—but everything he says could have come from a casual reading of the newspapers.[23] None of these stories in fact gives the reader a real feeling for place as do many of Maugham's stories of other foreign places.

[22] W. Somerset Maugham, *The Complete Short Stories of W. Somerset Maugham*, II, 18–36. Raymond T. Stott prepared a bibliography.
[23] Maugham, *Short Stories*, I, 469–503.

Joseph Hergesheimer (1880–1954) thought that he had come to Mexico in February 1925 as a guest of the government, until two Mexican poets, Genaro Estrada and Luis Quintanilla, called on him and informed him differently.[24] The novelist, then at the height of his fame, was in search of materials for a new work. He took some forty pages of notes on Maximilian and Carlotta, then turned to a movie script for Pola Negri set in the silver-mining area of Pachuca during the time of Huerta. The Mexican department of foreign relations continued to be so trying, however, that when *Flower of Night* was finally filmed, its locale was changed to gold-rush California.[25] Meanwhile Hergesheimer had found the idea for a novel and its title, *Tampico*, 1926. The excessively melodramatic story recounts the return of an American oilman to the fields, where he must confront sabotage, betrayal in love, and the realization of his own weakness, until he accepts the naturalist's view of an indifferent universe. Mexico served mostly as a rather exotic dash of local color, a fit place for casual killings and pleasure. Its one impressive moment comes when the hero moves surrealistically through a series of cantinas in the redlight district; here Hergesheimer anticipated Malcolm Lowry's nightmarish vision of Mexico. Otherwise *Tampico* is best forgotten.

Not so the work of John Dos Passos (1896–1970), for Mexico led him to the writing of the trilogy of novels, *U.S.A.*, 1930–1938. He came for a few months in 1926–1927 and again in 1932.[26] Like most visitors he was immediately captivated by the muralists. His first article, "Paint the Revolution!" published in *New Masses* in March 1927 and never reprinted, surveyed the work of Rivera, Orozco, and Montenegro. Dos Passos cited Rivera's attempts to bring the meaning of the Revolution directly to the people through his murals (an important task since so many of the people who needed to be reached could not

---

[24] Joseph Hergesheimer, *From an Old House*, pp. 193, 196; the University of Texas collection includes a telegram to Thomas S. Butler, February 5, 1925, and a letter to Jorge Juan Crespo, April 22, 1925; Witter Bynner, *Journey with Genius*, pp. 26–27. James J. Napier prepared a bibliography. Dorothy A. Bryan, Hergesheimer's niece, most kindly wrote to me.

[25] Joseph Hergesheimer, "Shapes in Light," *Saturday Evening Post*, March 20, 1926, p. 119.

[26] John Dos Passos, *The Best Times*, pp. 170–172; idem, *The Fourteenth Chronicle*, pp. 365–367, 404–406; Beals, *Glass Houses*, pp. 245–249; William Spratling, *File on Spratling*, p. 99; John H. Wrenn, *John Dos Passos*. Jack Potter prepared a bibliography.

read), but Dos Passos's greatest praise was for the purely pictorial qualities of Orozco's work.[27] He became a good friend of the young painter Xavier Guerrero, who may have served as a model for the revolutionary painter José O'Riely in *Nineteen Nineteen*, the second volume of the *U.S.A.* trilogy. Dos Passos and Guerrero took many walking tours, including one through Morelos in February and March 1927. Dos Passos has lamented that he, however, was the one who painted while the artist lectured the people on communism. Dos Passos was extremely nearsighted, but on these walks with Guerrero, Beals, and others, he studied the landscape through a pair of opera glasses.

Dos Passos's next article, "Relief Map of Mexico," published in *New Masses* in April (and collected in *In All Countries*, 1934), came from notes he had made in Mexico City just prior to the walking trip; therein he speaks sympathetically if superficially of "Juan Sin Tierra." In Yautepec and Cuernavaca he discovered the great failure of the Revolution: the ghost of Zapata still roamed unappeased; the land had not been restored to the people and lay idle. He met some who felt that the old days had been better, but this attitude was countered by the bitter memories of an old man who had been forced to build roads in Yucatan under Díaz. In Cuernavaca the people were excited by the *comunistas*, thinking that they could help. The notes of this walking tour formed a rather noncommittal article called "Zapata's Ghost Walks," published in *New Masses* in September and later in the collection. Dos Passos returned to the theme once again in March 1934 for *Esquire*, this time writing a history of Zapata's life and death (also collected in *In All Countries*).[28] None of the essays is very memorable; Dos Passos was at his best when he could manipulate his facts or when he was more impassioned.

But in Mexico City he met Howard Phillips, the editor of *Mexican Life* and a man "who already knew more about Mexico than anybody you could meet," and Gladwin Bland, a retired Wobbly full of stories about the old days when he had thought the IWW could rebuild society. Through Beals he also met many American journalists and Mexican writers. He swapped yarns with all these people; when he returned to New York in March, his head was filled with the anecdotes

[27] John Dos Passos, "Paint the Revolution!" *New Masses* 2 (March 1927): 15.

[28] Dos Passos, *In All Countries*, pp. 75–105; the essays are misdated a year. Charles Ludington, an English teacher at the University of North Carolina, suggested to me that O'Riely might be modeled on Guerrero.

that would expand into *U.S.A.* In a memoir, *The Best Times,* 1966, he remembered: "I was trying to organize some of these stories I had picked up in Mexico into the intertwined narratives that later became *The 42nd Parallel. Three Soldiers* and *Manhattan Transfer* had been single panels; now, somewhat as the Mexican painters felt compelled to paint their walls, I felt compelled to start on a narrative panorama to which I saw no end."[29]

This allusion to the muralists is intriguing. Dos Passos wanted to achieve a literary form into which he could crowd all contemporary life—personal, historical, and a fictional world somewhere in between—just as the artists were doing in their murals. He had already been taken by Reed's attempts in *Insurgent Mexico* to juxtapose a personal account of his adventures with an objective report of the issues and the people involved. In his own Spanish travelogue, *Rosinante to the Road Again,* he had experimented with uniting fiction and exposition in order to shed light on the immediate situation. Many other writers were of course groping along the same lines, but *U.S.A.* was to prove more complex than most contemporary works.

Mexico, as we would expect with a trilogy whose subject is the United States, appears seldom in its pages. It is an area less important than Europe to Dos Passos's heroes; people travel to Mexico mainly for escape or for business reasons. There is no mention of the mural renaissance. Only the Revolution impinges itself upon the characters' attention; Mexico appears as a threat to American political safety and to American industries there. The most references therefore occur in *The 42nd Parallel,* the novel that deals mainly with events before World War I; events of the Revolution and American reactions to it appear in at least five of the newsreels: Madero, the fighting, Huerta's coup, the Veracruz incident, and Pershing's expedition. Dos Passos relates the connections that four of his biographical figures had with the country: Reed, Paxton Hibben (who served in the Mexican embassy, 1905–1906), Woodrow Wilson, and Hearst. Four of his twelve title characters go to Mexico before World War I. Joe Williams, a sailor, touches port at Tampico and is impressed by the mescal and the prostitutes.[30] Joe's sister, Janey, goes down with her employer, J. Ward Moorehouse, who is connected with the oil industries. G. H.

[29] Dos Passos, *Best Times,* pp. 171–172.

[30] Dos Passos, *U.S.A.: The 42nd Parallel,* pp. 131, 167–169, 208, 239–240, 274; *Nineteen Nineteen,* pp. 14–15, 55, 179–181, 245; *The Big Money,* pp. 468–476.

Barrow is there to make a fast dollar if possible. These last three characters, however, we see only as they enter the life of Fenian O'Hara McCreary, nicknamed "Mac," the one character who ends up living in Mexico.

Mac has been a Wobbly in his youth (obviously Dos Passos used Bland for inspiration), but he marries and settles down. Since he feels that he has betrayed the order, however, tensions grow. In Los Angeles, he hears of Madero's rebellion and then his death. But not until his wife quarrels with him does he leave for Mexico. He crosses the border at Juárez, is introduced to the local IWW, then moves to Mexico City after Huerta's flight and picks up a job. All the Americans he meets, especially the oilmen, are hoping for intervention and spectacular gains, but Mac quietly settles down with a Mexican girl and her mother. By accident he finds himself the owner of a bookstore, but when it appears that another rebellion is coming, he sells the store and, like any other American, flees with the girl and her mother to Veracruz. He plans to take them with him to the States; when he can book only one passage, however, he buys it. The same day he learns that Obregón has taken Mexico City and there is no danger; he returns to the girl and her mother without their learning of his infidelity.[31]

In the course of Mac's story Dos Passos caught realistic glimpses of Mexican towns and the Mexican people, especially in their reactions to gringos, and gave some sense of Americans in Mexico and their typical attitudes. He made a number of factual errors, the most glaring being that of having Carranza's death occur at the same time as the United States enters World War I. But the Mexico that Dos Passos was describing was that of over a decade before. Whether the writers who came there after 1930 read the novels or not, it is unlikely that the trilogy would have affected their vision of the country.[32] In 1929 Dos Passos translated *Metropolis* by Manuel Maples Arce, and in 1935 he provided the subtitles for the film *Redes* by Emilio Gómez Muriel. But by then Cuba and Brazil interested him more.

B. Traven (Traven Torsvan, 1890–1969) has written more novels and short stories set in Mexico than any other "foreigner" (he became a Mexican citizen), and his interpretations and his ability to

---

31 Dos Passos, *The 42nd Parallel*, pp. 120–128, 304–325.
32 Hart Crane referred to *The 42nd Parallel* before his visit to Mexico. See *The Letters of Hart Crane, 1916–1932*, p. 366.

tell a story, whatever his other artistic failings, have been of high merit. Of all the writers of the twenties in Mexico only Traven can stand in the same company with Lawrence and Miss Porter. Steffens in a conversation in 1936 commented how Traven was "expressing the very heart and soul of Mexico." And Arthur Calder-Marshall, who himself had written a Mexican novel, felt in 1940 that Traven was the only author who could be compared with Mrs. Calderón and Flandrau when one was searching for a true representation of the country.[33] Other readers, however, have been mostly fascinated by the mystery of Traven's identity. From the beginning when his publishers sought biographical information, he refused to divulge any facts and tried to remain in seclusion. Even now we know only a very rough outline.[34]

Born in Chicago, Traven spent most of his life outside the United States. Part of his youth was spent in the merchant marine (he touched port at Mazatlán in 1913). Then he appeared as an itinerant actor named Ret Marut in Germany, under which pseudonym he had an active role in the founding of the short-lived Bavarian Republic (he was probably also Richard Maurhut, the author of an unheroic

---

[33] Lawrence Clark Powell, "Who Is B. Traven?" *New Masses*, August 2, 1938, pp. 22–23; Arthur Calder-Marshall, "Novels of B. Traven," *Horizon* 1 (July 1940): 522–528.

[34] To follow the tangle of facts set forth and errors made about Traven's biography, see in this order: "On the Traven Trail," *Publishers Weekly*, July 9, 1938, pp. 105–106; George Manfred, "B. Traven's Identity," *New Republic*, March 24, 1947, p. 35; Peggy le Bontillier, "Who Is B. Traven? What Is He?" *Modern Mexico* 20 (January 1948): 14–15; Hubert Jannach, "B. Traven—An American or German Author?" *German Quarterly* 36 (November 1963): 459–468; Charles R. Humphrey, "B. Traven," Ph.D. dissertation, University of Texas, 1965; William Weber Johnson, "The Traven Case," *New York Times Book Review*, April 17, 1966, pp. 1 ff.; Charles Miller, introduction to B. Traven, *The Night Visitor and Other Stories*, pp. vii–xiii, and idem, "B. Traven, Continued," *New York Times Book Review*, November 20, 1966, p. 84; Lewis Nichols, "B. Traven Again," *New York Times Book Review*, June 11, 1967, p. 51; "Who Is Traven?" *Times Literary Supplement*, June 22, 1967, p. 553; Judy Stone, "The Mystery of B. Traven," *Ramparts* 6 (September 1967): 31–49, and idem, "Conversations with B. Traven," *Ramparts* 6 (October 1967): 55–69; *Contemporary Authors*, vols. 19–20, pp. 433–435; Bernard Smith, "B(ashful) Traven," *New York Times Book Review*, November 22, 1970, pp. 2 ff.; and "B(ashful) Traven," *New York Times Book Review*, December 27, 1970, p. 10, including a letter from Lawrence Hill. Mrs. Traven (R. E. Luján) wrote to me, July 29, 1970; Lawrence Hill has been most helpful.

novel about World War I). When he had to flee for his life, he rejoined the merchant marine and in the early twenties settled in the state of Tamaulipas in or near Tampico. Probably he worked at a number of odd jobs; his books display knowledge of cotton picking, oil drilling, baking, cattle driving, and gold prospecting. He started writing under his newly adapted name, in German, the language in which all his books were initially published. Nevertheless, these early works show in their choice of characters that he still considered himself an American.

In 1926 Traven was in Chiapas, serving as a photographer for the scientific explorer Alfonso Dampf; the following year he published a travel work about the state, never translated into English, entitled *Land des Frühlings* (Land of springtime). It was illustrated with his photographs. About the same time he visited with the Bulnez family at the *finca* El Real.[35] Probably then he picked up some of the ideas for the jungle series he published in the thirties. By 1929 he was in Acapulco, there to pass unnoticed until 1947. In that year John Huston tried to contact him concerning the film version to be made of *The Treasure of the Sierra Madre*. Traven wrote several long letters full of helpful suggestions but refused to come forward in his own person, appearing instead as "Hal Croves," his "agent" (Esperanza López Mateos, sister of a later Mexican president, was his real agent until 1951).[36] Unfortunately for his peace, he let slip his address; the next year Luis Spota, a journalist and popular novelist, picked up the clue. Checking the immigration records for Acapulco, he discovered the name Berick Traven Torsvan. He went there and found "Croves" running a small restaurant. Bribing a servant to watch the mail, Spota intercepted a royalty payment to Traven and confronted "Croves" with the evidence. "Croves" claimed that Traven was his cousin, but shortly after this episode Traven disappeared again.[37]

In 1957 Traven married Rosa Elena Luján, his new agent, in San Antonio, Texas. Until his death they lived quietly on Calle Mississippi in Mexico City. There he worked on his last novel (about the United

---

[35] William Weber Johnson, "Who Is Bruno Traven?" *Life*, March 10, 1947, pp. 13–16; James Norman Schmidt, *Terry's Guide to Mexico*, p. 299.

[36] Dwight Whitney, "More about Traven," *Life*, February 2, 1948, p. 66. Two letters from Hal Croves appeared in *Life*, March 15, 1948, p. 23, and *Time*, March 15, 1948, pp. 12–14.

[37] "The Secret of *El Gringo*," *Time*, August 16, 1948, pp. 34–36.

States) and a number of movie scripts based on his work, including that for *Rosa Blanca*, directed by Gabriel Figueroa in 1962 but never released. (Other films made from his works have included *Die Rebellion der Gehenkten* by H. Wlen, 1956; *Macario* by Roberto Gavaldon, 1960; and *El Puente en la Salva* by Francisco Kohner and Huston, 1969.)[38] In the mid-1960's he finally broke his long silence and granted a number of interviews: to Charles Miller, Judy Stone of *Ramparts*, Luis Suárez of *Siempre*, the newspaper *Excélsior*, William Weber Johnson, and Lawrence Hill of Hill and Wang, the firm that has begun reissuing his works. His friend Federico Canessi meanwhile sculptured his bust.

In his first interview with Miss Stone, Traven cried out, "Forget the man! What does it matter if he is the son of a Hohenzollern prince or anyone else? Write about his works."[39] He was of course right, and in any case he has left little choice. The bibliographical problems that he poses are incredible, but nine of his ten Mexican novels are now available in English, as are some sixteen out of at least twenty-five short stories and legends; most of the novels and stories are in versions approved by Traven if not made by him. Two of the novels are narrated by Gerard Gales: *Die Baumwollpflücker*, 1929 (*The Cotton-Pickers*), and *Die Brücke im Dschungel*, 1929 (*The Bridge in the Jungle*). Then there is a cycle of six historical novels set in the jungle of southern Mexico during the opening years of the Revolution: *Der Karren*, 1930 (*The Carreta*); *Regiergung*, 1931 (*Government*); *Der Marsch ins Reich der Caoba*, 1933 (*The March to Caobaland*); *Der Troza*, 1936 (untranslated); *Die Rebellion der Gehenkten*, 1936 (*The Rebellion of the Hanged*); and *Ein General kommt aus dem Dschungel*, 1939 (*The General from the Jungle*). During the thirties Andrés Henestrosa, Gregorio López y Fuentes, and Mauricio Magdaleno were following Mariano Azuela's lead in creating the genre known as the Novel of the Revolution; they must have influenced Traven in his development. Finally, Traven wrote two novels that belong to neither series: *Der Schatz der Sierra Madre*, 1927 (*The Treasure of the Sierra Madre*), and *Die Weisse Rose*, 1929 (*The White Rose* or *Rosa Blanca*). Most of the short stories appeared in *Der Busch*, 1928, or *Una canasta de cuentos mexicanos*, 1946; separately published were *Sonnenschöp-*

[38] Allen Page of Los Angeles helped with information about these films.
[39] Stone, "Conversations with B. Traven," p. 57.

*fung,* 1936 (*The Creation of the Sun and the Moon*), and *Macario,* 1949.[40]

Certain themes recur in all these works. In several ways Traven's philosophy resembles Lawrence's. Both, fearing the ugliness of industrialization and its mechanical destruction of personality, romantically celebrated the sacredness of the individual man. According to them each person should seek to integrate himself with forces and rituals that preserve his humanity. He must not ignore the essential wisdom of the body and its correspondence to a harmonious and unified universe (hence partly the beneficence of the sexual act, which brings man a sense of closeness with another person without denying his own oneness and which corresponds to cyclical rhythms in nature). Looking for life's lowest common denominator, both authors turned instinctively to the primitive. But whereas Lawrence was distressed by his contact with the Mexican Indians, Traven praised the Indians' way of life. The Indian-owned hacienda in *Weisse Rose* and the villages in *Regiergung* are paradises that cannot be comprehended by American businessmen or the Mexicans corrupted by the city. The Indian governor in *Weisse Rose,* who has known only life in the city, gratefully feels a restoration of his heritage when he visits the hacienda: "Subjects and matters, heretofore vague to him, were now revealed, he thought, to his soul and heart, rather than to his brain. His brain seemed clouded over, while his soul and heart became more alive and alert."[41] Mexico as a nation was pulled this way as a result of the Revolution. It is the path also that the Americans Gales in *Brücke* and Howard in *Schatz* accept.

The Indian lives in harmony with the land, feeling a kinship for his small plot of ground. The owner of the Indian hacienda in *Weisse Rose* refuses to sell it to an oil company because "soil is eternal, as long as humans remain on this earth. Gold isn't eternal. It may change its value at any time, but soil never will." Although the natives live in abject poverty according to the standards of industrialized countries, "certain immaterial matters such as the infinite beauty of wild flowers, or the possession of a little desert-like place, or riding an Indian pony into the rising sun early on a tropical morning, or jour-

---

[40] For information about the first English publication of Traven's books, see Drewey Wayne Gunn, *Mexico in American and British Letters.* E. R. Hagemann also compiled a bibliography.

[41] B. Traven, *The White Rose,* pp. 143–144.

neying at night by a creaking carreta with a full moon popping up
between the large horns of the bullocks . . . are worth more than
certain amounts of money. . . ."[42] It is land for which the people are
fighting in the Revolution; the army in *General*, as soon as it has
successfully routed the oppressors who have enslaved them, settles
down. Howard, in *Schatz*, also feels this kinship with the earth; after
he and his partners finish their mining in the sierra, he insists that
they restore the mountain to its original appearance from gratitude
for what it has given them. Gales feels an intense relationship with
the jungle, indeed with all Mexico: "The land of perpetual summer.
Oh, beautiful, wonderful land of everlasting springtime, rich with
legend, dance and song! You have no equal anywhere on this earth,"
he says in *Baumwollpflücker*.[43]

Unfortunately this paradisal innocence has been repeatedly invaded
by the Spanish, the Mexican mestizo, and foreign exploiters. In Traven's view, Díaz's dictatorship epitomized the evil that had come to
Mexico. He told Miss Stone: "Write how he is against anything which
is forced upon human beings, including communism or Bolshevism.
See how, among all Traven's books, there goes one thought like a red
thread from the first line of his first book to the last line of his last
book."[44] The six jungle novels graphically show several examples of
the conditions that led to the people's rising up against Díaz's administration; the novels also defend the cruelty of the Indians as the
natural inheritance of an oppressive regime. Each novel focuses on a
new set of characters, but as the series develops, Indians from earlier
books reappear in minor roles, and finally most of the protagonists
come together at the same mahogany camp. There they rebel against
their tyrannical masters and destroy the camp. Then in order to retain
their freedom, they march against the punitive expeditions sent out
against them.

Like Miss Porter, Traven seemed convinced that the Revolution had
been successful. Occasionally he admitted its failures, as in *General*,
when he wrote that "the peons, accustomed for years to masters, ty-
rants, oppressors and dictators, were not in truth liberated by the
revolution, not even where the feudal estates were divided up among
the families of peons in little holdings, in *ejidos*. They remained

[42] Ibid., pp. 37, 169.
[43] B. Traven, *The Cotton-Pickers*, p. 183.
[44] Stone, "Conversations with B. Traven," p. 57.

slaves, with the single difference that their masters had changed, that mounted revolutionary leaders were now the wealthy, and that the politicians now used small-holding, ostensibly liberated peons to enrich themselves immeasurably."[45] But in *Baumwollpflücker* and *Weisse Rose* he depicts the Mexican officials who have come to power after the Revolution as exemplary governors and deplores mostly the wiles of foreign speculators.

His hatred of oppression explains his attack on the Catholic church. In his early books, especially, Traven returned to the theme again and again. In *Karren* he wrote that the Church was against the education of the Indian because it could enrich itself from his ignorance (when the Indian Juárez was educated and gained power, one of his first acts, Traven noted with approval, had been to confiscate the Church's wealth). Just as he defended the atrocities of the revolutionists in the jungle series, he questioned in *Schatz* how one could expect anything but cruelty from the Mexican bandits who have been

trained in their churches from childhood on. Their churches are filled with paintings and statues representing every possible torture white men, Christians, inquisitors, and bishops could think of. These are the proper paintings and statues for churches in a country in which the most powerful church on earth wanted to demonstrate how deep in subjection all human beings can be kept for centuries if there exists no other aim but the enlargement of the splendor and the riches of the rulers. . . . Instead of being shown the beauty of this religion, they had been shown only the cruelest and the bloodiest and the most repulsive parts of it. These abhorrent parts of the religion were presented as the most important, so as to make it feared and respected not through faith or love, but through sheer terror and the most abominable superstitions.[46]

Several of his short stories contain the same arguments, and in some of them he struck at the very essence of Christianity. He seems to have agreed with Lawrence that religion belongs to the land and that Christianity is wrong simply because it was imposed on the people. The Indians in *Brücke* turn back to their age-old beliefs, mingled with a corruption of Christianity, when they need help, and Gales says that the only real god in the universe is the sun. None of the Indians of the jungle series pays more than lip service to the Church. Obviously they need a schoolteacher more than a priest.

45 B. Traven, *General from the Jungle*, p. 58.
46 B. Traven, *The Treasure of the Sierra Madre*, p. 163.

Essentially Traven was a political anarchist who yearned for a natural government that had sprung up from the people, as in the primitive tribes of Mexico. He felt any artificial government was wrong because it was unnaturally arbitrary. Moreover, anything that stamps an identity upon an individual enslaves that person (the belief suggests an explanation for Traven's own elaborate masquerade). One of the jobs that the professor in *Rebellion* warns the revolutionaries to accomplish is to burn all government documents—deeds, birth certificates, statutes, whatever (the idea, he adds, is his contribution to revolutionary thought). And a character in "Der Nachtbesuch im Busch" tells Gales: "We don't destroy enough of the things and systems which we believe perfect . . . and by destroying them make room for absolutely new and different things and systems infinitely more perfect than the ones we destroyed."[47] Throughout his work Traven demonstrated his conviction that man can reach perfection whatever setbacks he may encounter. The patience of the Indian will restore Mexico to tranquility. Meanwhile individuals must chart their own destiny.

Perhaps the time of Traven's literary obscurity is coming to an end, so that his name will soon be known as well as the title of the film *Treasure of the Sierra Madre*. If his works do not approach the polished artistry of those by Miss Porter or the peculiar intensity of Lawrence's vision, few novels about Mexico surpass the sheer power of *Bridge in the Jungle* and *Rebellion of the Hanged* or the easy readability of *Treasure* and *Creation of the Sun*. For many readers who have looked at more than one of his books, the problems of style and narrative structure have disappeared and his ideas have hit with enormous force. Miss Stone summed up Traven's accomplishment well: "His writing may seem occasionally old-fashioned or awkward, but his storytelling is superb and his powerful, ironic foresight shows a contemporary 20th century vision."[48]

For a long time probably only Carleton Beals realized the significance Mexico had acquired for American and British letters, for only he seems to have known many of the important writers who were visiting Mexico, although even he would not have heard of Traven. These people were solitary travelers, each going his separate way and

[47] B. Traven, *The Night Visitor and Other Stories*, p. 7.
[48] Stone, "Mystery of B. Traven," p. 33.

refusing to mesh into cliques or to have much to do with the thriving Anglo-American colonies in Mexico City and Tampico. Thus while the entire expatriate scene in Paris has been chronicled rather minutely, we can so far just barely trace the lives of British and American authors in Mexico in the twenties.

# 6. "Second Country": Katherine Anne Porter

Without doubt D. H. Lawrence more than any other literary figure directed the attention of the literary world to Mexico, but in retrospect Katherine Anne Porter (1890–) seems to dominate this period in her use of Mexican materials. Perhaps she was prepared from birth to view the country with sympathetic but clear eyes. She grew up with Mexican Americans in Texas. Although she was not Catholic, she was sympathetic to that religious view, so that another often-present barrier for visitors to Mexico was absent.[1] Her father had spent part of his youth in Mexico. In a letter she wrote to *Century* in 1923 she remembered that he had told her "enchanting stories" about this life. As a result the land was her "familiar country" from the time of her first visit around the turn of the century; later it became her "much loved second country."[2]

She apparently made several visits before 1910. After the Revolution began in earnest, when San Antonio was full of exiles, she went

[1] George Hendrick, *Katherine Anne Porter*, p. 168.

[2] Katherine Anne Porter, *The Collected Essays and Occasional Writings of Katherine Anne Porter*, p. 355; idem, *The Collected Stories of Katherine Anne Porter*, p. v. See Roy Newquist, interview with Katherine Anne Porter, *McCall's* 92 (August 1965): 140–141.

to Mexico again; in the letter to *Century* she tells of watching a street fight between the *maderistas* and the *federales*. Then followed a long interval in her life that cannot yet be documented from published sources; if she made any Mexican journeys during this ten-year period, they have not been recorded, and I cannot be certain of her presence in Mexico until 1920. From her entry then until her departure for Germany in 1931 she was constantly, she has written, "running back and forth between Mexico and New York."[3]

It is impossible to say how she would have developed as an artist had she not gone to Mexico. Her first three short stories, published in *Century* in 1922–1924, and "Two Songs from Mexico," published in *Measure* in January 1924,[4] were all concerned with some aspect of Mexican culture. Apparently the country was somehow responsible for a sudden creative realization. One could speculate that, even though it was nine years before she would use the Revolution directly in her fiction, the vitality of that movement unleashed her full powers. Looking back at her visit of 1920–1921 more than forty years later, she recalled in an interview that it was her "most marvelous, natural, spontaneous experience," adding for another interviewer: "Mexico was wonderful . . . Mexico has meant something else to me, and I can't explain it any more than I can explain how you fall in love. I hear all the analyses and theories, and I can rationalize and give you a dozen reasons; but not one of them would be right, because there are no reasons. If there are, they're so hidden in my experience, so much a part of imagination and feeling, that they can't be isolated." Even in the 1923 letter she was speaking in similar terms.[5]

She went to Mexico in 1920 in anticipation of the artistic renaissance. In that year she had met Adolfo Best-Maugard and "Tata Nacho" in New York. When she mentioned her plan to leave for Europe, they persuaded her to go instead to Mexico, where great things were going to happen, they prophesied, in the arts. Also, according to one report, she was acting as a publicity writer for a New York movie company that was making a film in Mexico. If so, this job may have influenced her decision. She went to Nuevo Laredo;

[3] Porter, *Collected Essays*, p. 180. See "Contributors and Contributions," *Asia* 20 (August 1920): 653.

[4] Porter, *Collected Essays*, p. 486.

[5] George Plimpton (ed.), *Writers at Work*, p. 148; Newquist, interview with Porter, p. 141; Porter, *Collected Essays*, p. 356.

from there she took a train, literally covered with soldiers and their ammunition and women, to Mexico City, arriving in early December a few days after Obregón took office. She found an empty ballroom on Calle Eliseo for rent, bought some furniture, and settled in.

The Mexican renaissance was still a year or so away in fact; instead she became caught up in other adventures, including the Revolution. At the request of Best-Maugard, Manuel Gamio and the artist Jorge Encisco called upon her. They in turn introduced her to a number of revolutionists. She quickly saw that the Revolution had not proceeded according to an ideal pattern and insisted that the truth be told. It was also probably through these men that she met Mary Doherty, a chance glimpse of whom led years later to "Flowering Judas"; and certainly they must have introduced her to William Niven, an archaeologist. One biographer felt that Niven had probably given her the germ for "María Concepción," in which an archaeologist named Givens appears. The same biographer also asserted that Niven is the subject of a character sketch later entitled "The Charmed Life," which she wrote for *Vogue* in 1942.[6]

In an autobiographical sketch published in *Mademoiselle* in 1955 (later entitled "St. Augustine and the Bullfight") Miss Porter recounted how she ran with a rather wild international set and seekers of adventure, among them Shelley's great-great-nephew, who insisted on taking her to her first bullfight. (This was the same season that young Langston Hughes came down from Toluca.) Against her will she became fascinated by the spectacle of death. She returned to fight after fight until one day, while reading Augustine's *Confessions*, she realized that she was like the youth caught by the gladiatorial shows. Her weakness revolted her, and she ceased going.[7]

Meanwhile she earned her living by teaching dance at a girls' school. According to a note in one of her essays, she gave Best-Maugard a ballet libretto for Anna Pavlova, and the dancer used it. Best-

[6] Hank López (interview with Katherine Anne Porter), "A Country and Some People I Love," *Harper's* 231 (September 1965): 59–60; Plimpton, *Writers at Work*, pp. 148–149, 153; Donald Stalling, "Katherine Anne Porter," thesis, Texas Christian University, 1951, pp. 68, 70; Hendrick, *Katherine Anne Porter*, pp. 31, 148; Edward Weston, *The Daybooks of Edward Weston*, I, 59. Also Porter, *Collected Essays*, pp. 426–430; idem, *Outline of Mexican Popular Arts and Crafts*, p. 2.

[7] Porter, *Collected Essays*, pp. 91–101. The story is told in Chapter 6 of the *Confessions*.

Maugard had designed a Mexican ballet for Pavlova when she was in Mexico in 1918. Perhaps Miss Porter had known Best-Maugard earlier in Mexico, or perhaps he had continued to work on it and the libretto was a joint effort with Miss Porter. Pavlova's biographers are of no help in solving the problem. A friend also tells us that Miss Porter became the subject of a song, "La Norteña."[8]

Amid all this activity she somehow continued to read and write, especially about Mexico. She recorded in 1922 that she had then read works by Dr. Atl, Bancroft, Bandelier, Mrs. Calderón, Gamio, Humboldt, Prescott, and others—all historians, anthropologists, or travel writers.[9] Her creative writing took place in private since her closest friends were more interested in the Revolution than in fiction. Her first bibliographer denies that she wrote revolutionist pamphlets; nor has he accepted the statement that she wrote sketches for a Mexico City promotion magazine.[10]

The first published fruits of her visit were two essays concerning the Revolution. "The Mexican Trinity" was a long letter from Mexico City dated July 1921 and published the next month in the *Freeman*. It discussed with great honesty the enemies that Mexico had within. These were not individuals. Rather they were certain perpetual problems: the unrealistic approaches taken by both the corrupt and the idealistic politicians and reformers; the illiteracy of the peasant, into whose soul the meaning of the Revolution had not entered and who could not be reached through the feeble literature the Mexican writers were producing at the time; the manipulations of the Church; the lack of any real land reform; and foreign speculation in the oil industry—the last three forming "the great triumvirate" that would plague Mexico during the two decades 1920–1940 and beyond. Her second article, an essay for *Century*, July 1922, entitled "Where Presidents Have No Friends," continued her balanced analysis of Mexico's problems and potentialities, a refreshing attitude to find in

[8] Porter, *Collected Essays*, p. 33; Alma M. Reed, *The Mexican Muralists*, pp. 33–34; Glenway Westcott, *Images of Truth*, p. 31.

[9] Porter, *Outline of Mexican Popular Arts and Crafts*, p. 2.

[10] Edward Schwartz, "Katherine Anne Porter: A Critical Bibliography," *Bulletin of the New York Public Library* 57 (May 1953): 216. Schwartz was answering a review by Paul Crume, *Southwest Review* 25 (January 1940): 215–216. According to Crume, Miss Porter wrote a story, "Doves of Chapacalco," that she never published. Louise D. Waldrip has prepared a more up-to-date bibliography.

these years when the American government still refused to recognize Obregón. She carefully and thoughtfully explained the political machinery in Mexico, interpreting the article of the constitution that claimed mineral and oil rights for the government and setting forth the methods by which Obregón was attempting to fulfill the Revolution's ideals. She especially praised Vasconcelos, whom she knew by then, for his work with the Mexican school system.[11]

Subsequent articles and book reviews touched on other problems of the government during this period. She published in 1926 her slashing indictment against Rosalie Evans. "Leaving the Petate," 1931, was a more charming article for the *New Republic*. It humorously tells how some of Mexico's poor clung stubbornly to their old ways, as symbolized by their desire to sleep on the *petate*, the rush mat that the peasant uses, while others could hardly wait to climb onto a brass bed, symbolic of their new status. Miss Porter sympathized with both desires: Mexico wanted to be an Indian nation; yet it needed to be more modern. But she observed, tongue in cheek, that once the Indian had left the *petate*, his children would either "be added to the next generation of good little conservative right-minded dull people" or "become *mestizo* revolutionaries, and keep up the work of saving the Indian."[12]

Her first fiction strangely does not deal with the Revolution at all. Instead she entered into the minds of the people on a nonpolitical level. "María Concepción," published in December 1922, was unlike anything that had ever appeared about Mexico by an outsider. Miss Porter almost completely subordinated American society in the story, merely suggesting its attitudes through the presence of an archaeologist, and entered totally into the lives of an Indian community. Only a member of such a community could say whether she succeeded in her depiction, but everywhere the reader gains a sense of verisimilitude. The plot is simple. María Concepción discovers her husband, Juan, making love to María Rosa, and that same day the two lovers leave to join the army. Left alone, María Concepción withdraws into herself and does not cry even when her child is born and dies. Later Juan and María Rosa return, and María Concepción kills María Rosa.

[11] Porter, *Collected Essays*, pp. 399–415.
[12] Ibid., pp. 388–393; idem, "Mexico," *New York Herald Tribune Books*, November 2, 1924, p. 9; idem, "Paternalism and the Mexican Problem," *New York Herald Tribune Books*, March 27, 1927, p. 12; idem, "Mexico's Thirty Long Years of Revolution," *New York Herald Tribune Books*, May 30, 1943, pp. 1–2.

When the police arrive the neighbors protect the murderess with lies, and the story ends with María Concepción taking the dead woman's baby as her own.

Within this frame are a number of symbolic suggestions that the story may exemplify the spirit of Mexico at the time. Death and life are confused and mingled (there is a pulque shop named Death and Resurrection). The Indian is digging up his past for the archaeologist, yet neither understands nor has any use for it; moreover, it is another race that employs the Indian to do so. Outside laws are worthless. Only the religion of that other race actually has much effect on the Indian's mind, and even the religion is superficial, as María Concepción unwittingly shows when she crawls toward her husband after the murder exactly as she had crawled many times to the shrine at Guadalupe. Miss Porter gives support for such a reading in her *Outline of Mexican Popular Arts and Crafts*, published the same year.

The story is told with the same honesty Miss Porter would have used had her characters been Americans of her own class; nowhere does the author intrude with moral statements or a condescending attitude. As she says of the artist in the *Outline*, "He perceives and accepts the fundamental kinship of all human beings on the plane of natural emotion."[13] Perhaps her ability to enter completely the psychology of both races is shown clearest in the confrontation of the two. Juan works for Givens, the archaeologist, and the story begins with María Concepción going to feed the white man. For her his ways provide a source of amusement even though he mystifies her. He has no woman to cook for him but seems to feel no loss of dignity. He becomes excited over broken bits of pottery worth nothing, when any one of the villagers could make better ones and get good money for them from the visitors to the site. But he is Juan's chief, undoubtedly rich, and therefore to be respected and honored. On Givens's side, he too is amused by his Indians, in fact he likes to feel "a fatherly indulgence for their primitive childish ways." He delights in the number of times he must save Juan from jail and always knows how to "twit him with exactly the right shade of condescension."[14] Miss Porter's achievement is even more remarkable when one considers how almost every other American or British author who had written

[13] Porter, *Outline of Mexican Popular Arts and Crafts*, p. 4; see Newquist, interview with Porter, p. 138.
[14] Porter, *Collected Stories*, pp. 3–21.

about Mexicans had depicted, with an unconscious sense of Anglo-Saxon superiority, stereotypes of drunken, dangerous ne'er-do-wells.

Her next story, "Virgin Violeta," finished in 1923 but not published until December 1924, turned exclusively to upper-class Mexican society. It was as if she wished to prove her versatility. The story concerns the awakening of sexual desire in one of Mexico's carefully protected daughters. Violeta is about the same age as María Rosa; but unlike the Indian, she has no idea what is happening to her and is frightened into nervous hysteria by the kiss of her sister's boyfriend. Perhaps this story was easier for Miss Porter to write; her training in Catholic girls' schools must have made it possible for her to sympathize with the oppressive atmosphere that can hang over the home of a Mexican aristocrat. But much of the story's success lies in the fact that there is no attempt to provide local color; there is no sense that an outsider tells it. Though firmly set in Mexico City, "Virgin Violeta," like its predecessor, goes to the essentials of human nature and becomes universal.[15]

The long-awaited renaissance of the arts finally began, if such a movement can ever be dated precisely, in 1922. Miss Porter made no major contribution to the movement, though she was painting in tempera on wood panels and assisting—she has said—in her own small way. She was a friend of many of the artists. Best-Maugard had returned to Mexico and was now head of the federal department of art education (in a book review for *Nation*, 1927, she complimented his work). She met Miguel Covarrubias, not yet out of his teens, and later took his caricatures to *Vanity Fair*, where his drawings became a regular feature during the twenties. She knew Siqueiros, Rivera, Tina Modetti, Dr. Atl, Xavier Guerrero, Manuel Rodríguez Lozano, Carlos Mérida, and Winold Reiss. At some time Roberto Turnbull involved her in another burgeoning art form in Mexico, the motion picture. He was shooting a film about a man who falls in love with the legs of a girl he sees walking by his half-cellar window each day. Although a professional actress played the top half of the girl, Miss Porter's shapely legs were the ones used for the shots from the window.[16]

[15] Ibid., pp. 22–32.

[16] Porter, "Katherine Anne Porter," *New York Herald Tribune Books*, October 12, 1952, p. 8; idem, *Outline of Mexican Popular Arts and Crafts*, p. 2; idem, "Children and Art," *Nation*, March 2, 1927, pp. 233–234. Also López, "A Country and

In 1922 Best-Maugard, Covarrubias, Guerrero, Turnbull, and Miss Porter wanted to take an exhibit of Indian art to the United States. They assembled a collection of over eighty thousand pieces. While writing a monograph for the show, Miss Porter returned to the States to try to line up galleries. No one was interested; there were still political problems because the government had not recognized Obregón's government. Finally, the sponsors put the pieces on a train anyway and headed for California, to be stopped by customs officials and literally sidetracked for months. The exhibit was held only because a Los Angeles dealer bought the entire collection, paid the customs, and carried it to his city. Opening on November 10, the show was a hit; Miss Porter later claimed: "All the tremendous interest in Mexican art in the United States stemmed from that."[17]

The monograph, *Outline of Mexican Popular Arts and Crafts*, was published for the Los Angeles show with photographs by Turnbull. The work reveals a tight control over an extensive knowledge of Mexican culture, past and present, which she had gained from her wide reading and many friendships. The notes are clearly presented for an American audience. She begins with a discussion of the religious and social background, perhaps defending the Aztecs from charges of barbaric cruelty too much. She associates herself with the growing nationalism in Mexico and looks with mixed feelings at the collision of the Spanish and native cultures. The greater part of the work, however, is a survey of the native arts produced in Mexico from that time until the present. She sums up her position thus: "The artists are one with a people simple as nature is simple: that is to say, direct and savage, beautiful and terrible, full of harshness and love, divinely gentle, appallingly honest. No folk art is ever satisfactory to those who love smooth surfaces and artificial symmetry. They cannot approach a living thing that grows as a tree grows, thrusting up from its roots and saps, knots and fruits and tormented branches, without an uneasy

---

Some People I Love," pp. 60, 62, 65–66. See "Promise Kept," *Time*, April 10, 1939, p. 75; Reed, *The Mexican Muralists*, pp. 34, 96–97.

[17] Westcott, *Images of Truth*, p. 31; Crume, review of *Pale Horse, Pale Rider*, p. 216; López, "A Country and Some People I Love," p. 62; "Mexican Art Exhibit Opens," *Los Angeles Times*, November 11, 1922, sec. 2, p. 1; "Mexican Folk Music Planned at Art Exhibit," *Los Angeles Times*, November 19, 1922, sec. 2, p. 1. Eleanor C. Hartman of the Los Angeles County Museum of Art located the newspaper articles for me.

feeling that it should be refined a little for art's sake."[18] She notes that the cultured Mexican artist of late had returned to his native roots. The *Outline* is necessarily superficial, but it has been undeservably neglected both by students of Mexican art and by critics of Miss Porter's work, perhaps because of the scarcity of the publication. In a book review of Anita Brenner's *Idols behind Altars*, 1929, she presented another brief history of Mexican art.[19]

In 1924 *Survey* magazine asked Miss Porter to collect the art features for a special issue devoted exclusively to Mexico. It also included an article by her on *corridos*, a ballad form whose tradition continues alive in Mexico, especially given now to accounts of the exploits of Villa and Zapata; her translation of a poem by Sor Juana Inés de la Cruz, addressed to the poet's portrait; and her interview with Rivera, written in essay form, in which the artist discussed the way Mexican muralists had banded together in guilds.[20]

Miss Porter apparently met Rivera while he was working at the ministry of education; she recalls going to grind paint to be used in his murals, and in 1922 she acknowledged his help in the preparation of her *Outline*. She brought him before the American public again in January 1925 with her translation of part of his notebook in *Arts*. From then on she seems to have had a vacillating attitude about his work. In a book review in 1929 she praised him with restraint, pointing out that he was "a little too bucolic, maybe, at times a trifle inflated," but then she concluded that he was the most important living painter in the world. And in 1937 she wrote:

No single man in his time has ever had more influence on the eye and mind of the public who know his work than Diego Rivera; for he has made them see his Mexico, to accept his version of it, and often to think it better than their own. . . . For myself, and I believe I speak for great numbers, Mexico does not appear to me as it did before I saw Rivera's paintings of it. The mountains, the Indians, the horses, the flowers and children, have all subtly changed in outlines and colors. They are Rivera's Indians and flowers and all now, but I like looking at them.

But in interviews in the mid-sixties, after admitting that she had been

[18] Porter, *Outline of Mexican Popular Arts and Crafts*, p. 33.

[19] Katherine Anne Porter, "Old Gods and New Messiahs," *New York Herald Tribune Books*, September 29, 1929, pp. 1–2.

[20] "The Gist of It," *Survey*, May 1, 1924, p. 127. Miss Porter's work is found on pp. 157–159, 174–178, 182 of this issue of *Survey*.

taken in by Rivera, she angrily denounced him, saying that as a man he was treacherous and as an artist dishonest.[21] We can wonder whether she had not already symbolically killed him off in her third short story, "The Martyr," written back in 1923.

The story of Rubén, "the most illustrious painter in Mexico," is probably modeled from a number of figures, just as Ramón, though a caricaturist for magazines, is not solely Covarrubias. Nevertheless Rubén is certainly as fat as Rivera was and has as many marital problems as the real artist had. The narrative recounts how his favorite model ran off with another artist, making Rubén a martyr to love, because he slowly ate himself to death. The story is filled with such merry absurdities: his rival sells a painting because its colors match the decor of a new house; the doctor is afraid to prescribe worldly remedies to such a fat man of sensibility; Rubén dies in a cafe called The Little Monkies, an establishment Ramón promises to mention in his biography of the painter. The story is too slight to bear all the irony it holds, but the reader should welcome it simply because it deflates an artistic movement over which some of the most extraordinary rhetoric has been spilled. Perhaps Miss Porter's ability to mock something truly great partly explains her friendship with Covarrubias, who often made fun of his fellow painters. (Miss Porter paid tribute to him in the *New Republic* in 1925.)[22]

Not until 1929 did Miss Porter finish her first story set in the Revolution. "Flowering Judas" was published in *Hound and Horn* the following spring and collected in the same year as the title story for her first collection. It captures a sense of time and place, but the optimism of Obregón's regime is missing. The principal theme of the story is betrayal. Its main character, Laura, encased in a set of principles inherited from her Catholic training, finds that they do not function in revolutionary Mexico. Therefore, she turns altogether within, corrupting herself, and ends unable to love. She is untouched by a *zapatista*

---

[21] Porter, *Outline of Mexican Popular Arts and Crafts*, p. 2; idem, "These Pictures Must Be Seen: The Frescoes of Diego Rivera," *New York Herald Tribune Books*, December 22, 1929, p. 6; idem, "Rivera's Personal Revolution," *New York Herald Tribune Books*, March 21, 1937, p. 7. Also López, "A Country and Some People I Love," p. 65; Newquist, interview with Katherine Anne Porter, p. 141. See Diego Rivera, "From a Mexican Painter's Notebooks," *Arts* 7 (January 1925): 21–23.

[22] Porter, *Collected Stories*, pp. 33–38; idem, " 'Ay, Que Chamaco,' " *New Republic*, December 23, 1925, pp. 142–143.

captain who admires her; untouched by her students, who write "We lov ar ticher" on the board; untouched by the death of a prisoner, Eugenio, who has taken an overdose of the narcotic she supplied to bring sleep. Because she cares for nothing, she has ceased to exist; but this negation does not bring freedom. Braggioni, her suitor and a revolutionist, has betrayed the principles of the Revolution. Forgetting how he was once always hungry, the fat Mexican now uses hungry men for his personal gain and loves only when there is profit in it. The story ends with a double parody of the Last Supper, suggesting by implication the true meaning of love. Braggioni's wife, to whom he has returned for a moment, washes his feet, and "he is refreshed by the solemn, endless rain of her tears." Laura, in a dream, is forced to admit her guilt; Eugenio comes and, tearing off the flowers from the Judas tree, forces her to eat the symbolic betrayal of his body and blood. Awakened, she "was afraid to sleep again." Whether self-realization has really come to these people or not, whether they will change, the story does not say; it is finished.[23]

Miss Porter has spoken of "Flowering Judas" several times in interviews and has written about it once. As a result we know more about its origin than about those of most of her Mexican stories. Both major characters were based on real individuals she knew in 1921. Braggioni was a well-known Mexican general whom she never identified further, combined with the traits of others. Laura was based on her good friend Mary Doherty, combined undoubtedly with some of her own traits. Miss Porter has written:

The idea first came to me one evening when going to visit the girl I call Laura in the story, I passed the open window of her living room on my way to the door, through the small patio which is one of the scenes in the story. I had a brief glimpse of her sitting with an open book in her lap, but not reading, with a fixed look of pained melancholy and confusion in her face. The fat man I call Braggioni was playing the guitar and singing to her.

In that glimpse, no more than a flash, I thought I understood, or perceived, for the first time, the desperate complications of her mind and feelings, and I knew a story; perhaps not her true story, not even the real story of the whole situation, but all the same a story that seemed symbolic

[23] Porter, *Collected Stories*, pp. 90–102. See "Recent Southern Fiction: A Panel Discussion," *Bulletin of Wesleyan College* 41 (January 1961): 12. I appreciate the help of Louis D. Rubin, professor of English at the University of North Carolina.

truth to me. If I had not seen her face at that very moment, I should never have written just this story because I should not have known it to write.

But the story lay dormant for nearly nine years, to be suddenly dashed off in the present tense in five hours one cold night in New York.[24]

Another story, "That Tree," reflects the same period. It was first published in a shorter version (never reprinted) in the *Virginia Quarterly Review* in 1934 and, contrary to her usual practice, was extensively revised before it was collected in the second edition of *Flowering Judas* the next year. It is a long monologue, perhaps a somewhat drunken one, delivered by a well-known journalist in a cafe in Mexico City to an unidentified companion, through whose consciousness it is distilled. Filled with multiple ironies, it too recounts one betrayal after another. The journalist had become engaged to a Minneapolis schoolteacher named Miriam, but had quixotically run off to Mexico to write poetry that he knew was bad but that he enjoyed writing nonetheless. He had set up housekeeping with an Indian girl who modeled for some of his painter friends; but when time came for Miriam to arrive, the Indian girl had gone off "too cheerfully" with a painter, taking with her a baby the journalist could not be sure was his own. All this while Miriam had been writing letters from Minneapolis complaining about the drabness of her life. But when she arrived, Mexico was too much of a shock; she did not like their sexual life, his poetry, his artist friends, the Indians, the markets, or the food (in the story's first version she had obstinately refused to learn Spanish). Whatever happened, she reacted strictly according to her American instincts; thus when several generals, who had come into town with Obregón, began a fight among themselves (perhaps symbolizing how the Revolution had been betrayed), instead of swinging her husband around so that he formed a shield for her as all the Mexican girls did, to his complete embarrassment she dived under a table.

Nor was this the end of the series of betrayals. His artist friends left their ideal in search of an easier life. And finally Miriam left him. Unable to hold onto the dream or to transmute it into anything of value, having accepted finally his wife's judgment that only ma-

---

[24] Whit Burnett (ed.), *This Is My Best*, p. 539; cf. Porter, *Collected Stories*, p. 367.

terialistic gains proved personal worth, he too capitulated and began turning out appropriately liberal articles on Latin America that soon catapulted him to a position of authority: "Somehow he had never got to that tree he meant to lie down under." Now, as the final ironic thrust, Miriam wants to come back to him, and he plans to take her. Though successful in the eyes of the world, he has been so completely seized by failure that he cannot see anything clearly from under "his twitching lids." Carleton Beals has left us several such pictures of life in Mexico City. Miss Porter's first draft may recount rather closely some actual conversation. If so, she continued to mull it over, sharpening the various portraits of failure until it was no longer a tale of Mexico but a story simply located there.[25]

Both "Flowering Judas" and "That Tree" suggest the possibility that she had become disenchanted with the country by this time. Miss Porter said in an interview in the 1960's that she first saw signs of the coming of World War II in Mexico, although she added that she did not despair of the evil because "in Mexico there was always something good . . . always some *chance* of salvation."[26] Perhaps she believed thus in the late 20's and early 30's and the unpleasantness we sense comes from our dislike of her supreme realism. She will not become involved with her characters or take sides. Rather she lays them embarrassingly bare, revealing all their motives, their absurdities, their pitiful humanity no longer very pitiful because of her savagely ironic vision. Still she holds that some of these characters who seem to be the most unflattering portraits of man are really noble. She commented on her novel: "About *Ship of Fools* they say, 'No nobility.' Of course, there's nobility and there's goodness and love and tenderness and feeling and emotion, but with the instability of the human heart and the uneasiness of the human mind and the terrible stress and strain of human relations—these qualities are tempered and strained and frayed and aborted."[27] Consequently her stories are less easy to read than some critics think; several of them admit widely different interpretations, depending upon our understanding of her world view.

[25] Porter, "That Tree," *Virginia Quarterly Review* 10 (July 1934): 351–361; idem, *Collected Stories*, pp. 66–79. See Carleton Beals, *Glass Houses*, pp. 319–325.

[26] James Ruoff and Del Smith, "Katherine Anne Porter on *Ship of Fools*," *College English* 24 (February 1963): 397; Hendrick, *Katherine Anne Porter*, p. 51.

[27] Newquist, interview with Porter, p. 140.

Miss Porter's physical relationship with Mexico toward the end of the twenties remains obscure. Beals remembers her there about 1928, suffering from consumption, and she returned again in early spring of 1930. She was then working on a Mexican novel, *Thieves' Market*, which was scheduled for publication but dropped. About the same time she must have met Eugene Pressly, later her second husband. In 1931 several important events for her creative life occurred. She received a Guggenheim Fellowship on the basis of *Flowering Judas*. During that spring Hart Crane, who had also received a Guggenheim, stayed in and near her home in Mixcoac, stirring up a quarrel that unfortunately degenerated into a series of innuendos in their published comments, the whole issue being complicated by her relationship with Pressly. In July she visited the location for Sergei Eisenstein's movie on Mexico, an encounter that led to the writing of *Hacienda*. That August she left for Germany, not to return to Mexico for years. In the poem "After a Long Journey," first published in *Mademoiselle* in 1957, she looked back nostalgically to the warmth of Mexico.[28]

In 1932 the first draft of *Hacienda* appeared in the *Virginia Quarterly Review*. Written in the historical present, it gives no indication that it is not simply a reminiscence. The major characters are labeled "K——" and "A——"; other figures are "the famous director," "the main camera man," and "the art director." Two years later an expanded version appeared in a limited edition (it was collected into the second edition of *Flowering Judas*); it contained a note: "All characters and situations in this story are entirely fictional and do not portray an actual person." A reviewer retorted that "these nervous protests have come to be an unfailing sign that they aren't."[29] In its

[28] Beals, *Glass Houses*, p. 362; "In the Bookmarket," *Publishers Weekly*, October 11, 1930, p. 1747; Stanley J. Kunitz (ed.), *Authors Today and Yesterday*, pp. 538–539; Porter, *Collected Essays*, pp. 302–303, 272, 491–494; Peggy Baird, "Last Days of Hart Crane," *Venture* 4 (1961): 36–38; Philip Horton, *Hart Crane*, pp. 183–187; John Unterecker, *Voyager*, pp. 651, 658–662, 670–673. Matthew Josephson (*Life among the Surrealists*, p. 352) speaks of a Mexican marriage and divorce before 1929; Miss Porter does not mention such in her interview with Newquist, pp. 138–139. C. Carroll Hollis, professor of English at the University of North Carolina, was helpful.

[29] Porter, "Hacienda," *Virginia Quarterly Review* 8 (October 1932): 556–569; idem, *Hacienda*, p. 5. Also Elizabeth Hart, "Slight and Short Stories," *New York Herald Tribune Books*, December 16, 1934, p. 15.

examination of lost people isolated from their traditional setting, the work continues the basic themes of Miss Porter's fiction, but the details correspond fairly closely to actual events, including the central action of the story: an accidental shooting of an Indian girl by her brother. In any case, two works examining Eisenstein's experience in Mexico reveal that much of what Miss Porter observed while she was with him was unpleasant.[30]

Eisenstein had come to Mexico to make a film in December 1930, accompanied by his collaborator, Grigori Alexandrov, and his Swedish-born cameraman, Eduard Tissé. He had wanted to visit Mexico ever since he had dramatized London's "The Mexican" in 1920 in Moscow; and as his recent experience in Hollywood had been unpleasant, he felt the need to turn to something entirely different. All he and Upton Sinclair had in common was an aversion to liquor, but he turned to him and persuaded Mrs. Sinclair to raise the necessary funds, under the agreement that she would have complete control over the finished product. The fifteen-month visit was important to Eisenstein's development. It opened to him an epic spirit that he had never felt before. The country enchanted him, and the people accepted him as no one ever had. But the pleasantness was generally marred by the many problems that beset him. Although the contract called for the movie to be shot in three or four months, Eisenstein visualized a work of such proportions that, when he left, one section remained unshot. Absorbed in Mexico, seeing now what he had read about in Miss Brenner's survey of art, he developed a scenario that called for four individual stories, plus a prologue and an epilogue, and that would give by suggestion the entire history of the country and its people. The Mexican government was uncertain at first if it wanted a communist to make a movie at all. No diplomatic relationships yet existed between Russia and Mexico, even though both were revolutionary governments, and as soon as Eisenstein, Alexandrov, and Tissé arrived in Mexico City they had been arrested, taken to jail, and then released with confused apologies. Finally the government tried to protect itself by saddling Eisenstein with a body of advisors, chief among them Best-Maugard (through whose friendship Miss Porter probably met the filmmakers). Costs for the movie mounted; not being able to

---

[30] Marie Seton, *Sergei M. Eisenstein*, pp. 187–242; Harry Geduld and Ronald Gottesman (eds.), *Sergei Eisenstein and Upton Sinclair*, esp. pp. 112–113.

process his shots in Mexico, Eisenstein had to make several takes of each sequence. Government censors posed other problems. The Sinclairs had sent Hunter Kimbrough, Mrs. Sinclair's brother, to control finances. Kimbrough, a straitlaced southern gentleman, took an aversion to everything Mexican—food, customs, people, climate—and to Eisenstein, who often played the role of a coarse buffoon in order to hide his true sensitivity and thus protect himself. The Sinclairs did not cut off funds until January 1932, but by the time Miss Porter visited the set the tension was evident.

The crew was then at Tetlapayac, an old hacienda owned by Julio Saldívar in the state of Hidalgo. Eisenstein had chosen it especially for the setting of his third "novel," the story of maguey. This section of the film was ultimately culled from the unfinished work, but since the Sinclairs had complete control over the editing of *Thunder over Mexico* (as the section was called), Eisenstein's ultimate concept can only partly be judged from it. Miss Porter must have appreciated, however, the plot concerning a peasant rebellion during the days of Díaz; it was not difficult to shoot such a story in 1931. After the first hesitant reforms under Obregón and Calles, the latter, utilizing his puppet presidents, had betrayed the Revolution by slowing down agrarian reforms and pushing Mexico along an essentially conservative path. Nor had the peasant yet come to realize the meaning of the Revolution. Miss Porter wrote in *Hacienda* that "the money would flow silver-white into the government treasury: don Genaro and his fellow-hacendados would fret and curse, the Agrarians would raid, and ambitious politicians in the capital would be stealing right and left enough to buy such haciendas for themselves. It was all arranged."[31] This political setting, however, served only as the background for the story that began to develop in her imagination.

The portrayal of Kinnerly, one of the main characters in *Hacienda*, invites a critical comparison with Kimbrough. Kinnerly hates the Mexicans, is afraid of filth, worries over money, and is totally incapable of controlling this world of Russian filmmakers in Mexico: "His nerves were bundles of dried twigs, they jabbed his insides every time a thought stirred in his head, they kept his blank blue eyes fixed in a white stare." Besides, he feels guilty because he is drinking beer, being afraid of the water, since he knows his brother-in-law, "a violent

---

[31] Porter, *Collected Stories*, p. 168.

prohibitionist," would object. In contrast to Kinnerly is Andreyev, who suggests a fictionalized Alexandrov and who emerges as the most sympathetic person in the group. He remains undaunted by the seething tensions around him and is able to care for the director at once when he finds him ill, yet he enters easily into the Mexican time sense. The movie is taking a long time to film, but one need not worry: "When it is finished it is finished." The story is narrated by an unnamed woman, "a writer" whom Kinnerly "had never heard of" and "had never known anyone who had." (In 1931 Miss Porter's first collection, only a year old, had been in a limited edition.) The character who seems to represent Eisenstein is called Uspensky. The character named Stepanov strongly resembles Tissé, just as Best-Maugard seems to be represented by a character called Betancourt. Miss Porter, however, seems to fictionalize Betancourt more than the others in order to develop her theme.

As with the characters in "Flowering Judas" and "That Tree," the people in *Hacienda* are sterile souls trapped in a waste land. A passage near the end describes their predicament perfectly: "A silence like a light trance fell over the whole room in which all these chance-gathered people who had nothing to say to each other were for the moment imprisoned. Action was their defense against the predicament they were in, all together, and for the moment nothing was happening."[32] They are corrupt, as shown by their interest in fast machinery, by some questionable relationships (especially the lesbianlike attraction between Doña Julia and Lolita), by their interest in a person's social value, and by their inability to speak or interact with one another. The film world, which fixes a sometimes frightening reality into artificial patterns, serves as the perfect atmosphere. After Andreyev, the narrator comes closest to being a sympathetic character because she can judge Betancourt for his betrayal of a friend and Kinnerly for his lack of feeling for the poor Indian who, before he shot his sister, had played a similar scene in the movie. She can also understand the political corruption that one Velande (a Calles-like figure) has brought to the doomed landscape. This narrator then ironically sets the overly refined figures of the hacienda, and the many allusions to the failure of the Revolution, against the ragged Indians who are waiting for the days when the green corn will be

---

[32] Ibid., p. 169.

ripe and "there will be enough to eat again."[33] In her use of many morally frightening people, caught momentarily in the same environment and unable to act, she was moving toward *Ship of Fools*.

Miss Porter finished one other important Mexican work before she turned most of her attention to *Ship*: the first English translation of José Joaquín Fernández de Lizardi's novel, *El periquillo sarniento* (*The Itching Parrot*). She introduced the work, published in 1942, with a long history of the Mexican author, displaying again her talent for placing materials in a historical perspective. The same year she also wrote an introduction to a collection of Latin American stories, *Fiesta in November*, in which she commented on the difficulties a translator has, pointing out that even at best his work can be no more than paraphrase. *The Itching Parrot* was based on a translation Pressly had made over ten years before, after an intensive study of the Mexican common language in which the novel was written. Lizardi's style posed great problems because of this language, which utilized multiple puns and double entendres impossible even to approximate in English; only the obvious vulgarities could be retained easily. Miss Porter revised and abridged the narrative extensively, omitting the moral and political tracts that were interspersed throughout. The results may have been a wise compromise in order to present the work to an American public, but unfortunately the reader is left rather unenlightened as to why the book, the first novel written in Mexico (1816), has been so enormously popular in Spain and Spanish America. A minor controversy appeared in the pages of *Nation* about the translation's merits. It is worth noting that no one else has since attempted the job.[34]

Miss Porter must have been attracted by Lizardi's realistic depiction of the horrors of Mexican banditry and his intense, if probably unconscious, honesty concerning the Mexican psychology. The essential Mexican spirit seems to have changed little since it was written. The novel, however, does not portray all Mexican life. It never really looks at those born impoverished, only at the fashionable who have fallen into disgrace. Thus those extreme aspects of Mexico—the primitive native who suffers in silence and the self-satisfied aristocrat who cares

[33] *Ibid.*, pp. 135–170.

[34] José Joaquín Fernández de Lizardi, *The Itching Parrot*; Angel Flores and Dudley Poore (eds.), *Fiesta in November*, pp. 1–10; Porter, *Collected Essays*, pp. 385–387. See *Nation*, March 28, 1942, and March 6, 1943.

so little for his country, people Miss Porter has portrayed so well in her short stories and novel—are scarcely mentioned here. Lizardi's beggars are stereotypes, a world away from the deliberately mutilated cripple who crawls across the opening pages of *Ship of Fools*.

Also in 1942 she promised to publish her novel (then called *No Safe Harbor*). It was twenty years, however, before *Ship of Fools* was finished. In the meantime over half of it was published in sections in various magazines, almost the only pieces of hers that did appear in these years. The novel seemed to culminate her career and to sum up her views about man and his world. She received her first popular success; even though much of the early criticism was adverse, its sale was assured by its selection for the Book of the Month Club, and its transformation into a movie enhanced the paperback sale.

The setting and the characters of *Ship of Fools* are based on her voyage from Veracruz to Bremerhaven in 1931. Then she kept a letter-journal, which refreshed her memory when she came to write the novel. The ship is a sprawling Grand Hotel. The first-class passengers are a medley of Germans, Swiss, a Scandinavian, Spaniards, Cubans, Mexicans, and Americans, representing a number of religious and political principles. The interactions and discoveries of these people form the structure of the novel. Little in the way of external events happens; a bulldog is thrown overboard and a man drowns trying to save it; a party is held, in the course of which two men are badly cut up; a near riot occurs in steerage. But underneath as much happens as in any action-packed novel, perhaps more. The voyage is also one of discovery, and when it is over practically no one remains unchanged: Dr. Schumann realizes his fragility and his inattention to his true duties as a doctor and a Christian because of his relationship with the Spanish Condesa. Herr Fretag betrays his Jewish wife. Frau Hutten stands up against her abstracted husband, then submits, only to find that she has subtly changed him. Mrs. Treadwell realizes that she faces a life of continuing loneliness.

In spite of its title, the novel is not an allegory, but a realistic, even naturalistic, work. Miss Porter was, however, especially interested in exploring the nature of evil. Underlying the casual encounters of the voyage is the heavy threat of Nazism, which is lifted into a universal threat for all time. Miss Porter has credited her experience in Mexico with providing the key by which to understand the significance of her observations on the actual voyage which she took and for permitting her to capitalize on her original letter-journal. She said in an interview: "In Mexico, and later in Europe, I saw clowns like Hitler . . . and I was struck by an idea; what if people like this could take over the world! . . . For me as a writer, being on that ship was a godsent experience, and yet I wouldn't have been able to see any of these things in perspective if I hadn't seen them in Mexico."[35]

Only a few Mexicans are aboard. All but one of these represent types Miss Porter had not previously handled, but without exception they are minor characters. A bride and groom from Guadalajara have no names; in love only with each other, they exclude the rest of the world, oblivious to its existence. Likewise a political agitator in steerage remains unidentified except by his cherry-colored shirt. He is concerned for the world and attacks the Church as one source of its problems; as a result of his jeers at a religious service, he is knocked unconscious and remains so for the rest of the voyage. The two priests are treated slightly and rather unsympathetically by the author. In spite of her Catholic training Miss Porter (unlike Graham Greene or Evelyn Waugh later) was never blind to the realities of the Church in Mexico. The sixth Mexican is Señora Ortega, who is going to Paris to join her husband with their new baby and spends most of her time resting under the faithful gaze of her Indian servant, Nicolasa. With Nicolasa, for the first time since "María Concepción" and "Leaving the Petate," Miss Porter entered the mind of the primitive.

A few more Mexicans are treated in the opening scene in Veracruz (she published an early version of this scene in *Sewanee Review* in 1947); it reveals most strongly her political interests. For the only time in the novel the author intrudes at length with a heavy personal irony as she gives the differences between the *veracruzanos'* opinion of themselves and the reality of the situation. The scene is a bit one-sided; she is more interested in creating a mood than in depicting Mexico. The city is reduced to animality. Just as a parrot and a monkey tease each other, and a cat annoys both, to be harassed in turn by a dog, which receives a kick from a vagrant Indian—just as these animals prey upon each other, so do the humans. The Indian is picked up by the police for no apparent reason; the revolutionists kill a poor native they are trying to help when they bomb the wrong

---

[35] Ruoff and Smith, "Katherine Anne Porter on *Ship of Fools*," p. 397. See M. M. Liberman, "Some Observations on the Genesis of *Ship of Fools*: A Letter from Katherine Anne Porter," *PMLA* 84 (January 1969): 136–137.

house; the richer citizens prey upon the poor without mercy; and everyone tries to exploit the tourist.[36] The scene is frightening, presenting, for example, a much more vicious picture of Veracruz than either Jack London or Richard Harding Davis had. Yet there is a major difference. Whereas the earlier writers looked around smugly from their attitude of American superiority, Miss Porter was simply, if ironically, observing how things are in a port city. The unconscious distaste and distortion of the outsider's view have been replaced by a conscious hatred of evil from almost an insider.

The scene is the longest description of a specific Mexican locale in all her fiction. A few other memories of Mexico are scattered within the novel, chiefly in scenes with two American artists. The descriptions are so exact that one wishes Miss Porter had written her travel book. A feeling for the true Mexico underlies all the ugliness she depicts; hers is not a superficial glimpse of the native and his environment or the popular ecstasy over the primitive, although she approached such ecstasy in the *Outline* and in a 1923 essay, first published in 1970, "The Fiesta of Guadalupe."[37]

In 1960 Miss Porter returned to Mexico on an International Exchange of Persons grant and again in 1964 for speeches, a near brush with death from pneumonia in Guadalajara, and an interview with Hank López for *Diálogos*.[38] She translated the interview and published it in *Harper's* with her 1931 photograph made by Manuel Alvarez Bravo. By this time *Ship of Fools* and *The Collected Stories* (for which she won both a Pulitzer Prize and the National Book Award) had brought demands for many interviews. In almost all of them she stated her love for Mexico; and now that so much of her Mexican material is readily available in these two works and in *The Collected Essays and Occasional Writings*, more and more readers have become aware of the importance of Mexico to her development. It is to be hoped that they are also aware of the merits of her interpretations.

---

36 Porter, *Ship of Fools*, pp. 3–21; idem, "Embarkation," *Sewanee Review* 55 (January 1947): 1–23.

37 Porter, *Collected Essays*, pp. 394–398.

38 *Contemporary Authors*, II, 151; Haskel Frankel, "The Author," *Saturday Review*, September 25, 1965, p. 36. I talked briefly on the telephone with Miss Doherty's sister, in the summer of 1970; unfortunately, Miss Doherty was away from Mexico at the time.

# 7. Lawrence's Search for the Great Sun

In 1953 Sybille Bedford wrote in her Mexican travel book, *The Sudden View*: "The writer who first made people of my generation aware of Mexico as a contemporary reality was D. H. Lawrence in his letters, *Mornings in Mexico* and *The Plumed Serpent*."[1] Lawrence remains the most important author in the British-American literary world to have used Mexico as a setting. His Mexican works are in several ways flawed, but they display clearly his peculiar and at times overpowering genius. Moreover, his vision has influenced almost every subsequent writer about Mexico. Hart Crane, Lawrence Ferlinghetti, and Evelyn Waugh knew at least *The Plumed Serpent* well; Sherwood Anderson, Graham Greene, Malcolm Lowry, and Charles Olson seem to have known all his Mexican writings; Witter Bynner was at moments overwhelmed by Lawrence's personality; Conrad Aiken borrowed so much from him that the reader may legitimately question whether Aiken saw any of Mexico through his own eyes; and Aldous Huxley, Wright Morris, and Tennessee Williams, although they discovered a different Mexico in many ways, must have gone there under the influence of their literary mentor.

Even if a writer did not know Lawrence's work directly during the

1 Sybille Bedford, *The Sudden View*, p. 32.

1920's, Lawrence was the subject of much literary gossip, and soon after his death almost everyone who knew him in Mexico seems to have written a book or an essay about their relationship. When Edward Nehls compiled his composite biography in the mid-1950's, he elicited many new comments from Lawrence's friends. Thus we know more about his actions in Mexico and the background for his Mexican work than about any other author's.[2] Although Lawrence's portrait reveals a trying personality, his personal faults cannot eclipse his talent. Even the Mexicans have acknowledged his force and his revealing insights about their country.[3]

David Herbert Lawrence (1885–1930) came to Mexico by an indirect route. He became interested in the United States first, especially through an intense examination of American literature that he made during World War I and that culminated in *Studies in Classic American Literature*, 1923.[4] But he did not really distinguish between the cultures of Latin America and the United States; he meant the whole hemisphere when he used the word *America*. He was left with ambiguous feelings concerning what he found, or thought he found. America clearly held the destiny of the world; but it was convulsed, he felt, by destructive forces of will and rationality, and under all lay a vague urge toward death. Paradoxically, Americans were too self-effacing. One solution to the dilemma, which he proposed in an essay for the *New Republic* in 1920 ("America, Listen to Your Own"), was to turn back to the past, to the culture of the Indians, and pick up their thread to wind into the future. Consequently, he wanted most to visit the American Southwest and Mexico, where the Indian cultures

[2] Edward Nehls (ed.), *D. H. Lawrence*, II, 79, 212–249, 259–282, 353, 364–397; D. H. Lawrence, *The Letters of D. H. Lawrence*, pp. 565–571, 580–588, 618–630, and idem, *The Collected Letters of D. H. Lawrence*, II, 741–748, 754–764, 815–833; Frieda Lawrence, "*Not I, but the Wind . . .*", pp. 138–141, 146–151; Witter Bynner, *Journey with Genius*, pp. 19–186; Edward Weston, *The Daybooks of Edward Weston*, I, 101–103, 168, 181, 191, 198; Knud Merrild, *With D. H. Lawrence in New Mexico*, pp. 332–351; Mabel Dodge Luhan, *Lorenzo in Taos*, pp. 209–210, 217–221; Dorothy Brett, *Lawrence and Brett*, pp. 159–209; Harry T. Moore, *The Intelligent Heart*, pp. 284–285, 296–344; L. D. Clark, *Dark Night of the Body*, pp. 25–50. Warren Roberts prepared a bibliography.

[3] Clark, *Dark Night of the Body*, pp. 12, 32. Clark discusses the criticism of Bernardo Ortiz de Montellano, Alí Chumacero, Antonio Castro Leal, and José Vasconcelos. See also Martha Díaz de León in *Cuadernos Americanos* 139 (March–April 1965): 262–283.

[4] See Armin Arnold, *D. H. Lawrence and America*, pp. 23–36.

retained vitality. At the same time his soul was becoming sick of dying Europe and dead Christianity. In his Mexican novel, *The Plumed Serpent*, he would depict Christ as a dead god who brought only weeping into the world with a hope of a happier life after death. In a later short novel, *The Man Who Died*, he portrayed a Christ who realizes that his messianic attempt to turn men away from physical delight for the promise of an abstract heaven was wrong and who, having escaped the cross, takes on the robes of Osiris instead and comes into communion with a deeper spirit of the universe beyond time and space. This spirit is symbolized by a great sun, which Lawrence borrowed from early Mexican mythology. Somehow, in Mexico, Lawrence reached a new state in his understanding.

But in 1920 he had found no answer, not even a partial one, to his problems and only felt vaguely that America might hold what he needed. He spoke of his desire to find a farm somewhere in an isolated stretch of the continent. As if in answer, Mabel Dodge in 1921 issued an invitation to join her artists' colony at Taos, New Mexico. Lawrence hesitated, then turned instead to Ceylon and Australia. He found nothing in the Oriental religions or in the spirit of Australia to satisfy him, and finally in late 1922 he and his wife, Frieda, arrived in the States. Taos was only partly to their liking. Mabel Dodge demanded much of his time, until finally Frieda came to distrust the long conferences between the two and intervened. To these tensions were added renewed apprehensions about America. The mechanized pace of American life, which reached even into the mountains of New Mexico, disturbed him intensely, and he again began to wonder, as he later wrote in his novel, "whether America really was the great death-continent, the great *No!* to the European and Asiatic and even African *Yes!* Was it really the great melting pot, where men from the creative continents were smelted back again, not to a new creation, but down into the homogeneity of death."[5] Quite soon he spoke of returning to Britain. But the primitive Indians of New Mexico had appealed to his soul, awakening a desire to see the land of the Aztecs.

When the Lawrences prepared to visit Mexico in the spring of 1923, their New Mexico friends were understandably disquieted. Revolution remained an ever-present danger, and gringos were not being received warmly. Shortly before, an American from Santa Fe

[5] D. H. Lawrence, *The Plumed Serpent* (*Quetzalcoatl*), p. 73.

had been shot while he stood on his balcony at the Regis, a fashionable hotel in Mexico City. The Lawrences were not swayed; on March 21 they crossed the border at Juárez and began the long train ride to the capital. Bynner, whom they had met in Santa Fe, and his secretary, Willard ("Spud") Johnson, were to join them within a week. The Lawrences spent their first night at the Regis, but they disliked it and transferred to the Monte Carlo, a small Italian hotel on Avenida Uruguay. The *Excelsior* noted their arrival in its *viajeros* section, March 25, but no other newspaper took notice of them, a slight obliquely mentioned in Lawrence's novel.

Lawrence rapidly absorbed as much of Mexico as he could. He had read or was soon to read Bernal Díaz's history, Humboldt's *Vues de cordillères*, Dana's autobiography, Mrs. Calderón's journal, Prescott's history, Thomas Belt's *Naturalist in Nicaragua*, Bandelier's *The Gilded Man* and *The Delight Makers*, Pinchon and Gutiérrez de Lara's *The Mexican People*, Terry's *Mexico*, Lewis Spence's *The Gods of Mexico*, and several volumes of the *Anales del Museo Nacional*. Together, the Lawrences, Bynner, and Johnson traveled widely in the central part of the country, visiting both tourist attractions and obscure villages. They went to Cuernavaca, where Lawrence became upset over the ruins Zapata had left (he later praised Porfirio Díaz) and where Johnson became so ill that he had to drop out of the party for several days. The itinerary also included Puebla, Tehuacán, Orizaba, Cholula, and Atlixco, where Lawrence was the happiest that he had been in Mexico. Most important, perhaps, one day they went to see the pyramids at San Juan Teotihuacán. Lawrence was fascinated by the wall of Quetzalcóatl, the mysterious white and bearded god of Mexico worshipped in the guise of a feathered serpent. Bynner later mused: "Perhaps the germ of the novel's theme came to him then, his half-fascinated, half-frightened impulse to banish from Mexico the gods in human image and replace them with an animal, with . . . this 'snake of all snakes,' . . . Mexico's natural god and in many ways his own."[6] Bynner was not quite accurate about the gods as animals; Lawrence wanted rather to discover the spirit of the godhead within man. But this strange symbol, uniting land and air in phallic form, certainly appealed to him as an adequate vehicle to convey part of his message.

[6] Bynner, *Journey with Genius*, p. 24.

The first materials for the novel had already come several days earlier, however, with a bullfight the four had attended on Easter Sunday. The opening chapters of *The Plumed Serpent* give a fairly accurate account of that day. At the gate the men were frisked for firearms because Obregón was expected to attend. They sat in the sun with the poorer classes, who were in an excited state (Bynner was hit on his bald spot by an orange). Lawrence had been reading the history of bullfights; but when the first one began, he found that he hated the spectacle, especially the goring of a horse. At one point, to his friends' horror, he began denouncing the crowd in Spanish; luckily the people were too excited to pay any attention. The Lawrences left soon afterward; Bynner and Johnson stayed to see it through. After the fight the two men met a Polish professor, who invited them to meet one of the matadors; Johnson could not resist the invitation, so Bynner returned alone to the Lawrences. At supper that evening the professor came to their table. Lawrence contemptuously dismissed him and his *afición*; the Pole countered that Englishmen were inhumane to the fox and dismissed Lawrence. Only the last incident was omitted from the fictional description.

Lawrence wanted to meet the Mexican people, and made the acquaintance—through Fred Leighton, an American working in the capital—of several radical poets and other writers as well as of Luis Morones. One night in a Bohemian section of the city they met Miguel Covarrubias. The young caricaturist was attracted to the exotic Englishman and escorted the four visitors to see Rivera and other muralists at work in the ministry and the preparatory school; Jean Charlot took them around the patios. Lawrence disliked the frescoes and afterward debated their ugliness with Covarrubias.[7] In *The Plumed Serpent* he praised Rivera's craftsmanship but condemned Rivera's type of sympathy: "In the many frescoes of the Indian, there was sympathy with the Indian, but always from the ideal, social point of view. Never the spontaneous answer of the blood. These flat Indians were symbols in the great script of modern socialism, they were figures of the pathos of the victims of modern industry and capitalism. That was all they were used for: symbols in the weary script of socialism and anarchy."

Of Orozco's frescoes he wrote: "They were meant to be shocking,

7 Jean Charlot, *The Mexican Mural Renaissance, 1920–1925*, pp. 160–161, 237.

but perhaps the very deliberateness prevents them from being so shocking as they might be. But they were ugly and vulgar. Strident caricatures of the Capitalist and the Church, and of the Rich Woman, and of Mammon painted life-size and as violently as possible, round the patios of the grey old building, where the young people are educated. To anyone with the spark of human balance, the things are a misdemeanour."[8] Such an attitude precluded any real friendship with these artists. But Lawrence never became violent in his debates with Covarrubias, and Lawrence's portrait of him in the novel (fused probably with characteristics of Charlot) and in an early essay, "Au Revoir, U.S.A.," is kind. The artist did not understand then Lawrence's significance to world literature, but he later made several drawings of Lawrence from memory, one of which Bynner used as the frontispiece for his 1951 memoir of Lawrence, *Journey with Genius*.

Lawrence could often be charming. He conducted himself well at an unpleasant tea party—also described in the novel—given by Zelia Nuttall, an English anthropologist. Her study of myths, *The Fundamental Principles of Old and New World Religions*, 1901, probably influenced his concept of religion in *The Plumed Serpent* considerably. Although he declined her offer, she even invited the Lawrences to stay at her home. But Lawrence, already uneasy in Mexico and perhaps suffering even then from tuberculosis, compulsively engaged more and more in tyrannic outbursts against friends and the most casual acquaintances alike. Always there were quarrels with Frieda and to a lesser extent with Bynner. Meetings with other Mexicans were not happy. He had expressed a desire to meet Vasconcelos, so Leighton arranged a luncheon with the minister. On the day appointed they all gathered with Carleton Beals and others. After a long delay, a secretary finally apologized, saying that Vasconcelos was unavoidably detained, and would like to meet with them the next day instead. Lawrence flew into a rage and would not consider the invitation. Several days later he abruptly dismissed Leighton from his company. Such actions can only partly be excused by the physical and spiritual difficulties he was enduring.

Mexico increasingly placed Lawrence in a quandary. He saw the cruelty of the bullring displayed toward all animals, other Mexicans, and visitors. Over and over, a note of fear and disgust is found in his

[8] Lawrence, *Plumed Serpent*, pp. 47–48.

reported conversations, his letters, and his fiction and essays. He summed up at one point, Bynner reports, "It's all of one piece . . . what the Aztecs did, what Cortes did, and what Diaz did—the wholesale, endless cruelty. The land itself does it to whoever lives here. The heart has been cut out of the land. That's why hearts had to be cut out of its people. It goes on and on and will always go on. It's a land of death. Look at this dead soil around us—the dagger-fingered cactus— the knife-edged sun! It's all death."[9] This mood underlies his first piece on Mexico, "Au Revoir, U.S.A.," an essay published in Johnson's little magazine, *Laughing Horse*, in 1923. The essay distinguishes between the United States and Mexico as tension of the nerves versus exasperation of the temper. Lawrence stresses the rattlesnake that he believed to be coiled in the heart of Mexico, its fangs obviously showing, and he sneers at the attempts of anthropologists to make pretty myths out of the Aztec religion.[10]

To escape this exasperation he again spoke to his friends of returning to England. But he was still dissatisfied with that solution and decided finally, intrigued by Terry's account of the country around Lake Chapala, to go alone to discover whether perhaps they should all move there. Frieda was sure that he would like it; he always did like places he discovered on his own. While he was gone, she joined gaily with the two Americans in the celebration of May Day, staged in sympathy with the kindred revolution in Russia. The next afternoon Lawrence's telegram summoned them to leave for Chapala immediately. In a panic of haste the three got to the station with Leighton's help. In Guadalajara, Bynner and Johnson paused to visit Idella Purnell, a former student of Bynner's and editor of *Palms*, a little magazine to which Lawrence and Bynner contributed several poems (she has also written five children's books about Mexico).[11] Soon the Lawrences joined them, and the four went to Chapala—the Lawrences to Los Cuentales on Calle Zaragoza and the other two, at Bynner's insistence, to the Hotel Arzapalo.

Lawrence already was reading all he could find about Chapala; the novel was taking shape in his mind. He sat under a willow on the

[9] Bynner, *Journey with Genius*, p. 40.

[10] D. H. Lawrence, *Phoenix: The Posthumous Papers of D. H. Lawrence*, pp. 104–106.

[11] See Sue Watkins, "*Palms* from Mexico: The Story of a Little Magazine," *Texas Quarterly* 6 (Spring 1963): 73–79.

beach and wrote in a thick notebook, seldom erasing or correcting though he occasionally added a phrase or a passage. He was absorbing the life around him and putting it into the novel almost simultaneously. For the reader who visits Chapala, *The Plumed Serpent* takes on an added dimension, for the village in some of its most minute details became Lawrence's Sayula. The American characters with whom he began—his friends, scarcely disguised as Owen Rhys and Bud Villiers—he allowed to disappear after a few chapters; but his servants, Señora Isabel Delores de Medina and her children, become the servants of his heroine, who re-creates the Lawrences' experiences. Neither of the two male principals has a recognizable prototype,[12] but many other people at Chapala were transferred to the page with scarcely a change. For example, the tales of banditry Lawrence heard from Winfield Scott, the manager of the hotel, are retold in the novel by a hotel manager named Bell.

Meanwhile the two Americans were working: Johnson on his collection of poems, *Horizontal Yellow*, 1935, and a special Mexican issue of *Laughing Horse* in which would appear poems and articles by Lawrence, Bynner, Beals, Miss Purnell, Obregón, and the editor; and Bynner on *Caravan*, 1925, which included a poem about Mexico and two views of Lawrence as well as several poems written under Lawrence's influence. Bynner was also keeping notes on him, many of which went into *Journey with Genius*. Johnson, who served as secretary to both men, thus found himself in the amusing position of reading both sides of their quarrels—and discovering that each was saying nearly the same thing about the other.

Lawrence made several visits into the countryside, and in Chapala he generally regained his congeniality. John Dibrell, the ex-boxer, had come to the lake in search of the primitive; under his urging many of the foreign colony began wearing the native costume, which had been banned by the government in favor of work clothes. Dibrell succeeded in having the governmental prohibition temporarily lifted. This issue promptly entered the novel. Leighton came over, and Lawrence welcomed him. Then there were Miss Purnell and her father, with whom

[12] Clark, *Dark Night of the Body*, p. 29, lists various models for the two men that have been suggested by others: a Harvard radical by George Vaillant, John Dibrell by Witter Bynner, Vasconcelos by Lawrence's biographer Harry Moore and Lawrence's friend Luis Quintanilla, General Arnulfo Gómez by Howard Phillips. Clark himself suggests Juárez.

the four rented a *canoa* (a half-enclosed sailing vessel) to take an excursion on the lake. Idella became sick, and Bynner developed a painful rash that sent him to the hospital at Guadalajara. But the others remained for one of their happiest jaunts together. Johnson felt it was so perfect, indeed, that Lawrence hastened his departure from Mexico just so he might leave on such a pleasant note. Even Bynner and Lawrence came to a peaceful farewell in the hospital, where Lawrence taught Bynner how to mend serapes in order to pass the time. Near the middle of July the Lawrences returned to the States, carrying with them a nearly completed novel of some one hundred thousand words.

"Quetzalcoatl" was completely rewritten in Oaxaca in the winter of 1924–1925, becoming the next-to-last long novel that Lawrence ever finished. In the spring of 1926 it was issued at his publisher's insistence under the title *The Plumed Serpent*. Several details were added to the second draft from observations Lawrence made on later trips to Mexico, and a mythical journey of the soul through the spheres was omitted. But essentially the two drafts are the same in plot and theme. *The Plumed Serpent* is permeated with a sense of Mexico; Katherine Anne Porter wrote: "All of Mexico that can be *seen* is here, evoked clearly with the fervor of things remembered out of impressions that filled the mind to bursting. There is no laborious building up of local color, but an immense and prodigal feeling for the background, for every minute detail seen with the eyes of a poet. He makes you a radiant gift of the place."[13] Yet she recognized that these elements are so overlaid by Lawrence's fantastic vision of a resurrected early Mexican religion, and by his almost paranoid fear, that his intense feeling for the country can elude the reader. The story is relatively simple, but nearly every image and action opens into possible symbolic meanings to convey his basic themes, for he wanted this novel to be a full statement of his views on sex and the relationship of man to woman, on politics and the relationship of man to man, on the essence of life and death and faith.

Kate Leslie, Lawrence's heroine in *The Plumed Serpent*, knows that her past in Europe, the happy time when she had been the wife of a leader in the Irish Revolution, is finished; the life before her seems incredibly black, and she does not know where to turn. She finds only

---

[13] Katherine Anne Porter, *The Collected Essays and Occasional Writings of Katherine Anne Porter*, p. 423.

evil in the sterile and perverted rituals of Mexico, such as the bullfight with which the novel begins. All Mexicans seem to be caught up in purposeless violence or sunk in hopeless lethargy. Death broods over the land; not the horrible but meaningful Aztec ritual of sacrifice, but "death ragged, squalid, vulgar, without even the passion of its own mystery." Those who want to save the people want only to change the external patterns of life. Moreover, they still hate, wishing to murder the capitalists—although when they succeed, someone will step in to kill them. Political change has failed; President Montes (based on Calles, who took office while Lawrence was in Oaxaca) can do nothing to bring real meaning to his people. Yet Kate feels that somehow her destiny lies in this cruel, destructive waste land. She despairs. Then on her fortieth birthday she reads in a newspaper an account of a herald rising out of the waters of Lake Sayula to announce the return of Quetzalcóatl, the god who had gone away to be reborn into purity and strength. She is mysteriously moved by the sound of the god's name. When she discovers that two Mexican acquaintances, Ramón Carrusco and General Cipriano Viedma, have instigated the movement because they are convinced that Mexico is "entangled in the past, and unable to extricate itself," having no savior to redeem its people and bring them to the great sun, she decides to move to Sayula to learn what these two men have discovered.

She journeys over "the flimsy, soft, sperm-like water" of the lake, the visual symbol of creation, to the village. There she finds a home and servants, and, both repulsed and entranced by everything Mexican, enters into the life of Sayula. She participates in its festivities, battles against its hostile instincts, pays visits to Don Ramón and his wife in their hacienda. But all this time it is "the greater mystery, the higher power that hovered in the interstices of the hot air, rich and potent," that calls to her soul, and slowly she becomes aware of "the dark eyes of a deeper sun" behind the visual one and "a powerful heart . . . secretly beating" in the earth.[14] Don Ramón communes with this deeper presence, but he has realized that God must manifest himself concretely to the people. One manifestation, Jesus-Jehovah, has failed the Mexicans by bringing empty death and a meaningless promise; therefore, they must turn back to their old gods. To return to Quetzalcóatl, the benevolent god of civilization and one creator of man, to

[14] Lawrence, *Plumed Serpent*, pp. 104, 106.

Huitzilopochtli, the Aztec war god and sometimes alter manifestations of Quetzalcóatl, and to Itzpapalotl, the obsidian butterfly and one of the few attractive goddesses in the Mexican pantheon, may be to return to the horrors of the old Aztecs; but at least they are natural, not foreign, horrors.[15] The Mexican's soul, not his belly, must be reached if he is to be saved, and it cannot be with abstract solutions as both the socialists (these new "Juarezes," Lawrence calls them) and the Church have tried. So Don Ramón, for all these reasons, empties the local church of its Christian images and replaces them with images of the old gods for which he and Cipriano and Kate, if she will, are to become the living symbols. Man can be and must be swallowed up by god, and this he proposes to have happen to them.

This inner conviction makes Don Ramón into Quetzalcóatl, and he follows the course his deeper spirit demands, refusing to be swerved by the pleas of his Christian wife even when it becomes obvious that his conviction will kill her. Cipriano becomes the red Huitzilopochtli whom Ramón initiates into "the living darkness" of "undisturbed creation." (The two men complement each other just as the two gods often did.) And Kate, almost in spite of herself, accepts her position—except that she becomes Malintzi, probably named after a corruption of the name given to Cortés's Indian mistress—and with it marriage to Cipriano. Her Irish spirit troubles her, but she has discovered that she is incomplete in herself, that she must come into communication with the deeper sex in which man and woman meet to form the whole soul. Then Quetzalcóatl's symbol of the morning star, "the unfathomable life-mystery," will shine between them.[16] In a materialistic, mechanical world individuals can exist, but in the inner mystery to which she is appealing, Kate must give up her terrible, rationalistic will, which always tries to exert itself over others. All the elements come together in the novel at last; and as William York Tindall in an introduction to the novel has observed, "When the rains come to end the drought, it is impossible to tell whether these waters promise sexual, religious, or political regeneration, or all three at once, along with vegetable awakening."[17]

---

[15] Irene Nicholson (*Mexican and Central American Mythology*) gives a good introduction to the myths that Lawrence used; see Clark, *Dark Night of the Body*, pp. 102–127.

[16] Lawrence, *Plumed Serpent*, p. 271.

[17] William York Tindall, in ibid., p. x.

The sexual theme was an old one, appearing in almost all of Lawrence's work, but the religious theme had never been developed so clearly. The plight of Mexico provided an almost perfect vehicle. The conquest of one civilization by an alien one more than four hundred years earlier had perverted and crippled conqueror and conquered alike, but now Mexico was rediscovering through the Revolution its origins in the past. The vague unrest between church and state, exploding momentarily in the *Cristo rey* rebellion, must have contributed something to the novel, especially in Don Ramón's confrontation with the bishop and in the attack on his hacienda (one of the novel's more dramatic scenes, during which Kate kills a man in order to protect Don Ramón). Lawrence was wistfully dreaming, however, when he had Montes declare the worship of Quetzalcóatl to be the new state religion. Calles at one point wanted to establish a national church, but his intentions resembled those of Henry VIII of England. The primary sources for the novel's religion were Lawrence's reading and not life itself. Manuel Gamio told Edward Nehls that only historians and specialized archaeologists would have known the names or concepts of these gods and that the many surviving elements of pre-Columbian cultures among the people were not the forms Lawrence described.[18] Although the nonrational world of the Indian people, which imposed no false divisions between time and space, body and soul, heaven and earth, fitted neatly with Lawrence's own thoughts, the religion of Don Ramón is actually an arbitrary creation rather than a spiritual discovery. In the novel Lawrence's rituals and hymns—nearly twenty poems, most of them written in free verse without rhyme, and several prose litanies—are based on models of ancient songs of both Mexican and American Indians, but they are not truly religious. They were created in order to convey the basic themes of the novel in symbolic terms and not out of the deep spirit to which Lawrence was appealing. Therein lies part of the failure of the novel. If the idea was born of a deep conviction, the concrete demonstration really was not, since Lawrence himself never believed in these particular manifestations of God.

Further, it is one thing to return to the past and play with the conceit that Christ might have lived and come to regret his ministry, as in *The Man Who Died*; it is another to create a religion and place it in

---

[18] Nehls, *D. H. Lawrence*, II, 367.

the modern world. This asks the reader to suspend too much knowledge about the reality he has encountered for himself. Lawrence admitted in the novel, "The re-evoked past is frightening, and if it be re-evoked to overwhelm the present, it is fiendish." Amid all the fantastic procedures through which Lawrence puts his characters, the reader applauds Kate's sudden commonsensible revulsion: "For heaven's sake, let me out of this and back to simple human people. I loathe the very sound of Quetzalcóatl and Huitzilopochtli. . . . I've had it put over me." Some readers, most notably Huxley, felt that the ending, wherein she remains in Mexico, was forced.[19]

Worse, such a belief in the self-contained destiny of each people brought Lawrence to a position essentially one with fascism. This general tenor made the book popular in Fascist circles; it even became the model for one British group.[20] Concerning race Lawrence is contradictory, saying first that the half-breed is "a calamity" and "divided against himself," but later holding that there are natural aristocrats who can rise above race and commingle: Kate is to be married to Cipriano, but their union is not to become a demonstration of the engulfment of the white race by the darker one that Lawrence has suggested earlier.[21] The tone of the novel is shrill, and many of its ideas unworthy of Lawrence's talent. He may have been partly aware of these inner defects of the work. The contradictions within the second draft indicate more an uncertainty in aim than an attempt to get everything, both thesis and antithesis, into the work. Yet he spoke of it in his letters as the book that lay closest to his heart, adding, "I consider this my most important novel, so far."[22]

Certainly *The Plumed Serpent* for all its many faults exerts a strange fascination. It is interesting to compare it with *Manuel le Mexicain*, 1956, a French novel by the Italian writer Carlo Coccioli. This work depicts a similar search for a messiah in Mexico, but it is written in more realistic—and hence believable—detail. Yet the novel gives a flat, tourist's perspective and seems more strained than Lawrence's wild but deeply involved excursion into fantasy. In a mysterious and rather paradoxical manner Lawrence struck deep at the souls

---

[19] Lawrence, *Plumed Serpent*, pp. 332, 370; George Plimpton (ed.), *Writers at Work*, 2d ser., p. 209.
[20] William York Tindall, *D. H. Lawrence & Susan His Cow*, pp. 162–180.
[21] Lawrence, *Plumed Serpent*, pp. 59–60, 246, 145.
[22] Lawrence, *Collected Letters*, II, 845.

of all mankind, while Coccioli's novel seems too limited to a peculiarly Mexican experience. The very fact that no critic quite comes to terms with *The Plumed Serpent*, disliking now the theology, now the psychology, now the structure, yet feels compelled to make the attempt, expresses its baffling power. It has been the subject even of a book-length study, *Dark Night of the Body* (1964) by L. D. Clark.

But when the Lawrences left Mexico in 1923 only they realized how much he hoped to accomplish in this new novel. Frieda sailed from New York to England to visit her children. Lawrence turned back to California. There he renewed his friendship with Knud Merrild and Kai Gótzsche, two Danish painters he had known at Taos. Restless without his wife, Lawrence proposed that they accompany him down the west coast of Mexico to look for a place for him to settle, and Gótzsche accepted. On September 26 he began his second adventure in Mexico, described in his own and in Gótzsche's letters (published in Merrild's memoir). By train and car they crawled south through Guaymas, Navojoa, Mazatlán, and Tepic. This stretch of Mexico was extremely primitive, hardly more than a frontier, and Lawrence did not like it. Yet he was intrigued by everything, particularly the aboriginal Indians of the area. From Navojoa they detoured briefly to Minas Nuevas and Alamos, stopping to see a mine owned by a Swiss, Amos Yaeger, back in the Sierra Madre. The visit gave him part of the setting for "The Woman Who Rode Away," in which both the mine and market place at Alamos appear. From Tepic they turned east to the Mexican landscape of which Lawrence had become fond. They had to go by car and muleback now to Ixtlán del Río, where they could meet the Guadalajara train. Somewhere along the way they stopped for a bullfight, and there is no record of Lawrence's walking out on this one. In Guadalajara he visited the Purnells and designed several covers for *Palms*, apparently the only drawing that he did on either of the first two trips (one of these designs was reproduced in the *Texas Quarterly*, spring 1963). Gótzsche was painting and was particularly enchanted with Chapala when they visited it one day. But Lawrence felt that the village had already drastically changed its character, not realizing that it was he who had changed, especially without his wife along. He had again become temperamental; Gótzsche even suspected sometimes that he was insane. Yet the countryside was lovely, and Lawrence was still charged with the idea of finding a small farm. He wrote in a letter, "Mexico has a certain mystery of beauty for me, as if the gods were here."[23] But he had to return to England now, and on November 22 he sailed from Vera- cruz—little having been accomplished.

In England, Lawrence proposed to his friends that they follow him to America and create a colony. When the Lawrences sailed in March 1924, however, only Dorothy Brett and her ear trumpet accompanied them. They went to the Lawrences' ranch above Taos, where he rap- idly turned out several essays about the New Mexican Indians (col- lected in *Mornings in Mexico*) and two stories set in these mountains, both of which give some insight into the complexity of Kate's quest. *St. Mawr*, 1925, a short novel, tells of a woman who discovers the meaning of life in the primitiveness of a New Mexico ranch, having renounced the stupidities of British society; "The Princess," 1925, re- lates the tragedy of a woman who wants to exert her will over a Mex- ican hired hand and thus denies the possibility of love, remaining soli- tary and incomplete as a person. One day in exploring the mountains above Taos, Mrs. Dodge—now Mrs. Luhan—guided Lawrence to a cave used by the Indians for their ancient rituals. Behind a waterfall was a sacrificial altar upon which the sun shone at the winter solstice, piercing the frozen water. Imaginatively transferring the cave to the Sierra Madre of Chihuahua (higher than he had actually traveled), Lawrence had the second part of "The Woman Who Rode Away." This was his second piece about Mexico to be published, appearing in *Dial* in 1925; it was collected in 1928 in a volume titled after the story.

It tells the story of an unnamed woman married to a mine owner twenty years older than she. They live in a barren stretch of Mexican mountains close to a dead town. Their marriage is not really a mar- riage, and she has had one nervous breakdown. One day in autumn, when the mountains are briefly green, she hears of the Chilchuis, an isolated, primitive tribe of Indians who were descendants of Mocte- zuma and who still offer sacrifices to the old gods. She simply rides off one day, leaving her husband and children. On the quest she mysteri- ously loses her will power and moves to another kind of death than that she has lived among, the death of "her kind of womanhood, in- tensely personal and individual." She meets some of the Indians and tells them that she wishes to know more about their gods. They take her, caught in the curious trance, to a green valley magically opened

---

[23] Ibid., II, 757.

among the barren mountains. There, weary of the white man's God, she offers her heart to the gods of the Chilchuis.

The natives strip off her riding clothes and give her an Indian mantle of blue, symbolizing that she is to be the blue wind, which will carry a message to the lost god of the sun—imprisoned by the white man—saying that the Indians will open the gates to him and the moon again. At the winter solstice the Indians carry her to a cave, "an orifice" behind a curtain of ice that hangs like "a great fang." There the natives stretch her out naked on an altar and, holding a knife over her heart, wait for the sinking sun to send its ray through the ice to her open body. These last scenes can remind the reader of one of the various plots pornographers have reveled in: the sacrifice of the pure white woman to a dark race. But Lawrence explicitly denies that there is anything sexual about the Indians' regard for the woman, though her death is symbolic of the mastery of one race over another. These Indians are caught up in a religious passion too remote and great to be tempered by sexual desires.

This reading has followed the simplest thread of the story: other images reinforce the symbolic reading. For example, the miner has been digging up the bowels of the earth and leaving piles of refuse; the war turns silver into a dead market and the mine closes, forcing him to raise pigs instead. But Lawrence, as always, realized how complex the human organism is and contradicted his theme without worry. The dead town with its dead market and church is evil (though belonging to the Indians); the death of the woman seems somehow good. Her loss of power will be beneficial to her and to man; but the Indians are sacrificing her in order to gain the power they have lost to the white man. It is the method used with much the same theme in *The Plumed Serpent*; but in this story, narrowly compressed, the ambiguities enrich rather than perplex.[24] Lawrence did not seem to be caught up in the sickly dilemmas he was in when he rewrote the novel.

All this time the "Quetzalcoatl" manuscript demanded his attention, but Lawrence felt that he could work on it only in Mexico. He had been corresponding with Manuel Gamio. Apparently Lawrence wanted to discuss the religious background of *The Plumed Serpent* with the anthropologist, but the two never met. According to Mrs.

---

[24] D. H. Lawrence, *The Complete Short Stories*, II, 546–581.

Luhan, George Creel, a journalist and later author of *The People Next Door*, met Lawrence at Taos and offered to give him letters of introduction to both Gamio and the president-elect, Calles; but Lawrence was in some sort of black mood and refused. When he left Taos in late October 1924, with Frieda and Miss Brett, he intended to isolate himself in Oaxaca. He wished to saturate himself in another section of Mexico, and the south seemed appropriate because of his interest in the Zapotec and Maya Indians.

In Mexico City, Lawrence dined with Mrs. Nuttall and snubbed Maugham, who because of his stutter had asked his secretary to offer Lawrence a ride to the dinner after Lawrence had suggested that they meet. Lawrence took the secretary's calling as an intended slight. From Mrs. Nuttall he learned more about the murder of Mrs. Evans, an incident that may have colored his description of the raid on the hacienda in *The Plumed Serpent*. A guide's request that he remove his hat in the Museo de Antropología, another insult to him, likewise entered the work. He was photographed by Edward Weston (one of the photographs was used as the frontispiece for Mrs. Luhan's book *Lorenzo in Taos*, 1932). And having joined the recently organized PEN Club, he called upon the Mexican head of it, the poet Genaro Estrada, who in turn gave a special dinner in honor of the Englishman. At this fete Lawrence met Luis Quintanilla, with whom he struck up a brief but warm friendship. He asked Quintanilla to write a piece to accompany the Weston photographs when they were published. The resulting essay was not what Lawrence had ordered and was, he felt, oppressively pessimistic, but he could not resist polishing and rewriting it. "See Mexico After, by Luis Q.," which was published only after Lawrence's death in *Phoenix*, vents a Mexican's spleen against the typical American who tramps below the border seeking commissions —usually in oil—or sex or escape and who ends criticizing everything Mexican since "America . . . is CIVILIZATION." The fact that Mexico was the civilization of the past has been forgotten by the tourist; indeed the snake of civilization, which has crawled into the States, has forgotten where its tail rests. The last note sounds like Lawrence's addition, but the rest of the essay represents a viewpoint about the North American continent, especially in the feeling of a schism between the psychologies of the two nations, which was not his.[25]

25 Lawrence, *Phoenix*, pp. 111–116.

On November 8 the Lawrences left for Oaxaca. The town was still relatively isolated; the railroad, which had been destroyed during the Revolution, had been repaired only a short time before. A few Americans and Britons had remained throughout the various revolutions, but the Lawrences and Miss Brett were apparently the first foreign tourists in four years. Lawrence as usual was torn between a basic fear of the strangeness and a delight in the customs of the natives. With Miss Brett remaining at the Hotel Francia, the Lawrences rented a home on Avenida Pino Suárez from Father Edward A. Richards, the brother of the British vice-consul and probably the model for Bishop Severn in *The Plumed Serpent*. Lawrence hired a servant, Rosalino, and eagerly began exploring the markets and streets of the town. He was pleased to see that here the natives dressed in their ancient fashion instead of being forced into foreign work clothes. They, struck by his red beard, often called *Cristo* after him, and one day a crudely-drawn portrait of him appeared in a shop window. He met the governor of the state, and there were various diversions with the American and British residents. A group of them rode out to see the giant tree at Tule and the ruins of Mitla. About the middle of November he began rewriting *The Plumed Serpent*, but paused in December long enough to dash off four essays about Oaxaca. These were published separately in *Adelphi* and *Travel*, 1925–1927, and became the first half of *Mornings in Mexico*, 1927, a work dedicated to Mrs. Luhan.

All four describe in sensuous detail several aspects of the Lawrences' life in the town, but almost every scene served as a point from which Lawrence could begin an often lengthy exploration of the philosophy he was trying to fashion in the novel. In "Corasmin and the Parrots," internally dated Friday, December 19, he muses on the nature of the creation as he watches the parrots' imitation of his dog and his servant. He affirms his joy in the early Mexicans' belief in four convulsions of the sun by which the world has been successively created and destroyed. He intuitively felt, like some pre-Platonic philosopher, that the universe is continually trying to attain perfection, but that unity must always bring death and destruction. The violence of such cataclysmic creation seemed more satisfying to him than any doctrine of slow evolution, an idea he also asserted vigorously in the novel. In "Market Day," December 20, he wrote at length about their experiences with the Zapotec markets. He explored at the same time the idea that the barter was more than an economic institution, that in the great curve of space and time the market served like a religious ritual as a moment of still contact at the vortex. This mingling was another manifestation of his morning or evening star, hovering between night and day and "more wonderful than either."

"Walk to Huayapa," Sunday, December 21, is the most straightforward account of the four, Lawrence pausing only now and then to make fun of the Revolution or to puzzle over the nature of the Indian. He relates a tramp that he and Frieda took with Rosalino to the nearby village of Huayápam (Lawrence misspelled it "Huayapa"), describing the countryside and the natives they met, the town and their adventures in the shops. The last essay, "The Mozo," is a long portrait of Rosalino during Christmas week in which he became homesick for his own village. In it Lawrence admits briefly the horror and filthiness of the old Mexican gods, recounting a few legends about them, but the main theme of the essay is the difference between the Indians, who exist in a vast flux in which time and space are relative matters of the emotions, and the mechanical "white monkeys," who must fix everything to an exact point.[26] The curious collisions of fact and philosophy in these essays may be puzzling to any reader who does not know the rest of Lawrence's Mexican work, perhaps even irritating since the connections are often tenuous. They offer only a glimpse of the problems that he was worrying over in *The Plumed Serpent*, and they possess none of the explosiveness of the novel or the short stories. Yet the essays have their own vitality in Lawrence's great sense of place and are so low-keyed and fresh that they deserve a wider audience than they have gained (they are now out of print in the United States).

He had been dabbing in a few colors and figures in the paintings Miss Brett was doing of Oaxaca, but he had not yet turned to painting in that great burst of enthusiasm that would hit him in Italy. One scene she related to him did become the subject of a full canvas shortly afterward. December 23 was the Fiesta de Rábanos; huge red radishes were carved into the likenesses of little men with exaggerated genitals and hung for sale in the market stalls. Miss Brett bought one and brought it to Lawrence, who was sick in bed. His painting, reproduced in the *Paintings of D. H. Lawrence*, 1964, shows a crowd of men, some of whom are offering the radish figure to various women (the

[26] D. H. Lawrence, *Mornings in Mexico*, pp. 3–96. The book was reviewed by Conrad Aiken and Carleton Beals.

gift indicated love); Lawrence's self-portrait stands out prominently in the crowd. The painting resembles a fresco in both its apparent texture and its crowded composition.[27] No critic seems to have suggested that Lawrence may have been influenced by the Mexican muralists, no doubt because of his contempt for their artistry. Nevertheless, there are many curious resemblances, even when one considers that they were all Expressionists and that the similarities may be accidents of vision rather than direct borrowing.

By early January 1925 the tension between Frieda and Miss Brett had grown too strong for comfort, and Lawrence finally asked the young woman to leave. By the end of the month he had finished his novel and had given in to his growing illness, a combination of flu and malaria, he said. Frieda worried for his health and insisted that they return to Mexico City. In March the doctors there diagnosed the illness as tuberculosis in an advanced state. He rested several weeks at the Hotel Imperial, renewing his friendship with Quintanilla and making the acquaintance of George Conway, a British engineer and author, who had published a monograph on Thomas Gage and edited the works of other early visitors to Mexico. The *Revista de Revistas* printed a brief notice with photograph on March 22.[28] Lawrence returned to the ranch at Taos late in the month on the doctor's order; the Mexican adventure was finished.

Those last days in Oaxaca, combined with his 1923 departure from Veracruz, however, served as the opening for an uncompleted novel, *The Flying Fish*, first printed in *Phoenix*. It tells of the departure of Gethin Day, homesick and ill with malaria, from a lost town in south Mexico for England and his ancestral home. Again Lawrence showed his ability to depict vividly the Mexican landscape, creating here a hot lushness reminiscent in some ways of Henri Rousseau's tropics. Punning on his hero's last name, Lawrence describes what had actually happened to him in Mexico:

. . . in the last years, something in the hard, fierce, finite sun of Mexico, in the dry terrible land, and in the black staring eyes of the suspicious natives, had made the ordinary day lose its reality to him. It had cracked like some great bubble, and to his uneasiness and terror, he had seemed to see through the fissures the deeper blue of that other Greater Day

[27] D. H. Lawrence, *Paintings of D. H. Lawrence*, pp. 27, 67.
[28] "Illustre escritor inglés en México," *Revista de Revistas*, March 22, 1925, p. 10.

where moved the other sun shaking its dark blue wings. Perhaps it was the malaria: perhaps it was his own inevitable development; perhaps it was the presence of those handsome, dangerous, wide-eyed men left over from the ages before the flood in Mexico, which caused his old connexions and his accustomed world to break for him. He was ill, and he felt as if at the very middle of him, beneath his navel, some membrane were torn, some membrane which had connected him with the world and its day. The natives who attended him, quiet, soft, heavy, and rather helpless, seemed, he realized, to be gazing from their wide black eyes always into the greater day whence they had come and where they wished to return. Men of a dying race, to whom the busy sphere of the common day is a cracked and leaking shell.[29]

Lawrence told friends that he intended to end on a redemptive note for his sick hero, but he was unable to bring off the English sequence and left his hero crossing the Atlantic. Some of the dismay with the England that Lawrence confronted upon his two returns from Mexico was spelled out in two essays finally published in *Phoenix II*, 1968.[30] By 1925 Lawrence was a man without a country.

He had only one more Mexican story to tell, "None of That," first published in *The Woman Who Rode Away*. (Lawrence did give the hero of "The Lovely Lady," 1927, "a quite extraordinary collection of old Mexican legal documents" to brood over, but they have no bearing on the plot of the story.)[31] No one has said publicly when "None of That" was written or what the background of the story was. Because it is not only the most realistic of all Lawrence's American fiction but also the least concerned with the philosophy he was working out, it has been generally ignored. Perhaps it was based on some anecdote told to him after he had left Mexico; the narrative is related by a Mexican through an unidentified person in Venice. The narrative concerns the relationship between a Mexican bullfighter, Cuesta, "whose fame once rang through Spain and through Latin America," and a twice-divorced American, Ethel Cane, a figure who in many ways resembles Mrs. Luhan. Ethel is another variation on the Princess figure. She is filled with a terrible will, called by her the imagination, which she feels can rise above anything. She refuses to give in to the Mexican men, saying

29 Lawrence, *Phoenix*, pp. 780–798; quotation, pp. 782–783.
30 D. H. Lawrence, *Phoenix II: Uncollected, Unpublished, and Other Prose Works of D. H. Lawrence*, pp. 250–266.
31 Lawrence, *Short Stories*, III, 763.

that she will have "none of that." But then she goes to see the animal-like Cuesta in the ring, and when he plays a bull as if it were his lover, Ethel goes insane with desire like all the tiring women chasing hysterically after him. But she has wealth, and Cuesta comes to visit her. On her part she is now frightened, since her will cannot control her body; ironically she finds herself in the position of the women she has scorned, and she threatens to kill herself. Cuesta, inevitably, invites her to his home; there he turns her over to a group of men to do with as they please so long as they do not mark her. Three days later she kills herself, leaving half her fortune to the matador. Again the dark race has triumphed over the light. The scandal, occurring as it does in the period under Carranza, is forgotten among all the other turmoil.[32] The story is not inferior to Lawrence's talent and is of a piece with the rest of his work at this time.

This then is the Mexican legacy that the British author left. Carleton Beals has expressed rather poetically the strange impression it can leave on the imagination: "What Lawrence did was to shoot the sky-rockets of his morbid fancy over Mexico, and in the long glimpse of showering sparks he caught remarkable glimpses of the land, glimpses so strange, so fantastic and distorted, yet sometimes so grandiosely true as to make one wonder at the eerie quality of his genius."[33] These pieces form a significant segment of his total work, perhaps the vital center of his development as a writer. From Lawrence's Mexican experience a rather different personality emerged. Mexico had given him his fullest contact with the real primitive, and thereafter he ceased to praise that way of life as enthusiastically as he had. In Mexico he also came to a more intense awareness of the great sun behind the universe, which somehow led him to an understanding of one individual's true relationship with another. One of his friends summed up: "Mexico—horror and all—held something for Lawrence as a man and writer that he needed."[34]

[32] Ibid., III, 701–721.
[33] Carleton Beals, *Glass Houses*, pp. 188–189.
[34] Catherine Carswell, *The Savage Pilgrimage*, p. 177.

## 8. An Interlude: Three Quests in Time

The six years after Obregón's death emerged as a distinct interlude in the excitement generated by the Mexican Revolution. Although a great many novels about the country, especially westerns and mysteries, were being published, Archibald MacLeish, Hart Crane, and Aldous Huxley were the only major American and British authors to be attracted there. Ernest Hemingway had not seen Mexico when he published in *Winner Take Nothing*, 1933, his short story "The Mother of a Queen."[1] Nor were the Mexican poems of Wallace Stevens, published in *Harmonium* in 1931, based on actual experience.[2] The work of MacLeish, Crane, and Huxley reveals almost nothing about the contemporary scene in Mexico. One turned mainly to the romance of the Spanish Conquest; the others looked inward. Though Mexico

[1] Hemingway did not visit Mexico until 1940 or 1941, according to a letter to me from Carlos Baker, Hemingway's biographer, August 18, 1967. Baker thinks Hemingway based the story on an anecdote related to Hemingway by Sidney Franklin, an American matador, about an incident in the life of Ortiz.

[2] Malcolm Lowry was much taken by Stevens's descriptions in "Sea Surface Full of Clouds." See Malcolm Lowry, *Hear Us O Lord from Heaven Thy Dwelling Place*, p. 47.

formed a strong background for each, it seemed not (as many would argue about Crane) to have influenced their paths directly.

It was a sad period. Through these years Calles ruled from his expensive home in Cuernavaca as the real power, though three presidents nominally held office. Agrarian reforms almost ceased; Luis Morones's labor union was destroyed without any other rising immediately to take its place. Many Mexicans blamed the American ambassador for this state of affairs. Ironically, Dwight Morrow was perhaps the first American diplomat who sincerely tried to understand the Mexican people. He began the Good Neighbor Policy, which received official sanction under Franklin Roosevelt. He conducted interviews with Calles on the friendliest terms, bought a home in Cuernavaca and filled it with Mexican products, and employed Rivera to decorate the gallery of Cortés's palace. But Morrow was only too eager to offer Calles ample arguments for slowing down all reforms that ran counter to private enterprise. Historians are still divided over Morrow's ultimate service to the country, yet he cannot be held responsible for the pace at which Mexico then turned fascist. Although the breach with the Church was healed in 1929, state governments were allowed to impose their own restrictions on the clergy. Consequently, in some areas, especially Tabasco and Chiapas, priests were in effect outlawed altogether. Gold Shirts and Red Shirts were allowed to harass communists, Jews, and Catholics openly in many areas.

All this would influence later writers considerably, but neither MacLeish, Crane, Huxley, nor many members of the Anglo-American colony at the time seemed affected. The several historians, economists, sociologists, and political observers who were carrying on the work of Ernest Gruening, of course, must be excepted from this general observation. Important among their number were Hubert Herring (1889–1967), editor of *Renascent Mexico*, 1935, and author of *A History of Latin America*, 1956; Henry Bamford Parkes (1904–), author of *A History of Mexico*, 1938; and Lesley Byrd Simpson (1891–), author of *Many Mexicos*, 1941. Simpson's work is one of the few histories from this century that can be judged purely in literary terms. Interpreting history as the natural development of basic institutions, somewhat modified by dynamic leaders, Simpson was scholarly in his approach, yet he infused the work with his personality, reacting to the chief personages as actual humans in much the same manner as had Prescott and finding a style that lets the book be read as easily as fiction. For some readers Simpson has appeared too one-sided and iconoclastic, but he supported his viewpoints well; and whether the reader agrees with him or not, Simpson forces him to come to an understanding of Mexico in a way none of the more conventional historians can. He has also translated two novels of Mariano Azuela, 1956, and Gómara's history, 1964.

Although nothing occurred to attract socialists or artists as had the excitement of Obregón's revolution, the favorable rate of exchange brought in plenty of tourists, even during the worst of the depression, and new expatriates willing to gush over every strange sight. Travel books and journals were turned out at a phenomenal rate; between 1928 and 1942 over eighty appeared. Many of these revealed, as had earlier accounts, a romantic desire to find in Mexican primitivism a simple solution to all the social and economic ills that faced Western civilization. Thus it was with *America Hispana*, 1931, by Crane's friend and later editor, Waldo Frank (1889–1967), who had made a whirlwind tour of Latin America in 1929.[3] Another work, *Mexico: A Study of Two Americas*, shows the same attraction to primitivism more clearly than Frank's book. Its author, Stuart Chase (1888–), had spent some time in spring 1930 in Tepoztlán, a village near Cuernavaca. The same year Robert Redfield (1897–) had published his sociological study of the village. Chase decided to compare his findings with those of the Lynds about Middletown in order to review his own favorite theme, the impact of the machine on man. The handicraft culture is of course found to be almost perfectly integrated. Illustrated by Rivera, *Mexico* was extremely popular.[4] Both Crane and Huxley, although the latter quarreled with several of Chase's ideas, spoke of it with approval.

The search for the primitive by Richard Halliburton, Frank Waters, and J. Frank Dobie led them into perhaps the most strenuous exploits.

[3] Waldo Frank, *America Hispana*, pp. 233–259; idem, "Cárdenas of Mexico," *Foreign Affairs* 18 (October 1939): 91–101. Frank also translated an essay by Alfonso Reyes: "Modern Poetry of America Hispana," *Nation*, March 29 and April 5, 1941, pp. 376–379, 411–412. See also Paul J. Carter, *Waldo Frank*, pp. 91, 115, 125, 164; Arnold Chapman, *The Spanish American Reception of United States Fiction, 1920–1940*, pp. 57–74; Robert Spiller (ed.), *Literary History of the United States*, p. 1387. Reviews of *America Hispana* were written by Mary Austin and Ernest Gruening.

[4] Stanley J. Kunitz and Howard Haycroft (eds.), *Twentieth Century Authors*, p. 273; Stuart Chase, *Mexico*.

Halliburton (1900–1939?) visited Mexico in the summer of 1928 to follow Cortés's trail to the Valley of Mexico, with a slight detour to the crater of Popocatépetl, and then headed for Chichén Itzá to take two plunges into the sacrificial well. He appealingly recounted these adventures in *New Worlds to Conquer*, published the next year complete with photographs to prove the truth of his daring.[5] Waters (1902–) rode the length of Mexico alone on horseback and returned to explore the country several times in the 1930's and early 1960's. These experiences colored two of his novels, *Fever Pitch*, 1930, and *The Dust within the Rock*, 1940, and his extraordinary memoir of three years with the Indians of Arizona and northern Mexico, *Pumpkin Seed Point*, 1969.[6]

Dobie (1888–1964), growing up in Texas near the border, had always been familiar with Mexico, but he made his first extended visit in 1928, when *Country Gentleman* financed a pack trip for him, characteristically in search of a lost mine, across the Sierra Madre in Chihuahua and Sonora. In 1932 and again in 1933 he returned, part of the time in company with his wife, Bertha, and Henry Nash Smith, going by horse and mule, as he wrote, "through the vast, unpopulated mountains of Mexico, lingering at ranches and mining camps, living the freest times of my life." From these experiences came *Tongues of the Monte*, 1935, and the second section of *Apache Gold and Yaqui Silver*, 1939. *Apache Gold* is a collection of histories and legends about lost mines and secret hoards, with illustrations by the El Paso artist Tom Lea. *Tongues of the Monte*, which Dobie called "in some ways the strangest book that has ever been published about Mexico," records an idealized trip across northern Mexico in the course of which he picks up many folktales and legends of the region. He also scattered through the book many glimpses of a way of life seldom encountered by visitors. In addition Dobie wrote a number of articles, newspaper columns, and introductions to the works of others in which he further displayed his intimate knowledge, though romanticized, of the ways of Mexican cowboys, vagabonds, and kindred spirits.[7]

[5] Richard Halliburton, *New Worlds to Conquer*, pp. 6–76; idem, *Richard Halliburton*, pp. 285–288. Also Jonathan Root, *Halliburton*, pp. 141–144. Connie Hood introduced me to the adventurer.

[6] Martin Bucco, *Frank Waters*, pp. 3–4, 10–12, 15.

[7] J. Frank Dobie, *Coronado's Children*, pp. 158–181; idem, *Apache Gold and Yaqui Silver*, pp. xi–xv, 151–356; idem, *Tongues of the Monte*; idem, *Some Part of*

Others who admired the primitive were Mary Austin (1868–1937), who described her admiration of Rivera's primitive rhythms in her autobiography, *Earth Horizon*, 1932, and Erna Fergusson (1888–1964), whose *Fiesta in Mexico*, 1934, followed her trip to remote villages in search of their traditional celebrations.[8] But Mrs. Austin and Miss Fergusson, like Dobie, spent most of their lives in civilized surroundings. William Spratling (1900–1967) unintentionally revealed the impossibility of returning to innocence. When he settled in Taxco in 1929, Spratling wrote quietly and personally about the town and its people and about a few of his own explorations of the nearby countryside. Illustrated by the author and prefaced by a letter from Rivera, *Little Mexico* appeared in 1932. Reviews were good, but the publishing firm failed before many copies had sold; not until 1964 was it finally reissued, under the title *A Small Mexican World*. Meanwhile, Spratling had revived in Taxco the almost forgotten silver industry, his designs and craftsmanship bringing to the town fame, tourists, and wealth. Spratling also collected pre-Columbian artifacts. Pursuing these twin occupations, he met almost everyone of note in Mexico. The year of his death he decided to share that knowledge and compiled a *File on Spratling* with further illustrations by the author, a reproduction of his portrait by Siqueiros, and an introduction by Budd Schulberg. Extraordinarily candid, more than anything the autobiography reveals the emptiness of the lives of too many expatriates as they frantically searched for meanings that had eluded them at home and that equally eluded them in Mexico. Primitivism, attractive as it may appear in *Little Mexico*, can too easily grow stale and result in the sad posturing of *File*.[9] Crane became the tragic ex-

---

*Myself*, pp. 242–251. Also Winston Bode, *A Portrait of Pancho*, pp. 37, 57–58. Mary Louise McVicker prepared a bibliography; at least eight essays remain uncollected. Reviews of *Tongues of the Monte* were written by Erna Fergusson and Oliver La Farge.

[8] Mary Austin, *Earth Horizon*, pp. 364–366; T. M. Pearce, *Mary Hunter Austin*, pp. 57–58; David A. Remley, *Erna Fergusson*, pp. 20–22, 30. Miss Fergusson also wrote *Mexico Revisited*, 1955; it was reviewed by Hubert Herring.

[9] William Spratling, *A Small Mexican World*; idem, *File on Spratling*. Also J. P. McEvoy, " 'Silver Bill,' Practical Good Neighbor," *Reader's Digest* 47 (September 1945): 19–22; Robert D. Duncan, "William Spratling's Mexican World," *Texas Quarterly* 9 (Spring 1966): 97–104. Ruby N. and Jaime Castrejón prepared a monograph, published in Taxco after his death, *William Spratling*. Reviews of

treme; Huxley rejected explicitly the entire scene; MacLeish held aloof from it all.

Archibald MacLeish (1892–) in 1932 published *Conquistador*, an impressionistic account of the Conquest from the viewpoint of Bernal Díaz; the following spring it received the Pulitzer prize for poetry. He had begun it four years earlier in Paris as a result of reading Alfred Maudslay's translation of the *Historia verdadera*. But the poem would not go; MacLeish was too far from his setting and felt badly the need to see the countryside he was describing. Consequently he headed for Mexico City and from there took the train to Veracruz in order to retrace Cortés's route. The American Embassy had advised him not to go to Veracruz, as a rebellion was about to break out in the port city, but MacLeish felt that he could not miss the chance. He has written me in a letter that in the hills near Veracruz he found a young Mexican who wanted to improve his English, hired three mules, laid in some "ill-chosen" provisions, and set off. The only map he had been able to find was the frontispiece to Maudslay's edition, but once on the Sierra the choices that the Spaniards would have had to take were clear from the very lay of the terrain. When they paused at Jalapa, not far up country, MacLeish was already refreshed enough to resume work. Ultimately they arrived in Puebla and then crossed the pass between the two volcanos into the Valley of Mexico, which he remembers "even at that late date was heartbreakingly beautiful." In Mexico City, Ambassador Morrow gave him "a severe dressing down," then introduced him to Charles Lindbergh, who had made a goodwill flight south in February 1929. Getting together enough money to return to the States, MacLeish left Mexico soon thereafter.[10]

The journey had brought the poem to life for him, and he finished it a few months after his return; the *Yale Review* published a section late in the year. Finishing touches, however, were not added until 1931. When it was published, most critics, in spite of some mixed reactions, greeted the work with lavish praise. Almost every reviewer noted its Mexican origins, citing the poet's statement that he had ex-

---

the books were written by Stuart Chase and W. W. Johnson. In 1946 Warner Brothers filmed his life, *The Man from New Orleans.*

[10] All information about MacLeish's visit to Mexico comes from his letter to me dated June 21, 1967; see also MacLeish's introductory note to *Conquistador.*

plored the route on foot and muleback, but only Mrs. Austin attempted to relate the poem to its setting: ". . . no such curtailed sojourn in the country of his election accounts for the amazing vitality, the clarity and livingness of the work in hand. The feeling of Mexico is there, the high-keyed freshness and the immemorial sense of time past, the all but incommunicable beauty and subtler things still, the sense of meaning waters blue and green and gilt, which gives the mythical concept of the feathered serpent 'in those waters where the low sun paces.' Of what the eye can teach of Mexico, Mr. MacLeish has missed nothing; but he has captured much more."[11] We can understand her enthusiasm. But the sense of place is simply not that strong, although the cast of melancholy, the concern with death and despair, and the distaste for war, which were common in much of MacLeish's poetry, fit in well with one vision of Mexico. His descriptions are muted and occasional. The relation of Cortés's ascent into the Mexican highlands and his crossing into the valley is the most distinctive aspect and can remind one of MacLeish's actual experience, but one student who made a thorough study of the poem and its major source said that only certain features in Books VI and VII are not to be found in Bernal Díaz's history.[12] Yet by MacLeish's own testimony he could not use even Díaz's materials until he had re-enacted a similar experience.

*Conquistador* begins with a prologue spoken in the poet's voice in which he seeks to evoke from the dead their memories. Díaz appears to his imagination and takes the poet back to the time when the aged soldier had begun composing his history. The poem continues as an evocation of the old man's reveries, told from within. In the "Preface to His Book," Díaz gives the reader a glimpse of the reasons he had for recording his view of the expedition. In 1553 Gómara, Cortés's secretary, had published his version of the Conquest, so disgusting to Díaz by its exaltation of Cortés and consequent demeaning of the soldiers under him that he determined to tell the story himself. The rest of the preface is a rapid survey of the various explorations that Cortés's company had made before the epic journey began, gradually focusing

[11] Mary Austin, "The Story of the Conquest," *Southwest Review* 17 (April 1932): xiv.

[12] William J. Brown, "Influence of Bernal Diaz' *True History of the Conquest of New Spain* on Archibald MacLeish's *Conquistador*," Master's thesis, University of North Carolina, 1958, pp. 20–21.

on the vision of "the steep snow mountain on the sky" (Mount Orizaba) and the march west into Mexico.

The poem proper divides into fifteen books. There is some sort of narrative progression inherited from the *Historia*—the fifteen books group into three divisions—but no discernible emotional progression. The first five books are concerned with the departure from Cuba, the initial encounters with the Mexicans, and the scuttling of the ships so that the men must finish the expedition. Retreat impossible, they begin the march toward Moctezuma. The next five books are so heavily allusive that it is difficult to follow the narrative; the battle with the Tlaxcalans is given obliquely; the destruction of Cholula is so obscure that even MacLeish felt the need to identify the subject with a note. The reader returns to sure understanding only when Díaz's memory reaches "the pass and the down-going." Book X serves as an interlude, a center between two storms of battle; introduced by a paean to the halcyon, it ends—in preparation for what is to come—with the sacrifice of a boy on the altar. The last five books concern the fighting in Tenochtitlán and its environs, culminating in the *noche triste* (Book XIV) and the destruction of the city (Book XV).

The poem misleads the reader by beginning with epic intentions. MacLeish more clearly sought to recapture only the spirit of Díaz. He used an almost naturalistic language, slightly heightened by the artificiality of alliterative verse and an unorthodox terza rima. The sentences are broken, interrupted, creating a semblance of the thought patterns of the old; the vocabulary is common, occasionally earthy, such as a soldier might use. Diaz is presented as an honest man who was initially moved by indignation but soon was overcome by the melancholy distance between the heroic exploits of his youth and the dry reality of old age:

> Now time has taught us:
> Death has mastered us most: sorrow and pain
> Sickness and evil days are our lives' lot:
>
> Now even the time of our youth has been taken:
> Now are our deeds words: our lives chronicles:
> Afterwards none will think of the night rain . . .[13]

MacLeish was faced with a peculiar problem in choosing to base his work on another book easily available to his readers; he did not

[13] MacLeish, *Conquistador*, p. 14.

have the freedom from rivalry that Browning, for example, had with his Yellow Book for *The Ring and the Book*. And by allowing an elegiac mood to sweep over the narrative impulse, MacLeish put his reader into a muddle. We have a narrative that, fragmentary as it is, arouses interest, but then the poet asks the reader to forget that interest and to substitute for it a concern for the psychology of his dead hero. Legitimately one may ask whether it is worth reading nearly two thousand lines to emerge with an impression that an aging chronicler, thinking back sadly to his youthful adventure, might have many allusive, unconnected thoughts. Some of the lyrical moments are admittedly fascinating, but one can scarcely look at *Conquistador* as a collection of lyrics loosely held by a frame. MacLeish wrote me: "I don't think it is a great poem but I think it stands up with most comparable poems written in this Century."

In his note to the first edition, MacLeish spoke of "the strength of my attachment to the country of Mexico." Growing concern for the relationship between the United States and Europe, however, weakened that attachment, and although he made subsequent visits, speaking once at the Instituto Mexicano-Norteamericano, *Conquistador* remains his only creative work set in Mexico. He did publish one comment and two unsigned articles about Rivera's art. Like most tourists MacLeish sought out the artist's murals. He wrote in his notebook about the much admired frescoes at Chapingo (a comment published in 1948):

There is a new image of man in our time which many of us have dreamed but none seen . . . Rivera's new frescoes in the little chapel out across the lake bed . . . catch a refracted glimpse of it from the corner of the eye. It is true that Diego is a Communist. It is true also that no whole man can live on that dog biscuit. It is true finally that these frescoes betray the synthetic diet. But there is something else also. One says: What new dignity of man is this? Merely the noble savage repainted as the noble peasant or the noble pulque-drinker or the noble welder? Or something more? And one answers: Something more . . .[14]

In 1932–1933, while on the staff of *Fortune*, MacLeish prepared for the magazine two exhibits of Rivera's work in progress in New York and in Detroit. His textual comments reveal again his admiration for

---

[14] Archibald MacLeish, "Notebooks, 1924–1938," *Poetry* 73 (November 1948): 95.

the artist's vision and his uneasiness with his political affiliations.[15] He paid his final tribute when Rivera's fresco for Rockefeller Center, in which he had insisted on retaining a portrait of Lenin, was destroyed in 1933. MacLeish composed a series of poems entitled *Frescoes for Mr. Rockefeller's City*. Actually they have nothing to do with Rivera's composition, but the occasion provided MacLeish the inspiration for making another examination of his own country; he concluded that the United States was a strong land beyond the understanding of either the capitalists or the communists.[16] MacLeish wrote me: "As for Rivera, I never met him; I only know that he held a low opinion of me as a politician because of my views about Communism." And there MacLeish's Mexican chapter essentially ends.

Hart Crane (1899–1932) contributed to the legend of Mexico not so much by his life and work there—though that life seems to have been well known—as by his death.[17] He jumped from the ship returning him from Mexico, and the shock of his suicide threw a different perspective on the country he had left. Conrad Aiken thought of Mexico as the land where Crane had gone to die. And Malcolm Lowry wrote that Mexico was both "this pyre of Bierce and springboard of Hart Crane."[18] There seems to be no reason to believe that Mexico killed Crane; his dissipation had started long before, and threats of suicide had been almost habitual with him. But the country had already been tagged as a place of death, so Crane's first biographer wrote in 1937: "Mexico offered no reassurance to a person in need of spiritual and mental stability; and it cannot be doubted that Crane, with acute sensitivity to the most trivial influence, was further unhinged by the pervasive qualities of its profoundly mysterious and hos-

[15] Archibald MacLeish, "In Our Time: The Industrial Civilization of New York Seen in the Cross Section of a Rivera Fresco," *Fortune* 5 (February 1932): 40–41; idem, "Industrial Detroit by Diego Rivera," *Fortune* 7 (February 1933): 48–53. Arthur Mizener prepared a bibliography in which he identified these items.

[16] See Signi Falk, *Archibald MacLeish*, pp. 64–68.

[17] Hart Crane, *The Letters of Hart Crane, 1916–1932*, pp. 367–412; Philip Horton, *Hart Crane*, pp. 279–302; John Unterecker, *Voyager*, pp. 648–759; Hans Zinsser, *As I Remember Him*, pp. 334–339; Peggy Baird, "The Last Days of Hart Crane," *Venture* 4 (1961): 21–46; Spratling, *File*, pp. 98–102.

[18] Conrad Aiken, *The Collected Novels of Conrad Aiken*, pp. 436, 451. Also Malcolm Lowry, *Selected Poems of Malcolm Lowry*, p. 24; idem, *Selected Letters of Malcolm Lowry*, p. 67.

tile strangeness."[19] The truth cannot now be determined. Crane's letters, a vivid and frank account of his life there, only prove that he vacillated in his attitude. The important thing is the myth. It should be tempered, however, with the reminder that Crane did complete the first poem he had finished in two years while there—"The Broken Tower"—and experienced apparently his only heterosexual love affair.

In 1929, Crane had finished *The Bridge* and was left without any new purpose. Thus when he was awarded in March 1931 a Guggenheim fellowship, which stipulated that he live abroad, he did not know where to go. Several factors conspired to turn him to Mexico. Waldo Frank had just returned from his tour of Latin America; Malcolm Cowley had spent some time in Mexico recently; Katherine Anne Porter offered Crane the use of her home in Mixcoac. In preparation for the early portions of *The Bridge,* he had read William Carlos Williams's *In the American Grain,* with its chapter on the Conquest, and Prescott's history. At the time Crane had idly thought that the Conquest would make a fitting subject for an epic poem or drama. He had ordered *The Plumed Serpent* because of his "interest in Maya and Toltec archaeology." And now he was excited by MacLeish's work on *Conquistador,* which (according to MacLeish's letter) the two talked over. In April, Crane sailed for Veracruz.

On the boat he became friends with Dr. Hans Zinsser, a bacteriologist on his way to Mexico City to study typhus outbreaks. In the harbor at Havana, Crane became drunk and propelled the doctor into an embarrassing situation. Zinsser had thrown overboard some dying rats with which he had been experimenting; the water revived them and they made an effort to swim ashore. In his delirium Crane, who had come up to the deck unexpectedly, was convinced that Zinsser was trying to give the city typhus and began shouting his conviction aloud. Luckily the first officer assumed that Crane was making the whole thing up. The two men's friendship did not suffer; they remained together in Veracruz and for a while in Mexico City until the doctor departed. Zinsser tried to give Crane advice and to watch after him as well as he could. Crane recorded this friendship in "Havana Rose," a prose lyric written in phrases almost senseless to the reader who does not know the story behind it. It concludes with the doctor's

[19] Horton, *Hart Crane,* p. 282.

warning: "You cannot heed the negative, so might go on to undeserved doom . . ."[20] The line served as an omen for the year ahead.

Overwhelmed by the spectacular climb from Veracruz to the capital and delighted by the strangeness of the country, unlike anything he had known in Europe, Crane fell in love with Mexico. He told Miss Porter that he wished he had gone to Mexico first rather than to France: "Here I feel that life is real, people really live and die here."[21] Crane had lost control by now. Miss Porter recalled that during the day he would seem his old self as he helped her in the gardens or explored the city's markets, but that by midnight he was generally drunk and either in jail or in some brawl with a taxi driver. She remembered one occasion on which he began to curse the entire universe item by item: "But those were not the things he hated. He did not even hate us, for we were nothing to him. He hated and feared himself."[22] Finally she could not take his exploits any longer and begged him to find a place of his own. Unfortunately for her peace of mind, the house next door was vacant, and he rented it for a year, signing the lease with Eyler Simpson, a secretary for the Guggenheim Foundation and later author of a study of the *ejido*. The relationship, further complicated by Eugene Pressly, who Crane felt disliked him, moved from apology to apology, ending when neither Miss Porter nor Pressly came to a dinner he gave.

Crane's initial enthusiasm also was dampened in other ways. Through letters from Waldo Frank he met two Mexican poets, León Felipe Camino and Genaro Estrada, but neither received Crane warmly. On his part he rejected them as pallid imitators: ". . . not one of them is really interested one iota in expressing anything indigenous."[23] He was interviewed by the newspapers *Excelsior* and *El Universal*, but in general his reception was not what he had anticipated. Like many other visitors he was bewildered by the Mexican's habit of inviting guests to a dinner or a party that both host and guest were supposed to understand would never occur. As for the Indian, Crane wrote (in a letter to Frank): "I doubt if I will ever be able to fathom

---

[20] Hart Crane, *The Collected Poems of Hart Crane*, p. 153. Bibliographies have been compiled by Hershel Rowe and Kenneth Lohf.

[21] Hank López (interview with Katherine Anne Porter), "A Country and Some People I Love," *Harper's* 231 (September 1965): 67.

[22] Horton, *Hart Crane*, p. 287.

[23] Crane, *Letters*, p. 372.

the Indian really. It may be a dangerous quest, also. I'm pretty sure
it is, in fact. But humanity is so unmechanized here still, so immediate and really dignified . . . that it is giving me an entirely fresh perspective." This mood lay behind "The Sad Indian," a fragment that
contrasts the free vision of the Indian with his bound person, perhaps
symbolically enslaved by an airplane in the sky (technology), which is
no new eagle.[24] Crane does not really enter the Indian's nature except
in the most superficial manner; nor would he through later, more intimate contacts.

Incapable of making friends with either race, knowing few Americans and quarreling with them, he expressed his feelings in another
fragment, "Purgatorio":

> My country, O my land, my friends—
> Am I apart—here from you in a land
> Where all your gas lights—faces—sputum gleam
> Like something left, forsaken—here am I—
> And are these stars—the high plateau—the scents
> Of Eden—and the dangerous tree—are these
> The landscape of confession—and if confession
> So absolution? . . .[25]

On the proposed drama or epic (Crane kept referring to it both
ways, suggesting how little he had considered the matter) he did no
work. He felt so guilty about his laxity that, when he was called to the
States by his father's death, his first thought had been that the Guggenheim Foundation was bringing him back for discipline. Worse, he
was now unsure whether he retained any talent. He sailed back to
Mexico reluctantly in early September. Things were slightly easier
for him, however, since he had at least established a home. Peggy
Baird, who had come to Mexico to obtain a divorce from Cowley, also
welcomed him, and partly through her his circle of American friends
widened. Soon he knew Beals, Miss Brenner, Bynner, Pierre and Caroline Durieux, Marsden Hartley, the Lesley Simpsons, and Spratling,
among others. They provided him companionship and an excuse to
leave poetry alone.

He also met a young archaeologist exploring for Aztec artifacts

---

[24] Ibid., p. 371; idem, *Collected Poems*, p. 145.
[25] Crane, *Collected Poems*, p. 151; see Malcolm Lowry, *Dark as the Grave
Wherein My Friend Is Laid*, p. 63.

near his home. Through him the poet had his first encounter with primitive Mexico. They went on a five days' trip to Tepoztlán, arriving on the eve of the fiesta in honor of Tepozteco, the god of pulque. The two Americans were received with respect; and the next morning, to Crane's delight, he was invited to play the pre-Conquest drum the Indians had brought out. He lived like a native, feeding on tortillas and beans, bathing in the mountain streams with a young Indian. When he left, he was in ecstasy. The archaeologist came to live with him for a while. Perhaps under his influence Crane began reading more of Aztec mythology. An unfinished poem, "The Circumstance," is dedicated to Xochipilli, god of the sun and patron of youth, joy, poetry, and masculine fecundity. The fragment is too uneven to ascertain Crane's intentions. It seems to be a plea to escape time, but none of the god's elements, though they should have appealed to Crane, are clearly used as a means to live forever.[26]

In October Crane visited Miss Baird in Taxco, where she had taken a home. There he met Siqueiros and sat for a portrait. Crane's eyes were so alarming that the artist finally painted them lidded, having Crane look downward at a book.[27] When Siqueiros became ill with malaria in November and needed to return to Mexico City for attention, Crane invited him to stay in his home, generously asking many of the artist's communist friends to come also. The melée often bothered him so much that he had to escape to Tepoztlán or Taxco, but a full house seemed better than an empty one. Thus when Siqueiros recovered, Crane urged the others to stay. All this time Crane continued to write letter after letter explaining why he had not written anything creative. Mexico, in spite of its excitement, was becoming a dead end.

Then in December, appropriately at the Christmas season, his life turned again. He went to Miss Baird's for a party and either fell or willed himself into love. Under the stimulus of this new experience he excitedly began work on the last poem he finished, "The Broken Tower." There are two stories concerning its inception. Miss Baird said that Crane wrote the first three stanzas after hearing the festive bells ring out on the first night they had spent together. Lesley Simpson remembered his beginning the poem on January 27. He stated

---

[26] Crane, *Collected Poems*, pp. 146–147.

[27] The painting is reproduced as the frontispiece to *Collected Poems*. See Tennessee Williams, *Night of the Iguana*, p. 54; Selden Rodman, *Mexican Journal*, p. 99.

that the poet, troubled by insomnia, arose before daybreak and walked down to the main plaza. An Indian fiesta was to be celebrated, and Crane met the bellringer, an old friend now, on the way to the church. He went along to help; as he swung the clapper the tropical dawn came swiftly up; music and light flowed through him. Whatever the origin, both agree that he began composing in almost a frenzy of inspiration. For two months he worked over the poem and finally finished it in late March.

"The Broken Tower" ultimately has nothing to do with the Mexican landscape; it is rather a record of Crane's newly discovered and fragile happiness there:

> And so it was I entered the broken world
> To trace the visionary company of love, its voice
> An instance in the wind (I know not whither hurled)
> But not for long to hold each desperate choice.

The tower, broken by the music of the bells, is a symbol for the poet. The way of poetry is not easy and opens questions that cannot logically be resolved: the music of the poetry may even destroy him. Nevertheless, by acceptance of his power and divine inspiration, the poet builds anew a spiritual tower revealed in love. Crane's choice of words enriches the poem far beyond this, however; after using a relatively simple style for most poems written since *The Bridge*, he had returned to his earlier dense style, following "the logic of metaphor." He built into "The Broken Tower" a polarity between heaven and hell, movement up and down, the loud uproar of the beginning and the quiet serenity of the ending, in which the poem comes to rest in assurance in spite of these tensions.[28]

The final version was sent to *Poetry* but was lost in the mail. Crane mistakenly assumed that the resulting silence meant that his powers had failed and that his friends hesitated to tell him. Other problems were mounting. The relationship with Miss Baird was complex. Money was still an unsolved worry. At home his male servant—and drinking companion—had become completely insubordinate. Nor had Crane left his volcanic periods when he would rage in a drunken delirium against his friends. Miss Baird had come to live with him in Mixcoac but could do nothing to allay his turbulence. Early in April,

---

[28] Crane, *Collected Poems*, pp. 135–136. Williams used this stanza as an epigraph for *Streetcar Named Desire*.

in desperation, she invited Mary Doherty and Louise Howard over, hoping that they could take his mind off his troubles. When they arrived he was drunk, worse than she had ever seen him. The three women retired to a far room; Crane followed with Siqueiros's portrait. He verbally abused the artist, then suddenly slashed the painting with a razor. He dictated his will to Miss Doherty, swallowed iodine, and was finally quieted by a doctor. The next day, the attempt was blamed on tequila, but it served as a preview.

It seemed wise to return to the States; Crane and Miss Baird booked passage on the *Orizaba*, the same ship that had first brought him to Mexico. The last days were hectic, but by the time of departure he was again calm and was making plans for his and Miss Baird's life together. A letter from *Contempo* accepting an earlier poem perhaps reassured him; he thanked the editor and asked if he could review *Conquistador*. All seemed well until Havana. There Crane began drinking heavily and so exhausted Miss Baird that she gave permission for him to be locked in his cabin. He broke out and turned to the sailors' quarters, where he was robbed and perhaps beaten for attempted solicitations. The next morning, April 27, he returned to Miss Baird's cabin, bade her goodbye, went up on deck, and jumped. The body was not recovered.

In the winter and spring of 1933 Aldous Huxley (1894–1963) and his wife cruised through the Caribbean, stopped at Belize, explored Guatemala, and then entered Mexico through Puerto Angel, Oaxaca, to spend several weeks traveling through the southern and central parts of the country before departing from one of the Gulf ports. The journey provided the outline for a travelogue, *Beyond the Mexique Bay*, 1934, the last third of which records their experience in Mexico.[29] They rode on mules over the isolated trails of the Sierra Madre in company with Roy Fenton, the owner of a coffee plantation. Making the town of Oaxaca their temporary base, they explored the ruins of Mitla and Monte Albán, which especially intrigued Huxley, and spent a day in Etla to see the baiting of the bulls. Then they went on to Puebla, his favorite city because of its exquisite colonial architec-

[29] Aldous Huxley, *Beyond the Mexique Bay*, pp. 189–257; idem, *The Letters of Aldous Huxley*, pp. 367–370. Also John Atkins, *Aldous Huxley*, pp. 129–148. Claire J. Eschelbach and Joyce Lee Shobes prepared a bibliography. The short story "Little Mexican," 1924, concerns a sombrero in Italy and has nothing else to do with Mexico.

ture, and Mexico City, arriving in the capital in time for the Easter celebrations. He met "many men of letters" and inspected the murals. Concerning the murals he echoed the criticism of Lawrence ten years earlier:

Diego Rivera's frescoes in the *patio* of the Ministry of Education are chiefly remarkable for their quantity; there must be five or six acres of them. For quality one must go to the Preparatoria and look at Orozco's paintings. These have a queer merit, even when they are most horrible— and some of them are about as horrible as anything could well be. Their unsuitability as decorations in a school for adolescent boys and girls is almost absolute. But they are real pictures, by a man who knows how to paint. The formal inventions are often extraordinarily felicitous; the colour subtle; the modelling, for all the ferocious brutality of the subject, very sensitive and alive. They are pictures that remain, rather disquietingly, in the memory.[30]

The artists' colony at Taxco rather disgusted him. And of the country as a whole, he wrote in a letter: "Mexico was unpleasant, but very curious."

*Beyond the Mexique Bay*, however, is even more a travelogue of Huxley's mind. Each part of his journey inspired abstract speculation about such matters as the problem of language, the relationship of men in global economics, the nature of war, the threat of Nazism, and man's relationship with time. In Mexico two related subjects especially interested him: the nature of art and the nature of the primitive, including how a civilized man should react to primitivism. Concerning folk art, he held that much nonsense had been written by "the new William Morrises from the United States," who confused social and psychological values with aesthetic ones. Such values are enough to justify one's appreciation of folk art, but important art, he felt, is rare and generally found only in highly civilized societies. From this basis he attacked one of Stuart Chase's theses about Mexico (although he agreed that Chase's *Mexico* was the "most judicious" of the books about Mexico that had recently appeared). Both men wondered whether a culture could evolve that would combine the best of primitivism and civilization without the vices of either. Chase thought that Mexico could be introduced to many American comforts without changing the country's essential nature. Huxley held that American

[30] Huxley, *Beyond the Mexique Bay*, p. 252.

civilization must inevitably destroy the Mexican way of life. He also admitted that he could not really like the primitive. The problem became rather what segments of primitive life the civilized man should introduce into his society. Having just projected the horrors of *Brave New World*, Huxley felt that civilized man needed most to take over the primitive's "human wholeness" as a protection against the disasters of specialization.

Besides Chase, Huxley discussed the work of Thomas Gage, Humboldt, Stephens, Prescott, H. H. Bancroft, and Alfred Maudslay. But the writer who most impressed him and perhaps prompted his visit to Mexico was his late friend Lawrence. Huxley had already used Lawrence's descriptions of New Mexico for *Brave New World* and the same year had edited Lawrence's letters; for an even longer period he had thought that he had found in Lawrence's philosophy the wholeness he sought. In *Point Counter Point* the character modeled on Lawrence stands out as the only full human among all society's sterile and one-sided figures. But Lawrence's doctrine of blood consciousness was becoming unsatisfactory. In *Beyond the Mexique Bay*, Huxley made his first criticism of his mentor's beliefs. He noted that Lawrence could not turn to the primitive without occasionally refreshing himself through contacts with civilization; and he found the same failure when he reread *The Plumed Serpent*, a critique of which ends the travelogue. In Huxley's next novel, *Eyeless in Gaza*, 1936, through his persona he made a farewell to Lawrence's type of mysticism, rejecting specifically the animality of *The Man Who Died*: Lawrence "had insisted that the raw material should be worked up—but worked only to a certain pitch and no further; that the primal crawling energy should be used for the relatively higher purposes of animal existence, but for no existence beyond the animal. Arbitrarily, illogically. For the other ulterior purposes and organizations existed and were not to be ignored. Moving through space and time, the human animal discovered them on his path, unequivocally present and real."[31]

*Eyeless in Gaza* became a record of Huxley's move toward another mysticism. The novel was begun before he went to Mexico and finished two years after his return. Technically it juxtaposes sharply different moments in the life of its protagonist, Anthony Beavis. With

---

[31] Aldous Huxley, *Eyeless in Gaza*, p. 273.

the fluidity of a movie camera, it reviews significant events from Beavis's present, 1933–1934; his past, 1902–1931; and what might be called his future, 1934–1935. Altogether the different sections show Beavis developing chronologically from a self-centered, undirected young man to an active pacifist. The change takes place because of a chance meeting with a Scotch doctor in Mexico, undoubtedly modeled after Huxley's friend Gerald Heard but drawn too on "a most charming and saint-like Scotsman called Dr. MacPhail," whom he met at the United Fruit Company hospital in Quiriguá.

Beavis becomes so repelled by his life that, when a friend suggests he should accompany him to a coffee plantation in southern Mexico, he accepts. In December 1933 they land at the same port where the Huxleys had landed in March, though it now has a different name, and they wind up the same trails in the Sierra and experience the same problems. But Huxley's imagination also shapes the action. Beavis's friend injures his leg and gangrene sets in. Beavis rides off to find help and meets, as if by a miracle, James Miller, a doctor who ministers to the Indians. After amputating the leg, Miller discusses with them his doctrine that to treat men with love will bring peace even to a world caught in the coils of fascism. Beavis and Miller return to Great Britain to try to persuade their countrymen to follow their teachings.[32] All the projections into 1934–1935 are pages from a journal in which Beavis works out his new philosophy. Even though his turning point thus occurs in Mexico, it is doubtful that Huxley's visit was that significant for him. He simply needed to take Beavis on a pilgrimage away from the emptiness of Europe so that he could commit himself to a new life, and Mexico was handy because of the Huxleys' recent visit. However, Huxley must have felt it appropriate that his answer to the fascism of *The Plumed Serpent* should come from the same country.

In a curious way MacLeish searched for the past, Crane for the present, and Huxley for the future. To some degree each failed in his quest: Crane committed suicide; MacLeish's poem and Huxley's novel are largely ignored. Ironically, Crane's failure created a legend. And it was Huxley's look to the past that was successful: many subsequent writers have quoted with approval his comments on Mitla and Monte Albán.

[32] Mexican sections of *Eyeless in Gaza* are found pp. 312–313, 374–379, 400–409, 418–430, 433–444.

# 9. The Volcano and the Barranca

In 1947, ten years after the novel was first drafted, *Under the Volcano* was finally published. By Malcolm Lowry (1909–1957), it tells us more about Mexico than has any novel in English since Lawrence's. Moreover, a myth as great as those that surround Bierce, Lawrence, and Crane has sprung up about Lowry, concentrating particularly on stories of his ability to drink and rumors of the bizarre circumstances of his death. Buttressed by this sense of the author's personality, inescapable since his fiction is based with Wolfe-like directness upon his life, Lowry's work now greatly influences our vision of Mexico. Lawrence Ferlinghetti, for one, wandered through Mexico with fragments of the novel echoing in his mind.[1]

The British author arrived in Mexico by a roundabout route.[2] In

[1] Lawrence Ferlinghetti, *The Mexican Night*, pp. 1, 6, 13. See Jack Kerouac, *Desolation Angels*, p. 242.

[2] Malcolm Lowry, *Selected Letters of Malcolm Lowry*, pp. 11–15 [misdated a year], 26–27, 29, 91–112, 115; Dale H. Edmonds, "Malcolm Lowry," Ph.D. dissertation, University of Texas, 1965; "Malcolm Lowry," *Times Literary Supplement*, January 26, 1967, pp. 57–59; Conrad Aiken, "Malcolm Lowry," *Times Literary Supplement*, February 16, 1967, p. 127, and idem, *Ushant*, pp. 340–360; Robert H. Wilbur, interview with Conrad Aiken, *Paris Review* 42 (Winter–

1933 he had married Jan Gabrial, an American woman whom he and Conrad Aiken knew in Spain. The marriage turned out to be an unfortunate match; they soon separated, Mrs. Lowry returning to Los Angeles. Lowry followed in 1936. With the hope that a completely new setting for both would help, they sailed for Acapulco, landing (according to most of Lowry's statements) on November 2. From there they went to Cuernavaca and took a home on Calle de Humboldt, a long street below Cortés's palace that parallels the town's most awesome barranca. The change of scenery did not help, however, and often the deep crevice seemed symbolic of the depths into which Lowry had fallen as he embarked on one heavy bout of drinking after another. Nevertheless, he had also experienced the incident that formed the nucleus of his novel and thus shaped the rest of his life. Late in the year he, his wife, and two American friends took a bus for Chapultepec, a park on the outskirts of Cuernavaca. He has described the event in another Mexican novel, *Dark as the Grave Wherein My Friend Is Laid*:

About halfway there we stopped beside an Indian who seemed to be dying by the roadside. We all wanted to help but were prevented from doing so . . . because we were told it was against the law. All that happened was that in the end we left him where he was, and, meanwhile, a drunk on the bus had stolen his money out of his hat, which was lying beside him on the road. He paid his fare with it, the stolen money, and we went on to the bullthrowing. . . . The whole story grew out of that incident. I began it as a short story. It then occurred to me . . . that nobody had written an adequate book upon drinking, upon which I was now, to say the least, a considerable authority, and so while the first short version of the book was getting turned down by publisher after publisher, I began to elaborate upon that theme of drunkenness, both in my life, and in the book too . . .[3]

By the end of June he had finished the first draft. Both Aiken, who visited him that spring and summer, and Arthur Calder-Marshall read it with enthusiasm.

---

Spring 1968): 99, 109–110; Stephen Spender, introduction to Malcolm Lowry, *Under the Volcano*, pp. vii–xxvi; Douglas Day, introduction to Malcolm Lowry, *Dark as the Grave Wherein My Friend Is Laid*, pp. ix–xxiii (the latter novel is filled with biographical details), and idem, *Malcolm Lowry*, pp. 214–248, 310–317, 350–365.

[3] Lowry, *Dark as the Grave*, pp. 150–151.

Meanwhile, the relationship between Lowry and his wife became even more strained. Aiken, in his fictionalized autobiography, *Ushant*, seemed to blame Mrs. Lowry heavily: he described one episode in which the wife announced that she was going to spend a week with two engineers at the silver mines somewhere to the north ("Hambo" is Aiken's name for Lowry; "the heels" refers to Mrs. Lowry):

> . . . it was, and publicly, too, a flat declaration that the heels were damned well going to be unfaithful. From the parting at the bus station, where they had all gone to see her off, they had done their best to avert their eyes. The stonily beautiful little profile avoided the anguished and hang-dog gaze of poor Hambo, she was already looking ahead, over those propitious mountains to the wealth of those silvermines, and the promise of gay nights, and, as always on such occasions, the lavish and expensive gifts which awaited her there. And with this enthralling prospect before her, how could she possibly pay the slightest heed to the little gift which Hambo had brought, the little gift of silver earrings? They were for her birthday—he murmured—handing them awkwardly and shyly through the *camión*'s window . . . She accepted them with a glance of repressed annoyance, thrust them almost angrily into her handbag—as if they were a sort of rebuke, and perhaps they were—and then the bus shot away . . .[4]

Lowry, suffering too from lumbago, went on a series of drunks while she was away, disappearing for days at a time. Finally in December she left him for good. "It was the lowest ebb," he wrote in *Dark as the Grave*.[5]

Besides his marital problems, the friendship with Aiken also caused Lowry trouble. According to *Ushant* there were momentary irritations occasioned by Aiken's inability to understand Lowry's move toward "something like communism" (an argument about Marxism in *Under the Volcano* was supposedly a verbatim report of one of theirs). But the problem lay deeper. Lowry seems to have known instinctively that his new novel would be an important work, but before it could be totally his, he had to destroy the spiritual father from whom he had learned his craft; his first novel, *Ultramarine*, had been almost an extended footnote for Aiken's own fictional techniques. (Even in *Volcano* Lowry borrowed Aiken's theme of William Blackstone, the "man who went to live among the Indians.") Long, stormy

---

[4] Aiken, *Ushant*, p. 349.
[5] Lowry, *Dark as the Grave*, p. 77; see pp. 88–89.

sessions took place between the two men, some indication of which Aiken has given in *Ushant*. Their association continued, but the relationship had definitely cooled.

After his wife left, Lowry went to Oaxaca, where they had been sometime earlier. He traveled with a communist, but in this conservative town, it was Lowry's beard and his drinking that were singled out by the police, and he was the one to land repeatedly in jail. A few letters from this period indicate his intense despair. He realized that he was on the edge of insanity and that some of his fears must be imaginary; nevertheless, he was convinced that the police were working for a local fascist government and that they were deliberately persecuting him. This issue promptly became one of his novel's main themes. Also, he met Juan Fernando Márquez, a Zapotec Indian who worked as a carrier for the Banco Nacional de Crédito Ejidal, set up for poor farmers. Both in an essay written for the *United Nations World*, 1950, and in *Dark as the Grave*, Lowry recalled rides the two had made across the state delivering money. This friendship was to have an important influence on later drafts of *Volcano*, since Márquez became the model for both Juan Cerillo and Dr. Vigil. Probably through Márquez's influence, Lowry began to work out of the psychological problems into which he had fallen. In July 1938 he left Mexico via Nogales, to move finally to Canada with his second wife, Margerie Bonner, whom he had married in 1940, and to continue working on the novel.

The original short story out of which the novel grew was published in 1963 in *Prairie Schooner*. As he said, practically all the seeds of the final version of *Under the Volcano* are there. The story tells about a British consul who is going with his daughter, Yvonne, and her fiancé, Hugh, to a fiesta at Chapultepec. The consul is an alcoholic who has forced himself to go without drink this day for their sake. Thus he looks on with envy when the drunken *pelado* (shameless grafter) climbs on the bus. Woven into the simple plot are Popocatépetl, the barranca, an advertisement for *Las Manos de Orlac*, the *zopilotes* floating high in the air, a horse with a seven branded on its rump, and a sequence in which a lame Indian carries an old cripple on his back.[6] Only mention of the Day of the Dead is missing. As Lowry expanded

---

[6] Malcolm Lowry, "Under the Volcano," *Prairie Schooner* 37 (Winter 1963–1964): 284–300.

his story twelve times over, he would discover aggregating symbolic values in all these elements.

The story was taken almost intact into *Under the Volcano* as Chapter VIII, but the relationships among his characters have subtly altered. Yvonne (a composite portrait now of Lowry's two wives) becomes the consul's wife; Hugh is his half-brother and potential rival for her affections. Yvonne is a movie star who has failed to make a comeback; she had married the consul and then left him over a year before the story begins, partly because of her affair with Jacques Laruelle, a French movie director and an old friend of the consul. Yvonne returns early on the morning of November 2, 1938, the Day of the Dead, as we are constantly reminded. She hopes that they can begin their marriage over and holds out a vision of life together in a northern paradise (modeled on the Lowrys' Canadian home). The consul has long recognized the truth of the rather trite motto someone has emblazoned on Laruelle's house, "No se puede vivir sin amar," but it is too late for him. When he tries to make love to Yvonne, he is too drunk. Having to choose between Guanajuato, which comes curiously to stand for life, and Tomalín, a symbol for death because it involves Parián, he chooses Tomalín.

Yvonne, the consul, and Hugh go to Tomalín to see the bullthrowing. The consul becomes increasingly drunk and wanders to a cantina near Parián, although he knows that a fascist organization, which will threaten him merely because he is a gringo without considering other possible activities in which he may be engaged, has its headquarters there. While releasing the dead Indian's horse—marked by the mystic seven—which the vigilantes have tied nearby, he is shot and falls into the barranca. His end is ambivalent; the last words he hears are "compañero" and "pelado." Ironically, the horse careens down the very path that Hugh and Yvonne are taking in search of the consul. Giving in to his mad spirit, they have become drunk. She slips and the horse kills her. In her dying vision she is lifted up to the Pleiades, but she also sees the northern home going up in flames (as the Lowrys' Canadian home did in 1944).

The allusions and symbols that cluster around this plot lift it out of being merely a drunken domestic tragedy into a cathartic fall of Everyman. References are made to Atlantis, Dante's *Inferno* (the dark wood appears in multiple guises, including the translation of the old name for Cuernavaca, *Quauhnahuac*, "near the wood"), the cabala, the legend of Faust, Sophocles's *Oedipus*, and especially the story of

Adam's fall. The consul in one of his deliriums sees in his garden, which he has allowed to turn to weeds, a sign that he misreads thus:

¿LE GUSTA ESTE JARDIN?
¿QUE ES SUYO?
¡EVITE QUE SUS HIJOS LO DESTRUYAN!

He translates it: "You like this garden? Why is it yours? We evict those who destroy." (As Lowry realized on a return trip to Mexico, the actual sign reads more like "Do you like this garden which is yours? See to it . . . that your children don't destroy it.")[7] The theme recurs, and the last words in the book are these. Lowry himself set forth the best explanation of the multiple levels of the work in a long letter to a British publisher:

The scene is Mexico, the meeting place, according to some, of mankind itself, pyre of Bierce and springboard of Hart Crane, the age-old arena of racial and political conflicts of every nature, and where a colorful native people of genius have a religion that we can roughly describe as one of death, so that it is a good place . . . to set our drama of a man's struggle between the powers of darkness and light. Its geographical remoteness from us, as well as the closeness of its problems to our own, will assist the tragedy each in its own way. We can see it as the world itself, or the Garden of Eden, or both at once. Or we can see it as a kind of timeless symbol of the world on which we can place the Garden of Eden, the Tower of Babel and indeed anything else we please. It is paradisal; it is unquestionably infernal. It is, in fact, Mexico, the place of the pulque and chinches.[8]

Though moving thus on many levels, Lowry never lost sight of the concrete Mexico that he humorously suggests in the last sentence. His town is a composite portrait of Cuernavaca and Oaxaca, but enough glimpses of Cuernavaca occur to leave a visitor to the city haunted by the consul's movements.[9] There is no glimpse of the tourist's Mexico. Lowry says little about the muralists, although he does call Orozco an "indisputable genius" and uses Rivera's murals at Cortés's palace as a stimulus for one of his protagonist's hallucinations. Dominant features of the landscape are used only as they reflect the characters' sense of place and never as pretty pictures in themselves. Generally

[7] Lowry, *Dark as the Grave*, pp. 140–141.
[8] Lowry, *Selected Letters*, p. 67.
[9] See Muriel Reger, "Lowry's Quauhnahuac Today," *Vistas*, May 31, 1970, pp. 2–4.

he writes about the cantinas, the isolated trails, the fiestas, the often exasperating children, the more remote adults. And from these elements the novel provides an intense feeling for Mexico matched only by the best writers, never distorted even though his protagonist's drunkenness sometimes interferes with a clear vision of the plot.

Lowry utilized fully the political chaos of the time. In 1934 Calles had chosen his fourth candidate for the presidency: Lázaro Cárdenas. This obscure politician was expected to follow the directions of the *jefe máximo* as his predecessors had, but Calles had not reckoned upon Cárdenas's memory of life in a poverty-stricken village. The new president determined to be a leader for the people, and during both his campaign and his term of office he carried the government throughout Mexico, restoring meaning to the revolutionary slogans that had merely been mouthed for so long. Not until 1936 was he able to consolidate his powers as president and finally to deport Calles, although he had already closed the casinos in Cuernavaca and elsewhere by which the *callistas* had been fleecing the middle class. After this dramatic elimination of his political rival, Cárdenas rid himself of most of his opponents on the right and turned fully to making the Six-Year Plan, which had been drafted by the party when he took office, into a reality.

The president took the government into industrial ownership. He opened a sugar refinery near Cuernavaca to help the suffering economy there. He nationalized the railroads, which had become a disgrace. In his most dramatic move of all, on March 18, 1938, he struck at the arrogant oil companies, which had so long caused trouble in Mexico, by expropriating all their properties. The country was jubilant; Mexico had shown its power against foreign exploiters. Even the new archbishop, in an unprecedented move, urged all Catholics to support the government. The British ambassador reacted so angrily that Mexico broke diplomatic relationships with Great Britain for over three years. The United States responded less stridently. The American ambassador, Josepheus Daniels, was completely sympathetic with Cárdenas's aims, and President Roosevelt, facing the threat of a European war, wanted to consolidate hemispheric unity. The new Mexican oil company suffered a boycott, but the expropriation contributed immeasurably to the country's national pride.

Consequently, for a tragedy of such proportions as Lowry wanted, 1938 seemed a better year than 1936 in which to set his story. The consul is jobless and without protection because of the oil quarrel. Moreover, it is a country politically quite confused. The official program was obviously socialistic, some critics would say even communistic. During the Spanish Civil War, Mexico alone of all the governments in the Western Hemisphere supported the Loyalists, inviting refugees from the conflict to settle in Mexico. Yet Cárdenas had opposed Stalin and at Rivera's urging had granted Leon Trotsky political asylum in 1937. Then, too, during the oil boycott he was forced to turn to Germany, Italy, and Japan for trade agreements. But fascist groups agitated with increasing vociferation against his government. Catholics had generally supported Franco; the fanaticism that had led to the *cristero* movement in the twenties now burst out anew with the *sinarquistas*, whose goals, according to Anita Brenner, were to defend "religion, property, and the fatherland against bolshevism."[10] This friction between the official government program and the frantic efforts of the *sinarquistas* to create a fascist state became quite important to *Volcano*.

For example, most likely the dying Indian is a carrier for the Banco Ejidal and is murdered by the vigilantes of the fascist Unión Militar while the regular police are on strike. The *pelado*'s hands have become literally stained with the Indian's blood, and the Revolution seems to have left the people still enslaved in various ways: "Tierra, Libertad, Justicia y Ley. Did they mean anything? Quién sabe?"[11] Hugh telegrams a report to his London newspaper about the anti-Semitic propaganda being backed by the German legation: because the Nazis were interested in gaining a foothold in this hemisphere, German money flowed freely to all fascist groups in Mexico. Hugh's sympathies are communistic; the consul's position is less certain. Each time a question of politics comes up, he becomes guarded, but it is strongly suggested that he agrees with Hugh. He knows a great deal about the activities of the Unión Militar, and there is a distinct possibility that he is even some kind of spy. Certainly a number of mysterious persons—it is not clear whether they are protective or threatening—follow him about as if they are in some kind of communication with him.

Mexico's problems at this time reflect those of the entire world; the Spanish Loyalists are losing the battle of the Ebro; the Germans are

[10] Anita Brenner, *The Wind That Swept Mexico*, p. 101.
[11] Lowry, *Under the Volcano*, p. 249.

about to begin their march, as symbolized by the advertisement for *Las Manos de Orlac* (a movie about a German artist, who, having lost his hands in an accident, has those of a murderer grafted on); and the Pope is dying. Graham Greene and Evelyn Waugh, though deliberately writing about the 1938 political situation, do not present these conflicting attitudes so well as Lowry does incidentally.

The tragedy is not momentary either, as Lowry sees it. Mexico's past reveals how the record of man can be seen as a long series of betrayals and greedy invasions. Cortés conquered only with the help of his Indian mistress and the Tlaxcalans. After Spain had been thrust off, the United States exploited the country and then France through Maximilian and Carlotta (whose summer home was in Cuernavaca). And the *pelados*, including such figures as Huerta, whose statue Lowry imaginatively places in Quauhnahuac, were always there. The failures of the Revolution belong to the past, the present, and the future. The tiny scene in which an old lame Indian carries an "older and more decrepit" Indian on his back, "trembling in every limb under this weight of the past," Lowry wrote in his letter, "is a restatement and universalizing of the theme of humanity struggling on under the eternal tragic weight."[12] In preparation for the novel he obviously had read much, although only Prescott is mentioned openly, and Lawrence, whose works he knew thoroughly, did not apparently influence *Under the Volcano* at all.

The novel reveals its depths, both its intensely tragic vision and its equally powerful sense of comedy, only after several readings. By means of counterpoint conversations and the visionary quality of the consul's delirium tremens and fragmented memory, Lowry realistically wove all his motifs into the work. Barest hints are picked up and expanded later; related images reinforce each other. Stephen Spender noted in his introduction to a new edition that structurally the novel resembles a movie; he felt that Lowry was indebted heavily to Eisenstein. A film version has been scheduled several times, but it never seems to go into production.

Many of Lowry's Mexican poems, some fourteen of which were included in *Selected Poems*, 1962, come from this same period, and similar themes and images recur in them. Apparently one was even to have been incorporated into the text of the novel. The autobio-

---

12 Ibid., p. 280; idem, *Selected Letters*, p. 81.

graphical nature of "In the Oaxaca Jail" is clear; "Delirium in Vera Cruz," a poem about a lonely man who smashes all the glass in his hotel room, has a similar ring of reality. The need for love reappears, being explicitly raised in the sonnet "In a Mexican Church" to the religious plane suggested throughout *Volcano*. Inebriation is likewise constant.

Lowry's manipulation of some of the most complex forms in prosody complements his more remarkable accomplishments in fiction. His most ambitious poem is "Sestina in a Cantina." In a "waterfront tavern in Vera Cruz at daybreak" various personages speak figuratively of the horrors of life in this confused world in which dawn and sunset become alike:

> Such horrid beauty maddened all my mirrors,
> Has burst in heart's eye sanity of dawning,
> No chamber in my house brimful of horrors
> But does not whisper of some dreadful prison,
> Worse than all ships dithering through the ocean
> Tottering like drunkards, arms upraised at sunset.

The deliriums of the tavern's patrons merely reflect the tragedy without. The main speaker concludes:

> I see myself as all mankind in prison,
> With hands outstretched to lanterns by the ocean;
> I see myself as all mankind in mirrors,
> Babbling of love while at his back rise horrors
> Ready to suck the blood out of the sunset
> And amputate the godhead of the dawning.

The self-conscious mirrors will remain even when the horrors are gone.[13] But as always in Lowry's work self-knowledge itself is admirable. This explains why he saw even the consul as a noble and tragic figure.

While freeing himself of the influence of Conrad Aiken (1889–1973), Lowry was in turn influencing that man's work.[14] In Aiken's *Ushant*, "Hambo of Spain, of the bullfight, of Saltinge, of London, of

---

[13] Malcolm Lowry, *Selected Poems of Malcolm Lowry*, pp. 22–44, 78. Earle Birney and Margerie Lowry prepared a series of bibliographies. Two poems have not been collected.

[14] Aiken, *Ushant*, pp. 30, 39, 291, 296–297, 340–360; idem, *The Collected Novels of Conrad Aiken*, pp. 455–472.

Boston, and of Mexico" reviews Aiken's twenty-year friendship with
Lowry. The answer to the question, "How about Mexico?" provided
Aiken the last and strongest of the several muted climaxes of the fictionalized autobiography. Aiken's journey to Mexico in 1937 also
gave him the outline for an autobiographical novel, *A Heart for the
Gods of Mexico*, 1939. Both works together, although we must use
them warily, present a fairly detailed account of his trip and his state
of mind. It was not a pleasant experience; Aiken sums up about the
protagonist of his novel, "the truth was that he hated everything,
everything was wrong."[15]

In late spring of 1937 Aiken wanted to divorce his second wife and
wed Mary Augusta Hoover. Mexican jurisdiction seemed expedient
for both divorce and marriage; the couple could spend the necessary
time at Lowry's home in Cuernavaca. So they and the painter Edward
Burra boarded the train for the long, tiring journey "through unknown America to unknown Mexico City." The train moved slowly
across the midwestern states, down the Mississippi valley, and
through Texas. Finally at Nuevo Laredo, after dark, they crossed the
border and had their first encounter with Mexico:

Mexico! And then the sudden squalling and chattering rush of Indians
into the dirty car, the slamming of bags and boxes, the overturning of
chair backs, the human uprush as of a dark current from the underworld,
inimical, violent, and hot . . . Derisive and demonical laughter, full of
fierce and abandoned hatred, the pride of pridelessness, the arrogance of
the self-condemned; and the often-turning reptile-lidded eyes, which
slowly and malevolently scrutinized the three strange Americans, the
*gringos*—with what a loving and velvety pansy-darkness of murderous-
ness they glowed at these natural victims![16]

Not only the people but even the landscape disconcerted Aiken: "One
thought of Mexico as a jungle; and if one thought of mountains, too,
one didn't think of them as anything very formidable." But now the
train climbed over a mile in altitude to Mexico City, passing "miles
and miles of sagebrush and mesquite, the straggling rows of broken
prickly pear beside the railway line, the Spanish bayonet, the iron
and copper-colored mountains saw-toothed against the cloudless and
burning sky." There was occasionally relief from the frightening

---

[15] Aiken, *Collected Novels*, p. 464.
[16] Ibid., pp. 455–456.

strangeness. In the novel Aiken gives us glimpses of an Indian girl fascinated by his timetable, a blonde Mexican girl successfully putting down a cowboy who attempted to pick her up, and a violinist from San Luis Potosí. But like other Americans he had discovered that, if this were a Spain, it was a "dark, nocturnal Spain."[17]

It must have given the three travelers a sense of grace when Lowry met them in Cuernavaca, as they got off the bus from Mexico City, and led them to his home. But now the divorce proceedings dragged out at frustrating length. Miss Hoover and Burra painted some; Aiken worked on his Faulkner article. They saw bullfights in Mexico City and explored Cuernavaca. But nothing seemed right to them, and "the delay, and in that so tragic little house, with its discomforts, too, and the dreadful stench from the little sewage canal which ran directly beneath their bedroom windows, all this ended by depressing them to such a pitch—and with the bad food which the Indian cook provided for them, on her feeble charcoal fire—that all three of them became ill." Burra became so sick that he had to return to Massachusetts.[18] Finally the divorce was granted in Jojutla, a small town near Cuernavaca; Aiken and Miss Hoover, with the Lowrys for witnesses, were married on July 7. The couple departed immediately for Boston: "And then, that page . . . was turned. But not to be forgotten, not forgotten."

Aiken had taken many notes that found their way into the novel and the autobiography. *Ushant*, 1952, is controlled; and although his use of fictitious names for all the people he discusses is disconcerting (they are identified in the 1962 edition), it is yet delightful to read. But even Aiken conceded that *A Heart for the Gods of Mexico* was a failure. He wrote in *Ushant*: ". . . could there ever have been an adventure so vivid, so unique, which had been put, by a would-be author, to so poor a purpose—?"[19] The novel was published separately only in Britain; it did not appear in the States until the *Collected Novels* of 1964. Throughout the novel Aiken demonstrated his ability to delineate individual scenes sensuously; it includes some of the most lyrical descriptions of Mexico ever written. But the work as a whole is completely unsatisfactory. A woman, Noni, finding that she

---

[17] Ibid., pp. 456, 461, 455.
[18] Aiken, *Ushant*, p. 350.
[19] Ibid., pp. 357, 340.

is dying, decides to gain a Mexican divorce from her husband (whom she has not seen in ten years) in order to marry Gil before her death. She does not, however, want Gil to realize her condition and persuades a friend, Blomberg, to accompany them without telling him the truth. They take the long train ride from Massachusetts to Mexico. There they join Gil's friend, Hambo; and there, her mission unfinished, Noni suddenly and quietly dies. Blomberg is the center of consciousness for the novel and seems clearly to be a persona for Aiken.

This plot is slight and rather fantastic, but that is not the reason for the novel's failure. It tries to be an examination of the North American continent; that is the novel's theme and in a sense its true plot. As the train carries the three characters along, they become less important than the countryside. To put it another way, the landscape becomes a variation on their plight. They move first through Eliot's Waste Land, where past and future blend into the present moment. But the train is also "on the great circle to Mexico"; and the echoes of Eliot are soon overpowered by the penetrating influence of Lawrence. The very title must have come from "The Woman Who Rode Away," in which the phrase "heart to the god of the Chilchui" occurs. In *Ushant* Aiken admitted that he had written "a pseudo-lyric descant on Mexico: with a dash of D. H. Lawrence's blood-madness, blood-worship, and blood-sickness, thrown in."[20] The novel demands that he build to a grand climax then in his final scene in Mexico.

But if Eliot could be integrated into the novel, Lawrence could not; it would seem that familiarity with his Mexican works completely prevented Aiken from ever seeing the country with his own eyes. Having noticed Lawrence's hatred of Mexico without apparently seeing also his deep involvement in its spirit, Aiken was prepared for evil. One passage sums up the frightening world he therefore found:

Over the red palace of Cortez, on the far side of the square, the clouds had become of an unbelievable purple—there could be no doubt that they meant business, and soon. Not that anybody minded. The hubbub went on just the same; Indian boys on shiny new bicycles rode round and round the square, bumping in and out of the dusty holes, and displaying a positive genius for falling off. A blind beggar, with white slits for eyes, and as evil a face as he ever had seen, was led into the cafe, and out

[20] Ibid., p. 344.

again, by a frightened little girl. A starved dog with a broken back, the hind quarters twisted, dragged itself crookedly to the little parapet of flowerpots by the entrance, and lay there, mutely begging. No attention was paid to it. The eyes, tender and trusting, beseeching, were enough to break one's heart; and when at last it gave up hope, and began to drag itself away, it heaved such a sigh of pure and beaten despair as ought rightly to have ended the world.[21]

The reality of Cuernavaca for Aiken lay totally in the consul's deep barranca (when Aiken playfully retitled the work in *Ushant*, he even called it "A Heart for the Barranca").

Now one must grant the author his right to use a scene as he pleases, but Aiken still did not bring off his climax; rather he ended by giving a series of understatements, including—as it is written— the most minor of all, Noni's death. We do not have even a "descant on Mexico"; the novel is fifty-five pages long in the collected edition, but only seventeen of them concern Mexico directly. Blomberg's final cry, "Christ, but I'm a long way from home," suggests Aiken's aesthetic failure. Most readers will probably come to the novel for its portrait of Lowry.

In 1945, while Lowry was waiting to hear from publishers, he felt the need to return to Mexico in order to verify certain aspects of his novel. Too, he wanted to search out Juan Fernando Márquez, with whom he had lost touch. In early December, Lowry and his wife landed at the Mexico airport. They stayed briefly in the capital, checking out those of his old haunts that had entered the consciousness of the consul. They then took the bus to Cuernavaca, where they found an apartment on Calle de Humboldt in the very house, at the foot of Calle de las Casas, that he had assigned imaginatively to Laruelle. Making a few acquaintances, most notably Eduardo Ford, who became the Eddie Kent of the new novel, and taking a few side excursions, including one to Taxco, where they thought of Crane's drunken madness, the Lowrys spent most of the month retracing Lowry's steps in Cuernavaca. On the last day of the year he finally heard from a British publisher; the book was worthy but needed extensive revision. In despair—he attempted suicide on January 10— Lowry sat down and composed a chapter by chapter analysis, a superb explanation of intentions from which any student of *Volcano*

[21] Aiken, *Collected Novels*, p. 465.

must yet start.[22] The day after the letter was finished, they departed for Oaxaca.

Staying at the Hotel Francia, they explored Oaxaca, including trips to Monte Albán and Mitla. Lowry spied an old acquaintance (called John Stanford in *Dark as the Grave*), of whom he had unpleasant memories; they spent some time sidestepping each other before the inevitable confrontation. Awed always by coincidence, Lowry was taken aback at seeing the sign that the consul finds in his desolate garden. Finally Lowry found the new offices of the Banco Ejidal. There he learned that Márquez had been murdered in Villahermosa in 1939. The news profoundly affected him. After his return to Canada he began converting, with few changes, this section of his trip into *Dark as the Grave Wherein My Friend Is Laid*. A published version was edited in 1968 out of the enormous mass of notes that he had made for it.

*Dark as the Grave* is less intense, more intimate in scale than *Volcano*. Consequently, it is less impressive but perhaps more enjoyable to read. Because of its autobiographical quality, however, the reader must first know *Volcano* rather thoroughly. Hundreds of allusions to that novel are scattered throughout this one, and one can discover still more about *Volcano*'s background and Lowry's intentions while writing it. *Dark as the Grave* chronicles the return of Sigbjørn Wilderness and his second wife, Primrose, to Mexico, starting with their departure from Canada and ending with their discovery that his old friend, Juan Fernández Martínez, is dead. As the editors inform us, Lowry would have made many changes before a final draft emerged, essentially texturing it the same way he had *Volcano*. Even so, we can see clearly some of the directions he was taking. Again he used as a basic theme a conflict between life and death, between active and passive forces, between the way up and the way down. But in this case, he was fundamentally working with the ambiguity that an affirmation of life can sometimes come out of a discovery of death and the nadir of despair. Thus the day after the Wildernesses hear of his friend's death, they go to Mitla, and there "the inconceivable yet magnificent desolation of the whole place, an image, indeed, of death, reminded Sigbjørn for the first time, perhaps, since their fire, of the even greater magnificence of being alive." He realizes that he himself is responsi-

---

[22] Lowry, *Selected Letters*, pp. 53–89.

ble for his own destiny. And with that existential conclusion he leaves Oaxaca. A final image builds around the fruitfulness that the federal credit association, of which his friend had been a part, has brought to Oaxaca: "The Banco Ejidal had become a garden."[23]

The Lowrys returned to Cuernavaca via Puebla; early in March they set out for Acapulco. There they were fined for a violation he had allegedly committed on his prior visit, and through a series of misunderstandings—particularly Lowry's not having understood that the way to solve the problem was to bribe a minor official with *la mordida*, "the bite"—they were detained for several weeks. Returning to Cuernavaca, he discovered letters from both American and British publishers accepting *Volcano*. But the Mexico City bureaucracy insisted more strenuously that he had violated a number of technicalities. On May 4, 1946, the Lowrys were deported at Nuevo Laredo. This episode became the basis for another unfinished (and unpublished) novel, "La Mordida."

By now Lowry was planning a series to be called The Voyage That Never Ends, incorporating all the Mexican novels. A sort of divine comedy, it would end with a full vision of the Canadian paradise glimpsed from the Mexican hell of *Under the Volcano*. Wilderness, who has written a book similar to *Volcano*, would be the main character of the entire series. In "Through the Panama," a short story supposedly taken from Wilderness's journal (collected in *Hear Us O Lord from Heaven Thy Dwelling Place*, 1961), and actually based on a voyage the Lowrys made late in 1947 down the coast of Mexico and across the Caribbean, the relationship among these projections of Lowry's personality becomes even more Pirandellean by his having Wilderness create a character named Martin Trumbaugh, who has written his novel. Another mad stream-of-consciousness exploration of the effect of a writer's materials on him, coupled with this particular writer's need for alcohol, it shows Wilderness-Trumbaugh mulling over the problems Lowry was having with his two new Mexican novels (including his realization "at last that he is a Mexican dreaming of the White Cliffs of Dover").[24]

Throughout his association with the country, Lowry apparently had mixed emotions about Mexico. When a friend of his was planning

[23] Lowry, *Dark as the Grave*, pp. 246, 255.
[24] Malcolm Lowry, *Hear Us O Lord from Heaven Thy Dwelling Place*, pp. 29–98.

to go there in 1954, he wrote him that the country was "the most Christ-awful place in the world in which to be in any form of distress . . . All in all a good place to stay out of: (even though one dreams, quixotically of returning one day—a death wish, from my point of view, if there ever was one)."[25] But even while he had been experiencing the frightening horrors of the Oaxaca prison, he had said that the town was "so fantastically beautiful" that he did not want to leave. In his 1950 essay for the *United Nations World*, "Garden of Etla," he summed up his feelings:

The person who falls in love with Mexico falls in love with a colorful and proud and present entity . . . but he is also involved, in the deepest sense, with a mystery . . .

The sense of his past, of sorrow, of death: these are the factors intrinsic in Mexico. Yet the Mexicans are the gayest of people, who turn every possible occasion, including the Day of the Dead, into a fiesta. The Mexicans laugh at death; that does not mean they don't take it seriously. It is perhaps only by the possession of a tragic sense of life such as theirs that joy and mirth find their place: it is an attitude that testifies to the dignity of man. Death, defeated by rebirth, is tragic and comic at once. On many planes this is true.

Some people undoubtedly feel drawn to Mexico as to the hidden life of man himself; they wonder if they might not even discover themselves there.[26]

This ambivalence is found throughout Lowry's work. The hatred stands out most obviously and fits into the large pattern created by the reactions of so many others, but the love is always present.

[25] Malcolm Lowry, "Letters from Malcolm Lowry," *Canadian Literature* 8 (Spring 1961): 44.
[26] Malcolm Lowry, "Garden of Etla," *United Nations World* 4 (June 1950): 45–46.

## 10. Matters of Church and State, 1938

As Lowry shows so clearly, it was not pleasant to be a gringo in Mexico in 1938, even if one were not a drunk British consul. The expropriation of the oil industry caused many tensions. Yet Sherwood Anderson (1876–1941), his fourth wife, and several friends drove down to Mexico City and then over the newly opened road to Acapulco in February and March of 1938, and although, according to a letter (in which he felt that he needed to explain where Acapulco was), he observed in the Indians "something very bitter and cruel" along with "something very rhythmic and laughing," he seems to have encountered no real problems.[1] Anderson did include in his *Memoirs* (published by his fourth wife in 1942) a short story, "Mexican Night," about what befell three tourists from North Dakota. In the story, a man, his wife, and his sister-in-law have strayed off the main road to Mexico City into a small town for the night and are obviously terrified by the strangeness. A newspaper reporter down to cover the oil problem cannot resist the temptation to bribe the hotel proprietor to

[1] Sherwood Anderson, *The Letters of Sherwood Anderson*, pp. 395–397; idem, "An Impression of Mexico—Its People," *Southern Literary Messenger* 1 (April 1939): 241–242; idem, *Sherwood Anderson's Memoirs*, ed. Ray Lewis White, pp. 56, 537–540. Also William Spratling, *File on Spratling*, pp. 122–123.

make everything a bit difficult for the tourists; as the reporter and his fellow conspirators drink on into the night, they think of new ways to bedevil the unsuspecting Midwesterners. Finally, after a sudden on-slaught of roosters' crowing in the night about the same time some soldiers march by and a number of farmers arrive with their ma-chetes, followed by an outburst of the same noise within the hotel it-self, the three tourists flee in a panic, convinced that another revolu-tion is about to break out.[2] The note of anxiety that sounded in his letters, the short story, and an article published in the *Southern Liter-ary Messenger* (April 1939) may have come from reading Lawrence instead of from his own Mexican experiences, however.

Two British visitors, Graham Greene and Evelyn Waugh, did not have such an unruffled visit to Mexico. They came within a few months of each other, early in 1938, for the specific purpose of writ-ing a survey of the current situation. Although Greene was primarily interested in the conflicts between the Church and local governments in the south of Mexico (a heritage Cárdenas had received from Calles's disputes) and Waugh had come specifically because of the oil contro-versy, both writers in their respective travel journals expressed great dissatisfaction with the country in similar terms. Greene and Waugh of course have often been compared because they were both converted Catholics whose religious feelings shaped their development as novel-ists and because both men have tended to find much of their material in exotic locations. Mexico seems to provide another link in their paired development. But actually it marks a great divergence. Where-as Waugh's earlier journey to South America (British Guiana and Brazil) had resulted in a travel book, *Ninety-Two Days*, 1934, and had colored the ending of his novel *A Handful of Dust*, 1934, this time he wrote nothing else about the country he had visited, except indi-rectly in a review of Greene's work, and continued on essentially the same path as a writer. But Greene, without realizing it, had gathered the ideas for a short story and for the novel that is generally acclaimed as his masterpiece, *The Power and the Glory*. Perhaps the difference came from the great dissimilarity of their physical experiences in Mexico. As Waugh himself notes in his review of Green's journal for the *Spectator*, while he had made a homely journey in comfort

[2] Anderson, *Sherwood Anderson's Memoirs*, pp. 480–488. This version is al-most entirely different from the "Mexican Night" printed in White's edition of the *Memoirs*.

through the more European center of the country, Greene had made a "heroic" journey into one of the most isolated stretches of Mexico and had traveled, often ill, by various primitive means.[3] But if the reader looks closely at the two travel books, he will see that, in spite of similar objections to Mexico, they reveal basically two very different personalities to begin with.

Greene (1904–) came into Mexico late in February under a rather strange cloud.[4] Hollywood had sued him because of his comments about Shirley Temple in a film review; apparently there was even a threat of prison. It seemed a good time for him to leave Great Britain, and his publishers and several news journals commissioned him to write a book, *The Lawless Roads* (called *Another Mexico* in the United States), and articles on the religious situation in Mexico. Since the Mexican federal government had long ceased to uphold the anticlerical provisions of the constitution, the churches were by then open in most of the country. The priests had ended their strike nine years earlier, and the *cristero* rebellion had long spent its fury. But in Tabasco and Chiapas, farthest away from the capital and under the control of zealously anti-Catholic governors, worshippers were still actively persecuted by leftist organizations, especially Tomás Garrido Canabal's Red Shirts. Greene could not know that the conservative factions in Mexico were already returning to governmental power, but he avoided all mention of the obviously growing reconciliation between Church and State, ignoring for example the archbishop's unprecedented support of Cárdenas during the oil controversy, and concentrated entirely on signs of oppression. By the intensity of his conversion and through his artistic discovery of Catholic dogma as a source of his fiction, Greene was predisposed to find only unhappiness and terror. He defended, perhaps legitimately, the richness of the Mexican churches—so startlingly in contrast to the poverty of the people—by pointing out that man needs beauty. He honestly admitted the corruption to which the clergy could fall, but he distinguished between the infallibility of doctrine and the weakness of man. Nevertheless, some of his arguments seem irrelevant, and at no time could he dispassionately examine the reasons behind the conflict. In 1940, after he had written the almost impartial *The Power and the Glory*, he attacked in

[3] Evelyn Waugh, "The Waste Land," *Spectator*, March 10, 1939, pp. 413–414.
[4] Graham Greene, *Another Mexico*; idem, *The Power and the Glory*, pp. 1–5. Also John Atkins, *Graham Greene*, pp. 86–87.

a *Spectator* review a book by J. B. Trend, a Cambridge professor, for taking too little notice of the religious persecution and ill-temperedly called his attitude "symptomatic of the inhumanity of the academic brain."[5]

Greene entered Mexico at Nuevo Laredo. He spent several days at the border hoping, unsuccessfully, to obtain a car ride to Mexico City. While waiting, he found his setting and perhaps the plot for "Across the Bridge," a minor short story written in 1938 but not published until *Nineteen Stories* in 1947. (In 1958 it was made into a movie with the same title but bearing little resemblance to the story.) Its narrator, an unnamed Englishman, has been in a border town (obviously Nuevo Laredo) for several weeks when he hears that a British embezzler, Joseph Calloway, has come up from Central America, trying to escape extradition. All the natives are too awed by his enormous wealth to speak to him; Calloway has spent considerable time in the uncomfortable town, gazing wistfully across the river to the United States without discovering that practically everyone around him knows English and has been watching his activities with constant interest. Two detectives are sent over from the States, but they do not recognize Calloway even when the three sit on adjoining benches. When they finally discover the truth about each other, they hurry to the governor's palace, where the three convene. Extradition is denied; the detectives return across the bridge, stealing for some obscure reason Calloway's dog. He follows later that day, perhaps looking for the animal; the dog sees him go by and jumps from the detectives' car. The detectives follow, and in the rapid turn of events the car swerves to avoid hitting the dog and runs over Calloway. The narrator tells us: "It was comic and it was pitiable; but it wasn't less comic because the man was dead." Greene did not find the lightness of touch he needed in telling the story, however, and missed almost completely the humor he injected into *The Power and the Glory*. The finest quality in the story is his evocation of the hot, dusty border town, and even that he captured more firmly in his travelogue.[6]

Outside San Luis Potosí, Greene, in his role as a journalist, interviewed Saturnino Cedillo, the general who had been appointed to Cárdenas's cabinet as a concession to Mexican rightists because of his staunch support of capitalism and Catholicism. As Cárdenas consoli-

[5] Graham Greene, *Collected Essays*, pp. 337–339.
[6] Graham Greene, *Twenty-One Stories*, pp. 78–90.

dated his powers, however, he had eased Cedillo out of office. The general had returned to his home state, which he now ruled somewhat in the manner of a feudal king. Greene was allowed to interview him only because the author too was Catholic. In the manner of newsmen, he prepared a list of questions and watched the general sweat through the perils they posed. Cedillo was independent, yet the federal government was watching all the while. A few months after the interview, in fact, a series of pronouncements caused him to take to the hills; early in 1939, lacking by then even the support of the clergy, he was killed. The death, not condoned by the president, lends no credit to Mexico; but the circumstances do reveal the political stability Cárdenas had brought, for Cedillo was the last of the independent generals to so trouble the Mexican government. Greene, as usual concerned with the narrow religious question, failed to see the full political context of the problem and tended to treat Cedillo's death as another example of the powers of darkness triumphing over those of light—even though in this case he knew how murky the light was.

Already the ugliness and cruelty that are indeed part of Mexico had begun to bother Greene as much as the religious question. He attended a cock fight; he watched the obscene cripples at the train station in Mexico City; he walked through the capital's "high dark stony streets"; he noted that all the monuments in Mexico seemed to be "to violent deaths." The land appeared to him to be filled with hate; soon he was speaking like Lawrence of "some emanation from the evil Aztec soil," that brings about "sudden inexplicable outbursts of brutality." The pyramids at San Juan Teotihuacán depressed him, especially the wall of Quetzalcóatl, which was decorated for him with "horrors, serpents, and gas-masks"; he later felt much the same way about the ruins at Mitla. Only the Alameda on Sunday, the park at Chapultepec, later Puebla, and naturally the shrine at Guadalupe cheered him. He quickly came to hate the land and its people with an overwhelming intensity.[7]

Greene was far from being a typical tourist. He neither knew anyone in the country nor tried to meet any of the notables—Mexican, British, or American—unless one counts the general, a few priests, and two obscure Catholic poets. He visited the tourist attractions but found little that was exciting. He thought Taxco was a disgusting colo-

[7] Greene, *Another Mexico*, pp. 68, 88, 106–107, 91.

ny for American "escapists with their twisted sensuality and their hopeless freedom." Cuernavaca reminded him only of "Zapata's useless uprising," which he seems to have known about mainly from Rosa King's account published in 1935, *Tempest over Mexico*. The Mexican muralists obviously left him uncertain, however. In spite of their intense prejudices against the Spanish and the Church, he respected the artistry of some of Rivera's work (most of it he felt was "unbearably sentimental") and praised Orozco, saying that he— "however invalid one may believe his ideology to be—knows his own mind and his own world; it is very seldom that the great abstractions . . . bellow their sentimental draperies across *his* walls." Even those murals of Orozco depicting subjects that Greene could not like represented for him "emotions of pity and hate that one can respect."[8]

Most of the time he was far from the tourist spots. Pretending that he wanted to see the ruins of Palenque in the state of Chiapas (it seemed unwise to admit his actual reasons for wishing to visit that area, since the government could be quite sensitive about foreign reports), he planned to take a boat from Veracruz to Frontera and then somehow travel across the state of Tabasco into Chiapas. The boat turned out to be a rotting barge; the price for the ticket also included a life insurance policy. Villahermosa, the capital of Tabasco, was unbearably hot and was ruled with all the strictness of a puritanical state. No priests were in the state, nor were any of the churches open, even though Garrido Canabal had fled the country. From there Greene flew to Salto de Agua in Chiapas with an adventurous Mexican aviator. The village lay isolated in the jungle; his lack of Spanish became a hindrance, and without Greene's wanting to go, his letter of introduction destined him to visit the ruins. Early one morning a guide appeared, and the party set off by muleback across the mountains. The sun beat down; the flies droned after them; Greene lost his glasses. The trip left him so miserable that he scarcely looked at the ruins when they had reached them, and he welcomed the return to the depressing village.

From Salto he flew to Yajalón and waited for a plane to San Cristóbal de las Casas. All this time he was growing more and more depressed not only with Mexico but also with his own emotional reactions to the country. He later wrote: "Indeed, when I try to think back

8 Ibid., pp. 258, 75–76.

to those days, they lie under the entrancing light of chance encounters, small endurances, unfamiliarity, and I cannot remember why at the time they seemed so grim and hopeless."⁹ Although he had vowed never to go by mule anywhere again, he left Yajalón by that means. Holy Week was fast approaching, and the festivities were celebrated by the people in the isolated, semi-independent town of Las Casas even though no priests were allowed to enter its churches. Life there, however, was little better. The celebrations provided comfort for him, but he now encountered the hostility that had been directed against all gringos because of the oil controversy. And when he left, he had dysentery. Oaxaca interested him, but he was too sick to see much; Puebla he came nearest to liking of any city. By this time, whatever the reasons for his psychological depression, he "had taken such a distaste to Mexico that even an English prison promised relief."¹⁰ On the last day of April he sailed from Veracruz.

Looking at these circumstances, no one could be surprised by *The Lawless Roads*. It is one of the most ill-tempered books ever written about Mexico. Greene recorded in detail his disgust with the land, its government, and its people, excluding the priests and the aviators. Nor is it surprising that the book is seldom found in bookstores in Mexico, while *The Power and the Glory* in both Spanish and English editions is displayed everywhere. When the American poet Selden Rodman read the travelogue in Mexico in 1957, he reacted vehemently against Greene's "whines of self-pity," accusing him indirectly of having been a neurotic hypocrite. Even Greene seems later to have had mixed feelings about the book, for when the third British edition was issued in 1950, he wrote a prefatory note begging pardon for dwelling "too much on a religious situation liable to change at the expense of more permanent sides of Mexican life." In a cover blurb in 1968 he praised extravagantly ("the best book on Mexico written this century") *One Man's Mexico* by Maurice Cardif, a book that, if it admits heavily the despicable side of Mexican life, also cites often its virtuous sides.¹¹ Yet in Greene's 1962 preface to *The Power and the Glory* concerning the origins of the novel he showed no sign of having changed his mind about Mexico. And when he returned to Mexico

---

⁹ Ibid., p. 174.

¹⁰ Greene, *Power and Glory*, p. 1.

¹¹ Selden Rodman, *Mexican Journal*, pp. 147–148; Graham Greene, *The Lawless Roads*, prefatory note; Maurice Cardif, *One Man's Mexico*, jacket blurb.

City for a few days in the mid-1960's, he confessed to one of his hosts that he still found the country disagreeable.[12] Throughout *The Lawless Roads*, however, he is so honest that even when the reader disagrees totally with Greene's findings he must admire his directness and candor. Two historians of Mexico, Ernest Gruening and Hubert Herring, wrote reviews of the book when it first appeared. In spite of reservations, both basically liked it, and Herring felt that it was "a wholesome antidote to the flood of sentimental writing on Mexico."[13]

*The Lawless Roads* is carefully, beautifully written. Whereas with most travel books the reader is interested in the subject matter alone, with Greene's one can judge the work in strictly artistic terms. The plot becomes naturally one man's reaction to a country in which (he feels) his religion is held in disrepute. It begins with a two-part prologue. In the first part the author recalls that point in his childhood in England when he had come to believe in heaven because of a keen awareness of hell and when he slowly "began to have a dim conception of the appalling mysteries of love moving through a ravaged world." The second part recounts the story of Father Miguel Pro Juárez, who in 1927, while the *cristero* rebellion raged so fiercely, had been executed without trial for his alleged part in a conspiracy against Obregón's life. The rest of the work exemplifies Greene's faith in Catholicism and in the curious wonder of love through the record of his Mexican experiences.

After a short narrative recounting his initial reaction to Mexico, Greene gives a long account of Cedillo. The general's estate contrasts with the ungodly situation that Greene finds in Tabasco and in Chiapas—except for the festival of Holy Week, the climax of the book. General tourist notes on Mexico City and its environs provide other striking contrasts, before and after, to his lonely pilgrimage. The frame of the book is loose enough to allow him to interpolate many stories about the people he met (several of the stories were published as articles in British magazines and newspapers prior to the book's appearance). In an epilogue Greene reminds the reader of the violence about to burst on the entire world from Europe. The voyage from Veracruz to London is in miniature as sad as Katherine Anne Porter's

---

[12] Private conversation with me in Mexico, summer 1970.

[13] Ernest Gruening, "On Disliking Mexico," *Saturday Review of Literature*, June 17, 1939, p. 13; Hubert Herring, "Mexico and South America," *Yale Review* 29 (Winter 1940): 397.

*Ship of Fools.* In retrospect Mexico seems no different from all the other countries in the world.

In spite of the care Greene lavished on this book, one could not have expected him to use Mexico as a setting for a novel. He later recalled, "Nothing was further from my thoughts than a novel." But he had admitted in *The Lawless Roads*, "It was as if Mexico was something I couldn't shake off, like a state of mind."[14] The materials for *The Power and the Glory*, 1940, had begun to accumulate without his awareness. In Frontera he met a dentist; along the way to Las Casas he met a German and his sister at an isolated *finca* in the jungle (he also heard stories of a beautiful daughter, but she apparently had left). These people would evolve into minor characters in the novel: Mr. Tench, Mr. and Miss Lehr, probably the child Carol Fellows. The main character slowly grew from several casual remarks. In Frontera Greene had heard of a priest who had lived ten years in hiding in the jungle; "his few letters . . . recorded an awful sense of impotence—to live in constant danger and yet be able to do so little, it hardly seemed worth the horror." Later Greene heard of a priest in Chiapas who had to flee when the people told him that they could no longer protect him. He asked another dentist about this man and was told that he was "a whisky priest," so drunk at one baptism that he had named a boy with a girl's name. Greene mused: "He was little loss, poor man, a kind of Padre Rey; but who can judge what terror and hardship and isolation may have excused him in the eyes of God?"[15] From this question came the novel.

Greene stated in his preface to *Power* that it had been written to a thesis: he wanted to use the whisky priest as a means to show the great difference that can exist between a man and his office. To construct a good novel, however, he needed a strong foil for the priest. The foil would be a policeman whose allegiances at least reflected those of the Red Shirts. But Greene said: "I have not found the integrity of the lieutenant among the police and *pistoleros* I had encountered. I had to invent him as a counter to the failed priest; the idealistic police officer who stifled life from the best possible motives, the drunken priest who continued to pass life on."[16] From the conflict between these two men comes one of the finest novels ever written by an outsider about Mexi-

[14] Greene, *Power and Glory*, p. 2; idem, *Another Mexico*, p. 178.
[15] Greene, *Another Mexico*, pp. 123, 144.
[16] Greene, *Power and Glory*, p. 4.

co. It is also probably one of the best-known stories, because of the many editions of the novel and also because of the movie version, *The Fugitive*, directed by John Ford and Gabriel Figueroa, 1947, and a television adaptation.

The priest is a renegade who has become addicted to brandy, fathered a child, and gradually abandoned one principle after another. When the priests are ordered to leave the state or marry within ninety days, through pride he stays. He manages to escape, and though he knows that he is unworthy, he realizes that he is the only person left who can offer the people the gift of God: "If he left them, they would be safe; and they would be free from his example; he was the only priest the children could remember. It was from him they would take their ideas of faith. But it was from him too they took God—in their mouths. When he was gone it would be as if God in all this space between the sea and the mountains ceased to exist." He represents the mystery of God's grace. The lieutenant is as virtuous and morally upright as the priest is degenerate; he sincerely loves the people and wants to help them. To do so he is convinced that he must rid the state of foolish superstitions that bind their minds and bodies, but in his intensity he resembles a priest himself. Greene calls him a mystic who had experienced not God but "vacancy—a complete certainty in the existence of a dying, cooling world, of human beings who had evolved from animals for no purpose at all."[17]

So the chase begins; the priest in trying to escape follows the path Greene had taken across Chiapas. He finds momentary respite at an isolated German *finca*, near which the Indians have kept their church open. Here in this condition of physical safety he learns anew how little his hardships have changed him; with his position re-established, the sins that had initially damned him—pride and complacency—return in spite of all. He makes it safely across the state border, but realizing the corruption that awaits him, he is almost relieved when a poor mestizo comes and says that a priest is needed at the deathbed of an ambushed American gangster. There the priest, as he knew would happen, is finally taken by the lieutenant, carried back to the capital, and executed. Yet Greene is aware of the mysterious nature of God's love. The priest may have saved himself by his last acts. The novel concludes by recalling the benevolent effect the priest has had on sev-

17 Ibid., pp. 89, 33.

eral of the minor characters. In the conflict between the power and the glory (to interpret the title in one way) the glory proves mightier.

The novel evokes on almost every page, as well as Traven did, the jungle and the high mountains of southern Mexico, the small villages and the desolate capital. Scene after scene that Greene had rendered in *The Lawless Roads* become part of *The Power and the Glory*. But even things about which he could have known nothing, such as the conditions of prisons in Mexico, seem to be written from actual experience. Whereas in the travelogue one is always reminded (until the end) that it is essentially a description of Mexico, in *Power* one tends to forget the setting altogether and to remember best the powerful conflict between the ideals of the priest and those of the lieutenant. This fact probably explains why Arthur Calder-Marshall felt the book belonged more to "Greeneland" than to Mexico.[18] There is no sense that an outsider is telling the story with lots of local color. Greene the artist had come to some sort of terms with the land that Greene the Catholic never could.

The book is also important in his development as an author. He had written a number of novels in the late 1920's and early 1930's but then had turned to "entertainments," his label for a series of thrillers. In *Brighton Rock*, finished just before he left for Mexico, he had discovered his role as a Catholic novelist. This plot, however, followed essentially that which he had used in the entertainments, and powerful as the novel remains, there is a certain curious inconsistency between form and content. But *The Power and the Glory* is nearly flawless in its development. Though the chase still follows one essential pattern of a thriller, abstract thesis, characters, action, and setting all fit into a piece.

Greene went on to write a number of equally controlled and powerful novels. In all he continued to explore the mystery of grace, contrasting the limited knowledge of a man's heart with God's perfect understanding. One cannot say that Mexico made Greene the important writer that he is, but it is difficult to imagine his subsequent achievement had *The Power and the Glory* not been written. His early African experiences simply did not release his full powers the way Mexico did. He returned four more times to a Latin American setting for a long work: to Cuba for the entertainment *Our Man in Havana*,

18 Arthur Calder-Marshall, "The Works of Graham Greene," *Horizon* 1 (May 1940): 374.

1958; to Haiti for the novel *The Comedians*, 1966; to Paraguay for the last part of his comic *Travels with My Aunt*, 1969; and to Argentina for *The Honorary Consul*, 1973.

It is depressing to study Waugh's failure after Greene's demonstration of the power the artist can have over his own ego. But that failure offers an interesting warning of the possible nearsightedness an author can suffer when he allows things other than his sense of art to dictate the pattern of a book. By way of contrast, Waugh's failure makes Greene's achievement all the more remarkable.

Evelyn Waugh (1903–1966) and his second wife stayed in Mexico, most of the time with a Mexican friend, slightly less than two months in the summer of 1938.[19] They traveled the tourist circuit, visiting Veracruz, Mexico City, Cuernavaca, Taxco, Puebla, and Oaxaca. But Waugh, who had already made his mark as a satiric novelist and writer of popular travelogues, had come especially to write a book about the oil problem. Mexico had severed diplomatic relations with Great Britain in May, yet the British, even though they reacted more vehemently than the Americans to the expropriation, were likewise more concerned with the shape of affairs in Germany. Waugh could not understand such indifference; for him Mexico—in its handling of its political, economic, religious, and cultural development—represented the real anarchy in the world, rather than the fascist powers. He avowed that he was a conservative when he came (had he been totally honest he would have added that he was a snob). One would gather from his own comments that he read a few books about Mexico, primarily *Terry's Guide*, Gruening's *Mexico and Its Heritage*, and Lawrence's *Plumed Serpent*, and that he asked many questions of those Mexicans he met who spoke English. He then proceeded to lecture the world in a book entitled *Robbery under Law* (retitled *Mexico: An Object Lesson* in the United States).

At the very beginning of the book he anticipated his readers' argument that two months' acquaintance with a country is not enough time to understand it, insisting that such rapid surveys are part of the writer's normal course of work. As Greene demonstrated, a short stay may well reveal to a writer deep insights into a culture that might be missed by those who have grown too familiar with it. But Waugh thought that the artist could understand, in the same way as a special-

---

[19] Evelyn Waugh, *Mexico: An Object Lesson*; Malcolm Bradbury, *Evelyn Waugh*, pp. 25–27.

ist, complex institutions and movements. Therein lies the difference between the anger of Greene's book and the equal anger of Waugh's. Greene knew his limitations and worked within them, writing about himself and his personal observations. Consequently *The Lawless Roads* remains in print and is spoken of highly even by professional historians; *Robbery under Law* has been allowed to disappear.

When it was published in 1939, it salved the pride of many British subjects, and the reviews were favorable. But even then Henry Parkes, a British subject who had settled in the United States a decade earlier, contemptuously dismissed the book, writing: "Almost every statement which he makes about Mexican history is demonstrably false; and even his own experiences as a tourist, if correctly reported, seem to have been very peculiar . . . Indeed, when one contemplates the extent and variety of Mr. Waugh's misinformation, one begins to wonder whether his Mexican acquaintances made him the victim of an elaborate practical joke." He concluded, playing with the subtitle, that "the only true 'object lesson' of this book is the danger of writing on a subject about which one knows nothing."[20]

Waugh begins with a few notes about tourist Mexico and intersperses other such observations throughout the book. These are primarily comments on architecture; he dismisses the murals by merely mentioning "the fine crazy pictures of Orozco" and "the huge and clumsy frescoes of Diego Rivera." He agrees with Greene that Taxco was slightly depressing and that Puebla was "the only town in Mexico of dignity."[21] There are very few glimpses of the people he met. And none of the scenes sticks in the mind. The greatest part of the book is a rehash of Mexican history, emphasizing the role the United States played in its development, and an analysis of the current situation. Like Greene he deplored the persecution of the Catholics. Above all he disliked the destruction of the great civilization that he felt the Spanish had brought to Mexico. Waugh summed up:

It is a huge country with a long and proud history, taking precedence in its national unity over half the states of Europe; it has been rich and cultured and orderly and has given birth to sons illustrious in every walk of life; now, every year, it is becoming hungrier, wickeder, and more hopeless; the great buildings of the past are falling in ruins; the jungle is

[20] Henry B. Parkes, "Who Told Him All That?" *New York Herald Tribune Books*, September 24, 1939, p. 9.
[21] Waugh, *Mexico*, pp. 36, 80, 51.

closing in and the graves of the pioneers are lost in the undergrowth; the people are shrinking back to the riverbanks and railheads; they are being starved in the mountains and shot in back yards, dying without God. And General Cardenas and his gang stand on their balcony smirking at the applause of communist delegations; the tourists tramp round the Exhibition of his work marvelling at hammers and sickles in cross-stitch and clenched fists in plaster of Paris and the plans of monstrous public offices that no one is ever going to build.[22]

Waugh felt that the country might well spawn the fantastic religion that Lawrence had depicted. And what happened in Mexico, he concluded, could happen anywhere; that was the lesson we must learn before it was too late.

Since Cárdenas was undoubtedly one of Mexico's great statesmen, Waugh's comments seem all the more ludicrous. According to Selden Rodman, one of the Mexicans Waugh met (a somewhat addled man to be sure) told the Englishman: "Instead of assuming that the secular clergy is doing good and is being persecuted unjustly, why don't *you* hire yourself a cab and go out and talk to the average Indian who truly loves God and the saints and his own church, but hates the grasping priests with all his heart and all his soul? But you won't . . . because the truth would interfere with your dogma."[23] Though in a study of Waugh's development *Robbery under Law* has interest as the first clear statement of his political principles, it must remain the most irritating book about Mexico ever written by a highly respected author.

[22] Ibid., pp. 246–247.
[23] Rodman, *Mexican Journal*, pp. 187–188.

# 11. The End of an Era

In 1941 Wilbur J. Cash (1900–1941), fresh from his success with *The Mind of the South*, came to Mexico City on a Guggenheim fellowship to start work on a novel.[1] In the short time he was there he seems to have written only one thing: a minor article about Mexico, which was first published in 1967. His significance to a history of American and British writers in Mexico is akin to Ambrose Bierce's. Nervously depressed after the excitement of his book, ill from the new food and the high altitude, and worried about the war raging across Europe and the Pacific, Cash began to speak of Nazis who were plotting to kill him and his wife. She tried to quiet him as he rushed irrationally around their apartment one night clutching a kitchen knife, and the next day she arranged for him to see a doctor. But Cash eluded her and that night was found hanging from a bathroom door in the Hotel Reforma. His suicide seems to be the perfect symbol for the end of a nearly thirty-year period that had begun with Bierce's disappearance and had been punctuated by Crane's death. For it was during this time that American and British letters looked most intensely at Mexico.

[1] Mary Cash Maury, "The Suicide of W. J. Cash," *Red Clay Reader* 4 (1967): 8–13; Joseph L. Morrison, *W. J. Cash, Southern Prophet*, pp. 122–135, 305–309, which prints the essay.

Mexico itself changed about then, and the excitement that had undoubtedly stimulated earlier writers disappeared so that new visitors could not have access to the strength upon which their predecessors had pulled. For instance, Ernest Hemingway and his third wife (Martha Gellhorn, later author of a Mexican novel) came finally in 1941 to Mexico City for the bullfights, and Elizabeth Bishop spent the year 1943 there. But neither Hemingway nor Miss Bishop seems to have been impressed by Mexico as they were by Cuba and Brazil, respectively.[2] When Manuel Avila Camacho was inaugurated in December 1940, he announced that the Revolution had been finished and that Mexico would now stabilize its gains. The government began to bank on industrial expansion as a solution to its economic problems and let agrarian reforms slide. The Mexican cultural renaissance also lost its heady excitement. Painters continued working across the country, and one new artist, Rufino Tamayo, rose to an international reputation. A Mexican literature grew into similar recognition. But consolidation of a country's powers is never as exciting as the discovery of its dynamics. Even though Avila Camacho was led by political rhetoric to reverse his previous pronouncement and announce that the Revolution would continue forever, the movement was now an official party rather than a force from the people. The president's earlier characterization of his program as one of evolution rather than revolution has been accepted by Howard Cline and later historians as the direction that Mexico actually took. The country had achieved its place as a modern nation: as if to demonstrate its new status, in 1942 with the blessings of the archbishop it entered world politics by declaring war on the Axis.

World War II of course marked the end of one era and the beginning of another for Great Britain and the United States as well as Mexico. The British lost their previous importance in world affairs, and culturally the nation's artists seemed to turn inward to face sternly their own society and its problems. The United States uneasily accepted its position as a world power, but no cultural flowering kindred to that of the twenties and thirties occurred. It seems doubtful that the young writers of either English-speaking nation could have been capable of meeting a creative challenge had it come from Mexico. Still the country continued to have some significance for at least American lit-

[2] Letter to me from Carlos Baker, August 18, 1967; Anne Stevenson, *Elizabeth Bishop*, p. 18; *Contemporary Authors*, vols. 7–8, p. 58.

erature. Four important writers had come to Mexico during the last years of Cárdenas's presidency—John Steinbeck, Muriel Rukeyser, Saul Bellow, and Tennessee Williams—and they were working with their impressions during and long after the war. Katherine Anne Porter and Malcolm Lowry were still writing from memories of revolutionary Mexico. Several new authors headed south during the 1950's and 1960's; their work, if so far appearing less significant than that written by earlier visitors, adds something valuable. Perhaps we can consider it equally symbolic that Cash's suicide has never entered the mythology of Mexico in the way the deaths of Bierce and Crane did. And if Steinbeck, Miss Rukeyser, Bellow, and Williams mark the end of an era, then that era ended strongly.

Of the four, Steinbeck (1902–1968) arrived earliest, visiting the country in the late summer and fall of 1935.[3] It was natural that he should want to go there since he had grown up with Mexican Americans. They figure in most of his California stories: *Tortilla Flat*, his first popular success, is entirely about the *paisanos* of Monterey. He romanticized them into unbelievably simple but lovable rogues, but the novel retains a certain vitality. The royalties from it fittingly financed this trip for him and his first wife. He went south in deliberate search of materials for a new novel, but another California work, *Of Mice and Men*, seems instead to have occupied all his attention. When he was later asked about the visit, he replied: "Mexico fades very quickly. I can't remember it very well. I think possibly the people there live on a mental level about equal in depth to our dream level. The contacts I made there are all dreamlike."[4] He never lost this feeling about the country, but later trips, especially the series he made in 1940, were productive for his creative life.

He returned in March 1940, trying to escape the attention that *The Grapes of Wrath* had thrust upon him. His friend Edward Ricketts, the owner of a marine biology laboratory, asked him to go on an expedition to the Gulf of California, and for nearly a month they collected specimens along the shores. Being gregarious men, they took every opportunity to meet the natives along the Baja California peninsula:

---

[3] Peter Lisca, *The Wide World of John Steinbeck*, pp. 180–183, 218–231, 248–249, 291; E. W. Tedlock and C. V. Wicker (eds.), *Steinbeck and His Critics*, pp. 8–9, 14–15, 17–18; John Steinbeck, *The Log from the Sea of Cortez*. Hayashi Telsumaro prepared a bibliography.

[4] Tedlock and Wicker, *Steinbeck and His Critics*, p. 9.

they attended church in La Paz on Good Friday; they visited the cantinas; they went with three Mexicans into the sierra, ostensibly to
hunt bighorn sheep but really to get into the countryside; they hired
young boys from many of the towns to help them collect specimens.
There were also other encounters: in an isolated bay they ran into
three Americans whom they suspected of smuggling; they went on
board a Japanese shrimp boat, one of several the Mexican government
had allowed in the Gulf. But most of the time they spent on the boat
or peering into tidal pools along the littoral. From this trip Steinbeck
and Ricketts jointly published in 1941 *Sea of Cortez* (the old name for
the Gulf, which they preferred for its romance), consisting of two
parts: a journal of their expedition and a source book with illustrations of marine life.

The journal records the thinking of both men, but its style is un-
mistakably Steinbeck's, as he acknowledged when that section alone
was reissued in 1951 as *The Log from the Sea of Cortez*. It must be
one of the strangest records ever included in a modern scientific work.
Although the *Log* contains data on the methods and finds of the expedition, the concrete details always provide the basis for extended spec-
ulations about the nature of the world. Reminders of World War II
in forms other than the Japanese shrimp boats constantly intruded
upon their consciousness. The United States was then uneasily holding its peace; just after Germany's invasion of Poland the twenty-one
republics of the Americas had pledged the neutrality of the two continents unless one of the countries was attacked. The United States
was watching closely the development of events in Mexico, however,
since the Axis wanted an ally there and since many Mexican groups
were openly supporting Germany and Italy. Moreover, Mexico suffered from its usual problems at election time; a campaign by General Juan Andreu Almazán was being waged with great heat against
Avila Camacho, and it seemed possible that another civil war could
erupt. Nevertheless, the voyage was an idyllic retreat for Steinbeck
during which he tried to sort out many ideas that had long bothered
him.

*Sea of Cortez*, being mostly concerned with these personal ideas,
gives us few glimpses of Mexico. By holding that all men are basically
the same and therefore likeable, Steinbeck curiously blurred his portraits of the natives. Now appreciating more fully their "time-world,"
part of Steinbeck's mind still wanted to romanticize the apparently

simple Indians. He recognized the danger, writing at one point: "It is said so often and in such ignorance that Mexicans are contented, happy people. 'They don't want anything.' This, of course, is not a description of the happiness of Mexicans, but of the unhappiness of the person who says it." And later in the journal, he expanded on the idea: "To us, a little weary of the complication and senselessness of a familiar picture, the Indian seems a rested, simple man. If we should permit ourselves to remain in ignorance of his complications, then we might long for his condition, thinking it superior to ours. The Indian on the other hand, subject to constant hunger and cold, mourning a grandfather and set of uncles in Purgatory, pained by the aching teeth and sore eyes of malnutrition, may well envy us our luxury."[5] It is not altogether clear from the *Log* or from later Mexican works that Steinbeck remembered his own advice; the Mexican primitive appealed to him too much as a type of existential hero. Ultimately the descriptions of the unknown, mirage-filled Gulf, bordered by a fantastic, stony land, remain the most memorable aspect.

As soon as Steinbeck returned to California in late April, he set off for Cuernavaca to work on the script for *The Forgotten Village*, a film directed by Herbert Kline about life in a remote Mexican village. Steinbeck wrote an "elastic story" about the death of a child from typhoid fever. With this simple outline in mind he and Kline selected a number of villages as locations and moved in to absorb the life of the natives. Kline recorded in an article for *Theatre Arts* how complications quickly arose. The people distrusted the movie crew; when they were finally won over, Kline still could not persuade them to act out their lives. Professional actors who could play the parts were all busy in Mexico City. Finally Kline, in desperation, brought in natives who had had some contact with gringos to play the main parts. Seeing these peasants trusting the crew, some of the villagers, including an old herb doctor, came forward. There were other problems. The film had to be shot without dialogue since the people spoke an ancient dialect (narration was added later). The Mexican musician Silvestre Revueltas was to have composed the score, but he died. The film was released in the late fall 1941 to mixed reactions from the critics. Meanwhile, Steinbeck's script, illustrated with stills from the film, had been published.[6]

[5] Steinbeck, *Log*, pp. 98, 245.
[6] Herbert Kline, " 'Forgotten Village': An Account of Film Making in Mexico,"

*The Forgotten Village* traces an important moment in the life of one family in the village of Santiago, using as its hero an adolescent boy called Juan Diego. One of his brothers becomes sick, and though the herb doctor tries to cure him, he dies. Other children in the village are likewise taken ill. The schoolmaster tries to persuade the people that contaminated water in the village well is causing the deaths. Convinced, Juan carries a petition from the teacher to the hospital in Mexico City, making his first journey away from the village. A medical crew sets out in a rural service car; there follows "the clash of a medicine and magic that was old when the Aztecs invaded the plateau with a modern medicine that is as young as a living man."[7] The medical crew purifies the water, but the people drive them away. Juan believes in their science, however, and joins them to return to the capital and become a student. The ending has a forced optimism about it; and unfortunately the medical crew seems rather sterile in contrast with the intricate patterns of life in the village. Ricketts, who spent part of the time on location with the company, disliked the script and wrote for Steinbeck a fourteen-page model of the story as he thought it should have been told. But the film contains many beautiful moments, such as a harrowing birth ritual, the burial of a son, and the usual shots of fiestas that an American audience would expect.

Finishing this assignment—during which incidentally he met Richard Wright, down for a short stay and feeling paranoid about Mexico[8] —and the manuscript for the *Log*, Steinbeck was caught up by the war in Europe. In March 1944, however, and again that fall he was back in Mexico. An idea that had come to him in La Paz began to shape itself into a short novel, *The Pearl*. He had recorded in the *Log* how an Indian boy had found an exceedingly large pearl, which he expected to bring him a lifetime of ease: "In his one pearl he had the ability to be drunk as long as he wished, to marry any one of a number of girls, and to make many more a little happy too. In his great pearl lay salvation, for he could in advance purchase masses sufficient to pop him out of Purgatory like a squeezed watermelon seed." But when he took the pearl into La Paz, none of the brokers would offer

---

*Theatre Arts* 25 (May 1941): 336–343; John Steinbeck, *The Forgotten Village*, pp. 5–6; "New Pictures," *Time*, December 8, 1941, p. 96.

[7] Steinbeck, *Forgotten Village*, p. 5.

[8] Constance Webb, *Richard Wright*, pp. 187–188, 199.

him a decent price. That night he was beaten and searched; the next night the same thing occurred. Angrily he took the pearl from its hiding place and threw it back into the Gulf: "He was a free man again with his soul in danger and his food and shelter insecure. And he laughed a great deal about it." Steinbeck summed up: "This seems to be a true story, but it is so much like a parable that it almost can't be. This Indian boy is too heroic, too wise. He knows too much and acts on his knowledge. In every way, he goes contrary to human direction. The story is probably true, but we don't believe it; it is far too reasonable to be true."[9] The fall and winter of 1944–1945 he wrote his novel; it was published in December 1945 in the *Woman's Home Companion*.

In developing *The Pearl*, Steinbeck tried to avoid the improbabilities that he had sensed in the original. He changed the irresponsible boy into a father, Kino, who—in addition to his own desires for clothes, marriage in front of the altar, and a rifle—sees the pearl as the way to educate his son and thus save him from the miseries to which the Indian was accustomed. But Kino's great find enters the dreams of all the villagers, and suddenly he is their enemy by his new wealth. Greed stalks their thoughts; the first night someone attempts to rob him. Juana, his wife, is frightened and begs Kino to throw the pearl back into the Gulf. But the dream has become too real for him to give it up. He is "a man," and only after he has been forced momentarily to become an animal—to kill four men and to flee for his life—and after his son has been killed can he cast the pearl back, explicitly to end the evil that has descended on his family. The novel, however, is more than just a Mexican story. Steinbeck wanted it to be received by the reader as a parable; it becomes a complex study of the relationship between good and evil. The pearl is pure and capable of saving the family, but it unaccountably brings evil to them instead: "The essence of pearl mixed with essence of men and a curious dark residue was precipitated." Yet it proves the good in Kino's brother and his family, for they protect him and his family when their home is burned. And the tragedy brings new dignity to Kino and Juana: "The people say that the two seemed to be removed from human experience; that they had gone through pain and had come out on the other side; that there was almost a magical protection about them."[10]

Steinbeck showed an awareness of the problems of the Mexican

---

[9] Steinbeck, *Log*, pp. 102–103.
[10] John Steinbeck, *The Pearl*, pp. 34, 120.

nation that he had not displayed at all in the journal and only partly in the movie. In *The Pearl* he was moved to portrayals of the clergy and the upper class almost as damning as any Traven had drawn. When the baby is stung by a scorpion, the doctor refuses to help the poverty-stricken Indians at first; but as soon as he learns of the pearl, he hurries over and pretends to save the now-well child: "This doctor was of a race which for nearly four hundred years had beaten and starved and robbed and despised Kino's race, and frightened it too, so that the indigene came humbly to the door." The priest has already preceded the doctor, however, to remind Kino of his indebtedness to God. The priest considers the natives to be simply children, "and he treated them like children." Christianity of this sort obviously cannot be real to the people; thus they turn instinctively to their older religions for comfort. Kino's brother sums up that "we are cheated from birth to the overcharge on our coffins"; yet the brother does not clearly recognize the cupidity of the Church and the Spaniard.[11]

Steinbeck's late association with script writing apparently colored his development of the novel, or perhaps from the beginning he had in mind turning it into a movie. His visual sense was always strong. Kino's dive into the Gulf, his flight with Juana into the Sierra, the daily life of the village—all these pictorial scenes are delineated with authority. *The Pearl* was also developed in terms of theme music. Since the story so obviously begged for cinematographic development, Steinbeck easily turned out a script for the Mexican director Emilio Fernández, who shot it on location with an all-Mexican cast. *La Perla* was released in 1948 in both English and Spanish. The New York critics gave it widely disparate reviews, attacking and praising everything from its direction to the script itself.[12] Meanwhile, to coincide with the film's release, the original story was published late in 1947 in book form. Orozco provided the illustrations, one of three books he so honored. Whatever the worth of the film, the book has become one of Steinbeck's enduring works and ranks as a significant if extremely romanticized portrayal of one segment of Mexican life.

It was his last book about the country. He had originally conceived a Mexican setting for *The Wayward Bus*, a novel that had been on his mind for a long time, perhaps since his 1940 trip. But when he finally

11 Ibid., pp. 15, 40, 73.

12 "The Problem Pearl," *Newsweek*, March 8, 1948, pp. 83–84; " 'The Pearl,' " *New York Times Magazine*, February 15, 1948, pp. 34–35.

wrote it in 1946, although the hero is still a Mexican, the setting had changed to his native California. However, he did become involved with two lesser Mexican projects. For the *Collier's* 1948 Christmas issue he retold, without the humorous tone he had previously used toward aspects of Catholicism, "The Miracle of Tepayac," the legend of the Virgin's appearance at Guadalupe.[13] The same year he had a conversation with Elia Kazan that embarked him on a third Mexican movie script. Kazan was excited by the thought of a film about Zapata. Steinbeck mulled over the idea; he read Edgcumb Pinchon's biography and searched in Morelos for stories about the hero. From the fall of 1948 until May 1950 he worked on the script. He included a long introduction so that the company would understand just what he was after, and accompanied Kazan when he went on location in Texas. (The Mexican government refused to permit such a film to be made within its jurisdiction; it also temporarily banned the completed product.) *Viva Zapata!* was released early in 1952. The script has never been published, although *Argosy* printed a long synopsis by Merle Miller with illustrations from the film.[14]

Steinbeck chose to tell a tragedy of a man who wins his revolution only to discover that power corrupts. While trying to redeem his errors, he is betrayed by one of his own men who has come to love death and revolution more than people. But Zapata's death allows a myth to grow from which the people can take strength. The film's array of talent—the stars included Marlon Brando, Anthony Quinn, and Jean Peters—attracted some attention, but almost none of the reviewers were satisfied with the movie. They often singled out Steinbeck's script for being sentimental, turgid, and a bit blurred in its characterizations. All these criticisms are just. A viewer who knows Mexican history would be disturbed by historical inaccuracies that seem unnecessary and the omission of any references to the part the United States played in the Revolution (Huerta does make a cryptic reference to a "reception" after the murder of Madero, but no mention is ever made of Ambassador Wilson's role). The happiest aspect of the film remains Mexican-born Quinn's performance in the role of Zapata's brother. However, Zapata's biographer John Womack, though he felt some reservations about the distortion of "certain

[13] John Steinbeck, "The Miracle of Tepayac," *Collier's*, December 25, 1948, pp. 22–23.

[14] Merle Miller, "Viva Zapata!" *Argosy* 33 (February 1952): 52–53 ff.

events and characters," in general found the film "still subtle, powerful, and true."[15]

Muriel Rukeyser (1913–) went to Mexico in the spring of 1939 and returned there for several visits through at least 1969.[16] From her experiences grew a number of poems: six in *Beast in View*, 1944, and four in three later volumes. She has been much influenced by Octavio Paz, whom she encountered at Berkeley in 1944. She began then to translate his poetry; in 1962 she published a bilingual edition of his complex poem of changes, *Piedra de Sol*, included in her edition of *Configurations*, 1971; and in 1963 she finished *Selected Poems of Octavio Paz*. The two poets share a fascination for a lush flow of images, often hovering just below the level of a symbol, coupled with metaphysical ideas. Sometimes these two combine and reverberate with power; at other times they merely produce a catalogue of impressions and abstractions that overpower sense.

Several of her Mexican poems evoke different locales: Chapultepec Park and the streets of Mexico City, the plaza at San Miguel de Allende, the mountains of Chiapas, the churches around Cholula. In most of these she tried to capture the colors of the scene as light played across it. One or two almost reach perfection, as in her description of the park at dawn. Her description of an evening at San Miguel, however, is merely ornate. Rituals of both the past and the present fascinated her, especially in their juxtaposition of opposites. She described in one poem the effect of the ancient Indian ballgame and in another the present celebration of All Soul's Day, both of which mix a keen awareness of life and death. The same combination of opposites is found in the churches. All in all she seems to have felt rather at home in the country, although in the San Miguel poem she called it a strange land in which she was homesick.[17]

One would have expected Saul Bellow (1915–) as a former student

15 John Womack, *Zapata and the Mexican Revolution*, p. 420; "New Films," *Newsweek*, February 4, 1952, p. 78; Hollis Alpert, "Kazan and Brando Outdoors," *Saturday Review*, February 9, 1952, pp. 25–26; Laura Z. Hobson, "Trade Winds," *Saturday Review*, February 16, 1952, pp. 6–7, and March 1, 1952, pp. 6–7; Selden Rodman, *Mexican Journal*, p. 187. I have based my comments on my own reaction to the film, May 1968.

16 Muriel Rukeyser, *A Turning Wind*, preface and p. 46; Octavio Paz, *Configurations*, introduction.

17 Muriel Rukeyser, *Beast in View*, pp. 45–52; idem, *The Green Wave*, p. 38; idem, *Waterlily Fire*, p. 190; idem, *The Speed of Darkness*, pp. 26–27, 54–55.

of archaeology to have been especially intrigued by Mexico's pre-Columbian past when he spent three months there in 1940, and indeed one of his late stories is set partly at Mitla.[18] But his early Mexican work suggests that his imagination was more profoundly impressed by Leon Trotsky, against whose life an attempt had been made in May of 1940 and who was finally killed in August. "The Mexican General," Bellow's second story to be nationally published, depicts Trotsky's bodyguards as they return to their more normal activities after the death of the revolutionist, and the Russian serves as one of the characters in *The Adventures of Augie March*. Cárdenas had granted Trotsky political asylum in 1937, and that spring an international inquiry into his case had been held at Trotsky's home in Coyoacán.[19] After this stand against the Moscow trials, Trotsky then dropped out of the world's view until the attempts were made on his life. But the assassination, including his dramatic struggle to live, was so sensational, eclipsing even the news of World War II for a moment, that it is not surprising Bellow was fascinated.

"The Mexican General" appeared in the *Partisan Review* in 1942 and has never been collected. In it the author imaginatively entered the lives of several Mexicans vacationing at Pátzcuaro. One of them is an unnamed Jalisco general who had served as a guard for the outside of Trotsky's home without really understanding the stature of the inhabitant. After the assassination, however, he had seized the occasion as an opportunity for personal glory. Almost by instinct the general is a "history-ridden man—in a very egotistical fashion." Thus at every ceremony attending the death he had appeared before the photographers. But at last he has become exhausted and has now retired to the lake resort to rest with three women. The background for the story is traced in by one of the general's lieutenants talking to another who had been away when the Belgian stabbed Trotsky in his own study. Nowhere is the Russian's name mentioned, and the reader

[18] Robert Bate, Saul Bellow's assistant, in a letter to me, March 7, 1968, dated the trip. See Tony Tanner, *Saul Bellow*, p. 2. Harold W. Schneider prepared a bibliography.

[19] John Dewey returned to Mexico at the age of 78 to head the committee; Carleton Beals also served on it until the last day, when he dramatically resigned. The hearings attracted much attention. James T. Farrell was one of the correspondents, and later wrote an admiring essay about Dewey's conduct at the inquiry. See James T. Farrell, *Reflections at Fifty*, pp. 97–123. Farrell does not seem to have been otherwise influenced by the trip.

must put together the hints he is given in order to recognize Bellow's character, a small mystery designed to supply the interest of the story, since so little occurs at the lake.[20] Yet the author's ability to re-create imaginatively the psychology of these six Mexicans could have retained our attention without the rather annoying fakery of the plot.

*The Adventures of Augie March*, which won Bellow his first National Book Award in 1953, has little to do with Mexico. It is a picaresque novel, obviously based partly on the author's own experiences, and is set mainly in the United States. But over halfway through, the novel takes its Chicago-born Jewish narrator into Mexico. The land that Augie discovers is one familiar to readers of Lawrence and Conrad Aiken. Certain passages in which the protagonist thinks about the continuing influence of the Aztecs on modern Mexico, such as the following, echo in a less poetic fashion the remarks of the earlier authors:

Instead of racks or pyramids of skulls still in their hair and raining down scraps of flesh there are corpses of dogs, rats, horses, asses, by the roads; the bones dug out of the rented graves are thrown on a pile when the lease is up; and there are the coffins . . . sold in the open shops . . . Beggars in dog voices on the church steps enact the last feebleness for you with ancient Church Spanish, and show their old flails of stump and their sores. The burden carriers . . . lie in the garbage at siesta and give themselves the same exhibited neglect the dead are shown. Which is all to emphasize how openly death is received everywhere, in the beauty of the place, and how it is acknowledged that anyone may be roughly handled—the proudest—pinched, slapped, and set down, thrown down; for death throws even worse in men's faces and makes it horrible and absurd that one never touched should be roughly dumped under, dumped upon.

Even the beauty is fantastic, rather fearsome. Augie describes Chilpancingo, for example, hideously, with "decay in the town, the spiky, twisted patch of grave iron on the slope, bleeding bougainvillaea bubbles, purple and tubercular on the walls, vines shrieky green, and the big lips and forehead of the mountains begging or singing."[21]

Augie arrives with a woman named Thea Fenchel. She wants to return to Acatla (almost certainly modeled on Taxco), where she has a house, in order to divorce her husband and incidentally to hunt

[20] Saul Bellow, "The Mexican General," *Partisan Review* 9 (May–June 1942): 178–194.

[21] Saul Bellow, *The Adventures of Augie March*, pp. 338, 409.

iguanas with a trained eagle. The eagle proves to be a coward, and Thea angrily disclaims any further relationship with it. Nothing goes right between the man and woman; she goes off to Chilpancingo with another man, and Augie becomes mixed up with the American colony at Acatla. Bellow's picture of these expatriates, with their complete indifference to others, their perverse scandals, gossiping, gambling, and searches for obscene pleasures, is ruthless. Augie seems very much a part of them. He does help the mistress of a criminal to escape from him (much later in the book Augie is to marry her). After the escapade Augie merely drifts on to Mexico City. There he looks up an old friend whom he had seen earlier serving as Trotsky's bodyguard during one of the Russian's rare excursions. Augie is almost pulled into a scheme to protect the exile, whose home has just been attacked, but the plan—much to his relief—is rejected by Trotsky. And so Augie returns to Chicago, apparently unaffected by his sojourn in Mexico in spite of all his turbid activities there. True, he has rejected and been rejected by the way of life offered by Thea, but the fact leaves no discernible mark on his personality. It is difficult to understand what significance Bellow intended the visit to have.[22]

After this novel Bellow seemed to have forgotten Mexico. Then in 1968 he published in the *New Yorker* a story called "Mosby's Memoirs," which is set in Oaxaca and Mitla. The setting is almost incidental to the real story, however. Bellow merely needed a place for his protagonist to meditate away from either Europe or the United States, and the few Mexican views we get do not differ noticeably from those in the *Adventures*. The main character has come to Mexico on a Guggenheim fellowship to write his autobiography. Thinking that the memoir needs leavening with a comic touch, he decides to retell the story of Hymen Lustgarten, a born failure. But the humor is dissipated when Mosby reveals that he had been sleeping with Lustgarten's wife while her quixotic husband rushed about the Continent. This revelation occurs as he descends into one of the tombs at Mitla; the memory overpowers and frightens Mosby so badly that he wants to rush back to the surface. He recognizes his own spiritual sterility, but the understanding (unlike that in Lowry's novel) comes without any real aid from his brooding surroundings. Mitla serves as a metaphor rather than an integral part of the plot.[23] In the same

[22] Bellow, *Adventures*, pp. 334–418.
[23] Saul Bellow, *Mosby's Memoirs and Other Stories*, pp. 157–184.

year Bellow collected the story in a volume titled after it, published to mixed reviews.

In all three works Bellow depicted several aspects of life in Mexico that we have not previously encountered, yet his writing leaves few impressions. He could not respond vitally as others have done; he was far too intellectual to comprehend such an emotional country, too involved with a sense of city life to appreciate the awesome Mexican landscape, too tied to his own code of values to enter easily another, and finally too even-tempered to react with either great delight or hatred.

The last of the quartet of American writers to draw inspiration from the Mexico of 1939–1940 was Tennessee Williams (1911–). Idolizing both Lawrence and Hart Crane, he naturally had to travel there, and his observations had a greater influence on the playwright than is generally realized. His first visit was merely a jaunt into Baja California. Then he came to live in Mexico during the summer of 1940, in retreat from Broadway's commercialism. Having landed at Veracruz, he journeyed to Mexico City and then crossed over to Acapulco. The coast was still relatively isolated so that he spent a restful time lolling in his hammock, swimming, writing, and talking with other American writers: Andrew Gun and Jane and Paul Bowles. But in September he became ill and returned to Los Angeles.[24] He carried with him the ideas he would later develop into two of his most important plays, *Camino Real* and *The Night of the Iguana*, as well as the germ for a poem. Before he finished these, however, he returned for a series of visits to Mexico and picked up ideas for two new plays, produced first.

The success of *The Glass Menagerie* so frightened Williams that he wanted to return to Mexico in 1945 because, as he recalled in an essay for the *New York Times*, it had appealed to him as "an elemental country where you can quickly forget the false dignities and conceits imposed by success, a country where vagrants innocent as children curl up to sleep on the pavements and human voices, especially when their language is not familiar to the ear, are soft as birds'."[25] He vis-

---

[24] Tennessee Williams, "History of a Play," *Pharos* 1 and 2 (Spring 1945): 173–174; idem, *Night of the Iguana*, p. 5. Also Mike Stein, *A Look at Tennessee Williams*, pp. 144, 185; Edwina D. Williams, *Remember Me to Tom*, pp. 116–117.

[25] Tennessee Williams, *The Glass Menagerie*, p. xvi.

ited Cuernavaca very briefly and then spent the summer at Chapala
in order to begin work simultaneously on two plays called *Summer
and Smoke* and "The Poker Night" as well as a number of poems. He
spent the winter of 1945–1946 alternating between Texas and Mexico.[26] "The Poker Night" had now evolved into *A Streetcar Named
Desire*, which would bring Williams the Pulitzer Prize and his second
Drama Critics' Circle Award. *Summer and Smoke* opened the following year, but it did not receive full critical attention until its off-
Broadway production in 1952. Though both plays are set in the
South, they show clearly Williams's infatuation with Mexico. In
*Streetcar*, for instance, there is a poker player named Pablo Gonzales and a Mexican flower vendor. This woman adds a tragic counter-
point to the action: she cries out "Flores para los muertos" as the
heroine tries desperately to explain to her unsympathizing suitor why
she has become a nymphomaniac. The Mexican elements in *Summer
and Smoke* are even more obvious. The heroine of this play is named
Alma, "Spanish for soul." But this puritanical soul, disgusted by the
Latins who "dream in the sun—and indulge their senses," is defeated
by an elemental Mexican named Rosa Gonzales. Alma is in love with
John Buchanan, the young man next door, but, convinced that she
must remain a virgin, she repulses his physical advances. Rosa has no
such scruples, and she intends also to have John as her husband. In
explaining her love for the essentially clean, well-mannered man,
Rosa recalls her childhood:

I was born in Piedras Negras, and grew up in a one room house with a
dirt floor, and all of us had to sleep in that one room, five Mexicans and
three geese and a little gamecock named Pepe! . . . Pepe was a good
fighter! That's how Papa began to make money, winning bets on Pepe!
. . . we all slept in the one room. And in the night, I would hear the
love-making. Papa would grunt like a pig to show his passion. I thought
to myself, how dirty it was, love-making, and how dirty it was to be
Mexicans and all have to sleep in one room with a dirt floor and not smell
good because there was not any bathtub!

Alma foils Rosa's plan by calling John's absent father when Rosa and
her father have come to the Buchanans', for in the ensuing fracas the

---

[26] Paul Moor, "A Mississippian Named Tennessee," *Harper's* 197 (July 1948):
70; Benjamin Nelson, *Tennessee Williams*, pp. 114–115; E. D. Williams, *Remember Me to Tom*, p. 194.

drunken Mexican shoots the older Buchanan. But Alma does not win: she is left alone and ends up following the "Vamonos!" of a traveling salesman she has picked up to the promised delights of the Gonzales's casino.[27] Williams for some reason felt uneasy with these Mexican elements. When he revised the play as *The Eccentricities of a Nightingale*, published in 1964, he left out the Gonzales family altogether. The new version is not nearly so effective as the original.

The idea for a short story, "Rubio y Morena," probably dates from this same series of visits. Published in the *Partisan Review* in 1948 (collected in *Hard Candy*, 1954), it deals with "a rather singular relationship between the writer Kamrowski and a Mexican girl, Amada, which began in the Mexican border town of Laredo, one summer during the war when Kamrowski was returning from a trip through the Mexican interior." The writer, who is afraid of women, is visited in his hotel room during the night by the masculine half-Indian; their relationship is more that of two homosexuals than that of a man and woman. Kamrowski accepts her love, but, his ego bolstered by her attention, he becomes unfaithful, deserting her for other women and for his writing. Amada is taken ill, and, since he pays so little attention to her, she finally returns to Laredo. After several months he guiltily follows her and finds her dying on a pallet in her family's miserable hut. The story is interesting but it fails to cohere.[28]

Williams was now publishing materials that had grown out of memories of his 1940 trip. The earliest written was a poem, "The Christus of Guadalajara" (dated June 1941 in the University of Texas manuscript); it was first published in 1949 in *Botteghe Oscura* (collected in *In the Winter of Cities*, 1956). It is a complex rendering of the birth and death of Christ. Surrounded by the traditional symbols of Catholicism, the Christ lies in his tomb with "ashes of roses," waiting to be born. While the incarnation occurs, bells peal and the Indians wait in a shadowy room, "filled with the murmur of rain," and drink Lachryma Christi ("Tears of Christ," the name of a Mexican wine). When Christ becomes "the terrible Rose of the World," he will be crucified; for love leads to death, and no one can help, least of all Santa María, whose anguish is as great as the Christ's.[29] The rich,

---

[27] Tennessee Williams, *Summer and Smoke*, pp. 6, 73, 87, 130.

[28] Tennessee Williams, *Hard Candy*, pp. 125–144.

[29] Tennessee Williams, *In the Winter of Cities*, pp. 88–90.

symbolic texture of the poem makes it one of the outstanding lyrics to come from a Mexican experience.

When Williams had fallen sick in Mexico in 1941, he had thought he was going to die. His fears recalled the visions he had had as a child when ghostly figures had trooped in pageant through his imagination. He spent two months recording this new spectacle of lost, entrapped souls and then laid the sketches aside until a new attack of despair in 1947 reminded him of them.[30] He worked on the play further and the next year included "Ten Blocks on the Camino Real" in *American Blues*. By 1953 it was the full-length *Camino Real*, ready for a Broadway production under Kazan's direction. The Mexican elements are more explicit in the earlier version. The flower vendor from *Streetcar* appears there; the street vendors are all Spanish Americans. The setting is a plaza of "a small tropical port," and he added significantly, "It should have grace and mystery and sadness: that peculiar dreamlike feeling that emanates from such squares in Mexico and from the popular songs of that country."[31] By the 1953 version Williams was thinking of other ports he had seen, and he diluted the Mexican flavor. But from the beginning the drama was conceived in universal terms, and the Mexican elements were used more to suggest an exotic world of the imagination than to present a concrete setting. The locale of the play is not a seaport but rather the world itself, another kind of "port of entry and departure."

The public failed to understand the Broadway production, and it soon closed. Williams continued to brood over it and revised it extensively before it was published later that year. *Camino Real* is a fantasy whose characters are from history, real and fictional, and from the style of American comic strips; it works with certain ideas about death, love, and the necessity of illusions, but these form no clear pattern of relationships. Don Quixote, who has been deserted by Pancho, lies down to sleep; he will select from his dreams a new shadow to accompany him. That hero is to be the American Kilroy, whose bad luck has landed him in this place of last resort, along with others, most notably Jacques Casanova and Marguerite Gautier. As

---

[30] Nancy M. Tischler, *Tennessee Williams*, p. 182; Henry Hewes, "Tennessee Williams—Last of Our Solid Gold Bohemians," *Saturday Review*, March 28, 1953, p. 25.
[31] Tennessee Williams, *American Blues*, pp. 43–77.

Williams revised, the play became tougher, more pessimistic; the dancelike rhythms of the earlier version changed into wild flight. All the main characters are trying to escape, but Lord Byron has shown that the only way from this plaza where the Camino Real ends is through the Terra Incognita, "a wasteland between the walled town and the distant perimeter of snowtopped mountains." It is to this uncharted country that Don Quixote carries Kilroy at the end. Marguerite and Casanova remain behind, consoled by love.[32] An off-Broadway production directed by José Quintero in 1960 found a more receptive public, and it played again in New York in 1970. The play is surely one of Williams's most beautiful.

*The Night of the Iguana* began as a short story with the same title (dated April 1946 in the Texas manuscript); it was published in 1948 in Williams's first collection of fiction, *One Arm and Other Stories*. The main character, Edith Jelkes, is another variation of his neurotic Southern woman. Having suffered a nervous breakdown, she has begun to wander about the world, painting and idly living on her small inheritance. Since she needs desperately to keep in contact with other people, she is disconcerted to find herself in Acapulco between seasons with only two young writers at her hotel, both of whom pointedly ignore her. Utterly alone, she twice tries to return to Mexico City, where she has made friends in the Anglo-American colony. For some reason, however, she cannot leave the two men, whose relationship she has begun to understand. Then one night, when an iguana is tied under her bedroom window, keeping her awake, she seizes the opportunity to move closer. The men bluntly and loudly speak their feelings about her and she rushes into their room to protest. A thunderstorm has come up; it dramatically symbolizes the emotional storm that fills the small room. The younger man leaves in anger; while he is away, the other man attempts to rape her and desists only when he has spilled his semen on her stomach. She runs to her old room. But the storm has abated, and the iguana she discovers has been released; "in some equally mysterious way the strangling rope of her loneliness had also been severed by what had happened tonight on this barren rock above the moaning

---

[32] Tennessee Williams, *Camino Real*. David Deacon's 1970 production of the play at Texas A&I University helped my understanding of it.

waters." In spite of its melodramatic overtones, the story, narrated with gentle understanding, is extremely effective.[33]

As Williams developed *The Night of the Iguana*—first as a one-act play for the Festival of Two Worlds in 1959 and then into a three-act production that opened on Broadway in late 1961—only the symbols of the storm and the iguana remained. There is still a painter, named Hannah Jelkes, but she is strong in a way Edith Jelkes could never be. Significantly, this woman comes from New England; Williams's Southern neurotic is now a man, the Reverend T. Lawrence Shannon, defrocked for fornication and heresy. He has become a guide leading groups of tourists across Mexico, and on this trip, in the summer of 1940, he has a group from a Texas Baptist college for women. Ready to crack up mentally, Shannon brings them to the Costa Verde Hotel near Acapulco, where he hopes to find consolation from an old friend. But the friend is dead, and his lusty widow, Maxine Faulk, waits, rum coco in hand, to seduce Shannon into filling his place. Hannah and her ninety-seven–year–old grandfather arrive the same day. He was a minor poet and is now trying to complete the first poem he has begun in twenty years. He had wanted to come to Mexico, to the sea, "the cradle of life," but in the high Sierra he has suffered another cerebral hemorrhage. With these four people Williams composed perhaps his most mature play, the summation of a long struggle to understand how man may face the perverse darkness of life without giving in to it.

Under the goading of Maxine and the women on the tour, Shannon finally goes to pieces, and two Mexican servants are forced to tie him into a hammock in the same way they have earlier tied an iguana to a post at the edge of the veranda. Hannah tries to calm him, and in talking to him reveals Williams's faith that man can find "broken gates between people so they can reach each other, even if it's just for one night only."[34] Also at the hotel is a party of Germans, who are eagerly following the battle of Britain on their shortwave radio. But though the Nazis bring to light the cancerous evil that man can produce, such horror can be kept under control. *Iguana* ends on a muted but hopeful note. Shannon gives in to drink and will obviously stay

---

[33] Tennessee Williams, *One Arm and Other Stories*, pp. 169–196.
[34] Tennessee Williams, *Night of the Iguana*, p. 104.

to serve Maxine. The grandfather dies, leaving Hannah alone. But before that happens he has finished his poem, and Hannah and Shannon have played God and released the captured iguana. Even Shannon's defection may not be tragic, since he has freed himself from his ropes, an act symbolic of his calmer state of mind, and has been able to give up his cross, the symbol of his past. As the grandfather suggests in his poem, courage can come to dwell "in the frightened heart" of man. The Nazis will not win the battle.

Mexican elements, besides the iguana and the physical setting, permeate the play. Since the attention is always upon the Americans and their various dilemmas, the secondary characters tend to be caricatures: the two Mexican servants are essentially the oversexed primitives that Alma imagines. We are reminded through the presence of the Germans of the troubled situation in Mexico, which attracts Nazi agents to "the front door to South America—and the back door to the States." In Shannon's comments about his tour, he reveals Williams's knowledge of the tourist circuit: "the floating gardens of Xochimilco, Maximilian's Palace, and the mad Carlotta's little homesick chapel, Our Lady of Guadalupe, the monument to Juarez, the relics of the Aztec civilization, the sword of Cortez, the headdress of Montezuma. . . . Diego Rivera's murals."[35] And the playwright's portraits of the women tourists, though intentionally overdrawn so as to be comic, perfectly delineate at least one type of tourist.

As a result of the play, Mexico came alive to Williams in another way. In the fall of 1963 he joined John Huston's company at Puerto Vallarta and Mismaloya for a few weeks to watch part of the filming of *Iguana*. Williams assisted with the screenplay, but the movie failed to match the greatness of the play, which had won for Williams his fourth Drama Critics' Circle Award. And it is doubtful that he picked up new ideas from the turbulent and well-publicized meeting of Richard Burton, Elizabeth Taylor, Ava Gardner, Deborah Kerr, and Emilio Fernández in the tropical jungle, a meeting that profoundly altered the character of Puerto Vallarta.[36]

[35] Ibid., pp. 88–89. The play has been translated into Spanish and was for sale in several bookstores in Mexico City as early as the summer of 1965. One Mexican director whom I then asked about it felt that it would not be produced soon in Mexico, since the audience might be sensitive to some of Williams's comments. The film version deleted certain lines at the request of the government.

[36] "Stars Fell on Mismaloya," *Life*, December 20, 1963, pp. 69–73; Thelda Vic-

Williams's friends Paul Bowles (1910–) and his wife Jane (1917–1973) were not so deeply impressed by Mexico in their writings.[37] Bowles, having been awarded a Guggenheim fellowship in 1941, composed three works influenced by Latin American music: an opera, *The Wind Renews*, with a libretto adopted from the poetry of the Spaniard García Lorca; a ballet, *Pastorela*; and an orchestral work, *Danza Mexicana*. But the evidence of his macabre Spanish American short stories—eight collected in *The Delicate Prey*, 1950, and two in *The Time of Friendship*, 1967—as well as his novel *Up above the World*, 1966, suggests that as a writer he was more dramatically influenced by a later sojourn in Guatemala and knowledge of other parts of Spanish America than by his visit to Mexico. The same thing would be said of Jane Bowles in looking through her *Collected Works*, 1966: the novel, *Two Serious Ladies*, which she was working on in Acapulco while Williams was there, takes place partly in Panama, and the three short stories about Spanish Americans are set in Guatemala although a Mexican appears in one.

Few other writers visited Mexico during the war years. Edward Dahlberg (1900–) was in Mexico City writing just before the war, and his interest in Maya and Toltec mythology permeates two of the poems collected in *Cipango's Hinder Door*, 1965.[38] John Gunther (1901–1970) made a flying tour of all Latin America in 1940; the next year he published *Inside Latin America* with his usual mixture of history and straight reporting about the current situation. Such a work dates quickly, but Gunther's popularity undoubtedly led people who would never have looked at similar works to read this one. Randall Jarrell (1914–1965) and his first wife spent the summer of 1942 in Mexico. A small country market near Guadalajara inspired the poem "An Indian Market in Mexico," published in the *Arizona Quarterly* in 1945.[39] And Cole Porter (1891–1964) spent part of 1943

---

tor, "The Drama the Cameras Missed," *Saturday Evening Post*, July 11, 1964, pp. 27–28, 32.

[37] Stanley J. Kunitz and Howard Haycroft (eds.), *Twentieth Century Authors*, p. 107; *Contemporary Authors*, vols. 19–20, p. 53; Paul Bowles, *Without Stopping*, pp. 197–204, 225–232, 253–254.

[38] Edward Dahlberg, *Cipango's Hinder Door*, pp. 21–24, 65–66. Harold Billings prepared a bibliography.

[39] Mary Jarrell, his second wife, dated the trip for me in a letter, late January 1971. Randall Jarrell, *The Complete Poems*, p. 439.

in Mexico in search of atmosphere for his musical *Mexican Hayride*, which opened in New York in 1944.[40] But more and more it was would-be artists who now visited the country, running in their little cliques in Mexico City, Cuernavaca, Taxco, and San Miguel, occasionally producing works of a generally poor quality, and only occasionally would an artist of true genius flash across the scene.

[40] George Eells, *The Life That Late He Led*, pp. 209–212; Burns Mantle (ed.), *Best Plays of 1943–44 and the Year Book of the Drama in America*, pp. 451–452.

## 12. The Beat Trail to Mexico

"Behind us lay the whole of America and everything Dean and I had previously known about life, and life on the road. We had finally found the magic land at the end of the road and we never dreamed the extent of the magic."[1] Thus Jack Kerouac described Mexico as it appeared to many of his generation. This was in his book *On the Road*, 1957, which introduced to most Americans the new breed of Bohemians, the beatniks. Kerouac and his friends, particularly Allen Ginsberg and William Burroughs (to be joined later by others, like Gregory Corso and Lawrence Ferlinghetti), formed an inner circle of the Beat literary scene, sensitive to the new directions American youths were exploring. They held ambivalent feelings toward the United States, brought on by such circumstances as the threat of the atomic bomb, the destruction of the old left in an increasingly conservative atmosphere (climaxing in McCarthyism), and the general uncertainty of the cold war. Rejecting almost all the values of the middle class, which seemed somehow responsible, they were drawn variously to the criminal, the primitive, the exotic, and the hallucinatory—anything on the far edge of society.

[1] Jack Kerouac, *On the Road*, p. 276.

Consequently, Mexico, the nearest alien culture, provided magic. Since apparently none of them, contrary to what they thought, actually entered the life of that country, they easily imagined existing there whatever conditions satisfied their needs. Mexico was primitive. It seemed free, presenting, as Kerouac later explained in an essay (echoing undoubtedly Spengler's use of the word *fellaheen*), a "fellaheen feeling about life, that timeless gayety of people not involved in great cultural and civilization issues."[2] And drugs were easily available. Because drugs so often provided an escape, these five writers seem superficially to have followed the paths that Crane and Lowry had mapped. Perhaps Burroughs did, and Corso and later Kerouac experienced a disquieting sensation in Mexico; but Ginsberg and Kerouac at first plunged into the foreignness of the place with a kind of joyful abandonment, devoid of fear, even at their worst radiating a saintly innocence. Ferlinghetti alone of their number held Traven's political interests, the others having only a very generalized belief in anarchy; but Traven (as Kenneth Rexroth, a sort of elder statesman for the Beats, observed) was their real antecedent in Mexico.[3] Dean in *On the Road* summed up: "There's no *suspicion* here, nothing like that. Everybody's cool, everybody looks at you with such straight brown eyes and they don't say anything, just *look*, and in that look all of the human qualities are soft and subdued and still there. Dig all the foolish stories you read about Mexico and the sleeping gringo and all that crap—and crap about greasers and so on—and all it is, people here are straight and kind and don't put down any bull."[4]

Kerouac (1922–1969) first entered the country in the summer of 1950 in company with Neal Cassady—the Dean Moriaty of *Road* and perhaps the archetypal Beat—and another youth. Since the novel (written in 1951), like all of Kerouac's, provides a Wolfe-like transcription of actual events, it is fairly easy to follow the thread of Kerouac's Mexican life.[5] For two years he, Cassady, and others had whizzed back and forth across the United States. Kerouac was attracted by the apparently simple life of the Mexican Americans, and he lived with them in California for a while. Then he and Cassady

[2] Jack Kerouac, *Lonesome Traveler*, p. 27.
[3] Thomas Parkinson (ed.), *A Casebook on the Beat*, p. 186.
[4] Kerouac, *On the Road*, p. 278.
[5] Ibid., pp. 274–306. Also Ann Chartres, *Kerouac: A Biography*, pp. 124–125. Mrs. Chartres also prepared a bibliography.

turned south, crossing the Mexican border at Nuevo Laredo, and, "bearded, bedraggled," drove along the Inter-American highway almost nonstop to Mexico City. One respite did come in Ciudad Victoria. There they discovered a Mexican youth who provided them with marijuana and directions to the red-light district, where they spent a wild afternoon. Everywhere the police amazed them: the courteous officials at the border, the quiet ones outside the whorehouses, the sheriff at the little town below Victoria where they pulled the car over and slept the night. Of this man Kerouac wrote: "Such lovely policemen God hath never wrought in America. No suspicions, no fuss, no bother: he was the guardian of the sleeping town, period."[6]

Undisturbed by filth and poverty, they felt at one with the Indian earth and its people, excited equally by the gaunt landscape around Monterrey and Mexico City and the lush jungles in between. Yet ironically, although Kerouac wanted to identify with the natives, he was slightly depressed by their naïveté concerning the direction the world seemed to be taking since Hiroshima. He wrote about one group they met on the highway: "They had come down from the back mountains and higher places to hold forth their hands for something they thought civilization could offer, and they never dreamed the madness and the poor broken delusion of it. They didn't know that a bomb had come that could crack all our bridges and roads and reduce them to jumbles, and we would be as poor as they someday, and stretching out our hands in the same, same way." Still his general exhilaration continued all the way to the capital, "the great and final wild uninhibited Fellahin-childlike city that we knew we would find at the end of the road."[7] In Mexico City Kerouac stayed with the Burroughses, who had just arrived. The Mexicans seemed to them all completely free in contrast with the people in the tight American cities. Kerouac's happiness lasted even through his becoming ill and Cassady's simply leaving him to make his way back to the States as best he could.

Kerouac's next visit began in May 1952.[8] By now he had published one rather conventional novel, but no publisher liked the direction Kerouac had then taken, as he turned out almost automatically a stream of rambling, picaresque works. He felt at loose ends. Entering

[6] Kerouac, *On the Road*, p. 295.

[7] Ibid., p. 299.

[8] Kerouac, *Lonesome Traveler*, pp. 21–36; also Chartres, *Kerouac*, pp. 158–169.

Mexico at Nogales, he made his way down the west coast on a second-class bus, in company with two Mexican youths whom he had met at a rest stop. Together they sought out marijuana, opium, and other stimuli. By the time he arrived in Mexico City, he was completely broke and depended for the rest of his visit on the generosity of Burroughs. This trip Kerouac described in the essay "Mexico Fellaheen," published in *Lonesome Traveler*, 1960. He glimpsed this time something of Mexico's somber side. A bullfight, the bloody image of Christ in all the churches, reminders of the Aztec rites—all suggested to him the grimness of mortality. In June he worked on a novel, *Doctor Sax: Faust Part Three*, 1959, while sitting on Burroughs's toilet in order to escape all the junkies coming in and out of the house. This rather impressive novel concerns the nightmarish fantasies that come to a boy growing up in Massachusetts. Intertwined in them is Doctor Sax, a character considerably influenced in its delineation by the figure of Burroughs. By using symbolically the picture of the great Mexican eagle destroying the serpent, Kerouac ended his novel hopefully. Earlier he had said that "Doctor Sax made a special trip to Teotehua-can [*sic*] Mexico, to do his special research on the culture of the eagle and the snake—Azteca; he came back laden with information about the snake, none about the bird—."[9] But the Doctor too sees clearly the meaning of the final vision and thereafter "deals in glee" (here Kerouac was creating fiction, not a portrait of Burroughs). Throughout the novel are scattered other references to the country, and it is permeated with the ambivalent feeling Kerouac held toward Mexico at this time.

William Seward Burroughs (1914–), Kerouac's and Ginsberg's mentor, had come with his wife to Mexico in order to escape legal conviction as an addict.[10] Although he agreed, as he wrote in *Naked Lunch*, that "something falls off you when you cross the border into Mexico," he lacked the childlike wonder that Kerouac generally managed to maintain.[11] To Burroughs the land was "a sinister place."

---

[9] Jack Kerouac, *Doctor Sax*, p. 149; Ted Berigan, interview with Jack Kerouac, *Paris Review* 43 (Summer 1968): 84.

[10] William S. Burroughs, *Junkie*, pp. 98–126, with introduction by Carl Solomon, pp. 5–6; George Plimpton (ed.), *Writers at Work*, 3d series, pp. 145, 163, 167; William S. Burroughs, Jr., "Life with Father," *Esquire* 76 (September 1971): 113.

[11] William S. Burroughs, *Naked Lunch*, p. 14.

These were the years of Miguel Alemán's presidency, when spectacular gains were being achieved, including the building of the new University City, but when corruption was rampant. Many people went around armed. Burroughs too bought a gun; shortly afterward, while he was cleaning it, it went off and killed his wife. His drug-induced paranoia also distorted the scene. He tried several times to effect a cure, but cocaine, heroin, marijuana, peyote, and other drugs came to hand too readily. There were even dangers provided by tequila, as he discovered when he almost died of uremic poisoning. Nevertheless, he felt "safe in Mexico" to make his contacts and watch "refugee hipsters" fleeing from the growing conservatism of the United States, including William Garver. Yet Burroughs was bored. For a while he attended Mexico City College. Then about 1950 he began to write a number of letters to Ginsberg in which he tried to describe, as he has said in an interview, "in a more-or-less straightforward journalistic style something about my experiences with addiction and addicts."[12] From these grew his first book, *Junkie*, published in 1953 under the pseudonym "William Lee."

This book like all his works moves uneasily among fragmented memories, extended scenes, and expository digressions. Had he not gone on to make his later stylistic and structural experiments, beginning with *Naked Lunch*, we would ignore *Junkie*. But since it depicts objectively the experiences of an addict rather than attempting to re-create subjectively those experiences as the later books do, it provides a useful introduction both to Burroughs's world and to that of the hard drug scene. Here we find none of De Quincey's ornate descriptions; instead we possess simple and generally ugly insights into the routine life of a man totally committed to "junk sickness." The fictionalized autobiography begins with Burroughs's first acquaintance with morphine near the end of World War II and continues through several brushes with the law in New York and New Orleans. In these scenes he is in familiar surroundings, however, and the world does not seem particularly scary. But after his flight to Mexico, the pattern expands, spinning off increasingly abhorrent visions: "A series of faces, hieroglyphics, distorted and leading to the final place where the human road ends, where the human form can no longer contain the crustacean horror that has grown inside it."[13] The book finishes with

12 Plimpton, *Writers at Work*, 3d series, p. 145.
13 Burroughs, *Junkie*, p. 112.

his decision to move on to South America in July 1952 in order to look for "the final fix" in yage (an experience recounted in *The Yage Letters*, 1963, co-authored with Ginsberg, who likewise traveled there in 1960). By 1952 Burroughs seemed possessed.

After this journey he moved to Algiers. There he began creating the vignettes that he would eventually combine into *Naked Lunch*, 1959. His paranoia had convinced him that an intricate system, though it was slowly falling apart, controlled the world. Even before he went to Mexico, he had been fascinated by the undeciphered Maya codices and saw in the Maya calendar an earlier system whereby the priests could control even the most minute activities of the people. Drugs were another total control system: "Junk takes everything and gives nothing but insurance against junk sickness," he had written in his first book.[14] Thus if he examined his life as an addict, especially the horrible visions that had matured in those years in Mexico, he could explore these systems, past and present. Moreover, he thought that drugs provided a heightened sense of reality and an escape from the limitations of space and time. These thoughts in part inform the rationale behind *Naked Lunch*—and later *The Soft Machine*, 1961, especially in a chapter called "The Mayan Caper," and *The Wild Boys*, 1971. What we get in these novels is homosexual science fiction, sometimes frightening in the continual emphasis on death and pain, sometimes humorous, almost always nauseating. Totally devoid of plot and at times even sense, except perhaps to another addict, these books can be read by cutting into them anywhere one pleases. None of the experimental novels satisfies, but none can be easily forgotten.[15]

Allen Ginsberg (1926–) had planned to visit Burroughs while he was in Mexico, but the poet was unable to come until 1954.[16] Then he arrived by way of Cuba to explore the Maya country. He visited Chichén Itzá, Tulum, Uxmal, Kabah, Palenque, Piedras Negras, and Yaxchilán, camping out at several of the sites. It was his first encounter with an ancient civilization. Later he recalled, "Like Shelley in Italy, I was busy poking around big history-less Mayan ruins and

[14] Ibid., p. 106.

[15] Daniel Odier, *The Job*, pp. 28–36, 171; Kerouac, *On the Road*, p. 144. Also Burroughs, *Naked Lunch*, p. 233; idem, *The Soft Machine*, pp. 12–29, 85–97; idem, *The Wild Boys*, first section.

[16] Jane Kramer, *Allen Ginsberg in America*, pp. 40, 120, 137–138, 161; Chartres, *Kerouac*, pp. 201–202.

wandering all over alone, absorbing that kind of antiquity and sense of transience and thinking up big long poems about native grounds." The only one he has published is "Siesta in Xbalba," published in *Evergreen Review* in 1957 and collected as one of the *Reality Sandwiches* in 1963. He wrote it, according to his note appended to the poem, in the area believed by the Maya to be inhabited by the Xibalba (as the word is usually spelled), or people of the underworld, at the foot of a large tree to which "ancient craftsmen came to complete work left unfinished at their death." Musing upon the "alien hieroglyphs of Eternity," he used the moment to take stock of the present:

> above the abandoned
> labyrinth of Palenque
>         measuring my fate,
> wandering solitary in the wild
>         —blinking singleminded
> at a bleak idea—
>         until exhausted with
> its action and contemplation
>         my soul might shatter
> at one primal moment's
>         sensation of the vast
> movement of divinity.

All the associations of his past, framed as by a camera in his mind, juxtapose themselves against the incredible ruins he had explored, "sunken under the flood of years" and

> leaving many mysteries
> of deathly volition
> to be divined.

But the future also intersected, both his desire to visit the other classic places of the world (India and Greece later influenced him) and his pilgrimage toward the final "future, unimaginable God." The poem, grounded firmly in the realities of the area—his catalogue of the sites is unmatchable—remains one of his finest achievements.

Ginsberg must have met Karena Shields, to whom the poem is dedicated, at Palenque. A retired movie actress and later author of a memoir about her childhood on a rubber plantation in Mexico (*The Changing Wind*, 1959), she invited Ginsberg to her *finca* near the Guatemala border. Several months later he headed north to California to visit Cassady. This journey became the basis for a companion poem, "Return to the States." Though working with some of the same themes, especially in his contemplation of the mummies of Guanajuato, the poem fails to equal "Siesta." Bits of local color—a view of Lake Catemaco, a scene from San Miguel de Allende, the slums of Mexicali—and the frightening view of the United States with which the poem closes do not cohere, and the whole work seems anticlimactic after the perfection of "Siesta."[17] But he was preparing for "Howl" and its condemnation of America; from the introspective moment in Mexico he was "Returning / armed with New Testament." Ginsberg also alluded to the country in a number of his other poems, including a touching tribute to Burroughs's wife and her unvisited grave: "Dream Record, June 8, 1955," likewise included in *Reality Sandwiches*.

In the summer of 1955 Kerouac returned to Mexico City, living in the servant's room above Garver's house, where the Burroughses had lived. Kerouac met Esperanza Villanueva, an Indian girl, and began the affair with her described in his novel *Tristessa*, 1960.[18] In three weeks he improvised the 242 choruses of *Mexico City Blues*, 1956, a strong influence on Ginsberg's poetry. The poems are wild chants, composed—some while under the influence of drugs—more for sound than sense, but they seem appropriate for the depressed mood in which Mexico then left Kerouac. Later that summer he left for Berkeley to join Ginsberg and the large number of other poets who would effect the San Francisco poetry renaissance. That winter Kerouac returned home briefly to North Carolina, catching glimpses on the way there and back of Mexicali and Juárez (described in *The Dharma Bums*, 1958).[19] But both times nothing seemed right; he got a "vomity feeling." He was supposed to return to Miss Villanueva in the spring, but he had run out of money. They exchanged letters, in which he eventually confessed that he loved her. Some of the fantasies assembled in *Book of Dreams*, 1961, which often recall Mexico, may come from this same period.

---

[17] Allen Ginsberg, *Reality Sandwiches, 1953–1960*, pp. 21–39. Edward Z. Menkin prepared a bibliography.

[18] Jack Kerouac, *Tristessa*; Berigan, interview with Kerouac, pp. 91–92, 101; Chartres, *Kerouac*, pp. 217–229.

[19] Jack Kerouac, *The Dharma Bums*, pp. 124–126, 155–156.

In the fall of 1956 Kerouac returned to Mexico City.[20] He wrote in *Desolation Angels*, 1965, the record of this visit, that he always remembered Mexico at a distance as "gay, exciting," but when he returned he would find that he had "forgotten a certain drear, even sad, darkness."[21] The relationship with Miss Villanueva soon failed. As Kerouac remembered in the second half of *Tristessa*, finished almost as soon as the episode itself, she was now sick and looked at him with hatred, and her friends robbed him. At a party she fell over, spitting blood; thinking that she was dying, Kerouac tried to get help. "My poems stolen, my money stolen, my Tristessa dying, Mexican buses trying to run me down, grit in the sky, agh, I never dreamed it could be this bad—," he wrote. Their later reunion was tender; but obviously the affair would not work, and so they separated.

In October Kerouac learned that Ginsberg was coming down for a visit. Ginsberg dashed off a poem, "Ready to Roll," in San Francisco in anticipation of the journey; it too is collected in *Reality Sandwiches*. Ginsberg traveled down the West Coast with his companion, Peter Orlovsky, Orlovsky's brother, and Gregory Corso. The four men stopped briefly in Guadalajara to see Denise Levertov and Mitchell Goodman, and then walked casually into the Garver household. Ginsberg was perfectly content and rushed around to all the sights of the capital: University City, Teotihuacán, Xochimilco. But Corso (1930–) felt less assured, finding the same frightening conditions that he had observed in the United States. Kerouac in *Angels* remembered Corso's saying: "There's *death* in Mexico—I saw a windmill turning death this way—I dont *like* it here—." This attitude permeated *Gasoline*, 1958, a collection of poems Corso was writing during the trip. In one of them he summed up his disappointment less flamboyantly by pointing out:

> In the Mexican Zoo
> they have ordinary
> American cows.[22]

---

[20] Jack Kerouac, *Desolation Angels*, pp. 221–257, with introduction by Seymour Krim, pp. ix–xxviii. Also Chartres, *Kerouac*, pp. 272–277.

[21] Kerouac, *Desolation Angels*, p. 222.

[22] Gregory Corso, "Mexican Impressions," *Gasoline*, pp. 7, 23–26. Robert A. Wilson prepared a bibliography. Kerouac, *Desolation Angels*, p. 234; the possible Corso character is called Raphael Urso, while the possible Ginsberg character is called Irwin Garden.

At Corso's urging, the five men decided to return to the States, since at least there Corso could be comfortable if not content. Garver had become gravely ill (he died soon thereafter) and begged them not to leave him. But late that November they slipped out and made their way north to Nuevo Laredo. For the others it was apparently their last trip to Mexico, but Kerouac crossed at Juárez in 1957 to show his mother something of the country and returned to Mexico City in 1961 to finish the second half of *Desolation Angels*.[23]

These writers represented the East Coast in the Beat world; Lawrence Ferlinghetti (1919–) was a chief figure of the West Coast. He too went to Mexico, having visited the country first before World War II and then a few times in the 1950's. But most of the notes, poems (both in English and Spanish), and drawings collected in *The Mexican Night: Travel Journal*, 1970, date from the 1960's.[24] Though entertaining and oftentimes perceptive, Ferlinghetti's early comments offer no really new insight; "the new Mexico still the Old Beat Mexico," he jotted down. Narcotics and the stupidities of artificial borders remain a theme. In 1961 he re-explored Baja California, the towns of which he found hopelessly depressing. In 1962 he traveled over the new railroad opened between Chihuahua and Topolobampo through some of the most spectacular scenery in North America, but it was for him a "wild junkie landscape."

In his attack on borders, Ferlinghetti had echoed the revolutionary note that sounds in much of his writing. When he returned in the fall of 1968 to visit Oaxaca and Mexico City and again in the spring of 1969 to Guadalajara, this theme strongly focused his observations. In fall 1968 Mexican students were actively criticizing the government for spending too much money on the Olympics soon to open in Mexico City while so many of its people were going hungry. In one angry confrontation that October an unknown number were killed and more arrested. Thus Ferlinghetti had forced upon him the fact that life in Mexico is fully as complicated as that in the United States. He commented bitterly—and sometimes not very lucidly—on this state of affairs, the only notable American writer so far to have done so. He felt personally involved. Two of his friends, Margaret Randall and Robert Cohen, had lost the backing they previously enjoyed from

---

[23] Kerouac, *Desolation Angels*, pp. 342–346; Chartres, *Kerouac*, pp. 340–341.

[24] See Lawrence Ferlinghetti, *The Mexican Night*.

the government when their little magazine, *El Corno Emplumado*, supported the students, and they finally felt that they must flee the country. Ferlinghetti reproduced a letter setting forth their version of this troubled period in *Mexican Night* immediately following his poem commemorating the spirit of Che Guevara. But by mid-March 1969, when he settled in San Miguel to start working over Cassady's manuscripts, his notes seem like excerpts from Kerouac's apolitical vision. Obviously Ferlinghetti was fascinated by Mexico (he also visited South America in 1960) or he would not have returned so often, but it seems ultimately to have influenced his life much less than it did earlier Beats. *The Mexican Night*, however, is quite pleasant, often capturing some scene perfectly.

Other writers came during the 1960's, but they in general found little to incorporate into their writing. Thomas Pynchon (1937–) finished *V.* there early in the decade,[25] and the heroine of his second novel, *The Crying of Lot 49*, 1966, remembers a trip to Mazatlán. Terry Southern (1926–) may have visited about the same time; his Burroughs-like story "The Road Out of Axotle" appeared in *Esquire* in 1962 (collected in *Red-Dirt Marijuana*, 1967). Michael McClure (1932–) composed a number of his *Ghost Tantras*, 1967, in Mexico City.[26] Richard Brautigan (1935–) took the main characters of *The Abortion: An Historical Romance 1966*, 1971, to Tijuana. The most dramatic episode, however, was left for Ken Kesey (1935–), who arrived in 1966.[27] He had jumped bail, arranged for his second arrest on charges of possessing marijuana, had faked a suicide, and then had fled to Puerto Vallarta and later Manzanillo. For several months, in company with Cassady and others, he played an elaborate game of cops and robbers, described in a fragmented way in a series of fifteen letters to Larry McMurtry, published in 1967 in a limited edition and in a screen play, "Over the Border," published in *Kesey's Garage Sale*, 1973. Mexico scarcely presents itself in these works except as a fearful setting in which his pursuers could hide away: we return to the paranoia of Burroughs.

By now most of the hippies were demanding in the United States the same freedom to do as they pleased that the beatniks had sought

[25] *Contemporary Authors*, vols. 19–20, pp. 352–353.

[26] Michael McClure, *Ghost Tantras*, pp. 26–27.

[27] Tom Wolfe, *The Electric Kool-Aid Acid Test*, pp. 301–362; Jerome Charyn (ed.), *The Single Voice*, pp. 414–426.

in Mexico. Flight south would no longer suffice, as Kesey discovered—
he soon slipped back into the States—and as perhaps Cassady foresaw
before he fell dead on the railroad tracks outside San Miguel in
February 1968. The Mexican government, as the new youth movement became worldwide, also began to look upon the type in an
unfriendly fashion, and officials no longer greeted bearded and bedraggled visitors with the same warmth Kerouac and Cassady had received twenty years earlier. A number of communes managed to
spring up, especially in areas where peyote and the magic mushroom
grow, but these groups tend to be completely anti-intellectual and do
not express themselves in writing.

In fact, one of the surprising aspects of the Beat movement was its
extreme literacy. Though the writers (except Ferlinghetti) were less
knowledgeable about Mexico than other writers had generally been,
their reading ranged widely from European existentialists to Eastern
sages. Their ultimate worth as a group remains to be seen. Kerouac,
Ginsberg, and Burroughs, and to a lesser extent Corso and Ferlinghetti, have all been extravagantly praised and equally damned at
various points in their careers, but remarkably little attempt has been
made to examine their work critically.[28] Perhaps they were a fad.
As Imamu Amiri Baraka (LeRoi Jones) remarked in one of his poems
in the early sixties:

> Beatniks, like Bohemians, go calmly out of style. And boys
> are dying in Mexico, who did not get the word.[29]

Nevertheless, their influence at the moment was considerable, even
on Latin American writers, and their writing in a period of flaccidity
was among the best.

They also point up most clearly the American writer's repeated
need—not just the beatnik's—to escape from his own culture for
perspective, and they emphasize Mexico again as a possible direction
to go. In the oftentimes wildness of their flight, the Beats represent an
extreme, as they did in other aspects of their lives, but it was in a
direction perceived by almost every other visitor to Mexico from the
United States. They are set apart, however, by their gregariousness;

[28] Harry Russell Huebel, professor of history at Texas A&I University, who
helpfully criticized this chapter, finished a dissertation on the subject at Washington State University, 1970; Bruce Cook published *The Beat Generation*.

[29] LeRoi Jones, "The New World," *Black Magic*, p. 22.

they formed the only noteworthy group to have worked together in Mexico. And they differ from most other writers in their reactions to primitivism. Whereas Lawrence, Huxley, and others before the war rejected this way of life, the Beats (except Corso) left Mexico for the more alien worlds of South America, Algeria, and India, moving deeper and deeper into such cultures, before returning to America.

## 13. Fields of Vision

After the war, tourists continued to come into Mexico City and increasingly out into the provinces as more and more roads, railroads,
and airports were opened. Cuernavaca and Acapulco became sterile
international playgrounds. Travel books and memoirs naturally
proliferated, Terry's old guide even being revamped in the 1960's by
James Norman Schmidt (1912–); but none of these new works
matched the power of Flandrau or Greene, let alone the earlier giants.
Elizabeth Borton de Treviño (1904–) probably wrote the most popular
memoir, *My Heart Lies South*, 1953. The humorist H. Allen Smith
(1907–) wrote the delightfully chatty book *The Pig in the Barber
Shop*, 1958, but it has already dated badly. Selden Rodman (1909–)
made his second visit in 1956–1957; he took notes all the while, in-
tending to write a book to equal the masterpieces.[1] *Mexican Journal*,
1958, unfortunately fails to achieve his commendable goal. Still it
remains a valuable document. Rodman was a poet, and consequently
he was interested in the Mexican arts and in the reactions of American and British culture to that of Mexico. His interviews with various
members of the Mexican intelligentsia and of the artist colonies elicited much delightful and some malicious gossip. He also showed, by

[1] Selden Rodman, *Mexican Journal*; idem, *The Road to Panama*, p. 10.

recording the many variants he encountered of the same story, how impossible it is ever to recover the truth of a moment. Throughout his visits he spent most of his time in the area around the capital, but he traveled some in such isolated states as Chiapas and Yucatan.

Yucatan increasingly attracted tourists after the war. The British poet Sacheverell Sitwell (1897–) for instance was among those who flew into Mérida in 1960 to look around the Maya ruins, an incident he recorded in his Latin American memoir, *Golden Walls and Mirador,* 1961.[2] Charles Olson, as we shall see, spent many months in the same area in the early 1950's, and Ferlinghetti seems to have visited there briefly in 1969. Similarly, Baja California allured a surprising number of writers, including Ferlinghetti, in the three postwar decades. Mystery writer Erle Stanley Gardner (1889–1970) as usual was most proliferate, turning out between 1948 and 1969 eight travel books, several well illustrated, about the area.[3] But the best writing about Baja, even better than Steinbeck's journal, remains *The Forgotten Peninsula,* 1961, by Joseph Wood Krutch (1893–1970).[4] Quotations from it and other works by the critic and naturalist were incorporated into an outstanding Sierra Club edition, *Baja California and the Geography of Hope.*

No other really significant travel books appeared. There were, however, two splendid essays: one by Wright Morris, to be discussed later, and the other by Norman Mailer (1923–). During the mid-1950's Mailer spent several summers in Mexico City working on various projects.[5] After an initial dislike of bullfights, he became "a great lover" of the ritual; and out of this affection he created his only extensive comment on the Mexican scene, a preface entitled "Footnote to Death in the Afternoon" for a CBS collection of photographs, *The Bullfight,* 1967. It is more human in its approach than Hemingway's survey, although Mailer shared many of his assumptions, particularly the idea that the bullfight provides in the manner of Greek drama a catharsis by which the spectator might rid himself of all the accumu-

[2] Sacheverell Sitwell, *Golden Walls and Mirador,* pp. 247–281.

[3] Gardner wrote *Land of Shorter Shadows,* 1948; *Neighborhood Frontiers,* 1954; *Hunting the Desert Whale,* 1960; *Hovering over Baja,* 1961; *Hidden Heart of Baja,* 1962; *Off the Beaten Track in Baja,* 1967; *Mexico's Magic Square,* 1968; and *Host with the Big Hat,* 1969.

[4] Joseph Wood Krutch, *The Forgotten Peninsula; Contemporary Authors 2,* p. 93.

[5] Norman Mailer, *Advertisements for Myself,* pp. 205, 212, 216, 310.

lated horror of the week. Mailer saw only the *novillades*, in which hopeful novices appear, but he felt that a more genuine understanding of the human condition grew from his witnessing bad fights, with now and then an inspiring moment. He remembered one in which a most unlovely and unskilled *novillo* did everything wrong, receiving the complete contempt of the crowd, until the kill itself, perfectly executed. Mailer too had disliked him until that moment, when he discovered that this man too was human: "So this bad bullfight in the rain had given a drop of humanity to a very dry area of my heart," he wrote.

Most of the essay concerns the triumphal summer in 1954 experienced by a provincial given the nickname "El Loco" because of his completely unpredictable manner in the ring, moving from some of the wildest, most inept passes with one animal to a most brilliant execution with another. The lesson he provided, Mailer concluded, was of the highest importance:

... he spoke of the great distance a man can go from the worst in himself to the best, and that finally is what the bullfight might be all about, for in dark bloody tropical lands possessed of poverty and desert and swamp, filth and treachery, slovenliness, and the fat lizards of all the worst lust, the excretory lust to shove one's own poison into others, the one thing which can keep the sweet nerve of life alive is the knowledge that a man cannot be judged by what he is every day, but only in his greatest moment, for that is the moment when he shows what he was intended to be.[6]

Other authors would at about the same time discover affirmative qualities in the ritual so often dismissed by American and British visitors.

Students were attracted to Mexico more and more, many enrolling each year in the Universidad de México and in summer schools in various state capitals. Immediately after World War II many American veterans used their GI bill of education benefits at Mexico City College, an American school founded in 1940 (later renamed the University of the Americas and ultimately moved to Cholula). And in 1961 Ivan Illich opened his Center for Intercultural Documentation at Cuernavaca. The center attracted many famous educationalists, sociologists, political observers, and literary figures—but as Illich observed truthfully, in a conversation with me, they came not to Mexico

6 Norman Mailer, *The Bullfight*, unpaged.

but to CIDOC. At least two visitors, however—Paul Goodman (1911–1972) and Robert Lowell—did write poems about their impressions.[7]

In addition to playing host to the transients, Mexico remained as always a sort of permanent haven for would-be writers, painters, and mere escapists. The American colonies in Mexico City, Cuernavaca, and Taxco expanded and spilled over into San Miguel de Allende and several towns around Lake Chapala. George Woodcock in his travel book, *To the City of the Dead*, 1957, commented on the number of foreigners in San Miguel; the picture is pretty typical of all. There were, he noted, a few proud Germans, a number of "ambiguous English," and a few Spanish refugees from the Civil War:

But most of the expatriates were Americans and Canadians, and with few exceptions, they bore plainly the marks of frustration in their native environments. Minor painters, radio writers in search of the great novel that haunts every American broadcasting studio, professors in flight from minor colleges, divorcees living on alimony, dilettantish fairies, honest-to-God drunks with dwindling incomes who were attracted by the smell of rum at a guinea a gallon; most of them were people who had slipped the chains of home and come south in search of some Eden of fulfillment. How many of them found the Eden I cannot say, but I imagine that the drunkards were the most successful; few of the would-be creators did anything better than they had done at home, and those who sought liberty in libertinism seemed a singularly unhappy group. But all of them fell under the spell of the lotus, and, with the exception of a few strong spirits who made and kept the decision to live in comparative isolation, their lives assumed the traditional futility of expatriate Bohemianism. . . . it was a pale shadow of the Parisian twenties, but it was laced with neither a Hemingway, nor a Gertrude Stein, nor even a Henry Miller.[8]

Perhaps the expatriate scene in Mexico, save for the few strong characters, has always been so dismal, but in the 1920's there had been an alleviating spirit at work. Woodcock's evaluation now appeared only too deadly accurate. Moreover, the strong souls among the new expatriates often worked on projects having little to do with Mexico; Erich

---

[7] Randolph Wolfe, "Yanqui University in Mexico," *Holiday* 44 (July 1968): 91–93; Dan Dolan, "The Life of Ivan Illich," *New Republic*, March 1, 1969, pp. 18–19; Peter Schrag, "Ivan Illich: The Christian as Rebel," *Saturday Review*, July 19, 1969, pp. 14–19; Francine D. Gray, *Divine Disobedience*, pp. 231–322; Paul Goodman, *Homespun of Oatmeal Gray*, p. 19.

[8] George Woodcock, *To the City of the Dead*, pp. 123–125.

Fromm (1900–) and Budd Schulberg (1914–), for example, have given us almost nothing.[9] After the war, as always, the only commendable writing about Mexico—the sole exception being the Beats—came from those who made essentially solitary journeys, not from cliques.

A number of important poets—William Carlos Williams, Charles Olson, Denise Levertov, and Robert Hayden—went there in the 1950's; and Robert Lowell visited Illich briefly in 1967. Olson's major reflection was in prose, but the others composed lyrics of varying power. When we add to their work that of Ginsberg and Corso, we can see that poetry in these years found a subject in Mexico to an extent never before realized.

William Carlos Williams (1883–1963) touched Juárez in the fall of 1950. Dr. Williams spent two days in 1906 escorting a patient to San Luis Potosí but had not attempted to explore farther, a fact that seems surprising in view of his lifelong interest in Latin American culture. His mother came from the West Indies; he grew up hearing both Spanish and English. Before he turned to the more domestic materials in his impressionistic history of the early United States, *In the American Grain*, 1925, he retold some of the Spanish exploits, including a chapter on Cortés's conquest of Mexico; and for a while he thought of writing a sequel, continuing his history "to the present day to end with Pancho Villa."[10] And now Williams crossed the border for only an evening while he and his wife visited their old friend Robert McAlmon in El Paso. Nevertheless, out of that brief visit came one of Williams's most important poems, "The Desert Music." In 1951 he published it in *Botteghe Oscure*; in 1954 it became the title poem of a new collection.

In his *Autobiography*, 1951, Williams has described the occasion: "Juarez, across the bridge. Three cents the trip. *Sur le pont d'Avignon* —is all I could think of. The sparrows at night in the park—Bob and his brothers, George and Alec and their wives—tequilla [*sic*] at five cents a glass, a quail dinner and the Mexicans, the poor Indians—one huddled into a lump against the ironwork of the bridge at night—safe

---

[9] Fromm has co-authored *Social Character in a Mexican Village*, 1970; Schulberg published an article about the new Museo de Antropología, "Magnificent Showcase," *Holiday* 44 (July 1968): 47 ff.

[10] William Carlos Williams, *In the American Grain*, pp. 27–38; idem, *Autobiography*, pp. 72–75, 183, 237.

perhaps from both sides, incredibly compressed into a shapeless obstruction—asleep."[11] These elements remain in the poem, though we are no longer sure whether the Indian is asleep or actually dead. To them are added several other bits of local color; a glimpse of the bull-ring with booths around it filled with

> paper flowers (*para los santos*)
> baked red-clay utensils, daubed
> with blue, silverware,
> dried peppers, onions, print goods, children's
> clothing      ;

a street urchin begging for a penny; a worn-out stripper in some cheap bar; the restaurant in which American tourists avoid eating the lettuce. Such characteristic attention to detail partly explains why the poem is one of the best written by an American about Mexico. But local color was not ultimately Williams's real concern in the poem. Rather Mexico became a point of isolation in which he must define the nature of poetic inspiration for himself; and "William / Carlos Williams, the poet," is the poem's central character.

Questioned by one of the members of the party concerning why anyone should want to write a poem, Williams replies: "Because it's there to be written." Going further, he sets up the metaphor that the poem is really a dance, "counted . . . to an exact measure" of a mystical music that swells out of the very country itself and surrounds or intrudes upon the scene. The poet has heard this music, "subdued, distant," crossing the desert from California. He now catches it again in the depressing sight of the stripper and wonders about "so sweet a tune, built of such slime." And finally it becomes caught up in the image of that body curled up on the bridge. Frightened and attracted, he realizes that it is "Egg-shaped!" and sees "a child in the womb prepared to imitate life," guarded by "a mucus" of the "protecting music." Just so is the poem. From this realization that poetry can create life—just as nature can—out of even the elements of death grows Williams's reaffirmation of his role: "I *am* a poet!" With this assertion the poem triumphantly ends.[12] Williams's triumphal posture was amply justified by the last fifteen years of his life, for he represents

---

[11] Williams, *Autobiography*, pp. 388–389.

[12] William Carlos Williams, *Pictures from Brueghel*, pp. 108–120. Emily M. Wallace prepared a bibliography.

one of the rare examples of a poet who grew better as he grew older, this poem signaling the emergence of a newer, stronger voice. Later he somewhat belittled "The Desert Music," but Sherman Paul found it so central to an understanding of Williams's poetic career that he published in 1968 an entire study devoted to it, *The Music of Survival*.

During the last years of his life Williams also translated a number of Mexican poems. The work of Alí Chumacero attracted him, and he translated three of the poems included in that poet's *Palabras en reposo*. One of these poems appeared in *New World Writing* in 1958; the other two were included in 1959 in the special issue of *Evergreen Review* devoted to Mexican art and literature. Also in 1959 "Three Náhuatl Poems" were published in *The Muse in Mexico*, a miscellany.[13] All six pieces resemble many of Williams's own in their use of concrete images appealing strongly to the senses and in their somewhat unexpected juxtapositions.

To say that Charles Olson (1910–1970) was influenced by Williams and Pound, Melville and Lawrence, Blake and Mao Tse-tung partly explains what he would discover when he stayed with his wife in Lerma, a fishing village near Campeche, from December 1950 until July 1951.[14] The rector of Black Mountain College was captivated (as Dahlberg and Burroughs had been before him) by the idea that the ancient Maya had had "a culture and a civilization which was a contrary of that which we have known." As he scouted the northern part of the Yucatan peninsula, Olson found clear evidence, he thought, that this was so—that these people and their modern descendants had not become abstracted through humanism into the present existential dilemma but were still "part of [the] universe of things." For them things interpenetrated, and "time, in their minds, was *mass & weight*." Their hieroglyphs were verse, "design in language." (In 1952 Olson was awarded a grant for further study of the hieroglyphs, including a chance to press his claim that water and violence were more central to the Mayas' life than he thought archaeologists had admitted. They have paid no attention to any of his ideas.) The myths

---

[13] Williams, *Pictures*, pp. 59–60. Also Alí Chumacero, "Green Eyes," *New World Writing* 14 (1958): 92; idem, "Two Poems," *Evergreen Review* 2 (Winter 1959): 59–61.

[14] Charles Olson, *Selected Writings of Charles Olson*, pp. 53–130, 167–173. Newton Smith, former editor and now English teacher, brought Olson's Mexican trip to my attention. George F. Butterick and Albert Glover prepared a bibliography.

of the Mayas reflected the rambling and inconclusive nature of life, Olson added. Their forms "unfolded directly from content."

Olson found a solidity in the lives of the Yucatan natives missing from that of other moderns:

> . . . the individual peering out from that flesh is precisely himself, is, a curious wandering animal (it is so beautiful, how animal the eyes are, when the flesh is not worn so close it chokes, how human and individuated the look comes out: jeesus, when you are rocked, by the roads against any of them—kids, women, men—it's so very gentle, so granted, the feel, of touch—none of that pull away, which, in the States caused me, for so many years, the deepest sort of questions about my own structure, the complex of my own organism . . .[15]

Understandably, Olson disliked professional archaeologists and emphasized the role of the artist's intuition; only Stephens, he thought, had recorded an "intimate and active experience of the Maya." These ideas he set forth in an essay, "Human Universe," published in 1951, and in *Mayan Letters*, written to his fellow poet Robert Creeley and published by Creeley early in 1954.[16] Curiously, the sojourn, though it solidified Olson's ideas, seems to have had little direct influence on his poetry.

The lyrics of Robert Hayden and Denise Levertov, though not matching the power of Williams's poem and showing no change in the direction of their work, can only win our admiration for the felicity with which they have captured aspects of Mexico in words. Hayden (1913–), a professor of English at Fisk University, won a Ford Foundation Fellowship for creative writing and travel in Mexico, 1954–1955.[17] While working there he gave a poetry reading at Mexico City College and made a speech on the Baha'i World Faith in Puebla. His poems, eight of which were published in *Selected Poems*, 1966, record his impressions of a bullfight, a beggar in the market, a Cuernavaca street urchin, the pyramid and empty convent of Tepoztlán, Veracruz's harbor, Juchitán on the Day of the Dead. Image after image densely pile up in each, without ever obscuring the sense of the poem.

Although death or sadness hovers in each poem, each bears the

[15] Olson, *Selected Writings*, pp. 92–93.
[16] Robert Creeley (1926–) has a poem about Mazatlán in *Pieces*, pp. 67–68. He could easily have visited the seaside town from his home in New Mexico.
[17] "Robert Hayden," *Negro History Bulletin* 21 (October 1957): 15.

mark of a man who has intimately entered the spirit of Mexico and
tried to find some meaning to the puzzles of life. The empty convent
suggests that the conventional gods will not supply an answer; nor do
the Aztec gods promise a solution. Perhaps to escape the emptiness
sensed everywhere—the convent, the sky of Tehuantepec wheeling
with vultures, the harbor where even suicide momentarily attracts—
we must enter the only primitive ritual still very much alive in the
land, the bullfight. In the meeting of man and bull we have "mocking
truth," but out of participating in an encounter with death we gain a
keener sense of life. Significantly, Hayden's "Inference of Mexico,"
the section title under which the poems are published, begins with
"Day of the Dead" and ends with a litany in "La Corrida."[18]

British-born Denise Levertov (1923–) came to Guadalajara with
her American husband, Mitchell Goodman, for two years, 1956–
1958.[19] While he worked on a novel and popular articles for *Atlantic*
and *House Beautiful*, she studied ballet, translated some Mexican
poetry (including, like her friend Muriel Rukeyser, that of Paz), and
worked at her own poetry, now heavily influenced by the Black
Mountain school. In the years that followed, she collected sixteen
poems about Mexico, the majority of them in *Overland to the Islands*,
1958, and *The Jacob's Ladder*, 1961. In several of these she showed
an interest in the way the poet's perception of an image may generate
a poem. In the wind blowing a palm tree she sees the possibilities of a
"fabulous / poem," realizing, however, that it will come only in the
quietness after the battle; then

> does the scraping mind perceive
> what is possible:
> there are no miracles but facts.
> To see! (there might be work
> a challenge, a poem)
>
> The squat palm![20]

18 Robert Hayden, *Selected Poems*, pp. 27–36.
19 Linda W. Wagner, *Denise Levertov*, pp. 11, 66. Also Denise Levertov, *Here and Now*, pp. 29–30; idem, *Overland to the Islands*, unpaged; idem, *With Eyes at the Back of Our Heads*, pp. 4, 66; idem, *The Jacob's Ladder*, pp. 26–28; idem, *The Sorrow Dance*, p. 51. Also Thomas Mabry Cranfill (ed.), *The Muse in Mexico*, pp. 112–115; Octavio Paz, *Configurations*, pp. 61, 65–67, 73–81.
20 Levertov, "Overland to the Island," *Overland*, n.p.

In *With Eyes at the Back of Our Heads*, 1959, she laced her translation of the Toltec definition of the true artist at the head of the volume, an ideal that she would obviously like to match herself.

Each of the Mexican poems essentially begins with an image and then develops it emotionally the way a painter might play with his colors. "Tomatlán," printed in *Here and Now*, 1957, is fascinating for showing the artist at work. Taking as her basic images the sea wind and the coastal jungle, Miss Levertov created four variations on the theme.[21] Her most perfect rendering of Mexican scenes probably is "The Weave," included in *The Jacob's Ladder*. The poem typically mingles the earthy ("cowdung colored mud") and the lush (strange flowers and butterflies), accepting the interpenetration of all facts of life:

> Bite down
> on the bitter stem of your nectared
> rose, you know
> the dreamy stench of death and fling
> magenta shawls delicately
> about your brown shoulders laughing.[22]

It is difficult to keep up with all the poets of the 1960's, but apparently Robert Lowell (1917–) was the only important figure besides Ferlinghetti (and perhaps Robert Creeley) to visit Mexico. Lowell came to Cuernavaca in 1967, arriving two days after Christmas and staying several weeks. He apparently was much attracted to a younger woman, possibly a student at CIDOC.[23] This experience is recorded in a series of twelve poems entitled "Mexico," and published in *Notebook 1967–68*, 1969. They muse over the developing relationship, complicated by Lowell's feelings of guilt about his age, his experience, and his family and by his keen awareness of time. Unfortunately much of the writing describing his feelings for her seems trite, giving no indication that the poet was echoing ironically the usual clichés used to describe such a situation. The writing about Cuernavaca, however, is quite exact; Lowell mentions in passing "the tall red flowers" blooming in midwinter, the barranca below CIDOC, "a cleavage drop-

---

[21] Levertov, *Here and Now*, pp. 29–30.

[22] Levertov, "The Weave," *Jacob's Ladder*, p. 26.

[23] I am grateful to Rev. Ivan Illich for his conversation about Lowell one summer afternoon in 1970; he was reticent, however, to say much about his close friend.

ping miles to the valley's body," diarrhea and "mosquito spots, round as pesos"; he sketches in a few scenes:

> Mexicans, mostly kids, squared up by boxlike
> houses on a street where buses eat up the sidewalk.
> And New Year's midnight: three in the market drink beer
> from cans garnished with limes and salt; one woman, Aztec,
> sings her adultery ballads, and weeps because
> her husband has left her for three women . . .

More fully delineated are visits to the closed monastery of Emmaus, the Carmelite convent in which the young woman lodges, and the ruins of Xochicalco, south of the town.[24] But interesting though moments are, the poems rank as a minor production both in the poet's own body of work and in that about Mexico.

Nearly a hundred novels, over fifty additional works of fiction for children, and innumerable short stories about Mexico have been published since World War II. Science fiction now joined the westerns, mysteries, and romances always set there. But little of lasting impact has come so far from the American or British writers of consequence who worked there during these years. Tom Lea (1907–) has been admired for his three Mexican novels, especially *The Brave Bulls*, 1949, which describes the circumstances whereby a Mexican matador comes to meet a certain bull in the ring of a provincial town. The other two are historical novels: *The Wonderful Country*, 1952, set in the 1880's, follows the adventures of an American who fled to Mexico after avenging his father's murder and now feels torn between the two countries; *The Hands of Cantú*, 1964, concerns the apprenticeship of a sixteenth-century boy to a master trainer of horses.[25] Anaïs Nin (1903–) finished her novel series with *Seduction of the Minotaur*, 1961, set in a town modeled on Acapulco, and returned to the scene with a section of *Collages*, 1964. Robert Lewis Taylor (1912–) published his picaresque novel of the war with Mexico, *Two Roads to Guadalupé*, 1964. And Willard Motley (1912–1965) left his almost-finished portrait of lost expatriates, *Let Noon Be Fair*, 1966. (Gore Vidal carried the protagonist of his novel *The City and the Pillar*,

---

24 Robert Lowell, *Notebook*, pp. 101–107.

25 John O. West, *Tom Lea*, pp. 3–4, 9–18, 22–26; Stanley J. Kunitz and Vineta Colby (eds.), *Twentieth Century Authors: First Supplement*, pp. 562–563. Oliver La Farge reviewed *Wonderful Country* when it appeared.

1948, to Mérida and Chichén Itzá for a momentary confrontation with his problems, but if Vidal had visited the area himself it could have been only briefly.[26] Rather he knew Guatemala, where he lived immediately after the war and again in 1949, when he worked on *Dark Green, Bright Red*, a fictionalized account of the recent coup d'état there.) None of these, however, is so remarkable as the work of Ray Bradbury and Wright Morris.

Ray Bradbury (1920–) grew up with Mexican Americans in Tucson and Los Angeles.[27] During the war years he lived in one of the barrios of Los Angeles and, as he has written me in a letter, "got to know everyone in a tenement there, and celebrated in their celebrations and knew their miseries and their good humor amidst those miseries." Here he picked up the ideas for three short stories.[28] After the war he took an eight-thousand-mile jaunt through Mexico with the ceramic artist Grant Beach. On November 2 they ended up on the island of Janitzio in Lake Pátzcuaro, where one of the most elaborate celebrations of the Day of the Dead is held in the graveyard—all the families carry offerings of food and lighted candles to their relatives' graves and there wait through the night. Then the two men traveled to Guanajuato, where, Bradbury says, "the mummies scared the hell out of me." As a result of these two experiences he wrote five short stories and a poem about death.

"El Día de Muerte," published in *Touchstone*, 1947 (collected in *The Machineries of Joy*, 1964), gives a cross section of various events occurring across Mexico on this day, weaving back and forth from one action to another: the vigil at Janitzio, the tourists exploring the catacombs of Guanajuato, a bull being killed in the ring at Mexico City, the celebrants buying candy skulls with their names emblazoned on them and crowding the churches with the bleeding Christs. And a little boy running across a busy street in the capital is struck by a black car, his candy skull, bearing his name, rolling in pieces across the street to be seized by other children and eagerly devoured. "All

[26] Ray Lewis White, *Gore Vidal*, pp. 24–25.

[27] William F. Nolan, "Bradbury: Prose Poet in the Age of Space," *Magazine of Fantasy and Science Fiction* 24 (May 1963): 16–17; *Contemporary Authors*, vol. 4, pp. 42–43. Most of my information comes from a letter from Bradbury, dated "Dec. 2, Apollo Year Two" (i.e., 1970). Nolan prepared a bibliography in the same magazine.

[28] See Ray Bradbury, *Twice Twenty-Two*, pp. 148–153, 241–265, 368–373.

the land smelled of ancient death and dust and everywhere things ran toward death or were in death," Bradbury wrote.[29]

The controlled sense of impending doom in this story grew more tense in his tale of the grotesque end of a marriage in Guanajuato: "The Next in Line" (collected in *Dark Carnival*, 1947, and reprinted in *The October Country*). An American woman feels trapped: "she was in a town of people who said no words to her and she said no words to them except in blushing confusion and bewilderment. And the town was circled by desert and time, and home was far away, far away in another life." Actually her feeling comes from the gulf she feels between her husband and herself; they are unable any longer to communicate with each other. When she begs him not to visit the mummies, he laughs at her fears. She goes with him and is overwhelmed by the conviction that she will die in the town, that he in fact is subtly killing her spirit just as he eats unconcernedly a skull with her name on it. From the opening sequence in which a funeral procession winds across the tiny plaza while she looks on nakedly, the ending is as inevitable as any in Poe's stories.[30] The poem, "Death in Mexico," published in *California Quarterly*, 1954, found the reminders of death in Guanajuato as a way to affirm life.[31]

Three other macabre sketches are a mystery, "The Candy Skull," published in *Dime Mystery* in 1948 and never collected, a short section of the novel *Dandelion Wine*, 1957, and a black comedy, "The Life Work of Juan Díaz," first published in *Playboy* in 1963 and then collected in *Machineries*.[32] In "Juan Díaz," Juan's widow cannot afford to pay the rent on his grave any longer; finding that he has mummified, she steals his remains so that she can open a tourist attraction and thus support her family. With this story perhaps Bradbury managed finally "to lay the ghosts of those dire mummies."

In March 1953 Bradbury published in *Reporter* "Sun and Shadow." It won the Benjamin Franklin award for short fiction and was printed as a separate book as well as being collected in *The Golden Apples of the Sun*. Here he showed an interest in the values of primitivism. A

---

[29] Ray Bradbury, *The Machineries of Joy*, pp. 105–115.

[30] Ray Bradbury, *October Country*, pp. 18–57.

[31] Ray Bradbury, "Death in Mexico," *California Quarterly* 3 (1954): 11–13.

[32] I have not seen "The Candy Skull." Bradbury, in his letter, said that it was "not a good story," adding, "I am not a very good mystery writer, I fear." Ray Bradbury, *Dandelion Wine*, pp. 101–104; idem, *Machineries of Joy*, pp. 219–229.

fashion photographer is taking pictures of a model in front of Ricardo's house, wanting the contrast between its disrepair and her chicness, when Ricardo appears in protest. He warns the photographer that the town is not an impersonal studio to be treated with such lofty disdain: "We are people and must be given attention as people." The photographer naturally becomes annoyed and tries to escape Ricardo. But wherever he goes, there appears the Mexican. When the photographer attempts to incorporate him into a composition, Ricardo drops his pants. Nor will the policeman arrest him, insisting that Ricardo is doing nothing obscene since his hands are quietly at his side. Finally the photographer stalks off, and Ricardo returns quietly home, thinking of the meaning that each crack and stain of the home holds personally for him.[33]

Bradbury is generally thought of as a science fiction writer; these tales show how wrong that assumption is. Yet he did write two such stories about Mexico, both published in 1950 and collected in *The Illustrated Man*, 1951. "The Highway," which appeared in *Copy*, reflects the general fear of the atomic bomb that dismayed so many writers. A Mexican peasant watches uncomprehendingly as a vast convoy of cars rushes by on the highway in an attempt to escape the certain destruction when an atomic war breaks out. Bradbury apparently is suggesting that primitive values may be more sound than those engendered by the so-called progress of civilization. "The Fox and the Forest," first printed in *Collier's* as "To the Future," concerns a couple who have tried to escape in time from a deathly and impersonal future where all individuality can be crushed—the logical consequence of present progress—back into the quiet wholeness of Mexico in 1938. But the Searchers ruthlessly hunt them down, taking them to the Future—to the dismay of the hotel proprietor who can only assume witchcraft when their room thus mysteriously empties.[34] In both stories we have more emphasis on character than often occurs in science fiction, but neither so warmly involves the reader as do Bradbury's other Mexican stories. Of his entire trip there, Bradbury summed up for me: "Mexico delighted me and depressed me and frightened me."

Undoubtedly the best novel about Mexico published between 1947, when Malcolm Lowry's *Under the Volcano* appeared, and 1962, the

[33] Bradbury, *Twice Twenty-Two*, pp. 154–162.
[34] Ray Bradbury, *The Illustrated Man*, pp. 58–62, 157–173.

date of Katherine Anne Porter's *Ship of Fools*, was *The Field of Vision*. Written by Wright Morris (1910–), it won the National Book Award for 1956. Morris had spent the fall and winter of 1954 in Mexico; he returned the winter of 1958 while working on *Ceremony in Lone Tree*, the continuation of *Field of Vision*, and again in 1959.[35] In November 1959 *Holiday* published Morris's long essay "Mexican Journey." It gives the most concise insight into his attitude toward the country as he tried to answer for himself the question of why he kept returning. As he traveled along the west coast route to Guadalajara, around Lake Chapala and up to Guanajuato, through Mexico City and down into Oaxaca, he observed a primitive wholeness that seemed almost to have disappeared from the United States. Past and present met and mingled: "This is the land that levels the new, removes what is alien or blends it with what is timeless. Cultural innovations, artistic ambition, political slogans, and several thousand miles of highway, put down forever, all are chewed up. Day by day what is new as tomorrow blends with the massive inheritance of the past." Like Charles Olson, he felt the people were warmer. Morris remembered being in a crowd at a fairground in Mazatlán and there having a young woman naturally rest her head on his chest, accepting without comment his arm for support. "Why not?" he thought. "Don't we need all we can get? And yet, just a few weeks before, on a Philadelphia suburban local, the man sitting beside me shied away from me and pressed to the wall . . . Here in Mazatlán I am rubbed, supported, pressed, but seldom pushed. I take life in through my eyes, my lungs and my pores. I am a stranger, but they feel toward me neither affection nor malice. It is enough that I am human."[36]

Not that it is always easy to accept Mexico, Morris found. After Guanajuato he felt the need to visit Sanborn's in Mexico City and watch his fellow Americans. As he observed, one also travels "to see what one left behind." And in Izúcar de Matamoros he became nauseous. "What I cannot keep down," he diagnosed (speaking as one of his characters in *Field* had), "is Mother Mexico herself. She is simply too much for the stranger who feels obliged to put his thoughts in order. And if he cannot? Well, then he is sick." But poverty, filth all mat-

35 Wright Morris, "Mexican Journey," *Holiday* 26 (November 1959): 50–63 ff.; David Madden, *Wright Morris*, p. 14.
36 Morris, "Mexican Journey," pp. 104, 55.

ter little in comparison to the rich gift that Mexico makes to the spirit: the knowledge, "impersonal as rain, that life is living."[37]

In his article Morris described the bullring in Mexico City, making the comment in passing that it was "like a lens that brings all of Mexico into one focus." It had likewise functioned to bring *The Field of Vision*, begun in 1952, into focus; as his unifying idea, Morris took seven American characters to a bullfight and recorded what happens to them there. *The Field of Vision* may at first appear to be almost entirely about the United States, for each of the five central characters thinks more about his past in Nebraska or New York City than about the events he is witnessing. Tom Scanlon recalls his father's story about a near brush with death when he became lost in a dry canyon, the very symbol of the descent into hell that Scanlon thinks necessary before one can ascend into heaven. Scanlon's daughter Lois, her husband, Walter McKee, and his friend Gordon Boyd think back on their intertwined lives, especially the way in which Boyd's wildfire touched them as he quested, first for success and then for failure but always attempting to "touch bottom." And Dr. Leopold Lehmann recalls the transformation of his saintly protégé and how the discovery affected him. Each person finds to some degree his character, the pattern of his being, by searching out this inheritance of the past. But the events in the bullring somehow help to clarify this search.

For Lehmann (as in life for Robert Hayden) the ring symbolizes the labyrinth into which each person must go to find the truth that the minotaur holds. For Boyd it is T. S. Eliot's "still point" around which the dance of life wheels; and that point, not the kill—as Hemingway would say—is the real moment of truth. Whatever the symbolic value of the "field of vision"—hell, labyrinth, or still point— there each person becomes "his own bullfighter, with his own center, a circle overlapped by countless other circles, like the pattern of expanding rings rain made on the surface of a pond. How many had been traced on the sand of the bullring that afternoon?" They watch an alter ego for Boyd jump into the ring, witness a matador stabbed by the bull, and finally see Boyd lift the McKees' grandson into the bullring for an initiation of sorts into the life of the imagination. Mrs. McKee has already left, overcome by the apparent sadness of the ritual and the shock of meeting Boyd again. The moment has affected

[37] Ibid., pp. 60, 103, 104.

her profoundly: "The thing about Mexico was—and she would say so—that it had her guessing herself."[38] In *Ceremony in Lone Tree*, 1960, we are told that the McKees left Mexico the next day, but this time Mrs. McKee touched Boyd: "Hardly a moment, but long enough to finish what the bullfight had started. After thirty years of exile Boyd was back where his life had begun." He goes to Acapulco to forget the whole episode; but there he is summoned to a reunion at Scanlon's old home in Nebraska and the conclusion to the transformations begun in the bullring.[39]

After the richness of *Field*, Morris's second novel about Mexico, *Love among the Cannibals*, 1957, comes as something of a jolt. It was as if here the author had deliberately set out to create the best seller that has always eluded him. Though the reader can take the novel as a witty satire on the clichés of modern America (including an examination of the stereotyped view of Mexico), the rich black comedy of which Morris is capable never really appears, and the whole affair seems shallow. The novel revolves around two weeks in the lives of four people: Earl Horter and Irwin Macgregor, middle-aged songwriters who "are sometimes referred to as the poor man's Rodgers & Hart"; Billie Harcum, a Southern belle who is Mac's young discovery; and Eva Baum, who sets Horter completely aback by her beauty. Contracted to write a Hollywood musical with a vaguely Latin American setting, the two men decide they need to go to Acapulco for atmosphere. Naturally they will take the girls along. But once they arrive nothing goes right. They run their car into a ditch. They move into *mañana* Mexico, into a house that "any day" will have water, electricity, and all sorts of comforts—"any day now." And there Billie maneuvers Mac into marriage, and Eva runs off and leaves Horter— after having stripped Billie, tied her to the bed, and anointed her with the contents of a slop jar. As the men conclude, however: "It's been real, man! You know what I mean?"

The comment is not cynical. Through Mexico, the natural element for the pagan Eva, the other three move onto a deeper level of experience than they have previously known. In Mexico they are initiated finally into the meaning of love. Horter, the narrator of the novel, describes, in the third person, what has happened to him: "He had to

---

38 Wright Morris, *The Field of Vision*, pp. 193, 225.
39 Wright Morris, *Ceremony in Lone Tree*, pp. 25–28.

learn about loving and talking from scratch, and he saw that the first thing the lover destroyed was the mind in his body, since it had nothing to do with his body of clichés. The body was cannibal, the clichés were vegetable. Love among the vegetarians, that is, was verbal—it was made with participles, unmade with verbs, honored, cherished, and disobeyed with nouns. But love among the cannibals is flesh feeding on flesh."[40] Thus even Billie's anointment becomes symbolic; she must now face the realities of her body. The wrecked car, in a running joke (the nearest approach to true comedy in the book), is slowly stripped of all its parts until the natives possess it altogether. Likewise (Horter makes the comparison explicit) these three people finally get "down to the facts."

In *One Day*, 1965, Morris returned partly to his Mexican themes. The novel actually concerns what happened to a number of people in Escondido, an imaginary town across the Golden Gate Bridge from San Francisco, on November 22, 1963, the day President Kennedy was assassinated. But the family of Ignacio Chávez is Mexican. (It bears a striking resemblance to the Mexican family in *Love among the Cannibals*; Morris often resurrects, under different names, characters from his other works.) In the course of the day Chávez remembers his life in Yucatan and in Mexico City with his wife and children, especially the events concerning the death of his first son. Too poor to have the child buried, he had put it in a shoebox, taken the bus beyond Toluca, and then set out walking to find a burial place. Two pariah dogs, however, had followed him. Finally, fearing that they would dig up the box, he had gone into a church and there placed the dead child in the arms of the Virgin, taking the image she had held to his daughter for a doll. And another character in the novel, Cowie, had fled into Mexico while he was a young man to try to sort out essentially the meaning of life. (Morris and his first wife had also visited the land in the 1930's.) There, as if to prove that even accidents are part of the universe's plan, Cowie had run over two men in his car and had in turn been hit by an overcrowded bus. Taken into Izúcar de Matamoros and tended by a Mexican family, he confronted the problem of love and flesh in the figure of one of the daughters. Cowie, not being a cannibal, fled. Since then he has lived in Escondido among people but always alone.[41] As Dr. Lehmann ob-

[40] Wright Morris, *Love among the Cannibals*, p. 227.
[41] Wright Morris, *One Day*, pp. 174–201, 370–375.

served, some absorb and some resist. But Mexico will not leave one completely alone.

During the 1960's there was much discussion about the possibilities of the nonfictional novel. In such a genre the author would take a true event, either from his own life or someone else's, would preserve its truthfulness, but would structure its telling with the same attention to artistic development that novelists have traditionally followed. But the American anthropologist Oscar Lewis (1914–1970) carried the theory one step further, in a series of books he published about Mexican and Puerto Rican families, by letting the participants tell their own story, his function being one of editing.[42] Lewis wrote in the introduction to his first full "novel," *The Children of Sánchez*: "In preparing the interviews for publication, I have eliminated my questions and have selected, arranged, and organized their materials into coherent life stories. If one agrees with Henry James that life is all inclusion and confusion while art is all discrimination and selection, then these life histories have something of both art and life."[43] Unfortunately, this ambivalence between inclusiveness and selectivity prevents these books from being totally satisfying to either other anthropologists or general readers (although his study of Puerto Rican families won the National Book Award in 1967). But the general method, labeled by Lewis "ethnographic realism, in contrast to literary realism," still offers possibilities; and his four Mexican works that use this method add an extra dimension to the depiction of the country provided by conventional novelists.

Lewis went to Mexico in 1943 to restudy Tepoztlán, the site of Redfield's work over a decade earlier. He returned to the village several times and in 1951 published a casebook on the area. But by then he had also traced families who had emigrated to Mexico City and he had become fascinated by the whole problem of the culture of poverty. In an effort to understand this phenomenon, he interviewed several families in depth and in 1959 published *Five Families*, with illustrations by the Mexican artist Alberto Beltrán and an introduction by Oliver La Farge. Here Lewis first turned to writers of fiction for guidance (as had the Mexican anthropologist Ricardo Pozas); he selected an ordinary day as the unit of observation whereby to reveal each

[42] *Current Biography 1968*, pp. 221–233; *Contemporary Authors*, vols. 19–20, pp. 211–212.

[43] Oscar Lewis, *The Children of Sánchez*, p. xxi.

family, and he composed five unconnected sequences much like short stories. As Selden Rodman noted in a review, Lewis went further toward fictional methods than he acknowledged. For example, Rodman raised the question if it is "quite scientific or honest for the interviewer to leave himself entirely out of the finished interview, turning into casual family dialogue what must have been in many instances answers to his own questions, or at least conversation slanted to some extent by his alien presence in the crowded room." Rodman justly added: "Considered as fiction—and this aspect of 'Five Lives' almost compels us to—there are drawbacks quite as grave. In addition to the absence of drama and suspense or any description of the physical presence of Mexico, the principle of nonselectivity or all-inclusiveness contributes downright boredom."[44]

Lewis introduced in this book two families that were to occupy his attention further: the Martínez family of Tepoztlán and the Sánchez family of Mexico City (the names are pseudonyms). In 1961 he published *The Children of Sánchez*, his editing of interviews with Jesús Sánchez and four of his children. The candidness of their observations caused the Mexican government temporarily to ban the book—until the country's intellectuals laughed with such scorn that it reconsidered. Abridgment would have helped the book and Lewis could have profitably studied novelists more closely concerning structures of multiple narration. The prologue and the epilogue are spoken by Jesús; the major portion of the chronicle alternates among the memories of his children. As each character reveals what has happened to him, the reader learns more about the family than any member of it knows. And the reader can see clearly the discrepancy between a character's view of himself and the reality as revealed by his actions. Much the same thing happens with *A Death in the Sánchez Family*, 1969, a record of the circumstances surrounding the funeral of an aunt.

*Pedro Martínez* was published in 1964 with further illustrations by Beltrán. It details the life over a seventy-year period of one of the leaders of Tepoztlán (called Azteca) as revealed by himself, his wife, and one of their sons. The book has been less popular; Lewis pointed out in his introduction that "the world view of Pedro Martínez and his family is less familiar and less accessible to most American read-

[44] Selden Rodman, "After Westernization, Desolation," *Saturday Review*, July 4, 1959, p. 13.

ers than that of the children of Sánchez." The Sánchez family, even in the culture of poverty, represents the upwardly mobile, conditioned by mass media, and thus they speak a more familiar language than the Martínez family, who exist in a relative isolation where the father and the mother still think in a Náhuatl dialect. The Martínez family also possesses "less flux, less color, less joy," Lewis noted.[45] Even Pedro's memories of the Zapata revolution, in which he actively participated, do not come across vividly.

Carlos Castaneda (c. 1935–) is another anthropologist who used fictional techniques. His interviews with a Yaqui Indian *brujo* (a man wise in the ways of magic) about the religious use of drugs and the Indian's apprehension of the spirit of the world have become the basis for three books: *The Teachings of Don Juan*, 1968; *A Separate Reality*, 1971; and *Journey to Ixtlan*, 1972. The books have received much attention, especially from college students.[46]

Curiously, none of these postwar writers, except perhaps Lewis, was in any way influenced by the shape of political events in Mexico, either the reactionary government of Alemán or the progressive spirit of President Adolfo López Mateos. Rather they all turned within to explore in relative isolation their private visions. A. Alvarez, in a review of several travel books, commented how "travel is always a two-way process; you may go to observe the strange customs of a strange country, but in the process you yourself become a stranger; it is you who do the wrong things, eat in the wrong way, speak with the wrong accent. In the end, you may have found out less about the others than about yourself. The change of scene is a prelude to a change of heart." He then added significantly, "Perhaps this is why for some writers travel has been a precondition of creativity."[47] The postwar period was an extremely troubled time spiritually. E. M. Forster, during his visit to the United States in 1947, noted the American's longing to return to some idealized primitivism away from all problems of industrial progress, citing as another instance of this dream "the yearning for Mexico, whose peasants were drunk and

[45] Oscar Lewis, *Pedro Martínez*, p. xlix. Reviewers of the four books have included Saul Bellow, Carleton Beals, Carlos Fuentes, Mauricio de la Selva, as well as Rodman.

[46] "Don Juan and the Sorcerer's Apprentice," *Time*, international edition, March 5, 1973, pp. 30–35.

[47] A. Alvarez, "Travel as a Passport to Freedom," *Saturday Review*, January 2, 1971, p. 17.

dirty, but they did sing."[48] The Beats' total rejection of civilization was only a slight extreme of the stance taken by more conventional writers. When American and British writers came to Mexico they were in quest of a faith to sustain the spirit, hoping to find this faith in so different a culture or at least to be prodded into providing the answer for themselves.

In thus moving within, the writers generally moved beyond the particular. But none of them lost sight entirely of his physical circumstances. It is intriguing how so many writers after World War II were attracted to matters traditionally rejected by the British and the Americans alike. Excepting Hughes and Miss Porter, neither of whom wrote about bullfights directly, none of the pre-war authors had been attracted to the ritual; rather Lawrence's (and eventually Miss Porter's) disgust seemed typical. But after Hiroshima the bullfight somehow fitted the need of the moment on a more symbolic level than Hemingway's existential confrontation. If often despair was found in Mexico, a sort of wholeness of body, mind, and spirit also seemed to dwell there to cure the ill, an idea most fully stated by F. S. C. Northrop in *The Meeting of East and West*, 1946.[49] All these writers ended their work on a note of affirmation.

[48] E. M. Forster, *Two Cheers for Democracy*, p. 338.
[49] F. S. C. Northrop, *Meeting of East and West*, pp. 15–65.

# Afterword

Lesley Byrd Simpson wisely reminded us in the title of his history that there are many Mexicos; a person cannot possibly know more than one or two well. Still these writers altogether explored almost every section of the country and have left at least a glimpse of practically every segment of society. Each period of history since the Mexican War of Independence, save the time of Maximilian, saw the presence of one or more major writers from the English world being influenced by conditions there. Lesser writers witnessed even that moment of history, and for other periods they reinforce and expand the vision that the more important writers present. Generally, their observations are openly those of an outsider, whether the work is a travel account, a novel, or a poem. But even in works concerned almost entirely with foreigners, such as *The Field of Vision* and *The Night of the Iguana*, the setting remains indisputably Mexico; it is difficult to imagine the story taking place elsewhere, even in a similar environment like Guatemala. When all is considered, how much does their writing reveal about the land and its people?

The question is not easy to answer—and not just because the response necessarily depends so heavily upon one's own experiences. Stephen Crane faced the difficulties a foreigner has in interpreting another country. He wrote: "It perhaps might be said—if any one dared—that the most worthless literature of the world has been that which has been written by the men of one nation concerning the men of another. . . . Instinctively he will feel that there are similarities but he will encounter many little gestures, tones, tranquilities, rages, for which his blood, adjusted to another temperature, can possess no interpreting power." And George Woodcock in his critical essay warned "that the curious exaggerations and distortions which appear in various accounts of Mexico in fact represent the imposition, over the true map, of the individual's personal fears and hopes."[1] Often, however, the map and the reality do seem to coincide—even in the eyes of the Mexicans. Manuel Gamio commented that the national author could write most deeply of his own country but that his perceptions would be limited by that very environment out of which he created, while the visitor who stayed for quite some time in Mexico, although he could see things that limited the natives' horizon, would be too unrealistic. Then he concluded: "The foreigner who writes a novel after a very short stay in Mexico is even less realistic than the above, but frequently he is able to appraise more ably the events which occur outside the horizon referred to, and if he is intelligent, his novel might have as much appeal or more so as those of the previous kinds of authors."[2]

Certain patterns of interest recur in these visitors' observations: bright colors, light, music, the strange and exotic aspects of customs and of geography, violence, loss, drink or drugs, extremes of emotions, good manners, primitivism, superstition and religion, socialism, patient expectation. The writers sought in the culture for those elements they needed, or sometimes feared, in themselves. We can see how selective they were in their concerns when we compare their writings with Mexican literature. It is especially noticeable that the foreigners as a rule possessed little sense of history, and only a few thought deeply about the significance that various movements had for the development of the country. Neither casual visitor nor expatriate could become really involved in the institutions; thus he missed many implications. The poets especially (for example, Witter Bynner, William Carlos Williams, and Denise Levertov), though they painted

[1] Stephen Crane, *Stephen Crane in the West and Mexico*, p. 74; George Woodcock, "Mexico and the English Novelist," *Western Review* 21 (August 1956): 23.
[2] Edward Nehls (ed.), *D. H. Lawrence*, II, 367.

superb scenes, tended toward local color alone. In moving through Mexico the writer generally gained a moment of freedom in which to explore himself and his own background. As a result, Mexico more often became a symbol, a sort of microcosm, than a real place. Yet Mexican writers and American and British writers often agreed in their findings. A foreigner could indeed enter the deeper spirit of the land.

Still the Mexican culture poses problems for the English world not presented by the Latin countries of Europe, with which it seems initially to share so many characteristics. Hart Crane came to feel that Europe was "an environment not half so strange and distractingly new-old curious as this."[3] Since history books have so emphasized the Conquest, we tend to forget that Mexico—though it now has a government, an architecture, and a religion adapted from Spanish forms—is in many ways still an Indian nation with reminders of Aztec, Maya, and other ancient institutions in evidence. Almost 30 percent of the citizens remain pure Indian, often speaking their own languages, and more than 60 percent are mestizos. The visitor is lulled by the cosmopolitan character of the cities, especially the capital, into forgetting the background of the people; but let him venture into the country or even into an obscure corner of the city and he will first think, "How picturesque," and then probably become bewildered. A sense of uneasiness appears in much of the writing.

A singular number of these visitors—the British especially but Americans also—suffered in fact a sense of trauma. Often the reader encounters in their comments mention of death and brutality, sadness or despair, and a sense of barrenness. Henry Bamford Parkes noted that "the Mexican, more than most other people, were a race who always lived close to death—a closeness which had belonged both to those who worshipped Huitzilopochtli and to those who had introduced the Inquisition and the bull-fight."[4] The country has one of the world's highest murder rates, though few tourists would be aware of the fact, since many of the killings are matters of revenge. But none of this seems to explain the extreme fear to be found in several works. I confess that I could never understand the emotion until after my visit to San Cristóbal de las Casas. Meeting the Indians of

[3] Hart Crane, *The Letters of Hart Crane, 1916–1932*, p. 402.
[4] Henry Bamford Parkes, *A History of Mexico*, p. 123. See Octavio Paz, *The Labyrinth of Solitude*, pp. 47–64; and William W. Johnson, *Mexico*, p. 14.

that distant town, I felt that I faced an alien world from which I was forever excluded and which was therefore somewhat frightening. For some writers, apparently all Mexico became my Las Casas. As Woodcock noted, the image of darkly alien and hostile eyes appears often in their writing—a quality that I must state I never observed. Some, such as Conrad Aiken and Saul Bellow, felt that the very landscape conveyed a sense of danger. Yet many transmuted their initial feelings into some form of affirmation. Sometimes, as in Huxley's novel, the feeling of uneasiness or dread mars the potential power of a work; at other times, as in Hart Crane's poems and letters and Lowry's *Volcano*, it adds to the impact. But we must conclude that it always distorts the picture.

Quite a number of writers, with varying degrees of success, tried to compare Mexican culture with their own. Cultural relativism was a principle admired from the time of Dana and Stephens but seldom achieved. Frequently, the writer found it easy to cling to the prejudices directed against the Indian world, the Mediterranean world, and Catholicism—in Mexico all united. But few experiences emerged with simple outlines: often the writer came away with extremely intricate and ambivalent attitudes. Religious difficulties played their part, beginning with Robert Tomson, but several writers became fascinated by the legend of the Virgin of Guadalupe, and almost all were overwhelmed by the magnificence of the churches. Though the Americans tended to make fun of the Indian culture in the nineteenth century, the British found it intriguing. When the potential horrors of industrialization became apparent, the primitive life appealed to both as an escape route or as a model whereby they might examine and modify their society. But only the naïve could accept Mexico as a utopia. For the sensitive visitor, just as he felt that he might have in Mexico the answer he sought, the country would suddenly offer another face. Sometimes he was shocked, sometimes just unsettled. But Wright Morris observed that as a result he might even become physically ill. E. M. Forster's *A Passage to India* with its conflicts among widely differing values gives more insight into the visitor's encounter with Mexico than do Henry James's confrontations of two societies. However successful one believes Lawrence's novel to be, it can here serve as an archetypal model repeated endlessly in works before and after it.

Certainly these writers give us a rather limited view of Mexican

society. The small middle and upper classes had less effect on the
creative imagination than the lower. A few writers knew Mexican
artists and various public servants; still fewer entered the guarded
*salas* of the upper class. The portraits we have of the artists, priests,
government officials, army officers, *hacendados*, and merchants leave
little impression on the readers. Mrs. Calderón's journal and Miss Porter's "Virgin Violeta" are perhaps the most successful, though we
should also remember Langston Hughes's and Elizabeth Treviño's
autobiographies. Since several of these writers knew Spanish, it is surprising that so few of them met Mexican authors or seem even to
have known their work. (Perhaps there are more ties than are pres-
ently evident, and scholars, not realizing how many of our writers
would have reason to be interested in Mexican literature either in
the original or in translation, have failed to look for relationships.
From Stephens's time to the present the visitors have left us a surprising number of translations.) On the other hand, the life of the
lower class, Indians and mestizos, sprawled everywhere in open sight,
and most writers felt that they must attempt to comprehend this
world. Their degree of success is always questionable, even with anthropologists such as Oscar Lewis. Traven was sometimes bucolic, but
perhaps he was most able to convey a sense of verisimilitude. Miss
Porter was almost as good. But Stephen Crane and Steinbeck, though
writing aesthetically satisfying stories, show slight understanding.

It is difficult to estimate how well a work captures a sense of place.
The summer that I spent in Mexico City, I carried along a number of
books about the country. *The Plumed Serpent* I did not comprehend
at all; that is, the story seemed to have little to do with the life outside
my window. Yet when I made an intense study of the novel a few
years later in the States, I was amazed at my previous denseness, for
it recalled for me moment after moment from my own experiences.
Much the same thing happened with *The Lawless Roads*. Selden Rodman likewise reacted negatively to these two books when he read
them on his journey; I wonder if he had second thoughts. Only *The
Children of Sánchez* really intrigued me that summer, but I think it
was as much a form of voyeurism as it was the realization of a truth
about a section of the city I had explored just the week before; certainly the book interested me little when I reread it. On later visits I
felt the same dilemma with other works. I do not totally understand
the significance of my response, but I have had the same reaction

with Mexican writings. Perhaps the country provides too vivid an experience to manage in words: literature cannot compete with the reality of Mexico; it can only serve to recall it.

When we discuss the effectiveness with which a writer reveals the truths about another culture, we are somehow balancing matters of artistry and of content. Some pieces—Stephen Crane's and Ray Bradbury's short stories, for example; perhaps Mailer's essay—can be satisfying without giving the reader an entirely realistic view of the situation. A completely inaccurate picture, such as Waugh's book, leaves one so angry as to care little for its literary qualities. Then we have strange failures like Aiken's novel: the vision it presents of Mexico is extremely misrepresentative, yet its descriptions of the landscape are among the best. With writers like Traven we forgive them their errant sense of style out of gratitude for their honesty. Many of the lesser journalists probably have presented more factual pictures than most of these writers, but possessing little of genius they ultimately leave little impression on the reader. On the other hand, we have seen the problems that a work like Lawrence's novel can create. I long ago realized that the list of books about Mexico that I consider to be the best written was not the same as the list of those that I consider to portray Mexico best. Hence the importance of Flandrau, Mrs. Calderón, and Miss Porter: they combine both ideals.

I would conclude that Stephen Crane's summation of the value of such literature is overly negative, but certainly these writings do have a limited use as an introduction to Mexico. Gamio probably assessed their value accurately. For the Mexican they can show him how his country strikes an outsider and will reveal aspects of his culture that he would otherwise overlook. For the American and the Englishman they prepare the visitor by showing him the reactions of other representatives of his culture, recall for him later his experiences, and present aspects of Mexico different from those he has perceived. Their absolute worth must of course be judged in terms largely apart from their revelation of Mexico. And there we do not have to explain or justify; clearly, if some works are failures, several novels, journals, essays, poems, and plays are among the most outstanding of the last 150 years of our literary heritage. Therein Mexico, though having seen fewer foreign writers living within its borders than many a country in Europe, rivals the Continent's impact on our authors' creative imagination.

# BIBLIOGRAPHY

Aaron, Daniel. *Writers on the Left: Episodes in American Literary Communism.* New York: Harcourt, Brace & World, 1961.

Adams, Henry. *The Education of Henry Adams: An Autobiography.* Boston: Houghton Mifflin, 1918.

————. *Henry Adams and His Friends: A Collection of His Unpublished Letters.* Edited by Harold Dean Cater. Boston: Houghton Mifflin, 1947.

————. *Letters of Henry Adams (1892–1918).* Edited by Worthington Chauncey Ford. Boston: Houghton Mifflin, 1938.

Aiken, Conrad. *The Collected Novels of Conrad Aiken.* New York: Holt, Rinehart & Winston, 1964.

————. "Malcolm Lowry." *Times Literary Supplement,* February 16, 1967, p. 127.

————. *Ushant: An Essay.* Boston: Little, Brown, 1952.

Allen, Jerry. *The Sea Years of Joseph Conrad.* Garden City: Doubleday, 1965.

Alpert, Hollis. "Kazan and Brando Outdoors." *Saturday Review,* February 9, 1952, pp. 25–26.

Alvarez, A. "Travel as a Passport to Freedom." *Saturday Review,* January 2, 1971, p. 17.

Amory, Cleveland. "Celebrity Register." *McCall's* 90 (April 1963): 184.

Anderson, Sherwood. "An Impression of Mexico—Its People." *Southern Literary Messenger* 1 (April 1939): 241–242.

————. *The Letters of Sherwood Anderson.* Edited by Howard Mumford Jones and Walter B. Rideout. Boston: Little, Brown, 1953.

————. *Sherwood Anderson's Memoirs.* New York: Harcourt, Brace, 1942.

————. *Sherwood Anderson's Memoirs: A Critical Edition.* Edited by Ray Lewis White. Chapel Hill: University of North Carolina Press, 1969.

Arciniegas, Germán. *Latin America: A Cultural History.* Translated by Joan MacLean. New York: Alfred A. Knopf, 1967.

Arnold, Armin. *D. H. Lawrence and America.* New York: Philosophical Library, 1959.

Arvin, Newton. *Longfellow: His Life and Works.* Boston: Little, Brown, 1963.

Atkins, John. *Aldous Huxley: A Literary Study.* New York: Roy, 1956.

———. *Graham Greene.* London: J. Calder, 1957.

Austin, Mary. *Earth Horizon.* Boston: Houghton Mifflin, 1932.

———. "The Story of the Conquest." *Southwest Review* 17 (April 1932): xiv–xvi.

Babcock, Charles E., Catherine M. Rooney, and Leila Fern. *Children's Books in English on Latin America.* Washington, D.C.: Pan American Union, 1941.

Baird, Peggy. "The Last Days of Hart Crane." *Venture* 4 (1961): 21–46.

Bancroft, Hubert Howe. *History of Mexico.* 6 vols. New York, 1890.

———. *Literary Industries: A Memoir.* New York: Harper, 1891.

Barrett, Ellen C. *Baja California: A Bibliography of Historical, Geographical, and Scientific Literature Relating to the Peninsula of Baja California and to the Adjacent Islands in the Gulf of California and the Pacific Ocean.* 2 vols. Los Angeles: Bennett and Marshall, 1957–1967.

"B(ashful) Traven." *New York Times Book Review,* December 27, 1970, p. 10.

Bassols Batalla, Angel. *Bibliografía geográfica de México.* Mexico City, 1955.

Beals, Carleton. *Black River.* Philadelphia: J. B. Lippincott, 1934.

———. *Glass Houses: Ten Years of Free-Lancing.* Philadelphia: J. B. Lippincott, 1938.

———. *The Great Circle: Further Adventures in Free-Lancing.* Philadelphia: J. B. Lippincott, 1940.

———. *House in Mexico.* New York: Hastings House, 1958.

———. *The Stones Awake: A Novel of Mexico.* Philadelphia: J. B. Lippincott, 1936.

Bedford, Sybille. *The Sudden View: A Mexican Journey.* New York: Harper's, 1953.

Beer, Thomas. *Stephen Crane: A Study in American Letters.* New York: Alfred A. Knopf, 1923.

Bellow, Saul. *The Adventures of Augie March.* New York: Random House, 1953.

———. "The Mexican General." *Partisan Review* 9 (May–June 1942): 178–194.

———. *Mosby's Memoirs and Other Stories.* New York: Viking, 1968.

Berigan, Ted. Interview with Jack Kerouac. *Paris Review* 43 (Summer 1968): 61–105.

Bierce, Ambrose. *The Letters of Ambrose Bierce*. Edited by Bertha Clark Pope. San Francisco: Book Club of California, 1922.

———. "Seven Ambrose Bierce Letters." Edited by Mary Elizabeth Grenander. *Yale University Library Gazette* 32 (July 1957): 12–18.

Billings, Harold. "A Checklist of Edward Dahlberg"; "A Chronology of Edward Dahlberg." *Tri-Quarterly* 19 (Fall 1970): 163–168.

Birney, Earle, and Margerie (Bonner) Lowry. "Malcolm Lowry (1909–1957): A Bibliography." *Canadian Literature* 8 (Spring 1961): 81–88; 9 (Summer 1961): 80–84; 11 (Winter 1962): 90–95; 19 (Winter 1964): 83–89.

Bode, Winston. *A Portrait of Pancho: The Life of a Great Texan, J. Frank Dobie*. Austin: Pemberton Press, 1965.

Bontillier, Peggy le. "Who Is B. Traven? What Is He?" *Modern Mexico* 20 (January 1948): 14–15.

*Book Review Digest*. 66 vols. New York: H. W. Wilson, 1905–1971.

Bowles, Paul. *Without Stopping: An Autobiography*. Boston: G. P. Putnam, 1972.

Bradbury, Malcolm. *Evelyn Waugh*. Edinburgh: Oliver & Boyd, 1964.

Bradbury, Ray. *Dandelion Wine*. London: Rupert-Hart-Davis, 1957.

———. "Death in Mexico." *California Quarterly* 3 (1954): 11–13.

———. *The Illustrated Man*. Garden City: Doubleday, 1951.

———. *The Machineries of Joy*. New York: Simon & Schuster, 1964.

———. *The October Country*. New York: Ballantine Books, 1955.

———. *Twice Twenty-Two: The Golden Apples of the Sun; A Medicine for Melancholy*. Garden City: Doubleday, 1966.

Brenner, Anita. *Idols behind Altars*. 2d ed. New York: Biblo & Tannen, 1967.

——— (with George R. Leighton). *The Wind That Swept Mexico: The History of the Mexican Revolution, 1910–1942*. 2d ed. Austin: University of Texas Press, 1971.

Brett, Dorothy. *Lawrence and Brett: A Friendship*. Philadelphia: J. B. Lippincott, 1933.

Brown, William Jackson. "Influence of Bernal Diaz' *True History of the Conquest of New Spain* on Archibald MacLeish's *Conquistador*." Master's thesis, University of North Carolina, 1958.

Bryant, William Cullen. *The Poetical Works of William Cullen Bryant*. Edited by Parke Godwin. 2 vols. New York: D. Appleton, 1883.

———. *Prose Writings of William Cullen Bryant*. Edited by Parke Godwin. 2 vols. New York: D. Appleton, 1884.

Bucco, Martin. *Frank Waters*. Austin: Steck-Vaughn, 1969.

Burnett, Whit, ed. *This Is My Best*. New York: Dial, 1942.

Burroughs, William. *Junkie.* 2d ed. Introduction by Carl Solomon. New York: Avon, 1964.

———. *Naked Lunch.* New York: Grove, 1962.

———. *The Soft Machine.* New York: Grove, 1966.

———. *The Wild Boys: A Book of the Dead.* New York: Grove, 1971.

Burroughs, William, Jr. "Life with Father." *Esquire* 76 (September 1971): 113–115 ff.

Butterick, George F., and Albert Glover. *A Bibliography of Works by Charles Olson.* New York: Phoenix Bookshop, 1967.

Bynner, Witter. *Against the Cold.* New York: Alfred A. Knopf, 1940.

———. "Beach at Chapala." *Southwest Review* 32 (Summer 1947): 250.

———. *Caravan.* New York: Alfred A. Knopf, 1925.

———. "The Conquest of Mexico." *Forum* 95 (April 1936): 256.

———. "Foreigner in Mexico." *Rocky Mountain Review* 10 (Autumn 1945): 11.

———. "In a Mexican Hospital." *Laughing Horse* 8 (1923).

———. *Indian Earth.* New York: Alfred A. Knopf, 1929.

———. *Journey with Genius: Recollections and Reflections concerning the D. H. Lawrences.* New York: John Day, 1951.

———. "El Musico." *Saturday Review of Literature,* December 12, 1925, p. 401.

———. "A Night in Mexico." *Nation,* September 9, 1925, p. 280.

———. "On a Mexican Lake." *New Republic,* November 7, 1923, p. 275.

———. *Take Away the Darkness.* New York: Alfred A. Knopf, 1947.

———. "With the Gods." *Nation,* August 24, 1927, p. 182.

Calder-Marshall, Arthur. "The Novels of B. Traven." *Horizon* 1 (July 1940): 522–528.

———. "The Works of Graham Greene." *Horizon* 1 (May 1940): 367–375.

Calderón de la Barca, Frances. *Life in Mexico during a Residence of Two Years in That Country.* Introduction by Henry Baerlein. London: J. M. Dent, 1913.

———. *Life in Mexico: The Letters of Fanny Calderón de la Barca with New Material from the Author's Private Journals.* Edited by Howard T. and Marion Hall Fisher. Garden City: Doubleday, 1966.

Cardif, Maurice [John Lincoln]. *One Man's Mexico: A Record of Travels and Encounters.* New York: Harcourt, Brace, 1968.

Carswell, Catherine. *The Savage Pilgrimage: A Narrative of D. H. Lawrence.* New York: Harcourt, Brace, 1932.

Carter, Paul J. *Waldo Frank.* New York: Twayne, 1967.

Castrejón, Ruby N., and Jaime Castrejón. *William Spratling.* Taxco, n.d.

Castro, Adolphe de. *Portrait of Ambrose Bierce.* New York: Century, 1929.

Caughey, John W. *Hubert Howe Bancroft, Historian of the West.* Berkeley: University of California Press, 1946.

Cavitch, David. *D. H. Lawrence and the New World.* New York: Oxford University Press, 1969.

Chapin, Clara C. "Bryant and Some of His Latin American Friends." *Bulletin of the Pan American Union* 78 (November 1944): 609–613.

Chapman, Arnold. *The Spanish American Reception of United States Fiction, 1920–1940.* Berkeley: University of California Press, 1966.

Charlot, Jean. *The Mexican Mural Renaissance, 1920–1925.* New Haven: Yale University Press, 1963.

Chartres, Ann. *Kerouac: A Biography.* San Francisco: Straight Arrow, 1973.

———. *A Bibliography of Works by Jack Kerouac (Jean Louis Lebris de Kerouac), 1939–1967.* New York: Phoenix Bookshop, 1967.

Charyn, Jerome, ed. *The Single Voice: An Anthology of Contemporary Fiction.* New York: Collier, 1969.

Chase, Stuart (with Marian Tyler). *Mexico: A Study of Two Americas.* New York: Macmillan, 1931.

Chaundy, Leslie. *A Bibliography of the First Editions of the Work of Robert Bontine Cunninghame Graham.* London: Dulau, 1924.

Chumacero, Alí. "Green Eyes." Translated by William Carlos Williams. *New World Writing* 14 (1958): 92.

———. "Two Poems." Translated by William Carlos Williams. *Evergreen Review* 2 (Winter 1959): 59–61.

Clark, L. D. *Dark Night of the Body: D. H. Lawrence's "The Plumed Serpent."* Austin: University of Texas Press, 1964.

Coccioli, Carlo. *Manuel the Mexican.* Translated by Hans Koningsberger. New York: Simon & Schuster, 1958.

Cohen, Merton. *Rider Haggard: His Life and Works.* New York: Walker, 1961.

*Contemporary Authors.* 29 vols. Detroit: Gale Research, 1962–1971.

"Contributors and Contributions." *Asia* 20 (August 1920): 653.

Conway, George Robert Graham. *An Englishman in Mexico, A.D. 1625.* Mexico City, 1920.

Cook, Bruce. *The Beat Generation.* New York: Charles Scribner's Sons, 1971.

Copeland, Fayette. *Kendall of "The Picayune"; Being His Adventures in New Orleans, on the Texas Santa Fe Expedition, in the Mexican War, and in the Colonization of the Texas Frontier.* Norman: University of Oklahoma Press, 1943.

Corso, Gregory. *Gasoline.* Introduction by Allen Ginsberg. San Francisco: City Lights, 1956.

Covarrubias, Miguel. *Mexico South: The Isthmus of Tehuantepec.* New York: Alfred A. Knopf, 1946.

Cowan, James C. *D. H. Lawrence's American Journey: A Study in Literature and Myth.* Cleveland: Case Western Reserve University Press, 1970.

Cox, Edward G. *A Reference Guide to the Literature of Travel, Including Voyages, Geographical Descriptions, Adventures, Shipwrecks, and Expeditions.* 2 vols. Seattle: University of Washington Press, 1935–1938.

Crane, Hart. *The Collected Poems of Hart Crane.* Edited by Waldo Frank. New York: Liveright, 1933.

———. *The Letters of Hart Crane, 1916–1932.* Edited by Brom Weber. New York: Hermitage House, 1952.

Crane, Stephen. *The Complete Short Stories and Sketches of Stephen Crane.* Edited by Thomas A. Gullason. Garden City: Doubleday, 1963.

———. *Letters.* Edited by R. W. Stallman and Lillian Gilkes. New York: New York University Press, 1960.

———. *Stephen Crane in the West and Mexico.* Edited by Joseph Katz. Kent: Kent State University Press, 1970.

Cranfill, Thomas Mabry, ed. *The Muse in Mexico: A Mid-Century Miscellany.* Austin: University of Texas Press, 1959.

Creeley, Robert. *Pieces.* New York: Scribners, 1969.

Crume, Paul. Review of *Pale Horse, Pale Rider. Southwest Review* 25 (January 1940): 213–218.

Cruz, Juana Inés de la. "To a Portrait of a Poet." Translated by Katherine Anne Porter. *Survey* 56 (May 1, 1924): 182.

Cumberland, Charles C. *Mexican Revolution: Genesis under Madero.* Austin: University of Texas Press, 1952.

———. "The United States–Mexican Border: A Selective Guide to the Literature of the Region." *Rural Sociology* 25, special supplement (June 1960).

Cunninghame Graham, Gabriela. *The Christ of Toro and Other Stories.* London: Eveleigh Nash, 1908.

Cunninghame Graham, Robert B. *Brought Forward.* London: Duckworth, 1916.

———. *Progress and Other Sketches.* London: Duckworth, 1905.

———. *Thirteen Stories.* London: W. Heinemann, 1900.

*Current Biography.* 31 vols. New York: H. W. Wilson, 1940–1970.

Current-García, Eugene. *O. Henry (William Sidney Porter).* New York: Twayne, 1965.

Dahl, Curtis. *Robert Montgomery Bird.* New York: Twayne, 1963.

Dahlberg, Edward. *Cipango's Hinder Door.* Austin: University of Texas, 1965.

Dana, Richard Henry, Jr. *Two Years before the Mast: A Personal Narrative of Life at Sea.* Boston: Houghton Mifflin, 1911.

———. *Two Years before the Mast: A Personal Narrative of Life at Sea; Edited from the Original Manuscript and from the First Edition, with Journals and Letters of 1834–36 and 1859–60.* Edited by John H. Kemble. Los Angeles: Ward Ritchie, 1964.

Davis, Charles B., ed. *Adventures and Letters of Richard Harding Davis.* New York: Charles Scribner's Sons, 1917.

Davis, Richard Harding. "How Davis Got a Story." *Literary Digest,* May 23, 1914, pp. 1284–1288.

———. Veracruz dispatches. *New York Tribune,* April 30–June 23, 1914 (April 30, pp. 1–2; May 1, p. 2; May 3, p. 2; May 4, pp. 1–2; May 5, p. 1; May 12, pp. 1, 5; May 18, p. 1; May 19, p. 1; May 20, pp. 1–2; May 24, pp. 1–2; May 25, p. 1; May 28, p. 2; May 30, p. 4; May 31, p. 3; June 4, p. 2; June 9, pp. 1–2; June 14, p. 4; June 23, p. 2).

———. "When a War Is Not a War." *Scribner's* 56 (July 1914): 41–52.

Day, Douglas. *Malcolm Lowry.* New York: Oxford University Press, 1973.

Dewey, John. *John Dewey's Impressions of Soviet Russia and the Revolutionary World: Mexico—China—Turkey, 1929.* Edited by William W. Brickman. New York: Columbia University Press, 1964.

*Diccionario Porrúa de historia, biografía y geografía de México.* 2d ed. Mexico City: Porrúa, 1964.

Dickinson, Donald C. *A Bio-bibliography of Langston Hughes, 1902–1967.* Hamden, Conn.: Archon, 1967.

*Dictionary of American Biography.* 20 vols. New York: Charles Scribner's, 1928–1936.

*Dictionary of National Biography.* 28 vols. London: Oxford University Press, 1921–1971.

Dobie, J. Frank. *Apache Gold and Yaqui Silver.* Boston: Little, Brown, 1939.

———. "Babicora." *American Hereford Journal,* January 1, 1954, pp. 56–58 ff.

———. *Coronado's Children: Tales of Lost Mines and Buried Treasure of the Southwest.* New York: Grosset & Dunlap, 1930.

———. "Down the Road to Mexico." *This Week (New York Herald Tribune),* March 22, 1936, pp. 14–15 ff.

———. *Guide to Life and Literature of the Southwest.* Rev. ed. Dallas: Southern Methodist University Press, 1952.

———. "The Mad Mexican Millionaire." *Frontier Times* 35 (Summer 1961): 13 ff.

———. "Mexico City." *Holiday* 13 (March 1953): 34–40 ff.

———. "Mexico's Mines Come Back." *New York Herald Tribune Magazine*, March 11, 1934, pp. 14–15 ff.

———. *Some Part of Myself*. Boston: Little, Brown, 1967.

———. *Tongues of the Monte*. 3d ed. Boston: Little, Brown, 1947.

Dolan, Dan. "The Life of Ivan Illich." *New Republic*, March 1, 1969, pp. 18–19.

"Don Juan and the Sorcerer's Apprentice." *Time*, international edition, March 5, 1973, pp. 30–35.

Dos Passos, John. *The Best Times: An Informal Memoir*. New York: New American Library, 1966.

———. *The Fourteenth Chronicle: Letters and Diaries of John Dos Passos*. Edited by Townsend Ludington. Boston: Gambit, 1973.

———. *In All Countries*. New York: Harcourt, Brace, 1934.

———. "Paint the Revolution!" *New Masses* 2 (March 1927): 15.

———. *U.S.A.: The 42nd Parallel; Nineteen Nineteen; The Big Money*. New York: Harcourt, Brace, 1938.

Downey, Fairfax. *Richard Harding Davis, His Day*. New York: Charles Scribner's Sons, 1933.

Doyle, Helen MacKnight. *Mary Austin: Woman of Genius*. New York: Gotham House, 1939.

Dulles, John W. F. *Yesterday in Mexico: A Chronicle of the Revolution, 1919–1936*. Austin: University of Texas Press, 1961.

Duncan, Robert D. "William Spratling's Mexican World." *Texas Quarterly* 9 (Spring 1966): 97–104.

Dunn, Robert. *World Alive: A Personal Story*. New York: Crown, 1956.

Edmonds, Dale H. "Malcolm Lowry: A Study of His Life and Work." Ph.D. dissertation, University of Texas, 1965.

Eells, George. *The Life That Late He Led: A Biography of Cole Porter*. New York: G. P. Putnam's Sons, 1967.

Egan, Ferol. *The El Dorado Trail: The Story of the Gold Rush Routes across Mexico*. New York: McGraw-Hill, 1970.

Emanuel, James A. *Langston Hughes*. New York: Twayne, 1967.

Eschelbach, Claire J., and Joyce Lee Shober. *Aldous Huxley: A Bibliography, 1916–1959*. Berkeley: University of California Press, 1961.

Estes, Mary Caroline. "American Travellers in Mexico, 1810–1940." Master's thesis, University of Texas, 1961.

Ewing, Russell C., ed. *Six Faces of Mexico: History, People, Geography, Government, Literature & Art*. Tucson: University of Arizona Press, 1966.

Falk, Signi. *Archibald MacLeish*. New York: Twayne, 1965.

Farrell, James T. *Reflections at Fifty and Other Essays*. New York: Vanguard, 1954.

Fatout, Paul. *Ambrose Bierce: The Devil's Lexicographer.* Norman: University of Oklahoma Press, 1951.

Fay, Eliot. *Lorenzo in Search of the Sun: D. H. Lawrence in Italy, Mexico, and the American Southwest.* New York: Bookman, 1953.

Fergusson, Erna. *Fiesta in Mexico.* New York: Alfred A. Knopf, 1934.

———. *Mexico Revisited.* New York: Alfred A. Knopf, 1955.

Ferlinghetti, Lawrence. *The Mexican Night: Travel Journal.* New York: New Directions, 1970.

Fernández de Lizardi, José Joaquín. *The Itching Parrot.* Translated by Katherine Anne Porter. Garden City: Doubleday, Doran, 1942.

Fields, Annie A. *Charles Dudley Warner.* New York: McClure Phillips, 1904.

Fitts, Dudley, ed. *Anthology of Contemporary Latin-American Poetry.* New York: New Directions, 1942.

Flandrau, Charles M. *Loquacities.* New York: D. Appleton, 1931.

———. *Prejudices.* New York: D. Appleton, 1911.

———. *Viva Mexico!* Introduction by C. Harvey Gardiner. Urbana: University of Illinois Press, 1964.

Flores, Angel, and Dudley Poore, eds. *Fiesta in November: Stories from Latin America.* Introduction by Katherine Anne Porter. Boston: Houghton Mifflin, 1942.

Folson, James K. *Timothy Flint.* New York: Twayne, 1965.

Foote, Mary Hallock. "A Diligence Journey in Mexico." *Century* 23 (November 1881): 1–14.

———. "From Morelia to Mexico City on Horseback." *Century* 23 (March 1882): 643–655.

———. "A Provincial Capital of Mexico." *Century* 23 (January 1882): 321–333.

Forster, E. M. *Two Cheers for Democracy.* New York: Harcourt, Brace, 1951.

Frank, Waldo. *America Hispana: A Portrait and a Prospect.* New York: Charles Scribner's Sons, 1931.

———. "Cárdenas of Mexico." *Foreign Affairs* 18 (October 1939): 91–101.

Frankel, Haskel. "The Author." *Saturday Review,* September 25, 1965, p. 36.

Frémont, John Charles. *The Expeditions of John Charles Frémont.* Vol. 1, *Travels from 1838 to 1844.* Edited by Donald Jackson and Mary Lee Spence. Urbana: University of Illinois Press, 1970.

Gage, Thomas. *The English-American: A New Survey of the West Indies, 1648.* Edited by Arthur Percival Newton. London: George Routledge, 1928.

————. *Thomas Gage's Travels in the New World.* Edited by J. Eric S. Thompson, 2d ed. Norman: University of Oklahoma Press, 1969.

Gale, Robert L. *Richard Henry Dana, Jr.* New York: Twayne, 1969.

Gardiner, C. Harvey. "Foreign Travelers' Accounts of Mexico, 1810–1910." *Americas* 8 (January 1952): 321–351.

————, ed. *The Papers of William Hickling Prescott.* Urbana: University of Illinois Press, 1964.

Garrett, Eudora. "Laboring Colony in All Arts Grows in Cuernavaca." Newspaper clipping, January 25, 1952; source unknown.

Geduld, Harry M., and Ronald Gottesman, eds. *Sergei Eisenstein and Upton Sinclair: The Making and Unmaking of "Que Viva Mexico!"* Bloomington: Indiana University Press, 1970.

Gillis, Everett A. *Oliver La Farge.* Austin: Steck-Vaughn, 1967.

Ginsberg, Allen. *Reality Sandwiches, 1953–1960.* San Francisco: City Lights, 1963.

"The Gist of It." *Survey,* May 1, 1924, p. 127.

Godwin, Parke. *A Biography of William Cullen Bryant, with Extracts from His Private Correspondence.* 2 vols. New York: D. Appleton, 1883.

González Peña, Carlos. *History of Mexican Literature.* Translated by Guston Barfield Nance and Florence Johnson Dunston. 3d ed. Dallas: Southern Methodist University Press, 1968.

Goodman, Paul. *Homespun of Oatmeal Gray.* New York: Random House, 1970.

Gray, Francine D. *Divine Disobedience: Profiles in Christian Radicalism.* New York: Alfred A. Knopf, 1970.

Greene, Graham. *Another Mexico.* New York: Viking, 1939.

————. *Collected Essays.* New York: Viking, 1969.

————. *The Lawless Roads.* 3d ed. London: William Heinemann, 1950.

————. *The Power and the Glory.* 3d ed. New York: Viking, 1962.

————. *A Sort of Life.* London: Bodley Head, 1971.

————. *Twenty-One Stories.* New York: Viking, 1962.

Gregg, Josiah. *Commerce of the Prairies.* Edited by Max L. Moorhead. Norman: University of Oklahoma Press, 1954.

————. *Diary and Letters of Josiah Gregg.* Edited by Maurice Garland Fulton; introduction by Paul Hogan. 2 vols. Norman: University of Oklahoma Press, 1941–1944.

Grey, Zane. *Tales of Southern Rivers.* New York: Harper, 1924.

Gruber, Frank. *Zane Grey.* New York: World, 1970.

Gruening, Ernest. *Mexico and Its Heritage.* New York: Appleton-Century Crofts, 1928.

————. "On Disliking Mexico." *Saturday Review of Literature,* June 17, 1939, p. 13.

Gunn, Drewey Wayne. *Mexico in American and British Letters: A Bibliography of Fiction and Travel Books, Citing Original Editions*. Metuchen, N.J.: Scarecrow, 1974.

———. "Three Radicals and a Revolution: Reed, London, and Steffens in the Mexican Revolution." *Southwest Review* 55 (Autumn 1970): 393–410.

Hagemann, E. R. "A Checklist of the Work of B. Traven and the Critical Estimates and Biographical Essays on Him; Together with a Brief Biography." *Papers of Bibliographical Society of America* 53 (1959): 34–67.

Haggard, H. Rider. *The Days of My Life: An Autobiography*. Edited by C. J. Longman. 2 vols. London: Longmans, Green, 1926.

———. *Heart of the World*. London: Macdonald, 1954.

———. *Montezuma's Daughter*. London: Macdonald, 1948.

Haggard, Lilias R. *The Cloak That I Left: A Biography of the Author, Henry Rider Haggard, K.B.E.* London: Hodder & Stoughton, 1951.

Hakluyt, Richard. *The Principal Navigations, Voyages, Traffiques & Discoveries of the English Nation*. 10 vols. London: J. M. Dent, 1907.

Halliburton, Richard. *New Worlds to Conquer*. Indianapolis: Bobbs-Merrill, 1929.

———. *Richard Halliburton: His Story of His Life's Adventure as Told in Letters to His Mother and Father*. Indianapolis: Bobbs-Merrill, 1940.

Halsey, Milton. *John Dewey: A Centennial Bibliography*. Chicago: University of Chicago Press, 1962.

Harris, Ray Baker. *Bibliography of the Writings of Albert Pike*. Washington, D.C.: 1957.

Hart, Elizabeth. "Slight and Short Stories." *New York Herald Tribune Books*, December 16, 1934, p. 15.

Hayden, Robert. *Selected Poems*. New York: October House, 1966.

Hays, H. R. "The Importance of B. Traven." *Chimera* 4 (Summer 1946): 44–54.

Heilman, Grace E., and Bernard S. Levin. *Calendar of Joel R. Poinsett Papers in the Henry D. Gilpin Collection*. Philadelphia: Historical Society of Pennsylvania, 1941.

Helm, Mackinley. *Modern Mexican Painters*. New York: Harper, 1941.

Hendrick, George. *Katherine Anne Porter*. New York: Twayne, 1965.

Hergesheimer, Joseph. *From an Old House*. New York: Alfred A. Knopf, 1925.

———. "Shapes in Light." *Saturday Evening Post*, March 20, 1926, p. 119.

———. *Tampico*. New York: Alfred A. Knopf, 1926.

Herring, Hubert (with Helen B. Herring). *A History of Latin America from the Beginnings to the Present.* 3d ed. New York: Alfred A. Knopf, 1968.

———. "Mexico and South America." *Yale Review* 29 (Winter 1940): 397.

Hewes, Henry. "Tennessee Williams—Last of Our Solid Gold Bohemians." *Saturday Review,* March 28, 1953, p. 25.

Hicks, Granville (with John Stuart). *John Reed: The Making of a Revolutionary.* New York: Macmillan, 1930.

Hobson, Laura Z. "Trade Winds." *Saturday Review,* February 16, 1952, pp. 6–7; March 1, 1952, pp. 6–7.

Hollon, W. Eugene. *The Lost Pathfinder: Zebulon Montgomery Pike.* Norman: University of Oklahoma Press, 1949.

Horton, Philip. *Hart Crane: The Life of an American Poet.* New York: W. W. Norton, 1937.

Hoyt, Edwin P. *A Gentleman of Broadway.* Boston: Little, Brown, 1964.

Hueffer, Oliver Madox. "Jack London: A Personal Sketch." *New Statesman,* December 2, 1916, pp. 206–207.

Hughes, Langston. *The Big Sea: An Autobiography.* New York: Alfred A. Knopf, 1940.

———. *The Dream Keeper and Other Poems.* Folkway Records, 1955.

———. "In a Mexican City." *Brownies' Book* 2 (April 1921): 102–105.

———. *I Wonder as I Wander: An Autobiographical Journey.* New York: Rinehart, 1956.

———. "Mexican Games." *Brownies' Book* 2 (January 1921): 18.

———. "Up to the Crater of an Old Volcano." *Brownies' Book* 2 (December 1921): 334–338.

———. "The Virgin of Guadalupe." *Crisis* 23 (December 1921): 77.

———. *The Weary Blues.* New York: Alfred A. Knopf, 1926.

Hulet, Claude. *Latin American Poetry in English Translation: A Bibliography.* Washington, D.C.: Pan American Union, 1966.

———. *Latin American Prose in English Translation: A Bibliography.* Washington, D.C.: Pan American Union, 1964.

Humboldt, Alexander von. *Political Essay on the Kingdom of New Spain.* Translated by John Black. 4 vols. London: Longman, Hurst, Rees, Orme, and Brown, 1811.

———. *Vues des cordillères et monumens des peuples indigènes de l'Amérique.* Paris: P. Schoell, 1810.

Hume, Martin. *Spanish Influence on English Literature.* London: Eveleigh Nash, 1905.

Humphrey, Charles R. "B. Traven: An Examination of the Controversy over His Identity with an Analysis of His Major Works and His Place in Literature." Ph.D. dissertation, University of Texas, 1965.

Huxley, Aldous. *Beyond the Mexique Bay*. 2d ed. New York: Vintage, 1960.

——. *Eyeless in Gaza*. New York: Harper, 1936.

——. *The Letters of Aldous Huxley*. Edited by Grover Smith. New York: Harper & Row, 1969.

Iglehart, Fanny Chambers Gooch. *Face to Face with the Mexicans*. Edited by C. Harvey Gardiner. Carbondale: Southern Illinois University Press, 1966.

"Illustre escritor inglés en México." *Revista de Revistas*, March 22, 1925, p. 10.

"In the Bookmarket." *Publishers Weekly*, October 11, 1930, p. 1747.

Jackson, Helen Hunt. "By Horse-Cars into Mexico." *Atlantic* 51 (March 1883): 350–362.

Jannach, Hubert. "B. Traven—An American or German Author?" *German Quarterly* 36 (November 1963): 459–468.

Jarrell, Randall. *The Complete Poems*. New York: Farrar, Straus & Giroux, 1969.

Jebb, Mrs. J. Gladwyn. *A Strange Career: Life and Adventures of John Gladwyn Jebb*. Introduction by Henry Rider Haggard. Edinburgh: William Blackwood, 1895.

Johnson, William Weber. *Heroic Mexico: The Violent Emergence of a Modern Nation*. Garden City: Doubleday, 1968.

——. *Mexico*. New York: Time-Life Books, 1966.

——. "The Traven Case." *New York Times Book Review*, April 17, 1966, pp. 1 ff.

——. "Who Is Bruno Traven?" *Life*, March 10, 1947, pp. 13–16.

Jones, LeRoi. *Black Magic: Sabotage, Target Study, Black Art: Collected Poems, 1961–1967*. Indianapolis: Bobbs-Merrill, 1969.

Josephson, Matthew. *Life among the Surrealists: A Memoir*. New York: Holt, Rinehart & Winston, 1962.

Kendall, George W. *Across the Great Southwestern Prairies*. Ann Arbor: University Microfilms, 1966.

Kerouac, Jack. *Book of Dreams*. San Francisco: City Lights, 1961.

——. *Desolation Angels*. Introduction by Seymour Krim. New York: Coward-McCann, 1965.

——. *The Dharma Bums*. New York: Viking, 1958.

——. *Doctor Sax: Faust Part Three*. New York: Grove, 1959.

——. *Lonesome Traveler*. New York: McGraw-Hill, 1960.

——. *Mexico City Blues*. New York: Grove, 1959.

——. *On the Road*. New York: Viking, 1957.

——. *Tristessa*. New York: Avon, 1960.

Kirk, Betty. *Covering the Mexican Front: The Battle of Europe versus*

*America*. Introduction by Josephus Daniels. Norman: University of Oklahoma Press, 1942.

Kline, Herbert. " 'The Forgotten Village ': An Account of Film Making in Mexico." *Theatre Arts* 25 (May 1941): 336–343.

Kramer, Jane. *Allen Ginsberg in America*. New York: Random House, 1969.

Krutch, Joseph Wood. *The Forgotten Peninsula: A Naturalist in Baja California*. New York: William Sloan, 1961.

Kunitz, Stanley J., ed. *Authors Today and Yesterday*. New York: H. W. Wilson, 1933.

————, and Howard Haycroft, eds. *British Authors of the Nineteenth Century*. New York: H. W. Wilson, 1936.

————, and Howard Haycroft, eds. *Twentieth Century Authors: A Biographical Dictionary of Modern Literature*. New York: H. W. Wilson, 1942.

————, and Vineta Colby, eds. *Twentieth Century Authors: First Supplement*. New York: H. W. Wilson, 1955.

La Farge, Oliver. *Raw Material*. Boston: Houghton Mifflin, 1945.

Langford, Gerald. *Alias O. Henry: A Biography of William Sidney Porter*. New York: Macmillan, 1957.

————. *The Richard Harding Davis Years: A Biography of a Mother and Son*. New York: Holt, Rinehart & Winston, 1961.

Langford, Walter M. *The Mexican Novel Comes of Age*. Notre Dame, Ind.: University of Notre Dame Press, 1971.

Lawrence, D. H. *The Collected Letters of D. H. Lawrence*. Edited by Harry T. Moore. 2 vols. New York: Viking, 1962.

————. *The Complete Short Stories*. 3 vols. New York: Viking, 1961.

————. *The Letters of D. H. Lawrence*. Edited by Aldous Huxley. London: William Heinemann, 1932.

————. *Mornings in Mexico*. New York: Alfred A. Knopf, 1927.

————. *Paintings of D. H. Lawrence*. Edited by Mervyn Levy. New York: Viking, 1964.

————. *Phoenix: The Posthumous Papers of D. H. Lawrence*. Edited by Edward D. McDonald. New York: Viking, 1968.

————. *Phoenix II: Uncollected, Unpublished, and Other Prose Works of D. H. Lawrence*. Edited by Warren Roberts and Harry T. Moore. New York: Viking, 1968.

————. *The Plumed Serpent (Quetzalcoatl)*. Introduction by William York Tindall. New York: Alfred A. Knopf, 1951.

Lawrence, Frieda. *"Not I, but the Wind . . ."* New York: Viking, 1934.

Lea, Tom. *The Brave Bulls*. Boston: Little, Brown, 1949.

———. *The Hands of Cantú.* Boston: Little, Brown, 1964.

———. *The Wonderful Country.* Boston: Little, Brown, 1952.

Lee, William Storrs, ed. *California: A Literary Chronicle.* New York: Funk & Wagnalls, 1968.

Levertov, Denise. *Here and Now.* San Francisco: City Lights, 1957.

———. *The Jacob's Ladder.* New York: New Directions, 1961.

———. *Overland to the Islands.* Highlands, N.C.: Jonathan Williams, 1958.

———. *The Sorrow Dance.* New York: New Directions, 1966.

———. *With Eyes at the Back of Our Heads.* New York: New Directions, 1959.

Lewis, Oscar. *The Children of Sánchez: Autobiography of a Mexican Family.* New York: Random House, 1961.

———. *A Death in the Sánchez Family.* New York: Random House, 1969.

———. *Five Families: Mexican Case Studies in the Culture of Poverty.* Introduction by Oliver La Farge. New York: Basic Books, 1959.

———. *Pedro Martínez: A Mexican Peasant and His Family.* New York: Random House, 1964.

Liberman, M. M. "Some Observations on the Genesis of *Ship of Fools*: A Letter from Katherine Anne Porter." *PMLA* 84 (January 1969): 136–137.

Lindsay, Robert O. *Witter Bynner: A Bibliography.* Albuquerque: University of New Mexico Press, 1967.

Lisca, Peter. *The Wide World of John Steinbeck.* New Brunswick, N.J.: Rutgers University Press, 1958.

Lohf, Kenneth. *The Literary Manuscripts of Hart Crane.* Columbus: Ohio State University Press, 1967.

London, Charmian. *The Book of Jack London.* 2 vols. New York: Century, 1921.

London, Jack. "Law-Givers." *Collier's,* June 20, 1914, pp. 15–16 ff.

———. *Letters from Jack London.* Edited by King Hendricks and Irving Shepard. New York: Odyssey, 1965.

———. "Mexico's Army and Ours." *Collier's,* May 30, 1914, pp. 5–7.

———. *The Night Born.* New York: Century, 1913.

———. "Our Adventures in Tampico." *Collier's,* June 27, 1914, pp. 5–7 ff.

———. "The Red Game of War." *Collier's,* May 16, 1914, pp. 5–7.

———. "Stalking the Pestilence." *Collier's,* June 6, 1914, pp. 11–12 ff.

———. "The Trouble-Makers of Mexico." *Collier's,* June 13, 1914, pp. 13–14 ff.

————. "With Funston's Men: Our Army and Navy in Peaceful Action." *Collier's*, May 23, 1914, pp. 9–10 ff.

London, Joan. *Jack London and His Times: An Unconventional Biography*. New York: Doubleday, Doran, 1939.

López, Hank (interview with Katherine Anne Porter). "A Country and Some People I Love." *Harper's* 231 (September 1965): 58–68.

Lowell, Robert. *Notebook*. 3d ed. New York: Farrar, Straus & Giroux, 1970.

Lowry, Malcolm. *Dark as the Grave Wherein My Friend Is Laid*. Edited by Douglas Day and Margerie Lowry. New York: New American Library, 1968.

————. "Foul Acapulco." *Carleton Miscellany* 2 (Fall 1961): 34.

————. "Garden of Etla." *United Nations World* 4 (June 1950): 45–47.

————. *Hear Us O Lord from Heaven Thy Dwelling Place*. Philadelphia: J. B. Lippincott, 1961.

————. "Letters from Malcolm Lowry." *Canadian Literature* 8 (Spring 1961): 44.

————. *Selected Letters of Malcolm Lowry*. Edited by Harvey Breit and Margerie Lowry. Philadelphia: J. B. Lippincott, 1965.

————. *Selected Poems of Malcolm Lowry*. Edited by Earle Birney. San Francisco: City Lights, 1962.

————. *Under the Volcano*. 2d ed. Introduction by Stephen Spender. Philadelphia: J. B. Lippincott, 1965.

————. "Under the Volcano." *Prairie Schooner* 37 (Winter 1963–1964): 284–300.

————. "Wrecker of Gardens." *Prairie Schooner* 37 (Winter 1963–1964): 335.

Luhan, Mable Dodge. *Lorenzo in Taos*. New York: Alfred A. Knopf, 1932.

McClure, Michael. *Ghost Tantras*. San Francisco: City Lights, 1967.

McCormick, Medill. "Just Out of Jail." *Harper's Weekly*, May 30, 1914, pp. 6–7.

McCutcheon, John T. "With Davis in Vera Cruz, Brussels, and Salonika." *Scribner's* 60 (July 1916): 91–97.

McEvoy, J. P. " 'Silver Bill,' Practical Good Neighbor." *Reader's Digest* 47 (September 1945): 19–22.

McKee, Irving. *"Ben-Hur" Wallace: Life of General Lew Wallace*. Berkeley: University of California Press, 1947.

MacLeish, Archibald. "The American Experience." *Bulletin of Pan American Union* 73 (November 1939): 623.

————. *Conquistador*. Boston: Houghton Mifflin, 1932.

[————]. "In Our Time: The Industrial Civilization of New York Seen in the Cross Section of a Rivera Fresco." *Fortune* 5 (February 1932): 40–41.

[————]. "Industrial Detroit by Diego Rivera: A Selection from the Frescos Now in Process of Completion in the Detroit Institute of Arts." *Fortune* 7 (February 1933): 48–53.

————. "Notebooks, 1924–1938." *Poetry* 73 (November 1948): 95.

MacShane, Frank, ed. *Impressions of Latin America: Five Centuries of Travel and Adventure by English and North American Writers.* New York: William Morrow, 1963.

McVicker, Mary Louise. *The Writings of J. Frank Dobie: A Bibliography.* Lawton, Okla.: Museum of the Great Plains, 1968.

McWilliams, Carey. *Ambrose Bierce: A Biography.* New York: Albert & Charles Boni, 1929.

Madden, David. *Wright Morris.* New York: Twayne, 1964.

Mahoney, Tom. "The End of Ambrose Bierce." *Esquire* 5 (February 1936): 62 ff.

Mailer, Norman. *Advertisements for Myself.* New York: G. P. Putnam's-Berkeley, 1966.

————. *The Bullfight: A Photographic Narrative with Text by Norman Mailer.* New York: Macmillan, 1967.

"Malcolm Lowry." *Times Literary Supplement*, January 26, 1967, pp. 57–59.

Manfred, George. "B. Traven's Identity." *New Republic*, March 24, 1947, p. 35.

Mantle, Burns, ed. *The Best Plays of 1929–30 and the Year Book of the Drama in America.* New York: Dodd, Mead, 1930.

————. *The Best Plays of 1943–44 and the Year Book of the Drama in America.* New York: Dodd, Mead, 1944.

Mason, Gregory. "Reed, Villa, and the Village." *Outlook*, May 6, 1925, pp. 11 f.

Maugham, W. Somerset. *The Complete Short Stories of W. Somerset Maugham.* 2 vols. Garden City: Doubleday, 1952.

Maury, Mary Cash. "The Suicide of W. J. Cash." *Red Clay Reader* 4 (1967): 8–13.

Mayer, William. *Early Travellers in Mexico, 1534 to 1816.* Mexico City: Cultura, 1961.

Menkin, Edward Z. "Allen Ginsberg: A Bibliography and Biographical Sketch." *Thoth* 8 (Winter 1967): 35–44.

Mérida, Carlos. *Modern Mexican Artists.* Mexico City: Frances Toor Studios, 1937.

Merrild, Knud. *With D. H. Lawrence in New Mexico: A Memoir of D. H. Lawrence.* 2d ed. London: Routledge & Kegan Paul, 1964.

"Mexican Art Exhibit Opens." *Los Angeles Times*, November 11, 1922, sec. 2, p. 1.

"Mexican Folk Music Planned at Art Exhibit." *Los Angeles Times*, November 19, 1922, sec. 2, p. 1.

Miller, Charles. "B. Traven, American Author." *Texas Quarterly* 6 (Winter 1963): 162–168.

——. "B. Traven, Continued." *New York Times Book Review*, November 20, 1966, p. 84.

——. "Our Great Neglected Wobbly." *Michigan Quarterly Review* 6 (Winter 1967): 57–61.

Miller, Merle. "Viva Zapata!" *Argosy* 33 (February 1952): 52–53 ff.

Monroe, Harriet. "Pan-American Concord." *Poetry* 26 (June 1925): 152.

Moor, Paul. "A Mississippian Named Tennessee." *Harper's* 197 (July 1948): 70.

Moore, Harry T. *The Intelligent Heart: The Story of D. H. Lawrence.* New York: Farrar, Straus & Young, 1954.

——. *Poste Restante: A Lawrence Travel Calendar.* Berkeley: University of California Press, 1956.

Morris, Wright. *Ceremony in Lone Tree.* New York: Atheneum, 1960.

——. *The Field of Vision.* New York: Harcourt, Brace, 1956.

——. *Love among the Cannibals.* New York: Harcourt, Brace, 1957.

——. "Mexican Journey." *Holiday* 26 (November 1959): 50–63 ff.

——. *One Day.* New York: Atheneum, 1965.

Morrison, Joseph L. *W. J. Cash, Southern Prophet: A Biography and Reader.* New York: Alfred A. Knopf, 1967.

Nance, William L. "Katherine Anne Porter and Mexico." *Southwest Review* 55 (Spring 1970): 143–153.

Napier, James J. "Joseph Hergesheimer: A Selected Bibliography, 1913–1945." *Bulletin of Bibliography* 24 (September–December 1963 and January–April 1964): 46–48, 52, 69–70.

*National Cyclopaedia of American Biography.* 52 vols. New York: James T. White, 1898–1970.

Nehls, Edward, ed. *D. H. Lawrence: A Composite Biography.* 3 vols. Madison: University of Wisconsin Press, 1957–1959.

Nelson, Benjamin. *Tennessee Williams: The Man and His Work.* New York: Ivan Obolensky, 1961.

Nevins, Allan. *Frémont, Pathfinder of the West.* New York: D. Appleton-Century, 1939.

"New Films." *Newsweek*, February 4, 1952, p. 78.

"New Pictures." *Time*, December 8, 1941, p. 96.

Newquist, Roy. Interview with Katherine Anne Porter. *McCall's* 92 (August 1965): 89 ff.

Newton, Norman. *Thomas Gage in Spanish America.* New York: Barnes & Noble, 1969.

Nichols, Lewis. "B. Traven Again." *New York Times Book Review,* June 11, 1967, p. 51.

Nicholson, Irene. *Mexican and Central American Mythology.* London: Paul Hamlyn, 1967.

Niggli, Josefina. *Mexican Folk Plays.* Edited by Frederick H. Koch. Chapel Hill: University of North Carolina Press, 1938.

———. *Mexican Silhouettes.* San Antonio: Silhouette, 1931.

———. *Mexican Village.* Chapel Hill: University of North Carolina Press, 1945.

———. *A Miracle for Mexico.* Greenwich, Conn.: New York Graphic Society, 1964.

———. *Step Down, Elder Brother.* New York: Rinehart, 1947.

Nolan, William F. "Bradbury: Prose Poet in the Age of Space." *Magazine of Fantasy and Science Fiction* 24 (May 1963): 7–22.

———. "An Index to the Works of Ray Bradbury." *Magazine of Fantasy and Science Fiction* 24 (May 1963): 40–51.

*North Carolina Authors: A Selective Handbook.* Chapel Hill: University of North Carolina Library, 1952.

Northrop, F. S. C. *The Meeting of East and West: An Inquiry concerning World Understanding.* New York: Macmillan, 1946.

O'Connor, Richard. *Ambrose Bierce: A Biography.* Boston: Little, Brown, 1967.

———. *Black Jack Pershing.* Garden City: Doubleday, 1961.

———. *Jack London: A Biography.* Boston: Little, Brown, 1967.

——— (with Dale L. Walker). *The Lost Revolutionary: A Biography of John Reed.* New York: Harcourt, Brace & World, 1967.

Odel, Ruth. *Helen Hunt Jackson (H. H.).* New York: D. Appleton-Century, 1939.

Odier, Daniel. *The Job: Interviews with William S. Burroughs.* New York: Grove Press, 1970.

Olson, Charles. *Selected Writings of Charles Olson.* Edited by Robert Creeley. New York: New Directions, 1966.

"On the Traven Trail." *Publishers Weekly,* July 9, 1938, pp. 105–106.

Palmer, Frederick. *With My Own Eyes: A Personal Story of Battle Years.* Indianapolis: Bobbs-Merrill, 1933.

Parkes, Henry Bamford. *A History of Mexico.* 3d ed. Boston: Houghton Mifflin, 1960.

———. "Who Told Him All That?" *New York Herald Tribune Books,* September 24, 1939, p. 9.

Parkinson, Thomas, ed. *A Casebook on the Beat*. New York: Thomas Y. Crowell, 1961.

Partridge, Colin. " 'My Familiar Country': An Image of Mexico in the Work of Katherine Anne Porter." *Studies in Short Fiction* 7 (Fall 1970): 597–614.

Paul, Sherman. *The Music of Survival: A Biography of a Poem by William Carlos Williams*. Urbana: University of Illinois Press, 1968.

Paz, Octavio. *Configurations*. Introduction by Muriel Rukeyser. New York: New Directions, 1971.

———. *The Labyrinth of Solitude: Life and Thought in Mexico*. Translated by Lysander Kemp. New York: Grove, 1961.

———. *Selected Poems of Octavio Paz*. Translated by Muriel Rukeyser. Bloomington: Indiana University Press, 1963.

Pearce, T. M. *Mary Hunter Austin*. New York: Twayne, 1965.

" 'The Pearl.' " *New York Times Magazine*, February 15, 1948, pp. 34–35.

Penderast, David M., ed. *Palenque: The Walker-Caddy Expedition to the Ancient Maya City, 1839–1840*. Norman: University of Oklahoma Press, 1967.

Pike, Albert. *Prose Sketches and Poems Written in the Western Country (with Additional Stories)*. Edited by David J. Weber. Albuquerque: Calvin Horn, 1967.

Plimpton, George, ed. *Writers at Work: The "Paris Review" Interviews*. 2d ser. New York: Viking, 1963.

———. *Writers at Work: The "Paris Review" Interviews*. 3d ser. New York: Viking, 1968.

Poinsett, Joel R. *Notes on Mexico Made in the Autumn of 1822*. Introduction by A. Curtis Wilgus. New York: Frederick A. Praeger, 1969.

Porter, Katherine Anne. " 'Ay, Que Chamaco.' " *New Republic*, December 23, 1925, pp. 142–143.

———. "Children and Art." *Nation*, March 2, 1927, pp. 233–234.

———. *The Collected Essays and Occasional Writings of Katherine Anne Porter*. New York: Delacorte, 1970.

———. *The Collected Stories of Katherine Anne Porter*. New York: Harcourt, Brace, 1965.

———. "Corridos." *Survey*, May 1, 1924, pp. 157–159.

———. "Embarkation." *Sewanee Review* 55 (January 1947): 1–23.

———. *Hacienda*. New York: Harrison of Paris, 1934.

———. "Hacienda." *Virginia Quarterly Review* 8 (October 1932): 556–569.

———. "History on the Wing." *New Republic*, November 18, 1936, p. 82.

———. "Katherine Anne Porter." *New York Herald Tribune Books*, October 12, 1952, p. 8.

———. "Maya Treasure." *New York Herald Tribune Books*, February 8, 1925, p. 9.

———. "Mexico." *New York Herald Tribune Books*, November 2, 1924, p. 9.

———. "Mexico's Thirty Long Years of Revolution." *New York Herald Tribune Books*, May 30, 1943, pp. 1–2.

———. "Old Gods and New Messiahs." *New York Herald Tribune Books*, September 29, 1929, pp. 1–2.

———. *Outline of Mexican Popular Arts and Crafts*. Los Angeles: Young and McAllister, 1922.

———. "Paternalism and the Mexican Problem." *New York Herald Tribune Books*, March 27, 1927, p. 12.

———. "Rivera's Personal Revolution in Mexico." *New York Herald Tribune Books*, March 21, 1937, p. 7.

———. *Ship of Fools*. Boston: Little, Brown, 1962.

———. "That Tree." *Virginia Quarterly Review* 10 (July 1934): 351–361.

———. "These Pictures Must Be Seen: The Frescoes of Diego Rivera." *New York Herald Tribune Books*, December 22, 1929, pp. 5–6.

——— (interview with Diego Rivera). "The Guild Spirit in Mexican Art." *Survey*, May 1, 1924, pp. 174–178.

Potter, Jack. *A Bibliography of John Dos Passos*. Chicago: Normandie House, 1950.

Powell, Lawrence Clark. "Who Is B. Traven?" *New Masses*, August 2, 1938, pp. 22–23.

Prescott, William Hickling. *History of the Conquest of Mexico and History of the Conquest of Peru*. New York: Modern Library, 1936.

Preuss, Charles. *Exploring with Frémont: The Private Diaries of Charles Preuss, Cartographer for John C. Frémont on His First, Second, and Fourth Expeditions to the Far West*. Edited by Erwin A. and Elisabeth K. Gudde. Norman: University of Oklahoma Press, 1958.

"The Problem Pearl." *Newsweek*, March 8, 1948, pp. 83–84.

"Promise Kept." *Time*, April 10, 1939, p. 75.

Quinby, Henry Cole. *Richard Harding Davis: A Bibliography*. New York: E. P. Dutton, 1924.

"Recent Southern Fiction: A Panel Discussion." *Bulletin of Wesleyan College* 41 (January 1961): 12.

Reed, Alma M. *The Ancient Past of Mexico*. Introduction by Eusebio Dávalos Hurtado. New York: Crown, 1966.

———. *The Mexican Muralists*. New York: Crown, 1960.

Reed, John. "Bandit in Mountains Can Hold His Retreat." *New York American*, March 13, 1916, p. 3.

———. "The Causes behind Mexico's Revolution." *New York Times*, April 27, 1914, p. 4 [Reed's name is misspelled *Reid*].

———. *Daughter of the Revolution and Other Stories*. Edited by Floyd Dell. New York: Vanguard, 1927.

———. *Insurgent Mexico*. Introduction by Renato Leduc. New York: International, 1969.

———. "The Mexican Tangle." *Masses* 8 (June 1916): 11.

———. "Persecution of Mexican Refugees." *Masses* 8 (June 1916): 22–23.

———. "U.S. in Danger of Mountain Ambush, Declares John Reed." *New York American*, April 16, 1916, sec. 2, pp. 1–2.

———. Villa dispatches. *New York World*, March 1–April 4, 1914 (March 1, pp. 1–2; March 25, pp. 1–2; March 29, p. 5; March 31, pp. 1–2; April 1, pp. 1, 4; April 2, pp. 1–2; April 4, pp. 1–2).

———. "What about Mexico?" *Masses* 5 (June 1914): 11 ff.

———. "With Villa in Mexico." *Metropolitan*, February 1914, p. 72.

"Reed and Companion Had to Escape from the Front." *New York World*, March 31, 1914, p. 2.

Reger, Muriel. "Lowry's Quauhnahuac Today." *Vistas* (*The News*, Mexico City), May 31, 1970, pp. 2–4.

Remington, Frederic. *Pony Tracks*. Introduction by J. Frank Dobie. Norman: University of Oklahoma Press, 1961.

Remley, David A. *Erna Fergusson*. Austin: Steck-Vaughn, 1969.

Rexroth, Kenneth. *An Autobiographical Novel*. Garden City: Doubleday, 1966.

———. *The Collected Shorter Poems*. New York: New Directions, 1966.

Reyes, Alfonso. "Modern Poetry of America Hispana." Translated by Waldo Frank. *Nation*, March 29 and April 5, 1941, pp. 376–379, 411–412.

Rippy, J. Fred. *Joel R. Poinsett, Versatile American*. Durham: Duke University Press, 1935.

Rivera, Diego. "From a Mexican Painter's Notebooks." Translated by Katherine Anne Porter. *Arts* 7 (January 1925): 21–23.

"Robert Hayden." *Negro History Bulletin* 21 (October 1957): 15.

Roberts, Warren. *A Bibliography of D. H. Lawrence*. London: Rupert-Hart-Davis, 1963.

Robinson, Cecil. *With the Ears of Strangers: The Mexican in American Literature*. Tucson: University of Arizona Press, 1963.

Rodman, Selden. "After Westernization, Desolation." *Saturday Review*, July 4, 1959, p. 13.

———. *Mexican Journal: The Conquerors Conquered.* 2d ed. Carbondale: Southern Illinois University Press, 1965.

———. *The Road to Panama.* New York: Hawthorn, 1966.

Root, Jonathan. *Halliburton: The Magnificent Myth.* New York: Coward-McCann, 1965.

Rowe, Hershel D. *Hart Crane: A Bibliography.* Denver: Alan Swallow, 1955.

Rukeyser, Muriel. *Beast in View.* Garden City: Doubleday, 1944.

———. *The Green Wave.* Garden City: Doubleday, 1948.

———. *The Speed of Darkness.* New York: Random House, 1968.

———. *A Turning Wind.* New York: Viking, 1939.

———. *Waterlily Fire: Poems 1935–1962.* New York: Macmillan, 1962.

Runyon, Damon. Pershing Expedition dispatches and poems. *New York American,* March 23–May 27, 1916 (March 23, p. 2; March 24, pp. 1–2; April 1, p. 2; April 2, pp. 1, 6; April 4, p. 2; April 5, p. 2; April 13, p. 4; April 16, p. 2; [no issues available April 21–April 30]; May 1, p. 4; May 2, p. 18; May 5, p. 18; May 6, p. 6; May 10, p. 3; May 10, p. 3; May 22, p. 1; May 24, p. 1; May 27, p. 1).

———. *Poems for Men.* New York: Duell, Sloan & Pearce, 1947.

Ruoff, James, and Del Smith. "Katherine Anne Porter on *Ship of Fools.*" *College English* 24 (February 1963): 396–397.

Ruxton, George F. *Ruxton of the Rockies.* Edited by LeRoy R. Hafner from material collected by Clyde and Mae Reed Porter. Norman: University of Oklahoma Press, 1950.

Schmidt, James Norman [James Norman]. *Terry's Guide to Mexico.* 2d ed. Garden City: Doubleday, 1965.

Schneider, Harold W. "Two Bibliographies: Saul Bellow and William Styron." *Critique* 3 (Summer 1960): 72–86.

Schrag, Peter. "Ivan Illich: The Christian as Rebel." *Saturday Review,* July 19, 1969, pp. 14–19.

Schwartz, Edward. "Katherine Anne Porter: A Critical Bibliography." *Bulletin of the New York Public Library* 57 (May 1953): 211–247.

"A Score of Years Have Passed: The English Language Press—in War and Peace." *Vistas* (*The News,* Mexico City), July 5–11, 1970, pp. 2–5.

Scott, J. E. *A Bibliography of the Works of Sir Henry Rider Haggard, 1856–1925.* Takeley, Eng.: E. Mathews, 1947.

"The Secret of *El Gringo.*" *Time,* August 16, 1948, pp. 34–36.

Seton, Marie. *Sergei M. Eisenstein: A Biography.* New York: A. A. Wyn, 1952.

Simpson, Lesley Byrd. *Many Mexicos.* 4th ed. Berkeley: University of California Press, 1966.

Sitwell, Sacheverell. *Golden Walls and Mirador: Travels and Observations in Peru.* Cleveland: World, 1962.

———. *Journey to the Ends of Time.* Vol. 1, *Lost in the Dark Wood.* New York: Random House, 1959.

Smith, Bernard. "B(ashful) Traven." *New York Times Book Review,* November 22, 1970, pp. 2 ff.

Smith, H. Allen. *The Pig in the Barber Shop.* Boston: Little, Brown, 1958.

Spiller, Robert E., ed. *Literary History of the United States.* 3d ed. New York: Macmillan, 1963.

Spratling, William. *File on Spratling: An Autobiography.* Introduction by Budd Schulberg. Boston: Little, Brown, 1967.

———. *A Small Mexican World.* 2d ed. Introductions by Diego Rivera and Lesley Byrd Simpson. Boston: Little, Brown, 1964.

Stalling, Donald L. "Katherine Anne Porter: Life and the Literary Mirror." Master's thesis, Texas Christian University, 1951.

Stallman, R. W. *Stephen Crane: A Biography.* New York: George Braziller, 1968.

"Stars Fell on Mismaloya." *Life,* December 20, 1963, pp. 69–73.

Steffens, Lincoln. *The Autobiography of Lincoln Steffens.* New York: Harcourt, Brace, 1931.

———. "The Battle of Celayo." *Collier's,* March 11, 1922, pp. 3–4 ff.

———. "Bunk: A Story of Revolutionary Mexico." *Everybody's* 36 (February 1917): 200–211.

———. "Into Mexico and—Out!" *Everybody's* 34 (May 1916): 533–547.

———. "The Last Great Moment." *Everybody's* 36 (March 1917): 350–361.

———. *The Letters of Lincoln Steffens.* Edited by Ella Winter and Granville Hicks. New York: Harcourt, Brace, 1938.

———. "A Talk across the Border." *Masses* 8 (July 1916): 14–15.

———. " 'Thirty-Threed': A Tale of Our Border To-day." *Everybody's* 35 (July 1916): 41–51.

———. "The White Streak." *Collier's,* January 15, 1921, pp. 5–7 ff.

———. *The World of Lincoln Steffens.* Edited by Ella Winter and Herbert Shapiro. New York: Hill & Wang, 1962.

———. "The World's Interest in the Mexican Revolution." *Acción Mundial,* February 5, 1916, p. 2 (?).

Stegner, Wallace. "Joe Hill: The Wobblies' Troubadour." *New Republic,* January 5, 1948, p. 22.

Stein, Mike. *A Look at Tennessee Williams.* New York: Hawthorn, 1969.

Steinbeck, John. *The Forgotten Village.* New York: Viking, 1941.

———. *The Log from the Sea of Cortez.* New York: Viking, 1951.

———. "The Miracle of Tepayac." *Collier's,* December 25, 1948, pp. 22–23.

———. *The Pearl.* New York: Viking, 1947.

Stephens, John Lloyd. *Incidents of Travel in Central America, Chiapas, and Yucatan.* Introduction by Frederick Catherwood. 2 vols. New York: Dover, 1969.

———. *Incidents of Travel in Yucatan.* 2 vols. New York: Dover, 1963.

Stevenson, Anne. *Elizabeth Bishop.* New York: Twayne, 1966.

Stone, Judy. "Conversations with B. Traven." *Ramparts* 6 (October 1967): 55–69.

———. "The Mystery of B. Traven." *Ramparts* 6 (September 1967): 31–49.

———. "A Reader's Guide to B. Traven." *Ramparts* 6 (October 1967): 70–75.

Stott, Raymond T. *The Writings of William Somerset Maugham: A Bibliography.* London: Dodley House, 1956.

Sturgis, Cony. *The Spanish World in English Fiction: A Bibliography.* Boston: F. W. Faxon, 1927.

Sutton, Ann, and Myron Sutton. *Among the Maya Ruins: The Adventures of John Lloyd Stephens and Frederick Catherwood.* Chicago: Rand McNally, 1967.

Tanner, Tony. *Saul Bellow.* Edinburgh: Oliver and Boyd, 1965.

Tayloe, Edward Thornton. *Mexico, 1825–1828: The Correspondence of Edward Thornton Tayloe.* Edited by C. Harvey Gardiner. Chapel Hill: University of North Carolina Press, 1959.

Taylor, Bayard. *Eldorado, or Adventures in the Path of Empire; Comprising a Voyage to California via Panama, Life in San Francisco and Monterey, Pictures of the Gold Region, and Experiences of Mexican Travel.* Edited by Robert Glass Cleveland. New York: Alfred A. Knopf, 1949.

Tedlock, E. W., and C. V. Wicker, eds. *Steinbeck and His Critics: A Record of Twenty-Five Years.* Albuquerque: University of New Mexico Press, 1957.

Telsumaro, Hayashi. *John Steinbeck: A Concise Bibliography (1930–65).* Metuchen, N.J.: Scarecrow, 1967.

Terra, Helmet de. *Humboldt: The Life and Times of Alexander von Humboldt. 1769–1859.* New York: Alfred A. Knopf, 1955.

Terry, T. Philip. *Terry's Guide to Mexico.* 2d and 3d eds. Boston: Houghton Mifflin, 1922 & 1933.

Thompson, Henry T. *Waddy Thompson, Jr.: Member of Congress, 1835–41; Minister to Mexico, 1842–44.* Rev. ed. N.p., 1929.

Thompson, J. Eric S. *The Rise and Fall of Maya Civilization.* 2d ed. Norman: University of Oklahoma Press, 1966.

Thompson, Waddy. *Recollections of Mexico.* New York: Wiley & Putnam, 1846.

Tindall, William York. *D. H. Lawrence & Susan His Cow.* New York: Columbia University Press, 1939.

Tinker, Edward L. "The Devil's Lexicographer." *New York Times Book Review,* July 23, 1967, p. 4.

Tischler, Nancy M. *Tennessee Williams, Rebellious Puritan.* New York: Citadel, 1961.

Tocqueville, Alexis de. *Democracy in America.* Translated by Henry Reeve, Francis Bowen, and Phillips Bradley. 2 vols. New York: Alfred A. Knopf, 1945.

Toor, Frances. *A Treasury of Mexican Folkways.* New York: Crown, 1947.

Traven, B. *The Bridge in the Jungle.* New York: Hill & Wang, 1967.

———. *The Carreta.* New York: Hill & Wang, 1970.

———. *The Cotton-Pickers.* New York: Hill & Wang, 1969.

———. *The Creation of the Sun and the Moon.* New York: Hill & Wang, 1968.

———. *The General from the Jungle.* Translated by Desmond I. Vesey. London: R. Hale, 1945.

———. *Government.* New York: Hill & Wang, 1971.

———. *March to Caobaland.* London: Robert Hale, 1961.

———. *The Night Visitor and Other Stories.* Introduction by Charles Miller. New York: Hill & Wang, 1966.

———. *The Rebellion of the Hanged.* Translated by Esperanza López Mateos (?). New York: Alfred A. Knopf, 1952.

———. "A Saint in Pain." *Michigan Quarterly Review* 4 (Fall 1965): 266–273.

———. "Selections." *Texas Quarterly* 6 (Winter 1963): 169–207.

———. *Stories by the Man Nobody Knows.* Evanston, Ill.: Regency, 1961.

———. *The Treasure of the Sierra Madre.* New York: Hill & Wang, 1967.

———. *The White Rose.* London: Robert Hale, 1965.

——— [Hal Croves]. Letter. *Life,* March 15, 1948, p. 23.

———. Letter. *Time,* March 15, 1948, pp. 12, 14.

Tschiffely, Aimé Felix. *Don Roberto: Being the Account of the Life and Works of R. B. Cunninghame Graham, 1852–1936.* London: W. Heinemann, 1937.

Turner, John Kenneth. *Barbarous Mexico.* Introduction by Sinclair Snow. Austin: University of Texas Press, 1969.

Unterecker, John. *Voyager: A Life of Hart Crane.* New York: Farrar, Straus & Giroux, 1969.

Victor, Thelda (with Muriel Davidson). "The Drama the Cameras Missed." *Saturday Evening Post,* July 11, 1964, pp. 25–32.

Von Hagen, Victor. *Frederick Catherwood, Arch$^t$*. Introduction by Aldous Huxley. New York: Oxford University Press, 1950.

————. *Maya Explorer: John Lloyd Stephens and the Lost Cities of Central America and Yucatan*. Norman: University of Oklahoma Press, 1947.

————. *World of the Maya*. New York: New American Library, 1960.

*Voyages and Travels Mainly during the 16th and 17th Centuries*. Introduction by Charles Raymond Beazley. 2 vols. Westminster: Archibald Constable, 1903.

Wagner, Linda W. *Denise Levertov*. New York: Twayne, 1967.

Waldrip, Louise D., and Shirley Ann Bauer. *A Bibliography of the Works of Katherine Anne Porter and a Bibliography of the Criticism of the Works of Katherine Anne Porter*. Metuchen, N.J.: Scarecrow, 1969.

Wallace, Emily M. *A Bibliography of William Carlos Williams*. Middletown, Conn.: Wesleyan University Press, 1968.

Wallace, Lewis. *An Autobiography*. 2 vols. New York: Harper, 1906.

————. "A Buffalo Hunt in Northern Mexico." *Scribner's* 17 (March 1879): 713–724.

————. *The Fair God, or The Last of the 'Tzins: A Tale of the Conquest of Mexico*. Boston: Houghton Mifflin, 1873.

————. "The Mines of Santa Eulalia, Chihuahua." *Harper's* 35 (November 1867): 681–702.

Ward, Henry George. *Mexico*. 2d ed. London: Henry Colburn, 1829.

Warner, Charles Dudley. "Editor's Study." *Harper's* 95 (June and July 1897): 146–150, 312–314.

————. "Editor's Study." *Harper's* 97 (June and July 1898): 150–154, 312–316.

————. *On Horseback: A Tour in Virginia, North Carolina, and Tennessee; With Notes of Travel in Mexico and California*. Boston: Houghton Mifflin, 1888.

Watkins, Sue. "*Palms* from Mexico: The Story of a Little Magazine." *Texas Quarterly* 6 (Spring 1963): 73–79.

Wauchope, Robert, ed. *They Found the Buried Cities: Exploration and Excavation in the American Tropics*. Chicago: University of Chicago Press, 1965.

Waugh, Evelyn. *Mexico: An Object Lesson*. Boston: Little, Brown, 1939.

————. "The Waste Land." *Spectator*, March 10, 1939, pp. 413–414.

Webb, Constance. *Richard Wright: A Biography*. New York: G. P. Putnam's Sons, 1968.

Weeks, George F. *California Copy*. Washington, D.C.: Washington College Press, 1928.

Weiner, Ed. *The Damon Runyon Story*. New York: Longmans, Green, 1948.

West, John O. *Tom Lea: Artist in Two Mediums*. Austin: Steck-Vaughn, 1967.

Westcott, Glenway. *Images of Truth: Remembrances and Criticism*. New York: Harper & Row, 1962.

Weston, Edward. *The Daybooks of Edward Weston*. Vol. 1, *Mexico*. Edited by Nancy Newhall. Rochester: George Eastman, 1961.

White, Ray Lewis. *Gore Vidal*. New York: Twayne, 1968.

Whitney, Dwight. "More about Traven." *Life*, February 2, 1948, p. 66.

"Who Is Traven?" *Times Literary Supplement*, June 22, 1967, p. 553.

Wilbur, Robert H. Interview with Conrad Aiken. *Paris Review* 42 (Winter–Spring 1968): 97–124.

Wilgus, A. Curtis. *Latin America in Fiction: A Bibliography of Books in English for Adults*. Washington, D.C.: Pan American Union, 1941.

Williams, Edwina D. (as told to Lucy Freeman). *Remember Me to Tom*. New York: G. P. Putnam's Sons, 1963.

Williams, Stanley T. *The Spanish Background of American Literature*. 2 vols. New Haven: Yale University Press, 1955.

Williams, Tennessee. *American Blues: Five Short Plays*. New York: Dramatists Play Service, 1948.

———. *Camino Real*. New York: New Directions, 1953.

———. *The Glass Menagerie*. 2d ed. New York: New Directions, 1949.

———. *Hard Candy: A Book of Stories*. New York: New Directions, 1954.

———. "The History of a Play (with Parentheses)." *Pharos* 1 and 2 (Spring 1945): 173–174.

———. *In the Winter of Cities*. New York: New Directions, 1956.

———. *The Night of the Iguana*. New York: New Directions, 1962.

———. *One Arm and Other Stories*. 2d ed. New York: New Directions, 1954.

———. *A Streetcar Named Desire*. New York: New Directions, 1947.

———. *Summer and Smoke*. New York: New Directions, 1948.

Williams, William Carlos. *The Autobiography of William Carlos Williams*. New York: New Directions, 1951.

———. *In the American Grain*. 2d ed. Introduction by Horace Gregory. New York: New Directions, 1939.

———. *Pictures from Brueghel and Other Poems*. New York: New Directions, 1962.

Wilson, Robert A. *A Bibliography of Works by Gregory Corso, 1954–1965*. New York: Phoenix Bookshop, 1966.

Wolcott, Roger, ed. *The Correspondence of William Hickling Prescott, 1833–1847*. Boston: Houghton Mifflin, 1925.

Wolfe, Randolph. "Yanqui University in Mexico." *Holiday* 44 (July 1968): 91–93.

Wolfe, Tom. *The Electric Kool-Aid Acid Test*. New York: Farrar, Straus & Giroux, 1968.

Womack, John, Jr. *Zapata and the Mexican Revolution*. New York: Alfred A. Knopf, 1969.

Woodbridge, Hensley C., John London, and George H. Tweney. *Jack London: A Bibliography*. Georgetown, Calif.: Talisman, 1966.

Woodcock, George. "Mexico and the English Novelist." *Western Review* 21 (August 1956): 21–32.

—————. *To the City of the Dead: An Account of Travels in Mexico*. London: Faber and Faber, 1957.

*The World and Its Peoples: Mexico*. New York: Greystone, 1968.

Wrenn, John H. *John Dos Passos*. New York: Twayne, 1961.

Zinsser, Hans. *As I Remember Him: The Biography of R. S.* Boston: Little, Brown, 1940.

# INDEX